Language Teaching and Testing
Selected Works of Renowned Applied Linguists
世 界 知 名 语 言 学 家 论 丛（第 一 辑）

Series Editor: Rod Ellis

U0783581

Rod Ellis

语法学习与教学

LEARNING
AND
TEACHING GRAMMAR

上海外语教育出版社
外教社 SHANGHAI FOREIGN LANGUAGE EDUCATION PRESS

图书在版编目（CIP）数据

语法学习与教学 / （新西兰）埃利斯（Ellis, R.）著.
—上海：上海外语教育出版社，2010（2019重印）
（世界知名语言学家论丛）
ISBN 978-7-5446-2051-2

Ⅰ.①语… Ⅱ.①埃… Ⅲ.①英语－语法－学习方法－文集
②英语－语法－教学法－文集 Ⅳ.①H319.35-53

中国版本图书馆CIP数据核字（2010）第198654号

出版发行：**上海外语教育出版社**
　　　　　（上海外国语大学内）　邮编：200083
电　　话：021-65425300（总机）
电子邮箱：bookinfo@sflep.com.cn
网　　址：http://www.sflep.com
责任编辑：许进兴

印　　刷：江苏凤凰数码印务有限公司
开　　本：700×1000　1/16　印张32.75　字数500千字
版　　次：2010年12月第1版　2019年4月第3次印刷

书　　号：ISBN 978-7-5446-2051-2 / H·0895
定　　价：68.00元
　　　　本版图书如有印装质量问题，可向本社调换
　　　　质量服务热线：4008-213-263　电子邮箱：editorial@sflep.com

世界知名语言学家论丛

第一辑

Editorial Advisors：杨惠中　庄智象

Series Editor: Rod Ellis

Contributors to the Series:

Chales Alderson

Gaby Kasper

Paul Nation

Peter Skehan

Rod Ellis

Zioltan Dornyei

出　版　说　明

　　"世界知名语言学家论丛（第一辑）"由上海外语教育出版社约请国际知名学者、英语教育专家Rod Ellis教授担任主编。丛书作者均为国际应用语言学领域耳熟能详的权威专家。丛书中的每一本聚焦应用语言学领域的一个特定主题，收录一位在该研究领域最有建树和影响力的语言学家一生中最重要的经典文章，如：Rod Ellis:《语法学习与教学》；Paul Nation:《词汇学习与教学》；Charles Alderson:《语言测试》，等等。书中的每篇文章经由精心挑选，既有对某一领域理论主题的深入阐述，又探讨了对第二语言教学和测试颇具意义的话题；除了作者一生的代表性作品外，还有不少新作，体现了作者的思索过程和研究轨迹，也展示了应用语言学领域发展历程中理论和研究逐步完善的一个个精彩镜头。

　　相信本套丛书的出版定能为国内应用语言学研究提供一个新的平台，带来新的启示，进一步推动我国语言学研究的发展。

Preface

This book is a collection of articles for the series *Language Teaching and Testing — Selected Works of Renowned Applied Linguists*. This series collects articles written by a number of leading applied linguists. Each collection focuses on a specific area of research in applied linguistics — for example, on grammar learning and teaching (this book), vocabulary language learning and teaching, language testing, and task-based language teaching. The aim of each book is to bring together older and more recent articles to show the development of the author's work over his/her lifetime. The articles are selected to address both theoretical issues relevant to a particular area of enquiry and also to discuss issues of significance to the teaching or testing of a second language (L2). As a whole, the series provides a survey of applied linguistics as this relates to language pedagogy and testing.

Each book begins with an autobiographical introduction by the author in which he/she locates the issues that have been important in his/her lifetime's work and how this work has evolved over time. The introduction also provides an outline of the author's professional career. The rest of the book consists of chapters based on articles published over the author's lifespan.

Each book, then, will contain articles that cover the author's career (over thirty years in some cases). Not surprisingly there are likely to be shifts (and possibly contradictions) in the author's positioning on the issues addressed, reflecting the changes in theory and research focus that have occurred in the specific area of enquiry over a period of time. Thus, the articles will not necessarily reflect a consistent theoretical perspective. There is merit in this. Readers will be able to see how theory and research have developed. In other words, each book provides a snapshot of the kinds of developments that have occurred in the applied linguistic field under consideration.

My own book gathers together various articles on grammar learning and teaching as this has figured as one of my major concerns over the course of my professional life. The articles cover a twenty-four year period. The first was originally published in 1982 and the last in 2006. In addition to the Introduction and Conclusion sections there are two major sections, one dealing with research on grammar learning and the other one teaching grammar. In just about all the articles, however, I have been concerned with the interface between researching grammar learning and teaching grammar. Throughout my perspective has been informed by work in Second Language Acquisition (SLA).

Rod Ellis
Auckland
March 2010.

Contents

Section D   CONCLUSION

Section A

INTRODUCTION

Chapter 1

A Professional Life: Teacher, Teacher Educator and Researcher

This chapter was written for this book and has not been previously published.

INTRODUCTION

I have worked as a language teacher, teacher educator and second language acquisition (SLA) researcher for over forty years. During this time grammar has figured large in my thinking, in part because it has traditionally been so central to language pedagogy and in part because I became fascinated with how the human mind grapples with the task of learning the grammar of a second language (L2). Throughout this period I have sought to address what I still see as the key question — How can the grammar of a second language be taught in a way that will maximize the chances of students learning it? In other words, my interest lies in the relationship between teaching and learning an L2 grammar.

In this introduction to the collection of my published articles on grammar learning and teaching, I would like to provide an autobiographical sketch of my professional work as a teacher, as a teacher educator and as a SLA researcher. I want to use this sketch to contextualize the theoretical and pedagogical issues that I have seen as important and also to show how my own thinking about grammar has evolved over time and where it has arrived at now. I would also like to take the opportunity to identify some of the key figures in the field who have influenced me at different times during my career. Most importantly, I want to use this introduction to dispel the view, which some might hold, that I endorse a specific and fixed approach to the teaching of grammar and that this approach is reflected consistently throughout my work. My thinking has been and still is dynamic on this issue, informed as it is by both my early experience of teaching a L2 and my later efforts at researching L2 learning.

My career is characterized by three fairly well-defined stages. My first experiences were as a language teacher. Later I became a teacher educator. Later still, while continuing to work as a teacher educator, I also increasingly adopted the role of SLA researcher. I have organized this chapter accordingly.

TEACHING ENGLISH AS A SECOND/FOREIGN LANGUAGE

In 1965, when I completed my BA in English Literature at the University of Nottingham (UK), I had little idea of what career I wanted to follow and knew only that I wanted to travel. So I became a 'backpacker English teacher', taking a job at a Berlitz school in a small town in northern Spain where I received a few days' training in the 'Berlitz Method' (a version of the then popular direct method). This method, based on a structural syllabus, seeks to elicit correct grammatical sentences from students inductively (i.e. the teacher is expressly forbidden from providing metalinguistic explanations of the target structures). It aimed to achieve functional ability in English by ensuring that students developed correct grammatical 'habits'. I recall the frustration that I and my students felt when, despite my best attempts to help them produce the target structure correctly, they frequently failed to do so.

While I was in Spain, I was also a language learner. At school I had studied French and German by means of the translation method but achieved only moderate success. Now I was in a naturalistic setting where survival required that I learn at least basic communicative skills in Spanish. Interestingly, although learning Spanish 'directly', I did not follow the precept of the Berlitz method but instead often referred to a reference grammar of Spanish and attempted to memorize conjugations of the different verb classes — aping the technique I had used for learning French and German. But I also made use of other learning strategies. I visited bars and restaurants and attempted to get into conversations. I picked up some useful formulaic expressions — *me no gusta, no inteiendo, que tal, hasta la vista* — many of which have stayed with me up to today even though I have had little occasion to use Spanish since leaving Spain. I also used a transfer strategy — what Corder (1981) called 'borrowing'. I 'foreignized' Latin sounding English words (e.g. *cosmopolita*) and gambled that my interlocutors would understand. On the whole, I didn't do so badly as a learner.

Unfortunately, I did not stay long enough in Spain to become proficient in Spanish. After four months, I had had enough of my Berlitz experience and decided to return to England. However, this period was formative. I found that I enjoyed teaching (although not using the Berlitz Method) and also that learning an L2 did not necessarily entail the stultifying boredom of the translation method.

There was an interim year before I took off on my travels again. During this year I worked as a primary school teacher in a school in Dalston, London. I began as a supply teacher. My first school was an unmitigated disaster. I was faced with a class of unruly ten-year olds with little idea of what I should teach them or how to manage them. But I learned quickly and was much more successful in my next school, so much so that I was offered a fixed position there and remained there for the rest of the year. My primary school experience was invaluable. It taught me the importance of well-structured lessons and in particular the need for effective classroom management and communication skills. My belief in these aspects of teaching has remained constant over the years.

In January 1967 I left to work in a newly established secondary school in Zambia, Africa. Zambia had only very recently achieved independence from Britain and was prioritizing secondary school education as a central element in nation-building. Kaoma Secondary School was situated some 275 miles from Lusaka (the capital), accessible only by means of a dirt road that passed, *en route*, through a game park. When I arrived at the school I found spanking new buildings, lines of houses for the teachers, all of whom, with the exception of the Zambian headmaster, were expatriates like myself. There was no electricity and few resources. But there was, in general, a highly motivated student body, and an enthusiastic group of young teachers. This proved to be an experience of a life time, one that contributed enormously to my development as a person and as a teacher of English.

The English curriculum that I and the other teachers developed was built around the two central notions that learning English involved 'skill-getting' and 'skill-using' (see Rivers and Temperley (1978) for a detailed exposition of these concepts). Although, the term 'communicative language teaching' had not yet appeared on the scene, it is clear to me that the curriculum we devised and taught in fact conformed to many of the principles of this approach. 'Skill-getting' involved helping students develop the 'knowledge' of English they needed to communicate effectively and involved the intensive practice of the sounds, vocabulary and grammar of English. 'Skill-using' involved providing opportunities for the students to use their knowledge of English to communicate orally and in writing. Our curriculum consisted of a careful balance of activities that catered to these two aspects of learning.

Grammar was central to the 'skill-getting' component. Out of the seven 40 minute English lessons per week, two or three were devoted to teaching a structural syllabus. This syllabus listed the grammatical structures to be taught in a structure-a-day approach. Although I was not aware at the time, this was the period during which the 'language teaching controversy' (Diller, 1978) was prominent. There were those who espoused an empiricist, structural view of language (e.g. Bloomfield and Fries) and those who viewed language in rationalist terms (e.g. Chomsky). In language teaching, there were proponents of the audiolingual method (a development of the direct method I was already familiar with from my Berlitz experience) with its emphasis on mimicry, memorization and pattern drill and other proponents of the cognitive code method which emphasized the psychological reality of 'rules' and the importance of presenting these clearly and explicitly to learners.

The textbooks we experimented with reflected this controversy. We used substitution tables and drills of the kind found in Monfries' (1969) *Oral Drills in Sentence Patterns*. The following is a good example:

Simple present third person singular and plural

The teacher quickly asks the students the questions designed to elicit the use of the correct verb form:
Example:
T: What does a student do?
S: He studies.
T: What do singers do?
S: They sing.

1. What does a typist do?
2. What do typists do?
   etc.

The idea here was to prevent or eliminate common errors in our students' use of English by establishing correct 'habits'. But, at one time, we also used materials that called for a much more intellectual and analytical approach to learning grammar. Bright's (1965) *Patterns and Drills in English* presented students with highly detailed and explicit explanations of grammatical patterns and their transformations, followed by exercises that required students to engage in conscious analysis or manipulation of sentences, as in this example:

> Group of change of state or appearance patterns
>
> These consist of a subject, a linking verb and a complement:
>
> | S | LV | CN |
> |---|---|---|
> | The lady | became | his wife |
> | This | appeared | a good idea |
>
> Make up more examples and name the parts.

Both approaches proved problematic. There is a story I have often used in subsequent years when giving talks about grammar teaching that illustrates the kind of problem we experienced with the audiolingual approach. I was attempting to address errors involving verbs of possession such as this:

* I am having two brothers.

After extensive oral drilling during which the students successfully produced correct sentences, I set the students a written exercise and then noticed that there was one student at the back doing nothing. When I approached him and asked him why he was not working on the exercise he replied 'I am not having my exercise book'. Clearly, there had been no transfer of learning from the drill to communicative use! Some years later, when I began to study the SLA literature, I was able to understand why this might be. At the time, though, I put it down to the limitation of this particular student. Bright's textbook raised a different kind of problem. While some of the Zambian students benefitted from the systematic and detailed explicit explanations of grammar points, many did not. The emphasis on grammatical form and the analytical approach to language that this book embodied seemed to run counter to their natural inclination to treat language as a communicative tool. Thus, neither audiolingual drills nor cognitive explanations of grammar proved very successful.

Together with Brian Tomlinson, who arrived at the school one year after myself, I began to try out the approach that Brian had been exposed to while he completed a postgraduate diploma at the Institute of Education, University of London. This approach, known as the oral-situational method, originated in the London School of Linguistics established by Firth (see, for example, Firth's (1957) *Papers in Linguistics 1934–1951* (1957), which espoused the importance of studying language in relation to the 'context of situation'. That is, grammar was a resource for realizing meanings in relation to the specific situations in which language was used. Applied to language teaching, this meant that grammar should not be taught as a set of formal patterns or abstract grammar rules, but rather through situations that would demonstrate the meanings realized by specific grammatical forms. The oral-situational method differed from audiolingualism in that it viewed grammar as a means for realizing meanings rather than as a set of formal habits while it differed from the cognitive-code method in that much less emphasis was placed on the explicit explanation of grammar points.

As there were no textbooks based on the oral-situational approach suitable for the Zambian context, Brian and myself set about constructing our own grammar teaching materials. These were eventually published in 1973 as *English Through Situations* by Longman. The materials attempted to practice specific grammatical points in relation to situational information that demonstrated their meanings. They also sought to make grammar more interesting for the students by including activities that were humorous and, sometimes, zany. I recall the publisher censoring some of our more risqué ideas. For example, we developed a character called 'Mr Cabbage', but, reluctantly, agreed to change this name to the more mundane 'Mr Mwenda'. The example below from Book 1 of *English Through Situations* comes from a unit designed to teach the use of different prepositions of location and direction.

The following story should be dramatized by the teacher using either a piece of chalk or a cardboard cut out to represent Bessie Bee. The teacher should move the chalk around the room to show what Bessie did.

Bessie Bee was flying around outside the window of this room. She came into the room and flew onto the table. She then flew off the table and towards the door. Then she turned round and flew across the room away from the door. She landed on the floor under the table. She rested there for a few minutes and then flew into the open cupboard. Inside the cupboard Billie Bee was sleeping. He woke up and kissed Bessie Bee. The two bees then flew out of the cupboard, out of the window and across the field towards their home.

The teacher should tell the story again and then ask questions about what Bessie Bee did whilst illustrating her actions — e.g. What did Bessie do then?

A pupil should be asked to tell the story and then the class writes the story without looking at their book.

Such activities reflect a number of general principles about the teaching of grammar. One is that teaching grammar should involve input-based as well as production-based activities. Later, I was to develop this idea more explicitly by proposing the use of 'interpretation tasks' (Ellis, 1995a; see Chapter 12). Another principle — central to the oral-situational approach — was that grammar consists of form-meaning mappings and that 'correctness' involves the use of a specific form to express a specific meaning. A third principle is the 'real operating conditions principle' (see Chapter 18) according to which learners need to process grammatical forms in the same conditions in which they will experience them in real communication. However, I was not consciously aware of these principles at the time I was writing *English Through Situations*. They emerged in explicit form much later as a product of my work in SLA. At the time, my thinking about grammar was based on a view of language (i.e. what grammar is) rather than on any notion of how grammar is actually learned. It is interesting to note, however, that at least some of the time I was intuitively designing activities that accorded with what I now understand about L2 learning.

What both Brian and I were conscious of at the time was that grammar teaching was likely to be much more successful if it was fun — for both the teacher and the learner. Thus, apart from our commitment to showing how grammar made meaning, we aimed to make our grammar lessons enjoyable and indeed competed with each other to achieve this. I recall the student laughter that regularly emanated from our classrooms.

There was, of course, much more to the curriculum we taught than grammar. Many lessons were directed at 'skill-development'. We developed a classroom library system, taking boxes of carefully selected graded readers into our classrooms twice a week and encouraging the students to read at least one book per week. This was long before Stephen Krashen was to promote extensive reading as a primary source of 'acquisition'. We also had class readers (i.e. each student had a copy of the same book) which we read aloud to the students and then used as a source for various fluency activities. Recognizing that many of our students were extremely slow readers (some were reading no faster than 30 words per minute), we instituted faster reading lessons to train students in the techniques of rapid reading. We conducted intensive reading lessons using John Munby's (1968) *Read and Think*, which used carefully designed multiple choice questions to elicit small group and class discussion of the different levels of meaning in a text. Much of what we did would qualify as what is now called 'task-based language teaching'. We saw such work as an important complement to the 'skill-getting' lessons where grammar was taught.

The three years I spent at Kaoma Secondary School provided me with a truly concrete experience of language teaching — the opportunity to experiment with materials writing and to hone my own classroom skills as a language teacher. They were arguably the most formative and influential years in my career. A number of teachers I worked with at that time — Brian Tomlinson and Richard West come immediately to mind — have gone on to become major figures in the field of ELT. Through discussions with these people and through conferences I attended during this time I came to see that language teaching was not just a 'skill' but also an intellectual pursuit. It was not enough to know what worked and did not work in the classroom: I also wanted to know why. My appetite to study language and language teaching was whetted and in 1970 I returned to England to study for an MA.

LANGUAGE TEACHER EDUCATION

By the time I left Zambia I knew that teaching English as a second/ foreign language was no longer just a means of travelling the world and satisfying my thirst for adventure but a profession that I wanted to pursue. Thus, the next step was to obtain a qualification that would equip me to advance in the profession. I embarked on an MA in Linguistics and Language Teaching at Leeds University with an enthusiasm and commitment to academic study that was sorely lacking in my undergraduate years.

Postgraduate courses in TESOL or applied linguistics are now very common but in 1970 they were still a relatively new phenomenon. The Leeds programme offered courses in transformational generative grammar, field linguistics, sociolinguistics, psycholinguistics and language teaching. This was a time of paradigm change in linguistics, with the structural school of Bloomfield and Fries giving way to the generative school of Chomsky and with the corresponding shift from behaviourism to nativism in the psychological underpinnings of linguistic theory. It was an exciting time. However, the application of these new ideas to language learning and teaching was still in its infancy and was only weakly reflected in the content of the Leeds programme. My most vivid memories of the programme are the lectures that Bill O'Donnell gave on transformational generative grammar and psycholinguistics. I remember struggling with tree diagrams and feeling somewhat puzzled by Vygotsky's *Language and Thought*. In his advocacy of Vygotsky's sociocultural theory, Bill was nearly two decades ahead of the rest of the field as it was not until the 1990s that this theory began to receive serious attention from applied linguists. My other chief memory is of a lecture by David Barber on Newmark's ideas about language teaching. Newmark (1966) argued that we should not 'interfere' with language learning as this will take place naturally without the need for teachers to present and practice specific linguistic items. I found this proposal interesting but it was not till a few years later when I began to learn more about the processes of L2 acquisition that I took it seriously.

I do not think that the MA had a major effect on my ideas about language teaching. In retrospect its value to me was threefold. First, it opened my eyes to a whole range of interesting work on language and showed me that 'linguistics' constituted as exciting a discipline as 'literature' — which up to then was what I thought 'English' was all about academically. Second, it brought me into contact with teachers of English with experience of teaching in a whole range of countries, showing me that 'EFL/ESL' was a global phenomenon full of exciting possibilities. Third, with an MA under my belt I was equipped to explore these possibilities by applying for a range of jobs in both language teaching and teacher education.

However, I did not at first head overseas again. Instead I took a job working in an English for Academic Purposes programme at Huddersfield Polytechnic. This was not a success. I did not enjoy the work and felt like a fish out of water in Huddersfield, a northern English town that at that time was still very much marked by its industrial past. Luckily, during my very first term there I was invited by the UK Ministry of Overseas Development to apply for a position as lecturer in Nkrumah Teachers' College in Zambia. I leapt at the opportunity and in a few weeks it was settled — I was heading back to Zambia.

Altogether I spent five and half years at the College — years that in many ways were as formative as the years at Kaoma Secondary School. They were especially memorable because I was able to link up again with Brian Tomlinson, who joined the English staff of the College a year or so after my own arrival. The lectures on various aspects of teaching that we gave to the teacher trainees eventually formed the basis for a book that we jointly authored, *Teaching Secondary English: A Guide to Teaching English as a Second Language*, which was eventually published by Longman in 1980 (three years after I left the College). This book, then, affords a picture of the content of the training programme we devised. Its eighteen chapters covered the 'skill-getting' aspects of language teaching (pronunciation, vocabulary and grammar) and the 'skill-developing' aspects (speaking, listening, efficient reading, reading comprehension, extensive reading, composition writing, summary and note-making). In many respects, it was surprisingly comprehensive as a practical handbook for African teachers of English. There were, however, some notable absences, reflecting the limitations of our knowledge at the time. There was almost nothing on how learners learn an L2, on learner autonomy, or on the social and pragmatic aspects of language use. Nor was there anything that addressed 'learning teaching' and the need for the life-long professional development of teachers.

Three of the chapters addressed grammar in one way or another and I will focus on these as illustrative of my thinking at this time. The bulk of the chapter entitled 'Structure' consisted of descriptions and examples of different types of grammar activities. These were organized according to the approach we had adopted in Teaching *English Through Situations*. That is, they started with 'mechanical exercises' and then moved on to 'situational exercises'. There was also a section on planning structure lessons, where the traditional present-practice-produce (PPP) format was recommended, and another on actually teaching a structure lesson, which dealt with such aspects as how to conduct oral practice and deal with errors. The chapter concluded with some suggestions for 'follow-up lessons' (in recognition that even the most perfectly executed lesson

might not succeed in ensuring correct use of a target feature) and a
section on 'testing structure'. By and large, this chapter reflects what was
received opinion regarding how to teach grammar in the late 1970s. In
many respects, these views continue to reflect mainstream opinion about
grammar teaching today. There is probably not much in this chapter that
Michael Swan, for example, would disagree with!

Looking back at *Teaching Secondary English*, I can see what the views
about language learning that overtly or covertly underpinned what we
recommended for teaching grammar were. Interestingly, the chapter
on 'Structure' began by distinguishing two types of knowledge of
grammar — 'unconscious knowledge' and 'acquired knowledge'. The
former referred to 'the unconscious ability to use the structure of a language
to convey meaning' and the latter to 'information that has been deliberately
acquired through studying structural descriptions' (p. 8). This distinction
corresponded more or less exactly to that proposed by Stephen Krashen in
another part of the world (see Krashen, 1981a), although the actual labels
used differed somewhat! We emphasized the importance of 'unconscious
knowledge' on the grounds that this was needed 'to produce sentences
automatically'. However, we also argued that 'it is often useful to refer the
pupils to simple grammatical descriptions as a learning aid, i.e. as a means of
developing unconscious knowledge'. These are views that I was to develop
later on as I became more familiar with the SLA literature. They are also
views that, by and large, have withstood the test of time. In my later work I
have similarly argued that what I now call 'explicit knowledge' can facilitate
the development of 'implicit knowledge'.

Another important distinction to be found in the 'Structure' chapter
is that between 'initial teaching' and 'remedial teaching'. The former
assumes that the pupil has no knowledge of the structure to be taught,
while the latter aims to address errors that learners continue to make in
a structure that has been previously taught. We attached considerable
importance to remedial teaching on the grounds that secondary school
students would have already been taught most structures during

their primary school years but may not have mastered them. In fact, we included a separate chapter on remedial teaching. In this we recommended that teachers should not blindly follow the structural syllabus but rather first endeavour to find out which items on this syllabus their students were already able to use correctly so that they could focus on those that were continuing to manifest errors. We suggested a number of ways in which teachers could do this — by predicting errors through contrastive analysis, by closely observing their students' use of English, by setting diagnostic tests and by carrying out an error analysis. We also gave detailed suggestions for how to conduct remedial lessons (e.g. developing a bank of correction cards which could be given to individual students when they committed specific errors). Implicit in our views about remedial teaching was the belief that learning the grammar of an L2 is a slow and gradual process that will be characterized by errors which will only be eliminated over time. Explicit was our view that grammar teaching could assist this process although I do not think we had really worked out how.

However, we made some attempt to address this thorny issue in the sections of *Teaching Secondary English* that addressed how teachers should respond to learner errors. We advanced the view that was emanating from early work in SLA (as reflected, for example, in Jack Richards' (1974) collection of papers in *Error Analysis*, which we had read with great interest) that 'it was desirable for ESL learners to make errors' because these served as the means by which they tested out hypotheses about the target language. We pointed out that learners develop an 'interlanguage' that lies 'somewhere in between total non-competence and total competence' (p.262) but we made no real attempt to show how the teaching of grammar could be reconciled with such a view of L2 learning. It was not until much later that both Brian and myself came to question the validity of the present-practice-produce approach to teaching grammar. Our solution to the problem of recurring errors was simply 'more teaching'.

Also of interest is how we handled error correction. In the case of oral drills, we recommended that the teacher should clearly signal that an error had been committed and then repeat the stimulus, thus pushing the student to self-correct. We gave this example from a drill designed to practice 'used to':

> T: Where did you go to school before you came to this one?
> S: I used to going to Parker Primary School.
> T: No. Where did you go to school before you came to this one?
> S: I used to go to Parker Primary School.
> T: Good.
> (*Teaching Secondary English*, p. 38)

We also pointed out that if students persisted in making a particular error, it was necessary to stop the drill and provide a brief explicit explanation of the target feature. We were adamant that 'allowing errors to pass uncorrected negates the whole purpose of drilling' (p.39). Error correction also received attention in the chapter on 'Marking', with the focus on errors in written work this time. We recommended indirect correction (i.e. indicating that an error has been committed but without correcting it) and the use of an error correction code and remedial correction cards. We dismissed direct correction on the grounds that 'the pupil is not involved in any conscious activity and most of the corrections are unlikely to have any remedial value' (p.296). We also argued that it was better to select specific errors to correct rather than attempt to correct all errors. These views reflected those that were widely expressed in other teacher handbooks at that time (and indeed still are today). They did not draw on any empirical evidence of how teachers actually carry out corrective feedback or on the effect that such practices have on L2 acquisition. I am now somewhat embarrassingly struck by how sure and directive we were about what is in fact an extremely complex phenomenon. In recent years, I have addressed both oral and written corrective feedback in detail (see, for example, Chapters 7 and 16) in recognition of the importance of this aspect of language teaching for language learning.

In writing *Teaching Secondary English* Brian and myself drew both on our prior experiences of teaching in secondary schools in Zambia and also on the 'technical knowledge' we had obtained from our masters courses and our reading of applied linguistics texts such as Richards (1974). Looking back, there seems one glaring omission in how we conceptualized language teaching already hinted at in my comments about how we viewed error correction. We saw language teaching as a set of externally defined practices (drills, situational exercises, correction cards etc.) rather than as interactions that teachers and students engage in. I think we had very little sense of teaching as a classroom process and little idea of how this process created the contexts through which learning could take place. This, of course, is not surprising. At the time we completed our MA degrees 'classroom interaction' did not figure as a topic of enquiry. It was not till the mid seventies, for example, that research began to appear that documented corrective feedback as a classroom process and not until the eighties that researchers like Dick Allwright and Michael Long began to articulate theories that linked process to the product of learning.

Teaching Secondary English serves as a record of my early experiences of language teaching and my attempt to meld these onto the technical knowledge I had gleaned from my study of language, language teaching, and to a much lesser extent, language learning. If success is to be measured in terms of sales, then the book was a success. It was widely used in many African countries well into the 1990s.

Teacher education is, of course, not just about content. It is also about methodology. In this respect, my work at Nkrumah Teachers' College was perhaps more significant. The approach I adopted is one that survives in my work as a teacher educator today. It involved 'input' in the form of lectures supported by handouts and carefully selected readings followed by 'application' in the form of various activities that involved the trainees commenting on belief statements about language teaching, evaluating teaching materials, designing teaching activities, critiquing and preparing lesson plans and micro-teaching. In addition, our work at the College involved evaluating the trainees' teaching practice. Brian and I drove round the country visiting schools where our trainees had been placed, observing their lessons, and preparing evaluative reports. Apart from the sheer pleasure that our travels around Zambia gave us, the lessons we observed also provided us with valuable feedback on our own work as teacher trainers. In retrospect, though, I regret that we made no effort to make use of our observations as data for research. At that time, I did not see 'research' as part of my brief career as a teacher educator. In the years that followed my departure from Zambia in 1977, however, research was to figure in a major way.

RESEARCHING SECOND LANGUAGE LEARNING AND TEACHING

Looking back over the years in which I have been involved as a researcher of L2 learning, I can see that they fall into a series of periods reflecting my changing geographical and professional locations and the individuals in these locations who influenced me. I have organized this section accordingly.

Bristol University (1978 – 1979)

I returned from Zambia in 1978 and almost immediately started another masters course — this time a Master in Education — at Bristol University. I intended to use this as bridge to obtaining a suitable teaching position back in the United Kingdom. It was this course that introduced me to current work on language acquisition and also to the skills required of a researcher.

At Bristol, I studied with Gordon Wells and his co-researchers, who were involved in a longitudinal study of child first language acquisition — the Bristol Study of Language Development. This involved 'a fundamental study of language development from infancy to primary school' (Wells, 1985). Samples of children's talk with their parents and siblings were collected regularly using a radio microphone and recording device that was strapped to the children's backs. These samples were transcribed and then analysed in a variety of ways. Gordon's primary interest lay in how the interactions that the children participated in served as the matrix for their language development. The project drew heavily on earlier research on child language acquisition (e.g. the work undertaken by Roger Brown in the United States) but extended this in two major ways. First, in addition to examining the children's development of grammar, it also addressed the functional properties of their use of language, drawing on Michael Halliday's functional grammar. Second, it investigated the relationship between different properties of caretakers' talk and the children's language development. It was this latter aspect of the project that I worked on producing a thesis entitled 'Enabling Factors in Caretaker-Child Discourse'. A version of this thesis eventually appeared as an article that I co-authored with Gordon which appeared in *First Language*, a new journal devoted to studies of child language acquisition.

My time at Bristol was formative in two major ways. First, it exposed me to recent work in applied linguistics, in particular to research into first language acquisition but also to the exciting new areas of research in discourse analysis, conversational analysis and functional models of language. I became aware of the paradigm shift that had taken place since my days at Leeds University. In 1970 at Leeds the talk was all of Chomsky and formal models of language. In 1978, at Bristol, language was viewed as a communicative tool that was acquired through communication. Language learners underwent an 'apprenticeship in meaning', to use Gordon's catchy turn of phrase. Second, the Bristol course gave me the opportunity to cut my teeth as a researcher — to work with empirical data, to devise systems for analyzing it, and to learn how to use statistical tools. I found this enormously exciting and am indebted to Gordon Wells for the guidance and encouragement he gave me. In effect, the Bristol course changed my professional life. From that time onwards I wanted to be a researcher.

London: St Mary's College and the Institute of Education (1979 – 1984)

First, though, I needed a job. I successfully applied for the position of Senior Lecturer at St Mary's College, Strawberry Hill, London, and began my work there on undergraduate courses in language and the Diploma in TESOL in September 1979. This position provided me with the opportunity to continue my work in teacher education and also the time and financial support to undertake study for a PhD in the Institute of Education, University of London. There I came into regular contact with Henry Widdowson and Chris Brumfit in the weekly seminars that they ran for doctoral students. Among other students attending these seminars were Roger Hawkey and Cyril Weir, both of whom went on to become leading figures in their own areas of applied linguistics. We formed a mutually supporting group that saw us through our doctoral studies. The three years I spent studying for my PhD were, in many ways, the most stimulating and exciting of my professional life.

The key idea that informed my doctoral thesis was that L2 acquisition arose out of the discourse that learners participated in. In other words, I wanted to explore to what extent the claims I had investigated for child L1 acquisition were also valid for L2 acquisition. My starting point was to familiarize myself with the research that had investigated L2 acquisition. In 1979 this was still quite limited as 'SLA' at that time was still a very young field. I was struck by two major findings of the early research. First, like L1 children, L2 learners learned the grammar of the language gradually and incrementally, manifesting orders and sequences of acquisition that were remarkably uniform irrespective of their age or their first language. This finding could not be accounted for by the

Contrastive Analysis Hypothesis and the behaviourist learning theory that underpinned it. Rather it leant support to a mentalist account of L2 acquisition. Learners had their own built-in syllabus, which Selinker (1972) called 'interlanguage'. Second, like L1 children, L2 learners (both children and adults) participated in conversations with other speakers of the language, which afforded them the data they needed to activate their syllabus. Researchers reported marked similarities between the simplified input that L1 learners were exposed to in caretaker talk and that experienced by L2 learners in 'foreigner talk' and suggested that this helped learners to segment the stream of language they were exposed to and attend to its grammatical properties. Evelyn Hatch (1978c) went further, suggesting that the structure of the conversations that both child and adult L2 learners took part in provided them with an entry point to the grammar of the language. She famously wrote:

> One learns how to do conversations, one learns how to interact verbally, and out of this interaction syntactic structures are developed.

In short, I found clear support for the idea that motivated my thesis in the SLA literature. However, the bulk of the research had investigated naturalistic learners who were living in a country where the L2 was spoken and who therefore learned the L2 through the everyday conversations that were part of their experience of living. This led me to ask whether L2 classroom learners manifested the same order and sequence as naturalistic learners and in what ways the interactions they experienced in the classroom facilitated (or impeded) their L2 development. These were the questions I addressed in my thesis, which I rather grandly entitled 'Discourse Processes in Second Language Development'.

The research I undertook for my thesis involved a two-year longitudinal study of three ESL learners who were more or less complete beginners when I began the research. I collected data from within the classroom, keeping a pencil-and-paper record of all the utterances they produced and the situational context in which they occurred. I also audio-recorded a number of lessons in which they participated. My analyses examined the learners' use of formulaic speech, the order and sequence of development of negatives and questions and the nature of the different classroom interactions they participated in. At one stage, I conducted an experimental study in which the class the three learners were in received instruction in the formation of WH-questions, which my data showed the learners had not yet acquired. I completed my thesis in just under three years. I recall an exciting four-hour long oral viva with my external examiner — Dick Allwright — during which we discussed a variety of issues emanating from the thesis and, more generally, from the growing body of SLA research. The thesis led to a number of publications, including a book published by Pergamon in 1984 with the title *Classroom Second Language Development*. I have continued to make use of the data I collected for my PhD throughout my academic career.

At the same time I was working on the book version of my thesis I began an introductory text book on SLA for Oxford University Press. This brought me into close contact with Henry Widdowson, whose guidance in writing the book proved invaluable, and Cristina Whitecross, senior editor at OUP. The result was *Understanding Second Language Acquisition*, which appeared in 1985 and is still in print and selling well today. A Chinese version of the book appeared in 1990. A Japanese translation also appeared. The book was a landmark in my career. It was the start of a long and fruitful relationship with Cristina Whitecross, whose personal and publishing skills I came to respect more with each year. It provided me with the opportunity to review and synthesize the research on L2 acquisition and to identify the key issues in SLA. It also helped to establish me as one of the leading figures in SLA and thereby helped to shape the rest of my professional career.

London: Thames Valley University (1984 – 1989)

In 1984 I left St Mary's College to take up the position of Head of the ELT Department in Ealing College of Education (later to become

Thames Valley University), where I worked with a number of highly professional teacher educators, including Tricia Hedge, Pauline Rea-Dickens and Alan Fortune, all of whom have gone on to be influential in their respective fields. This was a period when I began to undertake a number of consultancies for the British Council and other professional bodies in various parts of the world, including Poland, Spain, South Africa, Cameroon, Thailand, India, Indonesia and Venezuela. This was also a period during which I began to regularly attend TESOL and SLA conferences.

I continued to research L2 acquisition and to write a number of papers. Drawing on data from my doctoral thesis, I focused on two key issues — the role of interaction in L2 learning and the variability of learner language — both of which were explored in relation to how learners acquired the grammar of an L2.

In my work on interaction, I sought to show how the conversations in which learners participate in the classroom provide them with units of different sizes which they then incorporate into their own utterances and how this can explain the incremental nature of L2 acquisition. This work drew on Dick Allwright's observation that whatever learners learned from instruction was ultimately what they took from the interactions they contributed to and that, therefore, what was important was the quality of these interactions, i.e. the extent to which they afforded opportunities for learning. To my mind, this involved a fundamental shift in the way in which language teaching was to be conceived. Language teaching should be viewed not so much as a set of techniques for imparting knowledge about the language but as 'interaction'. It followed that, in this sense, the learning that goes on in an instructed environment may not be so different from the learning that takes place 'naturalistically'. This view was espoused in an article that appeared in a book on the role of input in L2 acquisition edited by Sue Gass and Carolyn Madden and, later, in a whole series of articles that appeared in the 1990s.

My work on variability was motivated by the fact that L2 learners manifest enormous variation in their use of an L2 depending on such factors as whom they are addressing, the linguistic context of the grammatical structures they are attempting to use, and the extent to which they are able to plan what they want to say before executing an utterance. Drawing on sociolinguistic studies of language variation, I suggested that there was both 'free' and 'systematic variation' in learner language. I illustrated the former from data I had collected on 'J' (one of the learners studied for my doctoral thesis). In one lesson, where J was participating in a word bingo game, he produced in subsequent turns, to the same addressee and with the same pragmatic goal, the utterances 'No look my card' and 'Don't look my card'. I argued that at this stage of his development J possessed two negative forms and used these more or less randomly. I suggested that 'free variation' constituted a stage in a learners' development which occurred when they added a new form to their existing repertoire of forms. Over time, this would give way to systematic variation and, ultimately, to the elimination of the non-target form. This view of language learning proved controversial, with other researchers, such as Dennis Preston, challenging my claims about free variation. However, I continue to believe that my essential argument about the role of free variation in language learning is correct and note that subsequent to the 1985 article, where I first published my views, a number of studies have produced supporting evidence. My interest in variability in L2 acquisition led to me mounting a conference on the topic in 1985 and editing a collection of papers from the conference, which eventually appeared as *Second Language Acquisition in Context* (Pergamon). A subsequent development of this work was the research project on implicit and explicit L2 knowledge which I was involved in many years later at the University of Auckland.

While at Thames Valley University I also embarked on a new research project entitled 'The Acquisition of German in a Classroom Context'. With the help of a very able research assistant (Maria Rathbone), I undertook the study of how *ab initio* adult learners acquired a set of German word order rules, which previous studies of naturalistic learners of German had shown to be acquired in a fixed order of development. We investigated to what extent these classroom learners of German manifested the same order. We also examined the relationship between individual learner factors such as language aptitude, motivation and affective dispositions on the one hand and language achievement on the other. This project, then, was the start of my ongoing interest in individual learner differences. It was my first attempt to undertake qualitative research as we asked five learners to keep a diary of their learning experiences over a six month period. Ultimately the project led to a number of publications, including 'Are classroom and naturalistic acquisition the same? A study of the classroom acquisition of German word order rules' (see Chapter 3) and several articles based on the diary data, including 'A metaphorical analysis of learner beliefs'. My experience with this project convinced me of the merits of research that drew on both quantitative and qualitative traditions.

I also wrote a new book during this period — *Instructed Second Language Acquisition*, published by Blackwell. This attempted to draw together current research in SLA and how this could be applied to teaching. It was the basis for a number of ideas that were not fully developed until later, when I left Thames Valley University to work in Japan.

Tokyo: Temple University, Japan (1989 – 1993)

In 1988 I was invited to conduct a seminar on second language acquisition for Temple University Japan (TUJ). This proved another landmark in my professional career as it led to an offer of a one-year contract to work on the masters and doctoral programs in that university. I took a one-year leave of absence from Thames Valley University and moved to Tokyo in September 1989. Subsequently, this contract was extended and led to me spending a total of four years at TUJ. These proved to be enormously stimulating and productive years. They provided me, for the first time, with the opportunity to supervise doctoral dissertations and also to hone my ideas about grammar teaching. They also gave me the opportunity to live in one of the most exciting and remarkable cities of the world — Tokyo. I remain enormously grateful to Ken Schaefer, the Director of TUJ's graduate TESOL programme, for the opportunity to work there and for the support he provided for both my teaching and my writing.

A feature of TUJ's doctoral programme — one common to North American programmes at this level — was the provision of a series of courses which all the students had to complete before embarking on their dissertations. The purpose of these courses was to ensure that students were familiar with current research in applied linguistics and also to help them develop the technical skills needed to conduct research in a variety of different paradigms. As a result, when students reached the dissertation stage, they were thoroughly prepared to carry out empirical research. They possessed a clear idea of what they wanted to investigate, they were familiar with the relevant research and they had the tools they needed to design a study, collect data, analyse them, and write up their results in accordance with the conventions of their chosen research paradigm. In these respects, they differed markedly from doctoral students in the British tradition, including myself. I learned as much from them about how to research as they learned from me.

A number of the students I supervised produced exemplary dissertations. It is not possible to mention all of them but I would like to briefly summarise the research of three with whom I have continued to keep in contact up to today. The first student to finish her dissertation at TUJ was Tomoko Kaneko. She elected to examine the use of English and Japanese (the students' L1) in junior college English lessons. She was also interested in what the students 'uptook' from these lessons (i.e. were able to report having learned) and the types of interactions that promoted their uptake. One of her main findings was that the teachers in the classes she investigated used far more Japanese than English! The second student to finish was Sandra Fotos. She drew on my (and others') ideas about consciousness-raising (see below) to investigate the extent to which this was effective in helping learners learn grammatical structures in English. She was able to show that consciousness-raising via grammar discovery tasks worked as effectively as direct grammar explanations and also that the knowledge that learners gained from these tasks facilitated their subsequent noticing of the grammatical structures in input to which they were exposed. Gordon Robson finished his dissertation a year or so later. He examined the relationships among student participation in English lessons, their language proficiency and individual difference factors (personality and language anxiety). He found that extroverted learners and more orally proficient learners participated more and anxious learners less. I like to think that these dissertations were inspired by my own ideas about L2 learning in a classroom context. But supervising them also helped me to develop these ideas much further than I had been able to in my own research.

At TUJ I was busy teaching a variety of graduate level courses on such topics as language teaching methods, SLA, discourse analysis, individual learner differences, stylistics and the teaching of literature as well as supervising a large number of doctoral dissertations. There was no time left for personal research projects (although I did collaborate with some of my students in a number of small scale projects). However, this was perhaps a good thing as it gave me the time to use my understanding of SLA to put together my ideas about grammar teaching. These ideas were subsequently published in a series of articles and chapters that appeared in the early 1990s.

My work on grammar teaching is based on one central assumption: for teaching to work it must accord with how learners learn grammar. This assumption originated in my experiences of teaching grammar at Kaoma Secondary School, but my ideas about how to implement it only gradually solidified as a result of my work in SLA. During my time at TUJ, I explored a number of approaches for teaching grammar: (1) 'practice', (2) 'consciousness-raising', (3) input-based instruction and (4) 'pushed output'.

Perhaps the key article of this period was ' the structural syllabus and second language acquisition', which appeared in *TESOL Quarterly* in 1993 (see Chapter 11). In this, I tried to grapple with what many SLA researchers, myself included, saw as the central issue in grammar teaching — how to organize a grammar syllabus in a way that took account of the learner's own built-in syllabus. I argued that a structural syllabus could not serve as a basis for developing learners' implicit knowledge (i.e. the kind of intuitive knowledge needed for easy communication) because the acquisition of this type of knowledge was not a matter of 'accumulated entities' (Rutherford, 1987) but was an organic, learner-driven process. I also noted the difficulty of trying to match the teaching syllabus with the learner's syllabus given that teachers could not be expected to know precisely where each student was at. I concluded that, where implicit knowledge was concerned, a structural syllabus was simply not viable. However, such a syllabus could be used as a basis for developing learners' explicit knowledge (i.e. declarative knowledge of grammar 'facts'). I then went on to argue that explicit knowledge plays a facilitating role in grammar learning by enabling learners to 'notice' exemplars of grammatical features in the input, to 'notice-the-gap' between what they noticed and their own erroneous production of these features, and to monitor their output by self-correcting their errors.

Other articles addressed the limitations of traditional ideas of 'practice' (see Chapter 9) and to suggest that instruction should aim at explicit knowledge by means of 'consciousness-raising tasks' designed to assist learners to discover facts about the L2 grammar for themselves (see Chapter 10). I also argued that input-based instruction could help learners to pay attention to (i.e. 'notice') grammatical features in the input to which they were exposed (see Chapter 12).

In each case, I drew on research in SLA to support my claims.

In short, the theory of grammar teaching I developed proposed that instruction should be directed at promoting the cognitive processes that were involved in the development of implicit knowledge but should not attempt to teach implicit knowledge directly as the acquisition of this type of knowledge was controlled by the learner. By and large, this is a theory to which I still subscribe. It has not been without its critics, however!

This theory was directed at explaining how instruction could work for 'new' grammatical features (i.e. features that had not yet begun to enter the learner's interlanguage). However, not all grammar learning involves the acquisition of 'new' features. It also involves the development of control over features that have already been partially acquired (i.e. features that are being used by the learner variably) — a point acknowledged earlier in *Teaching Secondary English*. To address this, I drew on Merrill Swain's ideas about 'comprehensible output'. This staked out a role for learner production by proposing that learners did not just learn from input but also by being pushed to use the L2 more concisely and more accurately. In a small-scale study with Junko Nobuyoshi (see Chapter 4), learners received requests for clarification when they made a past tense error in their oral narratives. We investigated whether this resulted in the students correcting their own errors in what subsequently became know technically as 'uptake'. We were also interested in whether this treatment enabled them to use the past tense more accurately in a subsequent oral narrative when they were not 'pushed' to correct themselves. We found that for some of the learners uptake did occur and there was also subsequent improvement in accuracy. This was, in fact, an early study of corrective feedback (a topic that I was to explore much more fully later). It showed that, under certain conditions, output-based grammar instruction could be effective.

It was while I was at TUJ that I also began and completed work on *The Study of Second Language Acquisition*, published by Oxford University Press in 1994. This was an encyclopedic survey of the SLA field. It amounted to 824 pages, including 61 pages of references. Henry

Widdowson once joked that this heavy tome provided both mental and physical exercise! Its size reflected the exponential growth that had taken place in the SLA field since my earlier attempt to synthesize its output in *Understanding Second Language Acquisition*. SLA had become a distinct discipline within Applied Linguistics and now figured as a course in most masters and doctoral programmes across the world. The book received relatively few reviews (perhaps because of its length) but it won the Duke of Edinburgh prize for the best book in applied linguistics of its year. It was translated into Japanese (by Tomoko Kaneko) and a special Chinese edition was also made available. In many respects, I view it as my main publishing achievement.

During this time I also worked with Sarah Murray on writing a textbook (*Let's Use English*) for primary school learners of English in South Africa, visiting that country several times in the process. Textbook writing, which began with *English Through Situations* while I was in Zambia, has continued to figure in my professional work throughout my career. I have always seen it as an important element of an applied linguists' work as it serves as a means of creating the link between theory and the practice of language teaching. *Let's Use English* drew on many of the ideas about language teaching that I had developed through my study of SLA.

My years in Tokyo at TUJ were very happy ones — memorable not just for the opportunity for me to develop myself professionally but also for the many personal friends I made and the opportunity it provided my children to experience living in such an exciting city. But in 1993 I was ready to move on. Japan, however, was a country I was to continue to visit regularly throughout my professional career.

Philadelphia: Temple University (1993 – 1998)

The main campus of Temple University is located in Philadelphia and in 1993 I moved there with my family to take up a tenured position as Professor in the School of Education. I became the director of the

TESOL program, teaching a number of master level courses and also supervising doctoral students. Philadelphia itself did not prove to be one of the geographical highlights of my peripatetic career but I hugely enjoyed the work in the University and the students there.

The five years I spent in Philadelphia were highly productive in terms of research and publications. In all, I wrote two academic books and published some ten academic articles or chapters. I edited a series of graded readers for African primary school students and also wrote a teacher guide for using them. In addition, I contributed to the writing of an EFL textbook series (*Impact*) for Asian students under the guidance of Michael Rost. I also headed a team of writers who developed a new English course for the West Indies (*Let's Work with English*). In this way, my professional activities were a continuation of my previous years — a combination of research, academic book writing, and EFL/ESL text book writing.

The two books drew on my previous publications. Henry Widdowson invited me to write the book on *Second Language Acquisition* for a new series by Oxford University Press — the Oxford Introductions to Language Study (OILS), which was intended for readers new to the formal study of language. I was asked to provide an overview of the SLA field in 90 pages — a somewhat daunting task given that I had needed over 800 pages to do the same thing in *The Study of Second Language Acquisition*. I enjoyed the challenge and, with Henry's guidance, managed the task. The resulting book, published in 1997, continues to be widely used in introductory courses on SLA today. At the same time I put together a collection of my previously published papers in *SLA Research and Language Teaching*, also published by Oxford University Press in 1997. This attempted to systematically explain and illustrate my views about language (in particular grammar teaching). I drew heavily on my article 'Teaching and research: Options in grammar teaching' published in *TESOL Quarterly* to consider how research in SLA could best inform the practice of language teaching. In this article and the book, I discussed a number of options for teaching grammar — input-based instruction, explicit instruction, production-based instruction and corrective feedback — and tried to show how each of these could be informed by research in SLA. In the book I discussed ways of establishing a research-theory nexus: making the findings of SLA accessible to teachers (reflecting my attempt to do so in the OILS book), demonstrating how theory could be applied to the practice of teaching, conducting classroom-based research, and encouraging teachers to become researchers in their own classroom. This was an important book for me as it enabled me to articulate the belief that has guided my whole academic career — namely, that research and theory should not be divorced from the practice of language teaching but should both inform it and be informed by it.

My main research articles related to another of my major areas of interest — the role of interaction in classroom L2 acquisition. I (together with some of my students) devised studies to investigate Michael Long's Interaction Hypothesis. We examined the relative effects of simplified input, interactionally modified input and interactionally modified output on classroom learners' acquisition of vocabulary. We were able to show that all three types of input assisted acquisition but that a task that pushed learners to use the target words had the greatest effect. These studies all involved teachers performing a 'task' with the students and paved the way for my later work on task-based language teaching.

The textbook that best illustrates my attempts to implement my theoretical ideas about grammar teaching is *Impact Grammar*, co-authored with Stephen Gaies and published by Longman Pearson Asia in 1999. This adopted a 'grammar awareness' approach to teaching grammar, involving two distinct but related ideas:

1. The importance of 'noticing' a grammatical feature in the 'input' obtained from listening or reading. This drew on Dick Schmidt's seminal articles on the role that noticing plays in L2 acquisition (see Schmidt, 2001).

2. The utility of learners 'understanding' the grammatical feature (i.e. developing an explicit representation of the feature). This draw on my

own ideas about the role of consciousness-raising tasks.

The book was premised on the idea that being 'aware' of a grammatical feature (either in the sense of 'noticing' or 'understanding') is the not the same as 'acquiring' the feature but that awareness could facilitate grammar acquisition. The book also aimed to assist students to become autonomous learners of grammar through the use of discovery activities. Each unit dealt with a different grammatical point which SLA research had shown was likely to be problematic to L2 learners. There were activities in each unit: Listening for Meaning (where students listened to a short text containing the target structure just to understand the meaning), Listening to Notice (where they listened to the same text to attend to the exemplars of the target structure), Understanding (where they were guided into the formation of an explicit rule for the structure), Checking (where they applied the rule to some new data) and Trying It (where they completed a short task using the structure). The book was intended as a remedial grammar course that could be used either for self-study or in a grammar course. Below is an example of the 'Listening to Notice' and 'Understanding' activities from the unit dealing with subject-verb agreement in the Present Simple Tense. They constitute very different types of activity from those that figured in *English Through Situations* and *Teaching Secondary English* and illustrate the developments that had occurred in my own thinking about grammar teaching.

LISTENING TO NOTICE

Listen again. Choose the correct form of the verb in parentheses [ ].

1. Grace of My Heart
This drama _follows_ the singing career of Edna Buxton
    1 *(follow/follows)*

as she _____ through the pop music world of the late
    2 *(move/moves)*

'50s and '60s.

---

2. Big Night

This bittersweet comedy tells the story of two Italian immigrants who _____ a restaurant
3 (open/opens)

in New Jersey. But their American Dream _____ sour and things end up
badly.   *4 (turn/turns)*

3. Hoop Dreams

This documentary follows four years in the lives of 14-year-olds Arthur Agee and
William Gates, two exceptionally talented basketball players. They _____ up
5 (grow/grows)

poor in downtown Chicago and _____ of careers as highly-paid professionals.
6 (dream/dreams)

4. The Long Kiss Goodnight

This action thriller stars Geena Davis playing a school teacher who _____ from
7 (suffer/suffers)

amnesia. She hires a detective, played by Samuel L. Jackson, and together they
_____ for her past and true identity.
8 (search/searches)

UNDERSTANDING THE GRAMMAR POINT

1. Complete this table. Use the information in the movie listings.

Subject	Verb
1. *drama*	*follows*
2. *she*	
3. *who (two Italian immigrants)*	
4.	
5.	
6.	
7.	
8.	

2. Which form of the verb is used with singular subjects?
   Which form of the verb is used with plural subjects?

I had originally intended to return to Temple University Japan after
my five year period in Philadelphia but for a variety of reasons this did
not happen. When I left in 1998 I did so with mixed feelings. I was sad to

leave Temple University and the students who had made my time there so worthwhile but I knew I would not miss Philadelphia or the United States. While I had the greatest admiration for many of the academics I met during this period in North America (Jim Lantolf and Alister Cumming in particular come to mind) I did not feel that the American Dream was for me.

Auckland: University of Auckland (1998 to now)

My move to New Zealand and the University of Auckland in 1998 surprised many. But I had had the opportunity to visit this beautiful country in 1990 for a conference and knew that this was a place where I and my family could settle and be happy. I have never had reason to revise that opinion. I have received amazing support, not just from those I have worked with at the University of Auckland, but also from leading academics such as Graeme Kennedy and Paul Nation at Victoria University of Wellington. In many respects this stage of my life has proved the most rewarding professionally and agreeable socially.

I joined the University of Auckland as Professor in and Director of the Institute of Language Teaching and Learning, taking over this position from Jack Richards. When I joined, the Institute consisted of just four academic staff and a number of tutors who worked on EAP courses. However, this was a period of enormous growth in international students at the University and this gave me the opportunity to develop the curriculum of the Institute by adding a one-year taught masters degree and incorporating the EAP courses into the regular undergraduate programme. As student numbers increased, so too did the staff of the Institute. Cathie Elder, Gary Barkhuizen, and Shawn Loewen were among those appointed in the first few years. Alan Kirkness, who joined us from the Department of German in the University, where he had served for many years, contributed the institutional knowledge and wise advice that I needed to manage the exponential growth that was taking place in the Institute. Then with the support of the Dean of the Faculty of Arts, Doug

Sutton, a new department was formed with myself as its first Head — the Department of Applied Language Studies and Linguistics (DALSL). This incorporated the Institute of Language Teaching and Learning and the newly formed Institute of Linguistics and rapidly became one of the largest departments in the Faculty of Arts. The Department offered a variety of degrees in both language teaching education and linguistics at both undergraduate and graduate level. Additional appointments were made, including Rosemary Erlam, Jenefer Philp and Rob Batstone (from the Institute of Education, University of London) and Jim Miller (from the University of Edinburgh) as the first Professor of Linguistics and more recently Yan Huang. Today DALSL continues to thrive as both an academic unit and as a convivial community of individuals.

Much of my work at the University of Auckland has been directed at helping to form and develop DALSL. In many respects I consider this the major achievement in my time there, not least because I know that when I finally retire, DALSL will continue to go from strength to strength. During the 11 years I have spent in Auckland, however, I have continued to teach (developing a number of new courses), supervise a number of doctoral students, research and publish.

Supervising doctoral students proved somewhat more challenging at the University of Auckland than it had at Temple University, reflecting the fact that, in accordance with the British tradition, PhD students were not required to complete courses prior to embarking on their thesis. As a result they did not always possess the disciplinary knowledge and technical skills required for doctoral research and had to acquire these as they progressed. However, I was extremely lucky with my first few doctoral students. I took over the supervision of John Bitchener and saw his thesis through to completion. Shawn Loewen moved from Temple University to Auckland to take up a position as research assistant and, because of his experience as a postgraduate student in a US university, was fully equipped to undertake doctoral research. He completed an excellent thesis, became a highly valued member of the academic staff of the Department for several years, and, eventually, went on to take up a position at Michigan State University. Rosemary Erlam had no background in applied linguistics (although she did have substantial experience as a teacher of French). She was able to very rapidly develop the background knowledge and skills needed to complete a very accomplished thesis, demonstrating that, for some students at least, the British doctoral tradition works well. She too went on to join the academic staff of the department. Both Shawn and Rosemary were also to play major roles in a number of research projects in which I was involved. Over the years I have spent at Auckland I have supervised many other doctoral students — too many to mention — on a great variety of topics, including learner beliefs, corrective feedback, language testing, computer-assisted language teaching, teacher professional development, interlanguage pragmatics, motivation, second language writing, individual differences and classroom participation, and form-focused instruction. I remain indebted to my doctoral students — for their diligence, for tolerating my demanding and often impatient supervision, and, of course, for helping me to continue to develop the knowledge-base of my discipline.

I will mention four research projects that I completed during this period. The first, which I carried out with Helen Basturkmen and Shawn Loewen, investigated 'focus on form', a term used by Michael Long to refer to the incidental attention that is paid to linguistic form while learners are engaged in performing communicative tasks. Our methodology was as follows. A number of communicative lessons involving adult ESL students in a private language school in Auckland were recorded and transcribed. The transcripts were then examined in order to identify 'form-focused episodes', i.e. episodes where the teacher and the students departed from the main task to address a problem with a linguistic form that had arisen. These episodes were both teacher-initiated (as when the teacher provided corrective feedback) and student-initiated (as when a student asked a question about the use of a particular form).

We then developed a discourse analytic system to account for the structure of these episodes and the different kinds of moves they contained. Finally, we carried out an analysis of the episodes in terms of the linguistic focus (pronunciation, vocabulary or grammar), the source of the problem (i.e. whether the episode centred on a communicative problem or was more didactic in nature), the complexity of the episode (i.e. whether it involved just one or two or many turns), and the students' uptake of the information about a linguistic form that an episode provided. I gave a report of this project at a conference in Malaysia (see Chapter 6). The project — and a follow-up project led by Helen Basturkmen — also led to a number of co-authored publications, including 'Learner uptake in communicative ESL lessons' (*Language Learning*), 'Doing focus on form' (*System*), and 'Teachers' stated beliefs about incidental focus on form and their classroom practices' (*Applied Linguistics*). This project, then, brought together two of my principal lines of enquiry — classroom interaction and form-focused instruction (incidental focus on form constituting one option for conducting this).

The second research project was funded by the New Zealand Ministry of Education. I was invited to undertake a review of the literature on instructed L2 learning. This was eventually published by the Ministry and also led to an article — 'Principles of instructed language learning' (*System* — see also Chapter 15). There was also a follow-up to this project — 'Instructed Second Language Acquisition: Case Studies' — also published by the Ministry of Education. This project was carried out together with Rosemary Erlam and Keiko Sakui (one of my doctoral students). It made use of the principles I had identified in my review as a basis for carrying out case studies of four experienced teachers of foreign languages in New Zealand secondary schools. We devised a classroom observation scheme and a set of interview questions with a view to describing both the practices and belief-systems of the four teachers. The idea was to provide an evidence base in the form of illustrative material and exemplars of effective practice that could be used to assist teachers' professional learning and practice. This project, then, is another example of my life-long attempt to help teachers connect theory and practice.

The third project was an ambitious one. Cathie Elder and I received a grant from the Marsden Fund, a contestable fund administered by the Royal Society of New Zealand designed to support research excellence in a range of academic disciplines. Over the three years that the project lasted, a number of people were involved, including Shawn Loewen, Rosemary Erlam and Jenefer Philp and a number of research assistants. The project aimed to develop tests of implicit and explicit L2 knowledge, to examine the relationship between measures obtained from these tests and measures of general L2 proficiency, and to use the tests to investigate the effects of different kinds of form-focused instruction. It was motivated by the fact that although the distinction between implicit and explicit knowledge was now well-established and widely-accepted in SLA, there was no agreement about how these two types of knowledge could be empirically investigated and that until appropriate measures were developed a number of lines of enquiry in SLA (in particular the effect of form-focused instruction on L2 learning) would remain plagued with problems. Focusing on grammar, we developed and validated a battery of tests designed to provide relatively separate measures of the two knowledge types by administering the tests to samples of both native speakers and L2 learners. We explored the relationship between these measures and the learners' IELTS and TOEFL scores. Finally we used the tests to investigate the effects of different types of form-focused instruction on learners' acquisition of implicit and explicit knowledge. A variety of papers resulted from the study (including the one reproduced in Chapter 7) and a full-length book — *Implicit and Explicit Knowledge in Second Language Learning, Teaching and Testing* — published in 2009 by Multilingual Matters. The experience of conducting this project was enormously challenging, consuming endless hours of the time of those involved in it, but it was also immensely rewarding. It enabled me to test out and fine-tune many of my ideas about the nature of L2 learning as well as provide a basis for developing both my own research skills and those of the other people involved in the project. It is perhaps the most 'theoretical' of my research projects but it also aimed to address issues that were of potential practical use to both language testers and teachers.

In a way, the fourth project grew out of one strand of the Marsden project, where we had investigated oral corrective feedback. Together with Younghee Sheen, I successfully applied for a grant from 'The International Research Foundation for English Language Education' to investigate the effects of different types of written corrective feedback on L2 acquisition. We then linked up with two Japanese researchers (Hide Takashima and Mihoko Murakami) to carry out a study of the effects of focused versus unfocused feedback on Japanese university students' use of English articles in writing. Younghee Sheen carried out a parallel study on adult ESL learners in the United States. The resulting articles (both published by *System*) have contributed to the lively and ongoing debate that has taken place in the field of L2 writing studies regarding the role that written corrective feedback plays in L2 acquisition. The research project also motivated me to write an article for *ELT Journal* (see Chapter 16) where I presented a taxonomy of written corrective feedback types that I hoped would be of use in teacher education.

During my years in Auckland, my writing and publishing has carried on apace, perhaps more frenziedly than was desirable at times. In addition to the articles based on the various research projects and the book emanating from the Marsden fund, I completed a number of other books. *Learning a Second Language Through Interaction* (John Benjamins) was co-authored with a number of my Temple University doctoral students and brought together reports of the various research projects they had conducted. *Form-Focused Instruction and Second Language Learning* appeared in 'The Best of Language Learning Series', published by Blackwell on behalf of the journal *Language Learning*. It consisted of a selection of articles previously published in the journal and an introduction, where I surveyed the research on form-focused instruction.

Task-Based Language Teaching and Learning (Oxford University Press) was my attempt to synthesize research and theory on this topic. My advocacy of task-based language teaching in this book reflected my conviction about the centrality of 'interaction' in classroom instruction and the role that tasks could play in ensuring the kinds of interaction that would facilitate L2 acquisition. This book, like much of my work, aimed to connect research and theory in SLA and the practice of language teaching. *Analysing Learner Language* (Oxford University Press) was co-authored with Gary Barkhuizen. It was based on a course called 'Learner Language' that we were jointly teaching in our MA programme. The underlying idea was to replace a traditional expository approach to topics in SLA with a more hands-on, do-it-yourself approach where students were required to grapple with L2 data in order to investigate the kinds of questions that have figured in SLA research. *Planning and Task Performance in a Second Language* (John Benjamins) was an edited collection of studies of the effects of different kinds of planning on learner production. This book was an extension of my work on task-based teaching, one of my major areas of interest at this time. Finally, in response to pressure from Cristina Whitecross, my editor at Oxford University Press, I undertook a revision of *The Study of Second Language Acquisition*. The fifteen years that had passed since the first edition of this book had seen enormous developments in the field of SLA, both in terms of the research that had taken place and the theories that informed this research. In addition to thoroughly revising each chapter, I included two new chapters, one on sociocultural SLA and the other on neurolinguistic approaches to investigating L2 acquisition. The result was an even longer book — over a thousand pages. All of these books, in one way or another, drew on my knowledge of SLA and explored the relationship between theory/research and language teaching, in particular the teaching of grammar.

Looking back on my twelve years at the University of Auckland, I can see that in many respects they have been the pinnacle of my professional career. They have afforded me the opportunity to contribute to the development of a new department, to develop new programmes at undergraduate and graduate level, to supervise some extremely able doctoral students, to undertake a number of research projects, and to continue to write. All this has been made possible by the support I have received from members of my Department, which continues to be not just an exciting professional environment but a convivial, social community. I could not have asked for more.

CONCLUSION

In many respects my professional career has followed the traditional path of many British and some North American applied linguists. I began as a teacher of English as a foreign and then second language. I moved on to working as a teacher educator. Then, out of these experiences and influenced by a number of key figures in the field (Gordon Wells and Henry Widdowson in particular), I developed skills as a researcher and as a writer. Throughout I have been concerned with how a language can be taught in a way that will foster learning. I sometimes ask myself whether, if I could have my career all over again, I would make any changes to it. The answer is 'no'. While there are events in my personal life that I would certainly not want to repeat, there is nothing in my professional life that I would wish to omit. All its stages, from the Berlitz school in Spain to my work as a professor at the University of Auckland, have contributed to where I stand today.

How grammar is taught and how it is learned have been key themes through my professional life. Many of the articles I have written over the years reflect this concern. Indeed, my interest in SLA arose out of my wish to find ways of making grammar teaching more effective. I have taken a broad view of grammar teaching; I think it is best conceptualized as a series of methodological options that include not just the presentation and practice of a grammatical feature but also input-based and task-based approaches. Teachers of grammar need to be familiar with these options and how they are informed by what the research shows about their effectiveness. They need to develop the practical skills for combining the options into grammar lessons. They need to view grammar teaching not simply in terms of techniques but also as 'processes' that arise during the conduct of an actual lesson.

The articles in this book have been organized into two main sections. In 'Researching Instructed Language Learning' I include a number of articles that report studies that have investigated the effect of instruction on L2 learning. These articles span a period of twenty-five years, from my first attempt to conduct an experimental study of the effects of grammar teaching to my latest study of corrective feedback. The final article in this section spells out the kinds of issues that researchers need to consider when designing form-focused instruction studies. In 'Teaching Grammar' I include a range of articles that articulate my thinking about how teachers can set about teaching grammar in ways that reflect what is known about how grammar is learned. Hopefully this book will be of interest to both researchers interested in investigating grammar teaching and teachers who have to teach grammar.

Section B

RESEARCHING INSTRUCTED GRAMMAR LEARNING

Introduction

This section includes reports of a number of my studies that investigated the effects of form-focused instruction (FFI) on L2 acquisition. Form-focused instruction refers to any attempt to intervene in the process of L2 acquisition by drawing learners' attention to specific linguistic forms and the meanings they convey. The target forms may be phonological, lexical, grammatical or pragmatic. Thus FFI covers more than just grammar teaching. However, in all the studies in this section the instructional focus was either entirely or predominantly grammar.

The studies span a period from 1984 to 2007. They reflect the changes that have taken place in my ideas about grammar teaching over time (see Chapter 1) and also the increasing attention I paid to methodological issues in the design of such studies.

The first study — 'Can syntax be taught? A study of the effects of formal instruction on the acquisition of WH questions by children' — was published in *Applied Linguistics* in 1984. It was based on my PhD thesis and was my first attempt at an experimental study. Grammar teaching was conceptualized in terms of practice activities. There was no explicit presentation of the target structure. The learners completed controlled practice activities. However, I also viewed grammar teaching as 'interaction' (i.e. I saw it not just as a set of activities but also as a classroom process). There were some major methodological limitations in this study. I was not able to include a control group. The elicitation instrument I used to obtain data to measure learning was very contrived. The main value in the study today lies in the fact that it was one of the first to view grammar teaching not just as a set of techniques but as a 'process'.

The second study — 'Are classroom and naturalistic acquisition the same? A study of the classroom acquisition of German word order rules' — appeared in 1989 *in Studies in Second Language Acquisition*. It was non-experimental. I sought to investigate the effects of instruction on the learners' acquisition of a set of German word order rules by comparing the order of acquisition of classroom and naturalistic learners. No attempt was made to intervene in the instruction that the learners had received. I simply noted the order in which the different word order rules were introduced to the students in their textbook and in the actual teaching to which they were exposed. Observations of this teaching showed that the teaching was very traditional, largely consisting of grammatical explanations and various kinds of controlled practice exercises. This study supported the claim that learners follow their own syllabus rather than the teaching syllabus. However, such comparative studies cannot really show whether grammar teaching does have an effect on learning and they are unable to establish what effect (if any) different instructional practices have on learning.

'Focused communication tasks' was published in the *English Language Teaching Journal* in 1994. It was co-authored by Junko Nobuyoshi, one of MA students at Temple University Japan. It was premised on a very different view of grammar teaching from the previous two articles. I wanted to investigate whether pushing learners to self-correct by responding to utterances that contained a past tense error with a clarification request resulted in learning. Some readers may wonder if this really constitutes 'grammar teaching'. But to my mind it clearly is. The aim was to use an instructional technique to draw learners' attention to their errors and thereby to help them improve their grammatical accuracy. Any instructional technique that attempts this qualifies as 'grammar teaching'. This study was, in fact, an early experimental study of corrective feedback. It was better designed that the 1984 study — it had a control group and employed a more valid data collection instrument. Its limitation was the small sample size — just 3 learners in both the experimental and the control group.

The importance that I had begun to attach to how acquisition was measured in FFI studies is most clearly evident in the next article — 'Does form-focused instruction affect the acquisition of implicit knowledge? A review of the research', published in *Studies in Second Language Acquisition* in 2002. A key issue is whether FFI has an effect on learners' implicit knowledge or just on their explicit knowledge. To tap into learners' implicit knowledge it is necessary to obtain samples of their unplanned communicative use of the L2. In this article I reviewed the relatively few studies which have done this, most having taken the easier route of using grammaticality judgment tests or discrete-point production tests. I was able to show that FFI had an effect on implicit knowledge.

'Focusing on form in the classroom' also appeared on 2002. It reported the study of incidental focus on form which I had undertaken with Helen Basturkmen and Shawn Loewen (see Chapter 1). This study was descriptive rather than experimental in nature. It was premised on a very different view of FFI from that which informed my previous research. Rather than treating FFI as something that is planned (i.e. a specific linguistic target is chosen and instructional materials are developed to teach it) it viewed FFI as something that could arise incidentally while the students and the teacher were engaged in communicative activities. This is what is known as 'focus on form'. We found that focus-on-form episodes occurred regularly in the communicative ESL classrooms we investigated and that many of them involved grammar. This grammar teaching, unlike the teaching that occurs in grammar lessons, was extensive (i.e. the focus is on a large number of different grammar points rather than on a single grammar feature). The study convinced me that this kind of extensive, incidental attention to form was an important source of grammar learning. My view of what grammar teaching consists of had widened considerably.

This study also made me aware of the importance of corrective feedback as many of the FFI episodes we observed were 'reactive', i.e. involved the teacher correcting an error in a student's utterance. 'The differential effects of corrective feedback on two grammatical structures' appeared in 2007 in a collection edited by Alison Mackey. It sought to investigate the effects of two types of corrective feedback (recasts and metalinguistic explanations) on L2 acquisition. The design of this study incorporated a number of characteristics that I now saw as important — a control group, a pre-test, immediate post-test and delayed post-test, a clearly formulated instructional treatment, actual observations of the instruction as it took place, and measures of both implicit and explicit knowledge. A novel feature of this study was that it investigated two different grammatical features (past tense -*ed* and comparative adjectives) in an attempt to see whether the effect of the corrective feedback differed according to the complexity of the grammatical feature that was targeted.

The final article in this section — 'Researching the effects of form-focused instruction on L2 acquisition' — appeared in 2006 in a book edited by Bardovi Harlig and Zoltan Dornyei based on a colloquium given the previous year at an AILA conference. It constitutes my attempt to bring together my ideas about how to design studies of FFI. I attempt to define FFI broadly in terms of a set of instructional options. I discuss the choice of grammar targets in FFI studies. I suggest how the dependent variable of such studies — 'acquisition' — can be conceptualized and measured. My idea was to develop a framework that could both serve as a basis for reviewing previous research and for designing new studies.

Overall, these studies reflect the progress that has been made in investigating FFI. Early FFI research was primarily concerned with determining whether instruction had any effect on learning (i.e. whether it could alter the natural route of acquisition). Later research focused more on the effects of different kinds of FFI and the design of the studies became increasingly rigorous. Running through my own research on FFI was the conviction that 'grammar teaching' cannot be simply viewed as a set of externally-defined practices but needs to be viewed as a process that unfolds and affords opportunities for learning.

Chapter 2

Can Syntax Be Taught? A Study of the Effects of Formal Instruction on the Acquisition of WH Questions by Children

This chapter appeared originally in 1984 as an article in Applied Linguistics Vol. 5, pp.138–155.

INTRODUCTION

In 1973 Dulay and Burt published an article entitled 'Should we teach children syntax?'. The answer they gave was that syntax should not be taught to children. If children were exposed to a natural communication situation the 'natural processes' responsible for second language acquisition (SLA) would be activated and a resulting 'natural order' of development occur. In the decade that followed the publication of this study, the conviction among SLA researchers that formal instruction was not the best way to learn a second language (L2) grew. Krashen (1981a; 1982), in particular, has argued that because there is no 'interface' between 'acquired' and 'learned' knowledge, because there are constraints on the nature and number of rules that can be 'learnt', and because utterances are initiated only with 'acquired' knowledge, little time should be spent in teaching grammar. Krashen's position is not only that syntax *should* not be taught (to any great extent) but also that it *cannot* be taught.

However, it is a huge leap from advising against formal instruction for children, on the grounds that there is a better way to encourage SLA, to rejecting formal instruction for both children and adults on the grounds that it does not work. It runs contrary to the intuitions of many language teachers who operate on the basis that 'skill getting' precedes 'skill using' (Rivers & Temperley, 1978). According to this view, formal instruction may not be instantly successful, but it may act as an 'acquisition facilitator' (Seliger, 1979) by sensitizing the learner to a specific form which can then be fully acquired and more easily used later on. This is one version of the 'interface hypothesis', which states that knowledge derived from formal study can be utilized in everyday conversation if not sooner, then later. Protagonists of the 'interface' position (e.g. Bialystok and Frohlich, 1977; Sharwood Smith, 1981) argue that explicit (or 'learnt') knowledge can be converted into implicit (or 'acquired') knowledge, providing the learner has the opportunity and motivation to automatize new rules through practice. Even if formal instruction does not result in a different acquisition route (and there is no agreement about this), it is still desirable, because it can speed up development. 'Acquisition' is a slow process; the provision of carefully selected and graded input that is thoroughly practiced may accelerate it.

The 'interface' debate is conducted largely in theoretical and speculative terms. There is little in the way of hard empirical evidence. Krashen (1981b), responding to Sharwood Smith's (1981) arguments in favour of consciousness-raising, reviews his reasons for denying any seepage from 'learnt' to 'acquired' knowledge. There are learners like 'P' who are strongly motivated to practice, but who still do not 'acquire' rules like the third person singular of the present simple tense. 'Self-report' data do not support the view that rules are 'learnt' before they become automatized. The evidence for the 'natural order' is very strong, suggesting that learners cannot beat it. Finally, if development occurs via comprehension (as opposed to production) then it is unlikely that practice of formally presented language items will contribute to 'acquisition'. In Krashen's opinion the interface position consists of nothing but appeals to intuition.

Those empirical studies that have investigated the effectiveness of formal instruction have typically done so either by comparing learners who have received language teaching with those who have not (e.g. Fathman, 1975), or by correlational studies involving measures of target language proficiency (e.g. Krashen *et al.*, 1978). Krashen (1982:34ff.) reviews seven studies of the first type. He concludes that formal instruction can help, but only to the extent to which it provides 'comprehensible input'. He suggests that it is most successful in foreign language teaching situations, where the students are not exposed to the target language outside the classroom. In this interpretation, therefore, it is not consciousness-raising or practice that aids development, but simply exposure to input pitched at the appropriate level to facilitate 'acquisition'. However, Krashen *et al.* (1978) found that the proficiency of 116 ESL students correlated more strongly with the number of years of formal English study than with the number of years they had spent in an English-speaking environment. The conclusion they reached is in striking contrast to the view formulated in Krashen (1982): 'What may be inferred from the results is that formal instruction is a more efficient way of learning English for adults than trying to learn it "in the streets"' (p.260). The apparent contradiction can be resolved only by distinguishing 'exposure' and 'instructional' variables in language teaching. Is it the 'comprehensible input' or the 'consciousness-raising' that occurs in language teaching which contributes to development? This is a vital question, but the answer cannot be determined from studies that do not examine the nature of the classroom interactions that take place in the name of language teaching.

Some of the strongest evidence in favour of the non-interface position comes from studies that have investigated the relationship between explicit knowledge of grammatical rules and actual performance. Seliger (1979), for instance, found that there was no relationship between his subjects' ability to use 'a' and 'an' before a noun and their ability to state the rule involved. If this finding generalizes to a large number of other rules, it would appear that conscious knowledge of a rule is of little use in spontaneous communication. However, as Seliger recognizes, this does not mean that instruction is without value, as it may ease the way for later acquisition. His study does suggest that the processes responsible for learning about a rule are not those responsible for using it in ordinary conversation.

Rather surprisingly, however, the interface issue has not been subjected to the most penetrating form of empirical investigation, i.e. the study of the effects of formal instruction in *specific* grammatical rules on students' abilities to use these rules in informal contexts. An exception is the investigation by Lightbown *et al.* (1980). They studied the effects of classroom teaching on 175 French-speaking students' use of the [s] inflection, the copula in equational clauses, and locative prepositions of motion. They observed that scores on a grammatical judgement test improved on average 11% in comparison to a 3% improvement in a control group who received no instruction, although scores fell back to an intermediate level in a later administration of the test. This study suggests that formal instruction can have some effect in improving the general accuracy of learners' speech, but the grammatical judgement test may measure 'learning' rather than 'acquisition'; it gives no indication of whether formal instruction leads to an improved ability to use the target structures in ordinary conversation.

The kind of investigation undertaken by Lightbown *et al.* is problematic as a result of the difficulty in both identifying and controlling for the independent variables that may influence the success of formal instruction. There is a host of potential instructional variables. As

Sharwood Smith (1981) points out, 'consciousness-raising' can take place in varying degrees, depending on the level of elaboration and explicitness with which the rule is presented. Practice can vary in both amount and type. Some grammatical rules may be amenable to formal instruction and others might not — Krashen (1982) suggests that the third person singular is an example of the former, and WH interrogatives an example of the latter. It may also prove to be the case that whereas formal instruction is of little use where rules are concerned, it can prove very effective for formulaic speech (Ellis, 1983). In either instance, however, the student must be prepared to treat the formal instruction as a means of developing knowledge of the target language and not as a problem-solving task, otherwise it is likely that instead of 'interlanguage competence' developing, all that will result is 'reproductive competence' (Felix, 1977).

In addition to the above instructional variables, there is also a host of learner variables that may influence the success of formal instruction. The students' stage of development may be crucial. Vygotsky (1962) pointed out that for training to be effective, it must occur at the learner's 'zone of proximal development'. Also, beginners may be able to benefit more from instruction than advanced learners, or perhaps vice versa. [1] The importance of taking into account the age of the student in planning formal instruction is generally recognized; students who have reached the Piagetian stage of Formal Operations are likely to be better equipped to benefit from grammar teaching than those who have not. The attitudes and motivation of the students is likely also to be crucial. For example, students who expect language teaching to consist of formal instruction may be more receptive to it than others. A host of other variables could be considered — personality, cognitive style, the student's mother tongue, whether the student is literate or not in his mother tongue, the student's relationship with his teacher, etc. In general very little is known about how learner variables influence classroom language learning.

The difficulty of controlling for these (and other) instructional and learner variables is probably the major reason why there have been so few empirical studies of the direct effects of formal instruction on the acquisition of specific rules. Nevertheless, it is arguably time to lend support to theorizing about whether syntax can or cannot be taught by beginning the difficult process of submitting the arguments to empirical study. It is unlikely that any single study will resolve the issue, but the cumulative evidence of many studies may help to answer what has become the major question of applied SLA research — can syntax be taught?

The study that is reported in the subsequent sections of this paper has two major aims. The first is to make a start on examining empirically how the teaching of specific structures contributes to their acquisition, and the second is to identify a number of methodological issues that future studies will need to take into consideration. It must be emphasized that because of the difficulty of identifying and controlling for learner and situational variables that can influence acquisition, the study is to be viewed as exploratory.

THE DESIGN OF THE STUDY

The study was designed to investigate the effects of approximately three hours of teaching on the ability of thirteen children to ask WH questions that were semantically appropriate and that displayed subject-verb inversion.

The Participants

The thirteen children were aged between 11 and 15 years. They were full-time ESL pupils at a Language Unit in London. They differed in the amount of time they had been resident in Britain, the mean being approximately one year. All the children were exposed to English outside the classroom, particularly in the Language Unit, where English functioned as a lingua franca among teachers and pupils. The extent to which they used English outside the Unit is less certain. In many cases the pupils were socially 'distanced' from an English-speaking community, and in one or two cases probably did not use English at all. However, the possibility of acquisition occurring as a result of outside contacts cannot be excluded and should be borne in mind in evaluating the results.[2] The children varied considerably with regard to age, first language (Punjabi, Mandarin Chinese, Burmese, Arabic), time spent at the Unit, and mother tongue literacy. There were also differences apparent on other variables such as personality and learning-style. They were in many ways typical of the motley collection of 'first stage' learners found in Language Units throughout Britain.

Two of the children in the study were the subjects of a longitudinal study of classroom SLA. This study showed that at the time of the WH interrogative investigation, the two children had begun to use WH questions in spontaneous classroom speech, but that their development was by no means complete. Table 1 shows their development of questions in terms of four aspects at the time of this study. Both children typically relied on intonation rather than WH or inverted yes/no questions. Only about half of their total interrogative utterances contained a verb; only 'R' used subject-verb inversion in his interrogatives, and many of these consisted of routines (e.g. 'What's this?'). Table 1 is based on the spontaneous utterances the children produced in the classroom in the four weeks preceding this study.

Table 1: Development of interrogatives in two of the children
at the time of the WH interrogative investigation

Aspect of development	'R'	'T'
1. percentage of intonation questions in total interrogatives	53.3	68.8
2. percentage of interrogatives containing a verb	56.7	50.0
3. percentage of WH interrogatives in total interrogatives	36.7	31.3
4. percentage of interrogative utterances with subject-verb inversion	33.3	0

These two children, 'R' and 'T', were at the lower end of proficiency in the class as a whole. This is reflected in their 'when' development score (see below for an account of this); 'R' had a score of twenty-five and 'T' of nought (see Table 3). Therefore, given that both children were using WH questions in their spontaneous speech at the time of this study, it would seem reasonable to assume that WH interrogatives were within most of the thirteen children's 'zones of proximal development'. Indeed, WH interrogatives were carefully chosen with this point in mind.

The Formal Instruction

The children were used to a fairly eclectic teaching style. Any formal language work that normally took place was of the audiolingual type. There was little in the way of grammatical explanation, probably because this was considered difficult for this kind of child to grasp. It was decided, therefore, to base the formal teaching of WH interrogatives on an audiolingual approach.

The formal instruction consisted of three lessons, each lasting about one hour and taught on three consecutive days in the morning between break and lunchtime. A total of three hours of teaching is very little, so it was not expected that the children would have 'acquired' either the ability to use WH pronouns correctly or the ability to invert the subject and verb in the sense of reaching a 90% criterion level of success. It was felt, however, that three hours of teaching was sufficient to examine whether formal instruction had any impact on acquisition of the kind noted by Lightbown *et al.*

The aim of the first lesson was to ensure an understanding of the different meanings of four WH pronouns — 'who', 'what', 'where', and 'when'. In this lesson the teacher did not pay much attention to whether the children's interrogatives were inverted. The second and third lessons sought to actively teach subject-verb inversion. The plan of each of the lessons is sketched out below:

Lesson 1

The teacher grouped the children around a wall frieze displaying events taking place in a High Street. He began by asking a series of WH questions using first 'who' and 'what' and afterwards 'where' and 'when', and inviting individual pupils to respond. He corrected only when their responses were semantically inappropriate. For written practice the pupils were given a matching exercise — a series of questions about the frieze and jumbled answers.

Lesson 2

The teacher began by going over the written exercise of Lesson 1. He then again used the wall frieze to ask WH questions — this time only with 'who' and 'where' — but on this occasion corrected formal errors in the pupils' responses, in particular failure to invert questions. The pupils were then divided into groups and shown pictures to prompt 'who' and 'where' questions. Each pupil took it in turn to make a question, and another pupil to respond.

Lesson 3

The teacher revised questions with 'who' and 'where' by firing questions at the pupils. There then followed another session around the frieze during which the teacher asked 'what' and 'when' questions, concentrating on the latter, which posed the greater difficulty. Group work followed on the same pattern as in the previous lesson.

These lessons were taught by the children's normal class teacher. They were devised jointly by the researcher and the teacher, who was made aware of the purpose of the investigation. Each lesson was audio-recorded and transcriptions in normal orthography prepared.

The Elicitation Instrument

The elicitation instrument used to obtain a corpus of WH interrogatives from the children was an adaptation of the technique used by Beebe (1980). This required the children to make up WH questions about a picture of a classroom scene. To ensure that they produced a variety of WH questions, they were given cue cards for 'who', 'what', 'where', and 'when', and asked to produce an appropriate question for each card they took from the pile. There were also blank cards, when the children could use any question word they liked. A blank card was inserted after every fourth card. To diminish tension created by the elicitation procedure, and also to provide a more natural conversational framework, the pupils performed in pairs (except for the thirteenth child, who performed alone with the researcher) and were awarded points for each question they were able to ask and which their partner accepted as sensible. In this way the sessions were turned into a game. The scoring of points, however, did not contribute to the subsequent analyses.

The elicitation instrument was administered in an empty classroom with only a pair of children and the researcher present. It was used on the day before the first lesson was taught and three days after the last lesson (i.e. a weekend intervened between the last lesson and the second elicitation session). Both elicitation sessions were audio recorded and transcripts in normal orthography prepared.

RESULTS

The 13 children were asked to make 10 WH questions each in the first elicitation session. These were made up of 2 questions each for the 4 WH pronouns and 2 other questions of their own choice. In the second session the children were asked to make 15 WH questions, 3 questions for each of the 4 WH pronouns, and 3 others of their own choice.

Each question produced by the children was scored as follows:

1. According to whether it was meaningful irrespective or whether or not it was well-formed.

2. According to whether it displayed subject-verb inversion. For this analysis, only those questions that were semantically acceptable were considered, as some pupils treated 'where' and 'when' as free variants

of 'what' and inverted them through extension of the 'what+s' pattern. A question was counted as inverted irrespective of whether a second auxiliary was incorrectly used after the main verb (e. g. *When does she's eating?*).

3. According to whether it contained an auxiliary verb. The longitudinal study of two of the children showed that early interrogative utterances may omit the auxiliary verb. Thus an increase in the proportion of WH questions containing an auxiliary, irrespective of whether subject-verb inversion occurred, might be considered evidence of development. Questions which were suspected of being routines were excluded from this analysis.

4. According to whether it contained a main verb. The longitudinal study also showed that an early feature of interrogatives is the omission of the main verb. Thus an increase in WH interrogatives containing a main verb might also be considered evidence of development.

The scores that were obtained by the thirteen pupils in both elicitation sessions are given in Appendix A. A two-tailed t-test (Robson, 1973:78–79) was used to establish to what extent the difference in the scores between Time 1 and Time 2 was significant. The level of significance did not reach the 0.05 level on any of the measures. However, as Table 2 indicates, the mean scores at Time 2 were in each instance greater than at Time 1. Although the improvement in performance was not spread evenly across the thirteen pupils, there was a marked improvement in a number of children.

Table 2: Mean percentage scores at Times 1 and 2 and overall increase in scores

	Meaningful WH questions	Subject-verb inversion	Use of auxiliary	Use of main verb
Time 1	71.8	56.8	13	24.4
Time 2	81.4	66.7	20	28.7
Overall increase	9.6	9.9	7	3.7

An interesting feature of the results for the individual children is that a clear accuracy profile emerges. The accuracy order for the meaningful use of different WH pronouns correlates closely with that for subject inversion in the different WH questions. 'What' questions are easiest, closely followed by 'who'. 'Where' questions are substantially more difficult and 'when' most difficult of all. The application of the subject inversion rule is more likely in WH questions that employ WH pronouns whose meaning the learner has a clear understanding of. Thus the individual scores for meaningful use of the WH pronouns always exceed those for correct application of the subject-verb inversion rule. It would seem that learners first develop functional use of a WH question and then later develop the formal rules of usage.

The developmental order reflected in the accuracy orders at Time 1 mirrors that found in the longitudinal study of two of the children [3]. It would seem, therefore, that progress along this route may be facilitated by teaching, but that the effects are not general. Whereas some children benefit to a considerable degree from formal instruction, others do not benefit at all. Why is this so? The answer may lie in individual learner differences, but it may also lie in the nature of the classroom interactions in which individual children took part. In order to pursue the second possibility, it is necessary to peer inside the 'black box' itself.

The investigation of the relationship between the teaching and the acquisition of WH interrogatives was restricted to 'when' questions. Whereas many of the children had already achieved full competence with regard to 'who', 'what', and to a lesser extent 'where' questions, only one pupil had done so with 'when'. The hypothesis that was examined was that development of the subject-verb inversion rule for 'when' questions could be explained by the number of opportunities given to individual pupils either to comprehend or to produce a 'when' question in the lesson. Seliger (1977) suggested that 'high input generators' acquire a L2 more successfully and more rapidly than 'low input generators'. Seliger measured the amount of interaction that individual students participated in by counting every speech act that was performed in the classroom. However, because of the disorderliness of many of the interactions that took place in the 'when' lesson, an identical approach was not possible in this study. An alternative was to count the number of occasions when each individual pupil was nominated by the teacher either to produce or to answer a 'when' question. The advantage of this method was that such occasions could be readily and reliably identified from the transcript of the lesson and also that such occasions were representative of the mainstream 'instruction' offered by the teacher, and so were invariably supplied with feedback. The disadvantage was that every 'nominated' opportunity to use a 'when' question was also 'public', in the sense that any pupil could choose to attend to it if he wished and even to volunteer an unsolicited response which might or might not receive feedback.

A 'when' development score was calculated by awarding one point for each semantically appropriate 'when' question and a further one point if the question was inverted, converting the scores to percentages and then subtracting the difference between each pupil's percentage score for the first elicitation game from that for the second. The pupil whose 'when' questions appeared to be fully developed at Time 1 was not included in this analysis.

Table 3 shows the number of nominated 'when' exchanges that each pupil took part in, the total number of turns produced by the nominated pupils in these exchanges, and the 'when' development scores. The Fisher Exact Probability Test (Siegel, 1956) was used to establish the extent of any relationship between nominated opportunities for using 'when' questions and the development that took place between the two elicitation sessions. The twelve pupils were divided into two groups, labelled 'high interactors' and 'low interactors' in accordance with the number of 'when' exchanges they participated in, with the dividing line at three exchanges or more. The number of high and low interactors who showed a positive 'when' development score was then calculated. The result was quite startling; the expected relationship between high interaction and 'when' development did not emerge. In fact it was the slow developers who typically engaged in high interaction, and the fast developers who were typically low interactors ($p > 05$).

Table 3: Nominated 'when' exchanges, pupil turns,
and 'when' development scores for each pupil

Pupil	No.of exchanges	No.pupil turns	'when' development score
1	2	4	58
2	5	17	0
3	3	5	0
4	4	3	0
5	2	3	0
6	1	3	100
7	4	14	0
8	0	0	50
9	1	13	50
10	3	11	25
11	3	7	0
12	1	7	0

The results of the study can be summarized as follows:

1. For the group of thirteen children as a whole, there was no significant increase in their ability to use semantically appropriate and grammatically well-formed WH questions as a result of three hours of teaching.

2. Individual children showed a marked improvement in the ability to use semantically appropriate and grammatically well-informed WH questions.

3. An accuracy order based on the use of semantically appropriate and inverted 'what', 'who', 'where', and 'when' questions at Time 1 reflects a clear developmental progression which matches that observed

in the longitudinal study of two of the children.

4. With regard to development in the ability to use semantically appropriate and grammatically well-formed 'when' questions, it was the low interactors rather than high interactors who progressed.

DISCUSSION

Formal instruction can influence second language acquisition in two rather different ways. It can result in a different developmental *route*, or it can increase the *rate* at which learners pass along a standard route. Overall the results of the three hours of teaching of WH questions suggest that there were no effects on the route. The pattern of development that was observed cross-sectionally and from one elicitation session to the other was that observed in a longitudinal study of two of the children. It should be noted that the teaching did not completely follow the 'natural' order of development. The 'natural' order is (1) 'who' and 'what', (2) 'where', and (3) 'when'; whereas the teaching order was (1) 'who' and 'where', and (2) 'what' and 'when', although all four pronouns were presented together in the first lesson. Thus it is difficult to conclude that teaching does or does not influence the route of development. The results do suggest, though, that teaching does not lead to the dramatic appearance of 'new' rules but to a gradual improvement in the appropriateness and accuracy with which specific rules are developed and also to a slow accretion of syntactical complexity of utterances to which rules in the process of being developed are applied. Such an account is in accordance with current accounts of interlanguage as a variable system (e.g. Dickerson, 1975; Huebner, 1979).

It is also difficult from this study to decide whether teaching WH questions to the thirteen children helped the rate of development. It has been shown that some of the children made conspicuous improvement, but this improvement does not appear to be related to the amount of direct teaching specifically addressed to the children. The opportunity for plentiful practice did not lead to rapid development. This does suggest that practice of the kind provided in the three hours of teaching is not effective in aiding development. As has already been pointed out, however, there are innumerable instructional variables that can have a potential effect on the degree of success. Perhaps the teaching provided was of the wrong kind. Perhaps it is not active participation in practice, but listening to the attempts of other pupils that aids development.

The failure to find any significant effect for the amount of practice afforded individual children contradicts the results of Seliger's (1977) study. He found a significant correlation between the amount of interaction students took part in and their performance on achievement tests administered at the end of the course. What explanations are there for this contradiction? Seliger's subjects were adults, whereas in this study they were children. Seliger considered every utterance the students produced whereas this study considered only nominated exchanges. Also Seliger speculated that his results were best explained by the fact that high interaction inside the classroom was matched by high interaction outside, and that 'active learners' were successful because they made use of all language environments. The high interactors in this study were those selected by the teacher. It is possible that the teacher distributed opportunities for using 'when' to those pupils whom he considered most in need of formal instruction and that these were the pupils who were maximally socially 'distant' from an English-speaking community and thus the least likely to be high interactors outside the classroom. If this is the case, however, it would seem that formal instruction is not able to compensate for lack of general exposure to the target language.

The results raise an interesting and important question: why did those children who received the least practice improve the most? One possibility is that put forward by Allwright (1980) in his discussion of one high interactor. Allwright speculated that even if high interactors do not themselves benefit from using the language, their classmates might well benefit in a listening role. Another possibility is that it is not the quantity of interaction that counts, but the quality. One hypothesis might be that development is fostered by the consistency and accuracy of teacher feedback. Another hypothesis, one that is in tune with much current thinking on both first and second language development, is that communicatively rich interaction which affords opportunities for the negotiation of meaning may aid development, where more structured forms of interaction do not. In order to examine these 'quality' hypotheses, the transcript of the 'when' lesson was analysed.

There is little support for the first hypothesis. There are clear cases of pupils who received rigorous correction but who registered no improvement, and also of pupils who were allowed to get away with incorrect questions but who showed substantial development. Here are two examples [4]: (1) involves a zero developer, and (2) a fast developer.

(1)

> P7 When does her cooking?
> P2 When does the mother...

T. When does she cook the dinner?

> P7 When does she cooks the dinner?

T. When does she cook the dinner?

> P7 When does she cook the dinner?(exasperated)

T. All right OK. When does she cook the dinner.

(2)

T. Can you ask a 'when' question? When.

> PI When does she's she's going shopping?

T. When does she go shopping? Again.

> PI When does she goes shopping?

T. Right.

The second hypothesis looks more promising. Although there were obviously relatively few communicatively rich exchanges in a lesson designed to drill the use of 'when' questions, a number of occasions for more spontaneous conversation did arise and these always involved a pupil from the group that showed some development. Protocol (3) is an example of such an occasion.

(3)

T: Gurinder, would you like to ask
  a question?

                          P9 Who?

T: When. When does.

                          P10 In the park?
                          P? Ssh!
                          P9 In the park?

T. No, I think from the High Street
  I think.

                          P9 Oh.
                          P? Yes, come on.

T. I know. I'm going to help him a
  little bit.

                          Ps? No. No.

T. Ask me ask then a when
  question — the postman deliver.

                          P? When does...

T. Ssh!

                          P9 When does the postman
                          deliver ... What?
                          Ps? No. No.
                          P9 I know. What when does
                          the postman...

T. Deliver.

P9 Deliver.

P? Letter.

P? Letter.

P9 Letter?

T. Letters. Good. Stand up. Stand
up. Silence. Say it again, please.
Look at the class. Say it again.

P9 When does the postman.

T. Deliver.

P9 Deliver collect a letter.

T. No. Deliver.

P9 Deliver.

T. Letters.

P9 Letters.

T. Right. Who do you want to
answer?

P9 Raljip. (= name of
postman)

T. No. Anyone.

P9 Eh?

T. Anyone. You pick someone.

P? What Sir?

P? Oh!

T. When does the postman deliver
letters?

P2 In the morning.

Ps? (noise) In the morning.

T. In the morning.

This episode, which consists of forty-one turns, is the longest in
the lesson. Its length is the product of the need to negotiate the task
in a variety of ways. First, the pupil (P9) needs to establish what WH
pronoun he is supposed to use. Then he needs to establish the content of

the question (i.e. whether it should be about the pictures of the park or of the High Street). Later he requires specific help with the lexical content of the question (e.g. 'deliver'). Finally he misunderstands the teacher's instruction about choosing a pupil to answer his question and instead answers it himself — wrongly in fact, as he treats it as a 'who' question. The task is clearly a difficult one for this pupil, but there is no doubting his determination to succeed. The task itself serves to guide rather than dictate the structure of the episode. There is a lot of conversational work taking place just to stay on task, so it is not always clear where the cognitive focus lies. In the sequence dealing with the word 'deliver', for instance, the principal goal (constructing a 'when' question) appears to become of secondary importance. Arguably this is what occurs in natural conversations (see Schwartz, 1980). The exchange structure frequently departs from the three-phase pattern of most classroom interactions where the focus is on drilling a linguistic rule. It involves more of the topic-incorporation devices that characterize certain kinds of mother-child interaction and which have been found facilitative (see Wells, 1980). It is of course not possible to say what the pupil learnt from this exchange, but it is possible that the respite from the focus on form and the opportunity to negotiate an understanding did help him to achieve a better understanding of 'when' questions.

If this rather speculative argument has any legitimacy, it would seem that 'exposure' — for that is what it is suggested protocol (3) illustrates — is far more important than 'instruction' as represented in protocols (1) and (2). In other words, it is not focusing on the form of 'when' questions that helped some of the children to develop, but the opportunity to negotiate a communicative task.

An extension of this argument is that the development. that took place between the two elicitation sessions was not only the product of the exposure provided in the classroom, but also of that occurring in the elicitation sessions themselves. As Faerch (1980) has commented, interlanguage development may be the result of 'research internal' exposure just as much as 'research external' exposure.

An inspection of the transcript prepared from the second elicitation game lends some support to the view that the exposure in the sessions aided development. A good example is Pupil 10, who was one of the two children studied longitudinally. This pupil succeeded in producing a semantically appropriate 'when' question only in his final turn in the second elicitation game. Earlier, however, his partner, Pupil 9, had modelled 'when' questions for him. Also Pupil 10 appeared to seek out opportunities to practice 'when' questions by opting for 'when' on drawing a blank card. This contrasted with other pupils who typically chose an easy WH pronoun such as 'what' or 'who'. Protocol (4) is an example of the kind of practice that he constructed.

(4)

R. Blank. Any question you like,

R ...

P10 When is his (.) talking to him?

P9 What?

P10 When does his talking to him?

P9 Because he's happy.

P10 Happy?

R. Is that right, R ... ?

P10 No.

R. What's the answer?

P10 (.1.) Yes, right.

R. All right.

Although this exchange is not a successful one, it (and other attempts like it) may have enabled the pupil to experiment with a new form in a more or less communicative manner. Pupil 10's attempt in Protocol (4) seems to reflect a genuine effort to use 'when' meaningfully. As such it stands in marked contrast to the drill-like practice he took part in in the classroom, where Pupil 10 responded not so much by using language as with language-like behaviour.

The argument that is being tentatively put forward is that 'language teaching' involves both 'formal instruction' and 'exposure', and that for ESL children of the type investigated in this study, it is 'exposure' rather than 'instruction' that facilitates the development of WH questions. The illustrative evidence seems to indicate that when conditions are right (e.g. the learner is motivated and focused on meaning rather than form; the target rule is within the learner's 'zone of proximal development') acquisition can take place. In contrast, the statistical evidence indicates that the opportunity to practice the target rule in drill-like sequences does not aid acquisition. Implicit in this argument is the view that the L2 acquisition of English follows a uniform route in children learning English as a second language and that classroom teaching will influence only the rate of development. It must be emphasized, however, that this is a speculative interpretation.

CONCLUSION

The stated aims of the study of the thirteen ESL children were to make a start on directly examining how the teaching of specific structures contributes to their acquisition, and to identify a number of methodological issues important for this kind of research.

The Effects of Teaching on the Acquisition of Syntax

The study reported in the previous section cannot be said to have shown that teaching does not aid the acquisition of syntax for children. It indicated that for all the children the teaching did not subvert the 'natural' order of development, but then the teaching that was provided was not intended to achieve this. If the teaching had focused exclusively on 'when' questions and similar results achieved, then a strong case could have been made out for the failure of teaching to influence the developmental order. This may be a profitable line for future enquiry.

The study showed that the opportunity to take part in nominated teacher exchanges did not help acquisition of WH interrogatives. It is possible only to speculate why this was the case. A number of possibilities can be put forward:

1. It is not production but comprehension that aids development, as argued by Krashen (1982). The low interactors had the chance to learn by attending to interactions involving the high interactors.

2. It is not the quantity of interaction, but the quality, that ensures acquisition. Some illustrative evidence has been put forward to suggest that when the learner has the chance to negotiate meaningfully, acquisition may be facilitated. This suggests that the instruction may have worked when it provided the right type of interaction.

3. The kind of instruction provided worked for those who had already begun the process of acquiring 'when' questions, but not for those who had not. In other words, WH interrogatives (the 'when' type in particular) were not within the 'zones of proximal development' of all the children. Slender evidence for this can be found in the fact that 'R', who was more advanced at the time of the study, out-developed 'T' whose 'when' score was zero.

This study, however, was not tuned finely enough to be able to distinguish among these possibilities. What light can this study shed on current theories concerning the role of instruction in the acquisition of syntax? I shall conclude by attempting to relate the findings to two different positions — the 'interface' and the 'non-interface' position.

The 'interface' position states that formal instruction can contribute to development by providing the learner with the opportunity to practice and so to automatize new rules (Sharwood Smith, 1981; Stevick, 1980). It is through practice that 'explicit' knowledge, which is non-automatic, becomes 'implicit' knowledge, which is automatic. Instruction can both provide explicit knowledge and help to convert it into implicit knowledge. This study does not appear to support the interface position. Producing exemplars of a pattern in a drill does not foster their use in spontaneous communication (if that was what the elicitation session was) involving children of the type investigated. This study does not, of course, disconfirm the interface position. The instruction provided may have been of the wrong type, in insufficient quantity, at the wrong time, etc. It would be necessary to replicate this study several times with different structures and different learners before the interface position could be seriously challenged.

The main protagonist of the 'non-interface' position is Krashen. Briefly, Krashen argues that 'acquired' knowledge, which is internalized through participating in authentic communication, is stored separately from 'learnt' knowledge, which is the result of conscious study. Not only are the knowledge stores separate, but 'learnt' knowledge cannot be converted into 'acquired' knowledge. The findings of the interrogatives study are entirely compatible with Krashen's theory. The lessons provided two types of input — input where the focus was on form and input where the focus was on meaning. In the discussion of the study these have been referred to as 'instruction' and 'exposure'. The study provided no evidence that 'instruction' aided the ability of the learners to perform in the elicitation game, which (presumably) required the use of 'acquired' knowledge. However, 'exposure' in certain types of interaction, in both the lessons and the elicitation games, may have served to facilitate development. One difference between Krashen's position and that taken up in the discussion of the interrogatives study is that whereas Krashen talks of 'comprehensible input', this paper emphasizes 'meaningful interaction'. In other words, it may not just be a question of listening with understanding, but also of productive use of new structures that aids development.

It should be pointed out, however, that the findings of the interrogatives study are also compatible with other theories of SLA. Bialystok (1982), for instance, has proposed that L2 knowledge be characterized in terms of an *analysed* factor as well as an *automatic* factor. The analysed factor concerns the degree to which the learner is able to form a 'propositional representation' of target language knowledge.

Bialystok suggests that four basic types of knowledge can be identified by permuting the presence or absence of the two factors i.e. (1) – automatic, – analysed; (2) +automatic, – analysed; (3) – automatic, +analysed; and (4) +automatic, +analysed. This framework can account for what may have happened in the drills practising WH interrogatives; the pupils developed Type (4) knowledge. However, if spontaneous communication can call only on knowledge that is unanalysed (i.e. Types (1) and (2)), then Type (4) knowledge would be of little use in the elicitation game. Furthermore, the ESL pupils may not be motivated to develop analysed knowledge if they intuitively recognize that it is of little use in unplanned discourse. The 'exposure' to target language forms which the pupils received in both some of the lesson interactions and also in the elicitation games themselves may have aided the development of unanalysed knowledge in varying degrees of automaticity, depending on the amount and the quality of exposure available. Language drilling, in contrast, serves only to automatize analysed knowledge.

This study cannot be used, therefore, to decide in favour of Krashen's or Bialystok's theory. Krashen claims that 'learned' knowledge can be used only in highly restricted circumstances and that 'acquired' knowledge is primary in that it is used to initiate utterances. Bialystok claims that different kinds of knowledge are involved in the performance of different tasks. Future studies, therefore, might use several elicitation instruments in order to discover whether the kind of knowledge that children internalize from 'instruction' can be used in certain kinds of task but not in others.

Methodological Issues

The methodological implications of the study are somewhat clearer than the theoretical conclusions. They are:

1. A single study cannot hope to prove or disprove any specific theoretical position. The only solution to the problem of identifying confounding variables is a 'shot-gun' approach. Multiple studies that

provide similar results will enable these variables and their effects to be more clearly identified, and a 'general' position regarding the role played by instruction with different kinds of learners to be established.

2. It is important to take into account the 'zone of proximal development'. One way to achieve this is to relate studies of classroom instruction to longitudinal studies of specific learners, as attempted in this study.

3. One of the major faults of the comparative methodology studies of the sixties was their failure to examine what went on in the 'black box'. This study has shown that the nature of language teaching cannot be taken for granted, no matter how apparently prescribed the method is. All teaching provides both 'instruction' and 'exposure'. It is necessary, therefore, to examine the actual interactions that take place.

4. 'Research internal' exposure may be a crucial variable in 'treatment' studies that use some eliciting or testing device before and after the treatment. This variable can be handled by treating the elicitation sessions as 'exposure' (i. e. by recording and preparing full transcripts), as was undertaken in this study. Ideally it should also be handled through the use of control groups. If a control group had been used in this study, it might have been possible to determine more accurately what was gained from the instruction itself.

How instruction affects the route and rate of SLA is a crucial issue for ESL provision (and for language teaching in general). It has been the subject of much speculation. This paper is an attempt to begin the task of relating argumentation to empirical study.

Notes

[1] There are opposing arguments here. A common argument put by language teachers is that students need to be given some knowledge of the TL before they can begin to 'acquire' through natural communication. In this view, beginners need formal instruction more than advanced students. On the other hand, it can be argued that a basic knowledge of the TL can be 'picked up', but more complex knowledge (e.g. embedding and thematizing devices) requires formal explanations. In this view, formal instruction is best suited to advanced

students who have 'fossilized'.

[2] As the experiment was conducted within the space of a single week, the chance of acquisition occurring as a result of outside contacts with English was reduced.

[3] The order of development is also very similar to that reported in studies of WH interrogatives in naturalistic SLA.

[4] The following are the notational conventions used in the transcripts:

— the teacher's or researcher's utterances are given on the left-hand side of the page;

— the pupils' utterances are given on the right-hand side of the page;

— the teacher's utterances are labelled 'T'; the researcher's utterances 'R'; the pupils' utterances are labelled PI, P2 etc. if identifiable, and P? if not identifiable;

— pauses are indicated in brackets:

(.) indicates a pause of shorter than a second.

(.1.) indicates a pause of one second duration.

APPENDIX A

Scores obtained by the thirteen children in the two elicitation sessions.

1. Proportion of different WH questions that were (a) semantically appropriate and (b) inverted for the whole group at Times 1 and 2.

	Semantically appropriate				Subject-verb inversion			
	What	Who	Where	When	What	Who	Where	When
Time 1	100	.83	.69	.35	.85	.84	.50	.09
Time 2	1–00	.85	.82	.59	.92	.80	.68	.26

2. Proportion of WH questions that (a) contained an auxiliary verb and (b) contained a main verb for each pupil at Times 1 and 2.

	Auxiliary		Main verb	
Pupil	Time 1	Time 2	Time 1	Time 2
1	.10	.13	.30	.33
2	.40	.60	.60	.60
3	.20	.40	.40	.53
4	.00	.07	.40	.27
5	.11	.00	.25	.27
6	.00	.00	.00	.20
7	.00	.33	.00	.33

(continued)

Pupil	Auxiliary		Main verb	
	Time 1	Time 2	Time 1	Time 2
8	.00	.07	.07	.07
9	.22	.33	.22	.33
10	.10	.33	.50	.33
11	.00	.00	.00	.00
12	.00	.20	.00	.07
13	.50	.27	.50	.40

Are Classroom and Naturalistic Acquisition the Same? A Study of the Classroom Acquisition of German Word Order Rules

This chapter appeared originally in 1989 as an article in Studies in Second Language Acquisition Vol. 11, pp. 305–328.

INTRODUCTION

The study of classroom second language acquisition (SLA) has both a theoretical and an applied purpose. The theoretical purpose derives from interest in the role that input plays in the acquisition of a second language. Language instruction consists of the external manipulation of input; the learner is confronted with data specially contrived to provide exemplars of the linguistic feature that is the target of instruction. It is possible, therefore, to test hypotheses relating to the effect that exposing the learner to data rich in specific linguistic features has on their acquisition. The applied purpose concerns the relevance and efficiency of particular kinds of language instruction. Currently, language teaching methodologists are interested in whether classroom L2 acquisition can be best promoted by meaning-focused or form-focused instruction. They are also interested in establishing the best order for presenting grammatical items to the learner.

The study reported in this chapter was designed to contribute to both the theoretical understanding of the nature of SLA and also to language pedagogy. The general question the research addresses is 'Is the sequence of acquisition of grammatical structures the same or different in naturalistic and classroom SLA?' This question is of theoretical interest because it relates to the ongoing debate regarding the role of input in SLA (cf. White, 1987). It is of applied interest because it informs about the utility of form-focused instruction.

The comparison of acquisitional sequences in naturalistic and classroom SLA is one of two principal ways in which researchers have tried to investigate whether formal instruction can alter the 'natural' route of acquisition. Much of this research has relied on the methodology provided by the morpheme studies. The procedure followed by these studies involved collecting samples of learner language, identifying the obligatory occasions for the use of those grammatical morphemes that were the focus of the research, and establishing their degree of accuracy. The rank order of accuracy was then equated with the order of acquisition. The early 1970s saw a number of morpheme studies of naturalistic and mixed language learners (e.g., Bailey, Madden, & Krashen, 1974; Dulay & Burt, 1973; Larsen-Freeman, 1975). In the late 1970s and early 1980s, a number of morpheme studies of classroom learners were carried out (e.g., Fathman, 1978; Krashen, Sferlazza, Feldman, & Fathman, 1976; Makino, 1980; Pica, 1983; Sajavaara, 1981; Turner, 1979). In general, these studies lend support to the hypothesis that the order of morpheme acquisition is the same in formal and informal settings. It should be noted, however, that some of the studies have reported differences in the naturalistic and classroom orders (e.g., Sajavaara, 1981), while other studies have found that some structures (such as third person and plural -s) are performed more accurately by instructed learners, even though the difference was not sufficient to produce variations in the overall morpheme order. Also, the types of errors produced by the two kinds of learners have been shown to differ in some cases.

The morpheme studies have attracted considerable criticism (cf. Hatch, 1978a) and are no longer fashionable. There are grounds for believing that accuracy and acquisitional orders cannot be equated. The method of determining the accuracy of individual morphemes is suspect because it ignores the functions performed by the morphemes. Rank orders and rank order correlations (the principal means of comparing orders produced by naturalistic and classroom learners) conceal facts about the acquisition of specific features that may be significant. Also, there seems to be no theoretical basis for comparing the acquisition of one feature (e.g., articles) with another (e.g., aux. — be) which comes from a totally separate sub-system of the grammar of the language. The morpheme studies have not been motivated by any well-defined theory of grammar or by a theory of language learning. For many researchers, the results provided by the morpheme studies are of little theoretical or practical interest.

More recent comparisons of naturalistic and classroom SLA have tried to overcome these problems by:

1. carrying out longitudinal, rather than cross-sectional, investigations.

2. focusing on particular grammatical subsystems such as negatives or interrogatives or by carrying out in-depth analyses of individual grammatical morphemes.

Studies by Lightbown (1983), Ellis (1984b), Pienemann (1986), and Weinert (1987) have shown that, at least for some grammatical structures, the route of acquisition does not vary in any significant way from one setting to another. They support the claim that the effects of instruction are highly constrained. Weinert (1987), for instance, found that Scottish secondary school students manifested structures and processes in the classroom acquisition of L2 German negatives similar to those reported in naturalistic acquisition. Far from facilitating learning, the traditional instruction these learners received appeared to inhibit the processes of interlanguage construction by providing them with ready-made formulaic negatives that obviated the need for active processing of input. This and other studies suggest that the same acquisitional mechanisms operate, irrespective of setting.

The other way that researchers have tried to examine the effects of instruction on the sequence of acquisition is by means of experimental or pseudo-experimental studies (e.g., Ellis, 1984a and Chapter 2; Pienemann, 1984; Schumann, 1978a). These studies involve a standard pre-test/post-test design with the intervening treatment consisting of instruction in some grammatical feature. The purpose of the studies is to establish whether the treatment helps the learner to 'beat' the natural order of acquisition or whether it can push the learner from some pidgin-like, transitional stage in the acquisition of a grammatical structure to the target language form. In these studies, the choice of grammatical structure is an informed one; it is based either on a longitudinal study of the subjects or is motivated by a linguistic theory. The results suggest that instruction does not result in the acquisition of new grammatical properties unless the learner is developmentally ready to acquire them.

The study reported here is intended to further test the hypothesis that formal instruction does not affect the sequence of acquisition. The specific hypothesis tested is as follows: the route of acquisition of German word order rules apparent in the elicited speech of 39 adult classroom learners does not differ from that reported for naturalistic learners.

The study can be considered a strong test of the hypothesis on a number of grounds. First, the naturalistic acquisition of the target structure (German word order rules) has been the subject of intensive research that has demonstrated the existence of a robust acquisitional sequence. This research provides a solid basis for comparison. Second, the subjects of the study were totally reliant on the classroom for L2 input. They were foreign, rather than second, L2 learners and, therefore, were not 'contaminated' with naturalistic learning, as was the case with the subjects of several of the studies referred to earlier. Third, the subjects were all adult successful language learners with substantial experience of classroom foreign language learning. Thus, they were well-equipped — cognitively and in experience — to benefit from formal instruction.

I shall begin by describing the German word order rules that are the focus of the study and then will go on to review previous research that has investigated the naturalistic and classroom acquisition of these rules. There then follows an account of the classroom study. Finally, I shall consider the implications of the results of the study for both SLA theory and language pedagogy.

GERMAN WORD ORDER RULES

German has a number of word order rules. Their surface representation can be described as follows:

1. Subject-verb-object

The word order that many linguists consider canonical is subject-verb-object,

e.g., Ich trank ein Glas Milch.

'I drank a glass of milk.'

2. Adverb preposing

In German, adverbs can be shifted from sentence internal or final positions to sentence initial position.

e.g., Gestern trank ich ein Glas Milch.

'Yesterday drank I a glass of milk.'

Adverb-preposing requires inversion — see (4). The movement of the adverb is considered a separate rule, however.

3. Particle

This rule states that nonfinite verbal elements are moved to clause-final position. It applies in a number of linguistic contexts. For example, when the VP consists of modal+V infin.

e.g., Ich möchte heute abend ins Kino gehen.

'I would like tomorrow evening to the cinema go.'

when the VP consists of aux.+Ven,

e.g., Ich bin gestern abend ins Kino gegangen.

'I am yesterday evening to the cinema gone.'

and when the VP consists of a particle+V.

e.g., Ich rufe sie morgen abend noch einmal an.

'I call you tomorrow evening once more up.'

4. Inversion

This rule states that a finite verb form precedes the subject of its clause in certain linguistic contexts, such as when adverb-preposing occurs — see (2) — and after a sentence-initial direct object,

e.g., Fleisch esse ich nicht.

'Meat eat I not.'

In both cases inversion is the result of the requirement that the verb comes second in main clauses. Inversion also occurs in WH interrogatives.

e.g., Wann gehen wir ins Kino?

'When go we into the cinema?'

5. Verb-end

Finite verbs are placed in final position in all embedded clauses,

e.g., Ich trank das Glas Milch, während ich den Brief schrieb.

'I drank the glass of milk while I the letter wrote.'

The research reported in this article investigated three of these rules: (3), (4), and (5). Rules (1) and (2) were not studied because of the difficulty of determining obligatory occasions for their use.

PREVIOUS RESEARCH INTO THE ACQUISITION OF GERMAN WORD ORDER RULES

Naturalistic Acquisition

The following account of the naturalistic acquisition of German

word order rules is based primarily on the results of the ZISA
(Zweispracherwerb italienischer, spanischer, und portugiesischer
Arbeiter) project carried out in West Germany and reported in a series of
publications (Clahsen, 1980, 1984, 1985; Meisel, 1983; Meisel, Clahsen
& Pienemann, 1981; Pienemann, 1980). The project set out to describe
and explain the acquisition of German by adult migrant workers with
Romance language backgrounds and their children. Both cross-sectional
and longitudinal studies were carried out using natural language data
from informal interviews and free conversations. In addition, information
relating to such factors as the learners' origins, education, jobs, contact
with Germans and other foreigners, neighborhood, and use of mass
media was collected in order to determine the learners' attitudes towards
learning German. The particular analysis that concerns us here focused
on the acquisition of syntactic features and, in particular, word order.
Acquisition was defined by the ZISA researchers as the first appearance of a
word order rule in a non-formulaic utterance.

The results of the various studies indicate that for L2 learners with
Romance backgrounds there is:

1. a definite developmental sequence for the three word order rules.

2. individual learner variation within each stage of development.

In the first developmental stage, learners use a basic subject-verb-
object word order irrespective of the linguistic context. That is, they show no
control of the optional adverb-preposing rule or of the obligatory particle,
inversion, and verb-end rules. These rules are acquired sequentially.
Adverb-preposing is acquired first, particle second, inversion third, and
verb-end last. The sequence of acquisition comprises an implicational
scale:

Verb-end > Inversion > Particle > Adverb-preposing.

Thus, the acquisition of any one rule implies the acquisition of other
rules further down the scale, but not those higher up. For example, a
learner who has acquired verb-end would also have acquired the other
three word order rules, but a learner who has acquired adverb-preposing

would not necessarily have acquired any other rule.

Each word order rule applies to a number of different linguistic contexts (see previous section). One possibility, then, is that learners will not only acquire each rule sequentially, but also learn to apply each rule across contexts incrementally. That is, there would be a developmental ordering for the acquisition of the different linguistic contexts. However, this does not appear to happen. Within each stage of development there is considerable individual variation, and no ordering of contexts is apparent. Some learners (dubbed 'error-avoiders') seek to master a rule across a full range of contexts before moving on to the next rule. Other learners (dubbed 'communicators') display control of a rule in only one or two contexts before moving on along the scale.

Table 1 is based on Meisel (1983). It displays cross-sectional data for nine naturalistic learners. Three word order rules (the obligatory ones) are printed in italics, with the contexts for each rule beneath it. The figures represent the proportion of correct suppliance of each rule, both overall and in different contexts, by the 9 learners, X denotes that no obligatory occasions for the application of a particular rule were present in the data, while (0.0) shows that although there were obligatory occasions, there were fewer than five. The most advanced learner is learner 1, who has categorical control over all three word order rules. The least advanced is learner 9, who has not acquired any of the rules. Other learners are at various stages of development, displaying variable or categorical use of one or more of the rules.

There have been a number of other studies of the naturalistic acquisition of these word order rules in German and also Dutch and Afrikaans, which have a similar set of rules (see Jordens, 1988, for a review). This research covers learners with different language backgrounds — Turkish (Clahsen & Muysken, 1986), Moroccan (Coenen & Van Hout, 1987), and English (Duplessis, Solin, Travis & White, 1987). There is some disagreement about the interpretation of the results obtained and evidence to suggest that the learners' LI interacts with input in the process of acquisition.

However, clear regularities emerge. As Jordens shows, all learners cope with the problem of identifying L2 word order rules in similar ways and manifest a very similar sequence of acquisition to that reported by the ZISA researchers.

Table 1: Implicational scale for German word order rules
in naturalistic SLA (based on Meisel, 1983)

	Learners								
	1	2	3	4	5	6	7	8	9
Rules:									
Verb-end	1.0	0.56	0	(0–5)	X	0	0	0	X
Comp	1.0	0.67	0	0	X	0	0	0	X
Wh	1.0	0.67	X	X	X	0	0	X	X
Rel	1.0	0	0	(1.0)	X	X	0	X	X
Inversion	1.0	0.91	0.85	1.0	0.83	0.46	0	0	X
Wh	1.0	1.0	1.0	(1.0)	0	(1.0)	X	X	X
Adverb	1.0	1.0	0.70	1.0	1.0	0.40	0	0	X
Do	1.0	1.0	(1.0)	(1.0)	X	X	X	X	X
Comp	1.0	0	1.0	(1.0)	X	X	0	0	X
Particle	1.0	0.82	(0.93)	1.0	1.0	1.0	0.71	0.10	X
Mod+V	1.0	0.77	1.0	(1.0)	(1.0)	1.0	(1.0)	(0.50)	X
Aux.+V	1.0	0.71	1.0	1.0	1.0	1.0	0.70	X	X
P+V	1.0	1.0	(1.0)	(1.0)	(1.0)	X	X	0	X
Vcomp	1.0	1.0	0.67	(1.0)	X	1.0	(1.0)	X	X

Classroom Acquisition

There are a growing number of empirical studies of the acquisition of German word order rules in instructional settings. These have doubtlessly been stimulated by the strength of evidence demonstrating the presence of a natural sequence of acquisition in this area of grammar.

In an experimental study involving 10 children (ages 7–9), Pienemann (1984) found that instruction in inversion only resulted in the acquisition of this word order rule if the learners had already acquired the rule immediately preceding it in the sequence (i.e., particle). This led Pienemann to formulate the Teachability Hypothesis (Pienemann, 1985), which states that developmental features such as German word order rules can only be learned if the learner is psycholinguistically ready. Furthermore, Pienemann provides some evidence to suggest that premature instruction can have a negative effect. Two of the children he investigated regressed in the application of the adverb-preposing rule as a result of instruction in inversion, possibly because the learners sought to avoid a structure that required inversion. Pienemann's study is an important one. It is, however, based on a very small sample, so care must be taken in generalizing from it. Also, the subjects were young children who might be predicted not to benefit greatly from formal instruction.

In a subsequent longitudinal study, however, Pienemann (1986) investigated 3 adult classroom learners of L2 German in Australia. All three were complete beginners. He documents when specific word order rules were introduced and shows that the instruction only resulted in the acquisition of a new word order rule if the learners were developmentally primed. For example, the particle rule was explicitly taught in week 7 of the course, but was not acquired until weeks 15 and 17 by two of the learners, and not at all by the third learner. Pienemann also documents how the instruction resulted in avoidance behavior; the learners were taught the complexities of the perfect tense at an early stage, but because they were unable to handle the necessary processing operations, they tended to avoid using this form altogether.

Two other studies have investigated the effects of instruction on German word order rules. Daniel (1983; cited in Pienemann, 1986) carried out a cross-sectional study of adult beginners at a university in Australia. Her results revealed the same implicational order of acquisition as that reported for naturalistic learners. Finally, Westmoreland's (1983) cross-sectional study, which involved similar types of learners, showed the same developmental sequence.

The empirical study of the classroom acquisition of German word order rules, therefore, supports these claims:

1. The sequence of acquisition of these rules is the same in classroom and naturalistic settings.

2. Premature instruction can cause learners to regress by avoiding transitional rules that they know, resulting in ungrammatical utterances.

It should be noted that (1) holds true for adults as well as children. Even adults who are well-equipped in terms of experience and intelligence to benefit from formal instruction follow the natural sequence.

THE STUDY

In this section, I will describe the study carried out to examine the effects of instruction on three of the word order rules: particle, inversion, and verb-end. As already stated, the study was restricted to these rules because they are obligatory and their presence or absence in data can be clearly determined.

Participants

The learners were 39 students taking *ab initio* courses in L2 German as part of their first-year degree programs. They were taught in two separate institutions of higher education in London and were divided into groups ranging in size from six to nine. The subjects were administered a questionnaire at the beginning of their study in order to obtain general background information. This questionnaire revealed that there were 27 female and 12 male learners. The mean age of the learners was 20.95 years, the eldest being 41 years and the youngest 18 years. The LI backgrounds of the learners were varied: Spanish, English, French, Mauritian Creole, and Arabic.

All the 39 learners can be considered successful language learners in that they needed passes in the General Certificate of Education (GCE)

'A' Level or an equivalent examination in at least one foreign language in order to gain entry to the degree program. The learners differed in the extent and nature of their L2 experiences: 17 had knowledge of three L2s, 21 had knowledge of two L2s, and 1 student had knowledge of only one L2. All the learners had acquired at least one of their L2s in a classroom setting, but several of the subjects had acquired one or more of their other L2s naturalistically. The participants, therefore, comprised a group of experienced and sophisticated language learners.

Although the course was designed for complete beginners, 14 of the subjects had some previous knowledge of German. This varied from a few months of classroom study in school to contact with native speakers in Germany. The learners with previous experience were learners 5, 6, 8, 17,21, 22, 23, 24, 26, 27,28, 35, and 36.

The learners differed in one other way. Some of them were committed to continuing the study of German beyond the *ab initio* course in order to fulfill the requirements of their degree program. Others, however, had the option of abandoning German at the end of the year. This factor proved significant in determining the levels of achievement of individual students.

Type of Instruction

As the learners were divided into five different groups taught by different teachers, there was no uniformity in the instruction they received. Classroom observations of individual lessons that were carried out on a regular basis over two academic terms (22 weeks) revealed, however, that the similarities in instructional practices outweighed the differences.

The teaching received by Groups A, B, C, and D consisted of formal language instruction throughout and regional studies in the second term (this involved lectures and readings on social, economic, and political issues). The formal instruction was based on the *Grundkurs Deutsch Course* (Schapers, Luscher & Gluck, 1980). This is a traditional, structurally graded text book that emphasizes formal grammar study. The students also had the opportunity to work in language and microcomputer laboratories 1 or 2 hours a week. This resulted in further work that was essentially form-focused. Groups A and C received 12 hours of instruction, while Groups B and D received only 9 hours. Also, greater emphasis was placed on grammatical accuracy in Groups A and C. The nature of the instructional activities in all four groups was broadly similar, however. The instruction was text-based, involved frequent translation into English, teacher explanation of new grammatical points (often in English), and pattern practice exercises. There was little opportunity for real communication and hardly any small group work.

Group E was taught in a separate institution. The instruction was based on *Themen* (Aufderstrasse, Bock, Gerdes & Muller, 1983). This is a notional-functional course. The students also spent 1 hour per week using video materials from the television series *Deustch Direkt*. The general instructional style, however, followed a very similar pattern to that evident in the lessons experienced by the other groups. An analysis of the amount of time spent in meaning-focused (as opposed to form-focused) activity and in student-centered (as opposed to teacher-centered) work revealed no significant differences between Group E and the other groups. Altogether, this group received 6 hours of instruction per week, which was less than the other groups, although this was largely compensated for by an intensive 40-hour induction program.

Instruction in the Word Order Rules

None of the groups received specific instruction in the three obligatory word order rules. Instead, formal instruction was provided in the various grammatical structures that require the application of the rules. Thus, for example, no attempt was made to teach particle, but this rule was indirectly taught in lessons dealing with modal+V infin. and aux.+Ven. The presentation of the word order rules, therefore, did not conform to the process of acquisition observed in naturalistic settings.

The two text books used by the learners together with the teachers' records of work and the students' homework records were examined in order to determine (a) the order in which the three rules were introduced in the five instructional groups, and (b) the instructional emphasis given to each of the three rules over the 22 weeks of the study.

Table 2 shows the order of introduction of particle, inversion, and verb-end. It also shows the date when a structure requiring each rule was formally presented for the first time. All five groups experienced the same instructional order. That is, inversion was presented first, followed by particle and verb-end. In Groups A, B, C, and D, structures involving the three rules were introduced over a 6-week period and were evenly spaced. In Group E, structures involving inversion and particle were introduced more or less together, with verb-end appearing some 6 weeks later. In all the groups, verb-end — the most difficult of the rules — was the last to be introduced.

Table 2: Order of introduction of the three word order rules in the instruction

Word order rule	Groups A, B, C	Group E
1. Inversion	Lesson 3 (mid-Oct.)	Lesson 1, Bk. 1 (mid-Sept.)
2. Particle	Lesson 7 (early Nov.)	Lesson 2, Bk. 2 (late Sept.)
3. Verb-end	Lesson 9 (late Nov.)	Lesson 2, Bk. 3 (mid Dec.)

Table 3 shows the instructional emphasis given to each structure. This was calculated by ascertaining the number of explicit references to structures requiring each of the three word order rules in the text books, teachers' records, and homework records. The number of references is shown in brackets. There were differences in the order of emphasis between Groups A and B on the one hand and Groups C, D, and E on the other. Verb-end received the most attention in Groups A and B, while particle was the principal focus of instruction in the other groups. In all five groups, inversion received the least attention.

Table 3: Instructional emphasis given to each word order rule

Order	Groups A and B	Groups C and D	Group E
1	Verb-end (27)	Particle (33)	Particle (24)
2	Particle (22)	Verb-end (24)	Verb-end (15)
3	Inversion (6)	Inversion (13)	Inversion (7)

From this analysis, we can draw the following conclusions:

1. The order of introduction of the three word order rules did not correspond to the naturalistic order of acquisition reported by the ZISA project in any of the five groups of learners. The difference between the order of introduction and order of acquisition was least evident in Group E.

2. The order of emphasis given to the three word order rules in the instruction did not correspond to the degree of difficulty in their acquisition in a naturalistic setting. The mismatch between emphasis and difficulty was least evident in Groups A and B.

Hypotheses

In order to address the research question regarding whether classroom and naturalistic acquisition are the same, this study investigated the general hypothesis that adult classroom learners of L2 German would manifest the same sequence of acquisition of word order rules as that reported for naturalistic learners. Three operational hypotheses were tested:

1. The sequence of acquisition of three obligatory German word order rules would match the order reported for naturalistic learners by the ZISA researchers rather than the order in which the rules were first formally taught in the classroom.

2. The order of accuracy of three obligatory German word order rules would correspond to the order of acquisition reported for naturalistic learners by the ZISA researchers rather than to the degree of emphasis in the instruction given to the rules.

3. The order of accuracy of three obligatory German word order

rules obtained by each of the five instructional groups would correspond to the order of acquisition reported for naturalistic learners by the ZISA researchers. A corollary of this hypothesis is that there would be no differences in the order of accuracy of the rules among the different groups despite the fact that there were differences in both the order and emphasis of instruction.

Procedure

Data were collected from the 39 learners by means of a speech elicitation task. In this task the learners worked in pairs. A picture composition was cut up and two pictures given to each learner. Each learner was asked to describe his or her pictures in German without showing them to the partner so that they could jointly work out the story. This is an example of a two-way communication task, which Long (1983c) has claimed is the kind of task most likely to stimulate conversation containing plenty of interactional adjustments. In this case, the task ended with one of the learners being asked to tell the complete story in German (i.e., to produce an oral monologue). Each pair repeated the task three times, using different sets of pictures. The first time was treated as a warm-up and was intended to familiarize the subjects with the procedure. The second and third times required first one and then the other member of each pair to perform the oral monologue at the end of the task. The learners performed the task in a language laboratory large enough to seat two students at a booth. They were audio-recorded after they had completed the warm-up task.

The speech elicitation task was administered on two occasions — at the end of the first term (i.e., after 11 weeks of instruction) and at the end of the second term (i.e., after 22 weeks of instruction).

Transcriptions of the audio tapes were prepared in normal orthography. As the elicitation task had been designed to tap unmonitored, informal language use in order to afford comparisons with the ZISA research, which was based upon this kind of data, the transcripts were examined for evidence of monitoring of the word order rules. Evidence of monitoring would suggest that the learners were attempting to apply explicit knowledge of the rules. A problem would then arise, as the naturalistic learners could be assumed to have used implicit knowledge. In seeking to compare classroom and naturalistic acquisition, it is essential to ensure that the data used to make the comparison are indeed comparable.

Table 4 gives the number and type of linguistic corrections performed by the 7 learners who produced the highest number of corrections at Time 2. It shows that although the students did monitor their output, their efforts were directed at morphological features of German (e.g., articles and verb tense morphemes) rather than syntax.

Table 4: The linguistic corrections performed by seven learners at Time 2
Focus of linguistic correction

Learner	Morphology	Syntax	Other
4	5	0	1
8	4	0	0
19	3	1	0
22	5	0	0
23	4	0	0
28	7	0	0
38	3	0	1
Totals	31	1	2

Only learner 19 self-corrected a word order rule (verb-end) and only on one occasion:

einer Polizist erm (.2.) der ist erm der angekommt ist
'a policeman who is who arrived is'

It would seem, therefore, that the learners did not appear to pay conscious attention to the correct production of the three rules. In other words, the data produced by the speech elicitation task were comparable with those obtained by the ZISA researchers. Obligatory occasions for the three word order rules in the data collected from each learner at Times 1 and 2 were identified. The proportion of accurate suppliance of each rule was then calculated. Also, incidences of overuse of each rule were recorded. It should be noted that not all the learners produced sufficient obligatory occasions for each rule. For this reason, the results for some of the analyses reported here relate to subsets of the population for the sample studied.

RESULTS

Three sets of results will be presented, in accordance with the operational hypotheses described earlier. First, the order of acquisition of the three rules in individual learners is examined. Second, the level of accuracy of the rules achieved by the sample as a whole is indicated, and third, the results for the different instructional groups are presented.

Order of Acquisition

In order to establish the order of acquisition of the three word order rules, two analyses were carried out. First, an implicational scale was drawn up for those learners at Time 2 who produced three or more obligatory occasions for each word order rule. Second, the development that occurred between Time 1 and Time 2 was investigated.

As mentioned earlier, many of the learners failed to produce an adequate number of obligatory occasions for one or more of the word order rules. This is not surprising, as avoidance of 'difficult' structures is a familiar phenomenon in SLA. It conforms with similar results reported by the ZISA researchers for many of their subjects. It does, however, pose problems for the researcher. In particular, a decision has to be taken as to what constitutes a satisfactory number of occasions on which to base a judgment as to whether a particular rule has been acquired. In this case, the minimum number was set at three. This is rather meagre, but to have set a higher number would have reduced the sample size to an unacceptably low number.

Table 5 presents the implicational scale for the 17 learners who produced three or more obligatory occasions at Time 2. The learners have been scaled on the basis that a suppliance level of .75 or above for a particular rule constitutes acquisition of that rule. Hatch and Farhady (1982) rightly argue that the choice of criterion level must be justified. The .75 level was chosen on the grounds that if learners are able to supply a feature in three out of four instances, this constitutes sufficient evidence that a feature has been internalized. In contrast, two out of three instances is less convincing evidence. Using this criterion, the results show a perfect scaling (i.e., the Coefficient of Scalability = 1). In other words, there is no learner who has acquired verb-end who has not also acquired the other two rules, and no learner who has acquired inversion who has not also acquired particle. Of the 17 learners, 16 demonstrated acquisition of particle, 4 of inversion, and 2 of verb-end. The three rules can be implicationally ordered as follows:

Verb-end > Inversion > Particle

Table 5: Implicational scale for 17 learners at Time 2
Word order rules

Learners	Particle	Inversion	Verb-end
8	1.0	.89	.78
4	.83	.85	.75
14	1.0	.77	.15
23	.88	.86	.50
10	1.0	.66	.63
38	1.0	.66	.60
22	1.0	.60	.50
16	1.0	.46	.40
25	1.0	.33	.20

(continued)

Learners	Particle	Inversion	Verb-end
35	1.0	.33	.20
12	1.0	.29	.74
17	1.0	.25	.00
2	.88	.64	.00
15	.80	.44	.13
36	.77	.60	.00
9	.75	.33	.20
11	.25	.17	.18

NOTE Coefficient of reproducibility = 1.0; minimal marginal reproducibility=.43; improvement in reproducibility=.57; coefficient of scalability = 1.0

The implicational scale presented in Table 5 provides a cross-sectional analysis of the data. The study was also designed to allow for a longitudinal analysis of development of word order rules from Time 1 to Time 2. Table 6 presents the results of this analysis, based on 9 learners who produced three or more obligatory occasions for each rule on both occasions. Once again, the criterion level for acquisition was fixed at .75. Of these learners, 3 (learners 10, 17, and 23) displayed development from Time 1 to Time 2. That is, they progressed by adding the acquisition of a new word order rule. In each case, the process of acquisition conformed to the expected sequence.

Table 6: The acquisition of the three word order rules by 9 learners

	Time 1			Time 2		
Learner	Particle	Inversion	Verb-end	Particle	Inversion	Verb-end
10	—	—	—	+	—	—
14	—	+	—	+	+	—
17	—	—	—	+	—	—
18	+	—	—	—	—	—
22	+	+	—	+	—	—
23	+	—	—	+	+	—
25	+	—	—	+	+	—
27	+	+	—	+	—	—
38	+	—	—	+	—	—

For example, learner 10 displayed zero acquisition of all three rules at Time 1 but had acquired particle at Time 2: learner 23 had already acquired particle at Time 1 and added inversion at Time 2. However, not all the learners progressed. Learners 25 and 38 stayed at the same stage of acquisition. Learners 18, 22, and 27 took backward steps (i.e., displayed loss of an already acquired rule). In these cases, the loss reversed the natural sequence for acquisition. For example, learner 22 provided evidence of having acquired both particle and inversion at Time 1, but only particle at Time 2; in other words, he 'lost' the more difficult of the two rules. Only one learner, learner 14, showed an unexpected pattern, as at Time 1 she appeared to have acquired inversion, but not particle; however, by Time 2 she had acquired particle. None of the nine learners had acquired verb-end, even by Time 2.

Level of Accuracy in the Whole Group

Table 7 gives the proportions of accurate suppliance of the word order rules at Times 1 and 2 for the entire 39 learners. It can be seen that particle is performed more accurately than inversion, which in turn is performed more accurately than verb-end on both occasions. The accuracy order, therefore, is: (1) particle; (2) inversion; (3) verb-end. Particle is conspicuously easier than the other two rules; the difference between the accurate suppliance of inversion and verb-end is relatively small. The gain in accuracy in these two structures from Time 1 to Time 2 is noticeably greater than that for particle (.14 for both inversion and verb-end but only .08 for particle). This is largely explained by the high level of accuracy of particle at Time 1.

Table 7: Proportions of accurate suppliance of the
three word order rules by 39 Learners

	Time 1			Time 2		
Word order rule	Accurate suppliance	Obligatory occasions	Proportion	Accurate suppliance	Obligatory occasions	Proportion
Particle	150	192	.78	175	203	.86

(continued)

	Time 1			Time 2		
Word order rule	Accurate suppliance	Obligatory occasions	Proportion	Accurate suppliance	Obligatory occasions	Proportion
Inversion	63	168	.38	99	192	.52
Verb-end	38	119	.32	96	209	.46

Level of Accuracy in the Five Instructional Groups

Turning to the performance of the five groups at Time 2 (Table 8), it is evident that particle is performed with a high level of accuracy by all of them. There are, however, differences with regard to inversion. Group A achieves a high level of acquisition of this rule; Groups B, C, and E achieve average levels; but Group D shows no acquisition at all, although the learners in this group produced very few obligatory occasions for inversion. Differences are also apparent with regard to verb-end. Groups A and D manifest higher levels of acquisition than Groups B and C, with Group E showing the lowest level. In general, the different groups' accuracy orders mirror the natural order of acquisition, the only exception being Group D.

Table 8: Levels of accuracy (Time 2) of the three word order rules in the different instructional groups

	Obligatory Occasions	Accurate Suppliance	Proportion
Group A			
Particle	31	27	.87
Inversion	69	57	.83
Verb-end	46	31	.68
Group B			
Particle	37	32	.86
Inversion	59	27	.46
Verb-end	79	31	.39
Group C			
Particle	53	47	.89
Inversion	27	16	.59
Verb-end	46	17	.37

(continued)

	Obligatory Occasions	Accurate Suppliance	Proportion
Group D			
Particle	42	33	.79
Inversion	6	0	.00
Verb-end	18	12	.67
Group E			
Particle	40	35	.88
Inversion	21	9	.43
Verb-end	20	5	.25

DISCUSSION

It was possible to show that, although some learners did monitor extensively, they did not pay explicit attention to word order rules. Instead, they focused on morphological difficulties. This is not surprising, given that the instruction they had received focused primarily on morphological rather than syntactical features. The learners were, therefore, probably much more conscious of the need to produce articles, pronouns, and tenses correctly than word order rules. The absence of linguistic corrections targeted at these rules suggests that they were performed more or less spontaneously, although it is possible that some planning took place prior to production. In general, however, there are reasonable grounds for claiming that the word order data obtained from the communication task are comparable to the natural data obtained by the ZISA researchers.

The first hypothesis was that the instruction received by the 39 learners would not lead to a different order of acquisition from that reported for naturalistic learners. The results reported in the previous section lend support to this hypothesis. Implicational scaling of 17 learners (who produced three obligatory occasions for each word order rule) at Time 2 showed an identical order of acquisition. Also, an analysis of the development of 9 learners who produced three obligatory occasions for each rule at Time 1 and Time 2 revealed that progress consisted of the incremental acquisition of rules in accordance with the sequence found in naturalistic learners. Learners who regressed from Time 1 to Time 2 moved backwards along the sequence. It should be noted that the order of acquisition in these learners differed from the order in which the rules were introduced in the instruction. All five groups were introduced to inversion first. However, acquisition of particle far outstripped the acquisition of inversion in all the learners. It would seem, therefore, that learners have their own 'syllabus' for the acquisition of German word order rules and that this syllabus is the same for both tutored and untutored learners.

The second hypothesis was that the level of accuracy achieved in the production of the three word order rules by the 39 learners would correspond to the order of acquisition reported for naturalistic learners. The overall levels of accuracy of the three rules achieved by the whole sample at Time 2 matched the order of acquisition found in naturalistic learners by the ZISA researchers. Thus, particle was produced most accurately, followed by inversion, with verb-end last. Particle was, in fact, performed much more accurately than the other two rules. In contrast, the order of instructional emphasis experienced by any of the 39 learners is insufficient to explain the levels of accuracy achieved.

The third hypothesis concerned whether the five instructional groups manifested an accuracy order similar to the acquisition order of naturalistic learners, and whether there were any differences in the accuracy orders of the different groups that might be explained by corresponding differences in the instruction they received. Groups C, D, and E received more instruction in particle than the other two rules, while Groups A and B received more instruction in verb-end. Despite these between-group differences, all five groups demonstrated much higher levels of accuracy in the use of particle. Also, although inversion received the least attention in all the classrooms, four out of the five groups manifested higher levels of accuracy in this rule than in verb-end, which received greater instructional emphasis. In other words, despite differences in instructional emphasis among the five groups, the levels of acquisition of the three rules was surprisingly uniform, and accorded with the order of acquisition reported for naturalistic learners.

The one exception was Group D, which failed to display any acquisition of inversion while achieving a fairly high level of verb-end acquisition (.67). The learners in Group D were relatively poorly motivated. They did not need to continue with German beyond the end of the year. Classroom observation and a diary study kept by one of the learners showed how the group became disillusioned with their studies during the second term. This was reflected in irregular attendance by many of the students and in a poor response to the instruction. However, although these facts can explain the overall lower levels of achievement of this group on particle and inversion, it fails to explain why verb-end was performed more accurately than inversion. The order of instructional emphasis experienced by this group matches the level of acquisition of the three rules. This result is anomalous, therefore. No explanation is available. In particular, it is not clear why the learners in this group produced so few obligatory occasions for inversion (only 6 in total).

This study was set up to examine whether instruction had an effect on the route of L2 acquisition. The results reported suggest that they do not. The study lends support to claims that the acquisition of syntactical features, such as German word order rules, follows the same sequence in both untutored and tutored learners. The classroom learners followed this sequence even though the order of introduction and emphasis given to the rules in the instruction was different.

One interesting finding of this study is that many of the classroom learners achieved considerable success in acquiring the three word order rules, despite the relatively short period of instruction and despite the psycholinguistic difficulty of the rules themselves. Nearly all the learners acquired particle. Out of the 39 learners, 28 succeeded correctly in producing one or more utterances requiring verb-end (the most difficult of the rules). In contrast, many of the learners studied in the ZISA project failed to acquire inversion or verb-end after several years of living in West Germany, and several did not even acquire particle. Although comparisons between migrant workers and classroom learners of the kind investigated in this study may not be justified on the grounds of social and educational differences, it is striking that in such a short period of time the majority of the classroom learners achieved some degree of competence in all three word order rules. It does not follow, therefore, that instruction is worthless. Instruction may serve to accelerate acquisition and also may contribute to higher levels of ultimate success (Long, 1988). One of the central tasks facing classroom SLA researchers is to explain why learners who receive instruction seem to outperform learners who learn naturalistically despite the fact that instruction itself does not affect the route of acquisition.

CONCLUSION

The contribution of the research reported in the previous sections to the construction of a theory of L2 acquisition lies in the evidence it provides to show that the acquisition of features such as German word order rules is determined principally by internal mechanisms rather than by instructional input.

In order to explain the acquisitional sequence for word order, the ZISA researchers suggest that development proceeds in accordance with the cognitive complexity of the operations involved in the production of the rules. A rule that can be performed using a simple processing operation is acquired before a rule that requires a more complex operation. Thus, acquisition is subject to psycholinguistic restrictions; one processing operation serves as a prerequisite for another, more complex operation. Clahsen (1984) identifies a number of processing strategies that students have to learn to apply:

Canonical word order strategy. This strategy leads learners to produce sentences in accordance with a 'natural' word order that corresponds with the deep structure relations between sentence elements. In applying this strategy, learners avoid any processing that involves an interruption of the canonical order.

Initialization/finalization strategy. When learners master this strategy, they are able to apply permutations to the canonical order that entail moving elements to sentence-initial or sentence-final position. Elements in these positions are more salient and easier to memorize than sentence-internal elements.

Subordinate clause strategy. Clahsen suggests that subordinate clauses are processed differently from main clauses. Subordinate clauses are considered marked in relation to main clauses. The learner needs to recognize that the normal processing strategies that apply to main clauses will not apply to subordinate clauses. The subordinate clause strategy allows for the prediction that reorderings of sentence elements will be mastered in main clauses before subordinate clauses. These strategies — which are general in nature — can be applied to German word order rules in order to explain their sequence of acquisition.

Not all researchers explain the existence of a developmental sequence for German word order rules by means of general learning strategies. Researchers such as DuPlessis *et al.* (1987) and Jordens (1988) argue that L2 learners have continued access to Universal Grammar, on which they draw in systematic ways. These account for the sequence of word order acquisition. Jordens, for instance, claims that the main problem facing learners of L2 German is that of sorting out how two possible word orders — SVO and SOV — are related. Learners learn that the underlying word order is SVO when they discover the distinction between finite and nonfinite verb categories. Subsequently, they learn that this underlying word order needs to be restructured depending on whether the clause is main or subordinate. Jordens illustrates how deep structure representations of initial, intermediate, and final state grammars can account for this.

Irrespective of whether an explanation based on general learning strategies or Universal Grammar is invoked, the research can be used to support the general claim that instruction does not affect the sequence of word order acquisition. It would appear that the process of word order acquisition that learners follow is not influenced by learning context.

In reaching this conclusion, however, it is not intended to suggest that input is unimportant in L2 acquisition. Input is valuable because it acts as a trigger for the acquisition of learnable rules. In this respect, the position adopted by researchers like Pienemann (1986) who seek to explain acquisitional sequences in terms of general learning strategies is not dissimilar to that held by those such as White (1987) who invoke explanations based on Universal Grammar. Both Pienemann and White recognize that input interacts with the learner's current knowledge. Both are concerned with trying to specify what constitutes the most suitable input for learning to take place. Both acknowledge that it is possible to manipulate the input (e.g., by giving instruction in specific features or through the correction of overgeneralizations) in order to facilitate learning. Both draw attention to the internal factors that constrain it.

There is, however, one important difference between a cognitive theory of language learning and one based on Universal Grammar. In a cognitive theory, such as that propounded by Pienemann, instruction needs to be directed at the next stage in the acquisitional sequence for it to be successful. In a theory based on Universal Grammar, such as that advanced by White, instruction serves to trigger the setting of a particular parameter, which can in turn lead to further reorganization of the learner's grammar. Pienemann sees the relationship between input and acquisition as a direct one; White sees it as both direct and indirect.

Research based on typological universals lends support to the view that instruction can accelerate acquisition as a result of an indirect triggering effect. Zobl (1983) has suggested that learners have a projection capacity that enables them to acquire unmarked rules on the basis of input relating to associated marked rules. A number of studies based on typological universals (e.g., Eckman, Bell & Nelson, 1988; Gass, 1982; Zobl, 1985) lend support to this position. This concept of projection is an extremely powerful one, but it cannot be easily reconciled with the notion of acquisitional sequence as defined by Pienemann. Here is a case of different theories of L2 acquisition, drawing on very different background disciplines, offering opposing explanations, both of which find support in empirical research. It testifies to the need for different branches of SLA research to pay attention to each other's work in order to reconcile apparent contradictions.

The practical implications of the effects of instruction on the acquisition of German word order rules are also not entirely clear-cut. On the one hand, the research suggests that Krashen's (1985) claim that grammar instruction has no role in the 'acquisition' of new structures is not tenable. Instruction can result in acquisition (in Krashen's sense), providing that certain conditions are met. However, as Long (1985) has noted, it is more or less impossible for teachers to ensure that these conditions are met in the course of their day-to-day teaching. Teachers cannot be expected to know when learners are ready to acquire the next word order rule in the sequence. Also, individual learners will achieve readiness at different times, requiring the teacher to individualize instructional schedules to suit each learner. Another proposal might be to limit formal instruction to variational features. These are features that are not subject to processing constraints and that can be acquired at any time. Pienemann's (1984) study showed that formal instruction did have a positive effect on the acquisition of German copula. This proposal is certainly more feasible, but the problem is that not much is currently known about which features are variational and which are developmental. This proposal must remain no more than a future possibility. It would seem, therefore, that even though Krashen is theoretically wrong about what formal instruction can achieve, he may be right to advocate that teachers base their teaching on activities that lead to meaning-focused interaction. In other words, classroom learners should be invited to proceed in the same way as naturalistic learners. This would also safeguard against the possibly damaging effects of premature formal instruction, which Pienemann (1984, 1986) has reported.

There are, however, two major objections to this position. The first is that learners will fail to acquire the more difficult rules (e.g., inversion and verb-end) once they have achieved communicative adequacy. Learners may need form-focused instruction to make them aware of grammatical features that have little communicative importance and yet constitute target language norms. In other words, formal instruction may serve to prevent fossilization. The second objection is that naturalistic acquisition is often a very slow process; instruction may not alter the way in which learning takes place, but it may help to speed it up. Long's (1983a) review of the effects of formal instruction supports such a contention; classroom learners appear to learn more rapidly than naturalistic learners. The 39 learners investigated in the study reported in this chapter also seemed to outperform naturalistic learners. These two objections constitute powerful arguments in favour of formal instruction.

The question arises as to how formal instruction is able to prevent fossilization and accelerate acquisition if it only works when certain conditions have been met. There are a number of possibilities. One is that the advantages recorded for classroom learners may be the result of instruction in variational features. This is likely, but classroom learners also seem to do better in developmental features, so it cannot constitute a complete explanation. A second possibility is that by recycling the teaching of developmental structures, the teacher can ensure that every learner will be 'ready' sooner or later to benefit from the instruction. The principal objection to this is that premature instruction may have a deleterious effect on learning. Another possibility is that instruction has a delayed rather than an immediate effect. In other words, instruction at one point in time primes the learner so that acquisition becomes easier when a state of readiness is finally reached. As Lightbown (1985a, p.108) puts it, 'formal instruction may provide "hooks", points of access for the learner.' It should be noted that each of these possibilities does not exclude the others. Formal instruction may work in all three ways.

The study reported in this chapter has provided evidence to support the hypothesis that the sequence of acquisition of grammatical structures such as German word order rules is the same in naturalistic and instructed L2 acquisition. This, in turn, provides support for the view that instruction directed at a particular structure will not result in acquisition unless the learner is developmentally ready. It was noted, however, that the learners in this study progressed more rapidly than naturalistic learners reported on in other studies. One explanation for this (although by no means the only one) is that the instruction helped to accelerate acquisition. It has been suggested, therefore, that instruction may have a delayed rather than an immediate effect.

Chapter 4

Focused Communication Tasks and Second Language Acquisition

This chapter first appeared in 1994 as an article in ELT Journal Vol. 47, pp. 203–210.

INTRODUCTION

Communication tasks have been defined as tasks that 'involve the learner in comprehending, manipulating, producing, or interacting in the target language while their attention is principally focused on meaning rather than form' (Nunan, 1989, p.10). They contrast with other, more traditional language tasks that require learners to pay attention to specific linguistic properties (phonological, lexical, or grammatical) in order to learn them or to practice using them more accurately.

The pedagogic rationale for the use of communication tasks rests in part on the claim that they will help to develop learners' *communicative skills* and in part on the claim that they will contribute to their *linguistic development*. In other words, communication tasks are important for both 'fluency' and 'accuracy' (Brumfit, 1984). They aid fluency by enabling learners to activate their linguistic knowledge for use in natural and spontaneous language, such as when taking part in a conversation. One way in which this is achieved is by developing *strategic competence*, defined by Canale (1983) as the verbal and non-verbal strategies used to compensate for breakdowns in communication and to enhance the effectiveness of communication. They contribute to accuracy (i.e. *linguistic competence*) by enabling learners to discover new linguistic forms during the course of communicating, and also by increasing their control over already-acquired forms.

Second language acquisition researchers have suggested a number of ways in which communicating can lead to acquisition. According to the *interaction hypothesis* (Long, 1983c), learners acquire new forms when input is made comprehensible through negotiating for meaning, as in this example (Young and Doughty, 1987, p.213):

NS: Do you wear them every day?

NNS: Huh?

NS: Do you put them on every day?

Here the native speaker (NS) asks a question which the non-native speaker (NNS) does not understand. This leads the NNS to negotiate for meaning by means of a *clarification request*, which in turn causes the NS to paraphrase her initial question. Such negotiation may help to make new forms and their meanings transparent in the input, with the result that they can be more easily acquired.

According to the *comprehensible output hypothesis* (Swain, 1985), acquisition takes place when learners are 'pushed' into producing output that is more grammatical, as in this example:

NNS: He pass his house.

NS: Sorry?

NNS: He passed, he passed, ah, his sign.

Here the NS negotiates for meaning — by means of a clarification request — when she fails to understand the non-native speaker's initial utterance, causing the learner to reformulate the utterance.

The purpose of this chapter is twofold. It aims to report a small-scale study that provides some evidence to suggest that 'pushing' learners to produce more accurate output does indeed contribute to acquisition — as claimed by the comprehensible output hypothesis. It also aims to illustrate how this can be achieved by means of *focused communication tasks* and to consider the place of such tasks in language pedagogy.

FOCUSED AND UNFOCUSED COMMUNICATION TASKS

Communication tasks have the following characteristics (Ellis, 1982):

1. There must be a communicative purpose (i.e. not just a linguistic goal).

2. There must be a focus on message rather than on the linguistic code.

3. There must be some kind of 'gap' (e.g. an information or opinion gap).

4. There must be opportunity for negotiation when performing the task.

5. The participants must choose the resources — verbal and non-verbal — required for performing the task (i.e. they are not supplied with the means for performing the task).

Individual tasks can be more or less 'communicative', depending on whether all or just some of these characteristics are present.

A distinction can be drawn between focused and unfocused communication tasks. In the case of the latter, no effort is made in the design or the execution of a task to give prominence to any particular linguistic feature. The language used to perform the task is 'natural' and only very broadly determined by the content of the task. For example, a one-way picture description task that requires a learner to recount the information shown in a series of pictures to the teacher or another learner and, ultimately, to work out the story is an unfocused communication task, because there is nothing in the task that requires the participants to attend to or use specific linguistic features.

A focused communication task, in contrast, does result in some linguistic feature being made prominent, although not in a way that causes the learner to pay more attention to form than to meaning. Communication tasks can become focused either through design or through methodology. Loschky and Bley-Vroman (1990) observe that 'different tasks can put different requirements on particular grammatical knowledge, and it is correspondingly possible to construct tasks which involve grammatical knowledge in various ways and to varying degrees'. They distinguish tasks in which the use of a particular grammatical structure is 'natural', those in which it is 'useful', and those in which it is 'essential'. In a communicative task that is fully focused, the grammatical structure must be essential (i.e. its use is required by the task), but as Loschky and Bley-Vroman acknowledge, such tasks are difficult to construct, especially if the aim of the task is learner production [1].

The inherent redundancy of language and the availability of rich contextual clues in many tasks obviate the need for learners to use any particular grammatical structure. For this reason, most production tasks are focused only to the extent that a particular structure is 'useful' or 'natural' and, as a consequence, may not actually result in its use. It may be possible, however, to bring about a substantial degree of focus in the performance of a communication task through the manner in which it is carried out — that is, through methodology rather than design. Consider the one-way picture description task outlined above. Let us imagine that a learner is performing the task with a teacher and is given these instructions after receiving the pictures: 'The pictures tell a story about what happened last weekend. Tell me about your pictures'. These instructions make the use of the past tense 'natural', but by no means 'essential'. If, however, the teacher deliberately requests clarification of any utterance the learner produces containing a past tense error — irrespective of whether the teacher has or has not understood the utterance — the use of the past tense becomes a focus of the task. From the teacher's perspective, the task is not a truly communicative one, as the focus has shifted from message to code (see characteristic 2 of communication tasks above). However, from the learners' perspective the task remains communicative providing, of course, that they treat the teacher's request for clarification as a demand to improve the quality of the message rather than to display correct language.

The two examples below were taken from an actual performance of a one-way picture description task by a teacher and a learner. Although we cannot be sure that the learner did not become 'conscious' of the need to pay attention to the past tense, there was nothing in the actual discourse—or indeed, in the overall performance of the task—to suggest that this was the case. The learner appears to be focused primarily on conveying meaning. However, when faced with a request for clarification, she responds by correcting her past tense error:

1. Learner: Last weekend, a man painting, painting 'Beware of the dog'.

   Teacher: Sorry?

   Learner: A man painted, painted, painted on the wall 'Beware of the dog'.

2. Learner: He pass his house.

   Teacher: Uh?

   Learner: He passed, he passed, ah, his sign.

In effect, the learner is being 'pushed', in the course of trying to communicate, to produce utterances that employ correct use of the grammatical feature (i.e. past tense) which the teacher, unknown to her, has elected to focus on.

Focused communication tasks, in particular those where the focus is achieved methodologically, offer the teacher a means of 'teaching' grammar communicatively. Such tasks provide a means of encouraging learners to produce output that is comprehensible and, at the same time, grammatically correct. The question that arises is 'Do such tasks contribute to acquisition?'.

THE STUDY

The purpose of the study was to undertake a preliminary investigation of whether methodologically focused communication tasks lead to more accurate learner production that is sustained over time. Two research questions were addressed:

1. Does 'pushing' learners by means of requests for clarification result in more accurate use of past tense verb forms in communication?

2. Do learners continue to show improved accuracy in the use of past tense verb forms in subsequent communication when there is no attempt to 'push' them?

Participants

There were six participants in the study. They were all adult learners of L2 English enrolled in weekly-held conversational classes at Kanda Institute of Foreign Languages in Tokyo. They were of fairly low-level proficiency, but all of them were capable of using at least some past tense verb forms correctly.

Tasks and Procedure

The learners performed two picture jigsaw communication tasks of the kind described in the previous section. They were told that the pictures they held described events that happened the previous weekend (for task 1) and the day before at the office (for task 2). They performed the tasks individually with their regular teacher.

Three of the learners comprised the experimental group and the other three the control group. All the learners performed the two tasks twice. On the first occasion the experimental group received requests for clarification every time they produced an utterance in which the verb was not in the past tense, or the past tense was incorrectly formed. On the second occasion, however, they received only general requests for clarification (i.e. when the teacher genuinely failed to understand something they had said) and never when an utterance contained an incorrect verb form. The learners in the control group received general requests for clarification, none of which followed an utterance containing a verb incorrectly marked for past tense, on both occasions. There was a one-week interval between the two occasions for both groups. To ensure that the learners did not practice performing the task in the intervening week, they were not told that they would be asked to repeat them.

To confirm that the tasks did provide a natural context for the use of the past tense, baseline data from two native speakers were collected. These showed that except when background information (e.g. concerning the personality of one of the characters shown in the picture) was being provided, the task did indeed result in use of the past tense.

Analysis

The oral interactions between the teacher and the individual learners were recorded and transcribed in normal orthography. Obligatory occasions for the use of the past tense were then identified [2]. This led to some of the learners' utterances being excluded from the analysis, as when the sequence of events was interrupted by background information (e.g. 'Last weekend a man was painting a sign. He *has* a dog. The dog *is* dangerous. So he painted 'Beware of the Dog'.). For each obligatory occasion a learner was scored as supplying or not supplying the correct past tense verb form. If a learner successfully self-corrected in the course of producing an initial utterance, he/she was credited as supplying the past tense form. In the case of the experimental group on the first occasion, all utterances that were subsequently reformulated as a result of the teacher's focused requests for clarification were examined to determine whether the learner had corrected the original past tense error.

RESULTS

Table 1 gives the total number of obligatory occasions for the use of the past tense by each learner together with the number of occasions it was used correctly and incorrectly and the percentage of correct and incorrect use on both occasions. In the case of the experimental group, the number of times the learners correctly reformulated initially incorrect past tense verbs during the first administration of the task is also given, together with a revised percentage of correct forms.

Table 1: Correct and incorrect use of the past tense in two administrations of communication tasks

	Experimental			Control		
	1	2	3	1	2	3
First administration:						
Obligatory occasions	13	20	24	14	19	17
Correct	4	9	3	7	9	0
Incorrect	9	11	21	7	10	17
% correct	31	45	13	50	48	0
Correctly reformulated	4	7	2	–	–	–
% correct after reformulation	44	64	10	–	–	–
Second administration:						
Obligatory occasions	9	26	24	15	12	16
Correct	8	16	1	7	6	1
Incorrect	1	10	23	8	6	15
% correct	89	62	4	47	50	6

Most of the learners produced a substantial number of errors in the use of the past tense during the first administration of the task. In the case of the experimental learners the teacher's requests for clarification led to two of the learners reformulating their utterances in a way that corrected their past tense errors. However, the third learner paid less attention to past tense verb forms in his reformulations, correcting hardly any of his original errors.

The two experimental learners who had successfully reformulated their utterances to increase the use of correct past tense verb forms during the first administration of the task sustained the gain in accuracy during the second administration, even though on this occasion the teacher made no attempt to 'push' them into correct use. Both learners improved on their initial level of accuracy, learner 1 moving from 31% to 89%, and learner 2 from 45% to 62%. The third learner, however, showed no overall gain in accuracy. Neither did any of the learners in the control group.

DISCUSSION

This study provides some support for the claim that 'pushing' learners to improve the accuracy of their production results not only in immediate improved performance but also in gains in accuracy over time. Two of the learners in the experimental group showed significant gains in accuracy, whereas none of learners in the control group did so. This augurs well for the comprehensible output hypothesis. However, one of the experimental learners failed to show any immediate or long-term improvement in the use of past tense verb forms. His level of accuracy remained essentially the same in his initial and reformulated utterances produced during the first administration and in the utterances he produced during the second administration. In other words, this learner did not seem to benefit from being 'pushed'.

One possible interpretation of the results is that 'pushing' learners to make their output more comprehensible leads to linguistic development only in some learners, while others do not benefit. A number of researchers (e.g. Meisel, Clahsen & Pienemann, 1981; Clyne, 1985) have distinguished functionally-and structurally-oriented learners. The former tend to display good comprehension skills and have well-developed communication strategies. The latter have more interest in how language works, take greater efforts to keep the first and second languages separate, and are more inclined to engage in self-correction. It is possible that the first two learners in the experimental group were structurally oriented, while the third was functionally oriented. Thus, whereas the first two made efforts to improve the linguistic accuracy of their output when 'pushed', the third was content to simply get the message across. Such an interpretation is supported by an examination of the kinds of reformulations the third learner produced when the teacher requested clarification. These typically consisted of partial or complete repetitions of previous utterances, as shown in this example:

> Learner: But he sleep. He becomes a sleep.
> Teacher: Sorry?
> Learner: But he sleep. He become asleep.

In other words, this learner was more concerned with general fluency than with accuracy. If this explanation is right, it suggests that the comprehensible output hypothesis will need to be modified to take account of the type of learner.

This study was based on an extremely small number of learners and for this reason can only be considered exploratory. It will need to be replicated with a larger sample and with different linguistic features before any definite conclusions can be arrived at. The results it has provided, however, are intriguing.

CONCLUSION

One of the purposes of this chapter was to explain and illustrate what a focused communication task consists of. It is extremely difficult to bring about a focus on a specific linguistic feature while at the same time maintaining true communicativeness. Once learners realize that the task is intended to provide such a focus, they are likely to stop treating it as an opportunity to communicate and switch into a 'learning' mode. One way in which this can be prevented is if the focus is induced methodologically by means of requests for clarification directed at utterances containing errors in the feature that has been targeted. The data from the study reported above indicate that focusing in this way need not disturb the communicativeness of a task.

Methodologically-focused communication tasks, however, will only be of practical use if they can be used to 'teach' a range of different structures. It is not clear, yet, how possible this is. It is fairly easy to design a task that encourages the use of the past simple tense. It may also be possible, with ingenuity, to design tasks that afford opportunities for using such structures as present perfect, future forms, relative clauses and conditionals. But it is less clear whether they can be designed to 'teach' morphological features such as articles and third persons that are largely redundant, contributing little to the meaning of a message, or syntactic structures such as adjectival order and adverbial position, where, again, adherence to native speaker norms contributes little to message conveyance. As a number of second language researchers have suggested, it may be that certain types of grammatical features cannot easily be acquired through interaction (White, 1987).

It is also possible, as the study indicated, that some learners will not benefit much from being 'pushed' while interacting. This raises the question as to how these learners are to succeed in developing acceptable levels of grammatical accuracy. One answer might be to argue that it does not really matter if they remain grammatically incompetent, as long as they are communicatively competent. If there has to be a choice between the two, it is surely better to go for communicative skill. However, this might not satisfy some teachers. The alternative is to provide 'formal' instruction consisting of tasks designed to focus the learners' conscious attention on specific linguistic features. Indeed, it is not the purpose of this chapter to suggest that focused communicative activities should replace traditional grammar work, only that, for some learners at least, it can serve as a way of helping them to acquire interactively.

Finally, it is necessary to consider in what way focused communication activities can aid 'acquisition'. In this respect, it is useful to distinguish two meanings of acquisition — (1) acquisition as the internalization of new forms, and (2) acquisition as the increase in control over forms that have already been internalized. Arguably, the first occurs as the product of comprehending input, as claimed by the interaction hypothesis, while the second is aided by 'pushing' learners to improve their output, as claimed by the comprehensible output hypothesis. Focused communication tasks would seem better suited to increasing control than to 'teaching' new forms [3]. They provide a means for encouraging learners to maximize their linguistic competence under real operating conditions.

Notes

[1] It is much easier to construct communicative listening tasks in which attention to a specific linguistic property is essential. This is because in listening tasks the designer rather than the learner has control over the linguistic content.

[2] An obligatory occasion consists of an occasion when a learner creates a context that requires the use of a specific linguistic feature — irrespective of whether the feature is or is not actually used. For example, the following both constitute obligatory occasions for the use of the past simple tense:

Yesterday we visit the Tate Gallery.

Yesterday we visited the Tate Gallery.

[3] It is interesting to speculate that different pedagogic techniques may be needed for (a) teaching new forms and for (b) helping learners acquire greater control over forms that they have already learnt, as the psycholinguistic processes involved in these two aspects of acquisition appear to be different. To some extent, this is already acknowledged in language pedagogy, as in the distinction commonly made between 'skill developing' and 'skill using' activities.

Chapter 5

Does Form-Focused Instruction Affect the Acquisition of Implicit Knowledge? A Review of the Research

This chapter first appeared in 2002 in an article published in Studies in Second Language Acquisition Vol. 24, pp. 223–236.

INTRODUCTION

There is by now ample evidence to show that form-focused instruction (FFI) has a positive effect on second language (SL) acquisition. That is, by and large learners seem to learn the grammatical structures they are taught. Long (1983c) in an early review of some 12 studies asserted that the answer to the question 'Does SL instruction make a difference?' is 'a not-so tentative "yes"' (p.380). Norris and Ortega (2000) in a meta-analysis of 49 FFI studies found even more conclusively in favour of FFI, noting that not only did FFI make a difference but that 'it seems to make a substantial difference'. Their analysis also found that explicit instruction was significantly more effective than implicit instruction and that the effects of FFI were durable. N. Ellis

(2002) reiterates these views, claiming unequivocally that 'language acquisition can be speeded by explicit instruction' and, somewhat more contentiously, that 'without any focus on form or consciousness-raising, formal accuracy is an unlikely result' (p.175).

Nevertheless, despite the apparent strength of the evidence in favour of FFI, there are theoretical grounds for caution. Krashen (1981a; 1982; 1993) has argued consistently that the effect of FFI is only peripheral; it can affect only the 'learning' of 'simple' structures as explicit knowledge, not the 'acquisition' of implicit knowledge. N. Ellis' account of how learners acquire implicit knowledge also raises doubts as to whether focusing attention on specific forms is likely to have any impact. We are told that the typical route of acquisition is from formula through low-scope patterns to constructions and that this process is the result of a human categorization ability that enables learners to figure out the sequences and their frequencies in the input. Acquisition, then is a process of 'counting', 'it is all unconscious' (p.148) and it is subject to the basic power law of learning (i.e. practice effects are most evident in the early stages of learning but progressively tail off). Furthermore, the sheer number of words and patterns to be learned ensures that learning is a slow and gradual process. Implicit knowledge is knowledge about the distributional properties of language, which can only be revealed to the learner through substantial and repeated experiences with input. There are no rules but only a complex network of weighted connections adjusted in accordance with input frequencies so that eventually learner production becomes rule-like. Given such an account, it is not easy to see how a few hours, several days or perhaps even a number of weeks of FFI directed at some specific grammatical property can ensure that learners develop implicit knowledge of this feature. There are several reasons for these doubts. First, FFI is invariably based on explicitly formulated rules derived from a reference grammar of some kind or another. Thus what it seeks to teach, whether through implicit or explicit methods, may bear no resemblance whatsoever to how this feature is represented in the learner's store of implicit knowledge. Second, by artificially adjusting the frequency and distribution of a property through instruction, FFI may artificially distort the input and actually mislead the learner, as Lightbown (1983) found when Grade 5 classroom learners were taught Progressive Ving. Third, it is not clear that even highly intensive FFI is capable of providing the sheer number of exemplars needed for implicit knowledge to develop. On the face of it, then, there appears to be a marked mismatch between what FFI is capable of offering the learner and what the learner requires in order to build implicit knowledge.

How then can we reconcile the empirical finding that FFI 'works' and the theoretical probability of it failing? One possibility, the one favoured by Krashen, is that FFI 'works' only in the sense that it contributes to explicit knowledge; it has no effect on implicit knowledge. This is a very plausible claim, made even more plausible by N. Ellis' account of the nature of implicit knowledge and the process of its acquisition. In accordance with this claim, Krashen has argued that the effects of FFI will be evident when acquisition is measured by means that allow for 'monitoring' but not when it is measured in terms of unplanned, meaning-focused language use, which forces learners to draw on their implicit knowledge. Krashen's position, which would seem entirely compatible with N. Ellis' account of implicit knowledge, is empirically testable. However, it has not been tested until recently, mainly because of a lack of studies that have included a measure of acquisition based on free production.

Another way of reconciling the apparent contradiction between the findings of FFI and N. Ellis' theoretical account of implicit knowledge can be found in Long's (1988; 1991) proposal that FFI is only effective if it consists of a 'focus-on-form'. In contrast to a 'focus-on-forms', which involves the intensive teaching of specific grammatical features in a structure-of-the-day approach, 'focus-on form' entails incidental attention to form in the context of communicative activity. In this kind of FFI, forms and the meanings they realise are made salient to learners while they are grappling with the need to communicate, thus affording opportunities for the form-function mapping seen by N. Ellis as an essential aspect of implicit language learning. Again, though, to test the efficacy of focus-on-form instruction, it is necessary to demonstrate that it affects the accuracy with which the target forms are used in free production.

Does FFI contribute to the acquisition of implicit knowledge? Is FFI only effective when it consists of a focus-on-form? These questions will be addressed by considering studies of FFI that have included (1) a control group and (2) a measure of acquisition based on communicative free production (i.e. an activity that calls for unplanned language use directed at fulfilling some communicative purpose) [1].

SELECTION AND ANALYSIS OF THE FFI STUDIES

Out of the 49 studies Norris and Ortega (2000) investigated only eight studies included a measure of acquisition based on free production (i.e. only 16% of the sample). This probably reflects the difficulty of designing-focused communicative tasks that make the use of the target feature 'essential' (Loschky & Bley Vroman 1990). Six of Norris and Ortega's studies were included in the present analysis [2]. An additional five recently published studies were added [3].

Summaries of the 11 studies included in the analysis were prepared. The summaries, shown in Table 1, provide information about the learners, the target structures, the nature of the instructional treatments, the measures of acquisition and the results obtained. The learners differed with regard to age, their instructional context (immersion, university FL classes, intensive language programmes, private school SL classes, public school SL classes). A notable characteristic of the learners is that they were all non-beginners. The need for this is obvious; only learners with established proficiency in the SL are capable of undertaking free production tasks. The target structures of the FFI were taken from French, Spanish, English and Japanese. They varied from the relatively 'simple' (e.g. English past tense forms) to the complex (e.g. English passive sentences). The instructional treatments varied enormously in terms of length and type (see below). The measures of acquisition were all based on free-production and included narratives, picture description, role-plays, information-gap tasks and reports. Most of the free-production activities were oral but some were also written.

Table 1: Summaries of the 11 FFI studies involving measures of acquisition based on free production

Study	Subjects	Target structure	Treatment	Measure of acquisition	Results
Harley (1989)	319 Grade 6 early immersion students	French passé compose and imparfait	8 weeks of analytic-functional grammar materials	(1) Oral interview — 3 questions eliciting use of imparfait (% error score). (2) Written compositions (ratings of accuracy on both tenses).	(1) On immediate post-tests difference between experimental and control group scores significant (p<.05). (2) On delayed PT differences non-significant.
Day and Shapson (1991)	315 Grade 7 early French immersion	French hypothetical conditions	5–7 weeks of analytic-functional grammar materials	(1) Oral interviews— with prompts to rephrase more politely; (2) Written composition with prompts. Both scored for accuracy in obligatory contexts.	(1) On immediate PT the difference between experimental and control was NS in the oral interview but significant in the written composition; (2) Results were the same for the delayed PT.

(continued)

Study	Subjects	Target structure	Treatment	Measure of acquisition	Results
Lyster (1994)	106 Grade 8 early French immersion students	Various sociolinguistic expressions of politeness (especially 'vous')	Explicit explanation; Input highlighting in written texts; contextualised production practice	(1) Oral production — role-played responses to slides depicting formal and informal situations; (2) Written composition — formal letter.	(1) Differences between experimental and control group significant on written composition (p<.00001) and oral production (p<.0001) (2) Similar results on delayed PT. Results on OP largely due to increased use of 'vous'.
VanPatten and Sanz (1995)	44 3rd semester university students of L2 Spanish	Pre-verbal object pronouns; word order	2 days of input processing instruction consisting of explicit explanation and structured input activities	Oral story telling task — subjects watched videos twice and then told the story. Oral and written production.	No statistically significant differences on oral version of story; experimental group significantly better on written version.
Salaberry (1997)	65 3rd semester university students of L2 Spanish	Pre-verbal object pronouns; word order	1.5 hrs of input processing instruction/production based instruction consisting of explicit explanation and structured input activities/production practice	Oral narrative based on one minute silent video clips. Both immediate and delayed PT.	No significant differences between either experimental group and control group. Number of tokens of target structure very low.
Mackey and Philp (1997)	35 adult ESL learners	English question forms	Subjects performed three information gap tasks two conditions; interaction (1) with and (2) without intensive recasts.	Performance on similar information gap tasks to those used for treatment; analysis in terms of developmental stages.	Group that was developmentally 'ready' and received intensive recasts showed significantly greater stage increase.

(continued)

Study	Sub-jects	Target structure	Treatment	Measure of acquisition	Results
Long, Inagaki and Ortega (1997)	Study 1: 24 young adult learners of L2 Japanese	Study 1: Japanese adjectival order-ing and locative construc-tion	Study 1: A communica-tion game that supplied subjects with (1) models and (2) recasts	Study 1: Oral picture de-scription task	Study 1: Differences between control and experimental groups were NS.
	Study 2: 30 young adult 3rd semester Spanish students	Study 2: direct object topicaliza-tion and adverb place-ment	Study 2: 2 communica-tion games that supplied subjects with (1) models and (2) recasts	Study 2: Oral picture de-scription task	Study 2: Experimental groups scored sig-nificantly higher than control groups for adverb placement but not for direct object topicalization.
Mackey (1999)	34 adult ESL learn-ers	English question forms	Subjects performed three infor-mation gap tasks under 2 conditions (1) as interac-tors, (2) non-interactors.	Performance on similar information gap tasks to those used for the treat-ment; analysis in terms of Pienemann's 5 develop-mental stages.	(1) Interactors showed significantly greater stage increase ($p = .0053$) (2) Interactors produced more stage 4 and 5 ques-tions (marginally significant). Signifi-cant gains evident between pre-test and PT2 and PT3 but not PT1.
Dough-ty and Varela (1998)	34 middle school inter-medi-ate ESL ESL stu-dents	Past tense	Feedback in the context of tasks requiring sub-jects to produce three oral and written science reports; feed-back consisted of 'corrective recastings i.e. (1) repetition and (2) recast of student ut-terance. Tasks spread over four weeks	Similar oral and writ-ten science reports to those used in the treatment; data subjected to 'interlan-guage analysis to show development even when students did not perform target struc-ture.	Control group showed little im-provement from pre-test to PT2; experimental group differed significantly from control group on written and oral measures; gains in experimental group largely maintained over time (2 months).

(continued)

Study	Subjects	Target structure	Treatment	Measure of acquisition	Results
Williams and Evans (1998)	11 intermediate adult ESL students enrolled in writing classes	Passive verb forms	(1) Input flooding; (2) explicit instruction + input flooding in context of survey task about cultural values.	Short written essay based on a series of 5 or 6 pictures designed to elicit use of the passive. 2 weeks after completion of instruction. Dictogloss task.	None of the groups showed any significant improvement in use of the passive in the written essays or dictogloss task.
Muranoi (2001)	91 Japanese learners of English — first year college students	Articles — definite and indefinite	(1) Input/output enhancement plus formal debriefing; (2) input/output enhancement plus meaning-focused debriefing. Instruction lasted $1\frac{1}{2}$ hours.	(1) Oral story description task — silent movie scenes; (2) oral picture description task; (3) written picture description task.	Two experimental groups outperformed control group on indefinite article in PT1 but only group receiving formal debriefing outperformed control group in PT2. On the definite article the group that received formal debriefing outperformed the control group but not the group receiving meaning-focused debriefing in both Pt1 and PT2. These findings hold for both speech and writing.

A detailed analysis of the studies was then carried out, referring back to the original articles where necessary. The analysis was based on the following categories:

1. Effectiveness of the instruction (i.e. Did the instruction result in significantly greater gains in the accurate use of the target structure in comparison to the control group?).

a. In the immediate post-test.

b. In a delayed post-test.

2. Age of subjects (i.e. young learners were defined as those aged 12 years or below).

3. Nature of the target structure (i.e. formulaic, morphological or syntactical).

4. The extent of the treatment (i.e. 'extensive' consisting of several hours of instruction or many different tasks completed or 'limited' consisting of less than two hours or just one or two tasks completed).

5. Type of instruction (i.e. 'focus-on-forms' vs. 'focus-on-form' [4]).

6. Measure of acquisition (i.e. oral vs. written free production).

RESULTS

Table 2 shows the results of the analysis of the eleven studies. Seven of the studies report results that show FFI was successful in improving accuracy scores based on free production. In the six studies that included both oral and written free production tasks, if FFI was effective in the oral task it was invariably effective in the written task. However, the reverse was not the case; in one study (Day & Shapson, 1991) FFI was found to be effective only in the written free-production task. Four results report that FFI was unsuccessful, although one of these (Long, Inagaki & Ortega, 1997) found it worked for one of the four structures investigated. The effectiveness of the FFI was evident in both immediate and delayed post-tests. In fact, in studies that included both an immediate and a delayed post-test, there was no study that reported a statistically significant result in the immediate post-test and not in the delayed test. There is some evidence (Mackey, 1999; Muranoi, 2001) that the effects of FFI were stronger in the delayed than the immediate post-test.

FFI was successful in all four studies that involved young learners. Again, though, in Day and Shapson (1991), this success was only evident in the written task; in this study the oral task did not reveal any evidence of learning. The FFI was successful in three of the studies with older subjects. In all four studies where the FFI proved unsuccessful the subjects were older learners.

In all four studies that examined the effects of FFI on morphological/ formulaic features the instruction proved successful. It should be noted that three of these studies involved young learners. The results were more mixed for syntactic features. Out of seven studies, FFI was effective in only three and in one of these (Day & Shapson, 1991) only in the case of the written task. Thus, only Mackey's studies provide clear evidence that FFI works where syntactical structures are concerned.

Table 2: An analysis of the 11 studies

Study	Effectiveness (immediate PT)	Effectiveness (delayed PT)	Age	Target structure	Extent of FFI	Type of FFI
Harley (1989)	Yes (oral and written)	Yes (?)	Young	Morphological	Extensive	Focus-on-form
Day and Shapson (1991)	No (oral) Yes (written)	No (oral) Yes (written)	Young	Syntactical	Extensive	Focus-on-form
Lyster (1994)	Yes (oral and written)	Yes	Young	Formulaic	Extensive	Focus-on-form
VanPatten and Sanz (1995)	No (oral) Yes (written)	No delayed PT	Old	Syntactical	Limited	Focus-on-forms
Salaberry (1997)	No (oral)	No (oral)	Old	Syntactical	Limited	Focus-on-forms
Mackey and Philp (1997)	Yes (oral)	Yes (oral)	Old	Syntactical	Extensive (?)	Focus-on-form
Long, Inagaki and Ortega (1997)	No (oral) (but yes for 'adverb placement')	No delayed PT	Old	Syntactical	Limited	Focus-on-form

(continued)

Study	Effectiveness (immediate PT)	Effectiveness (delayed PT)	Age	Target structure	Extent of FFI	Type of FFI
Mackey (1999)	Yes (oral)	Yes — better still (oral)	Old	Syntactical	Extensive (?)	Focus-on-form
Doughty and Varela (1998)	Yes (oral) Yes (written)	Yes (oral) Yes (written)	Young	Morphological	Extensive	Focus-on-form
Williams and Evans (1998)	No (written)	No delayed PT	Old	Syntactical	Extensive	Focus-on-form
Muranoi (2001)	Yes (oral) Yes (written)	Yes (oral) Yes (written)	Old	Morphological	Limited	Focus-on-form + explicit instruction

In seven of the studies, the FFI was extensive in nature (i.e. consisted of several hours of instruction spread over several days or weeks). Included in these are Mackey's two studies. The instructional treatment in these studies involved only three information-gap tasks. However, the pre-test also consisted of a similar task, as did the three post-tests. Altogether, then, the subjects completed six tasks spread over several weeks before they took the final post-test. It is noticeable that the effects of the treatment became stronger the more tasks the learners completed. In six of the seven studies with extensive treatment, FFI proved effective. It was ineffective only in Williams and Evans (1998), where the target structure (passives) was of notable complexity. In contrast, FFI was less successful in the studies with limited FFI, with only Muranoi's study, which linked communicative practice to explicit instruction, producing a positive result.

Only two studies provided instruction of the focus-on-forms type. Neither study showed any effect for FFI on unplanned communicative language use. Of the 9 studies where the instruction was of the focus-on-form kind, seven produced results showing a clear effect for FFI.

DISCUSSION

Norris and Ortega's (2000) meta-analysis showed that the average FFI effect size in the eight studies involving free production that they investigated was much lower than in studies that utilized measures based on selected responses or on controlled production (k=0.55 as opposed to k=1.46 and 1.20 respectively) [5]. This result, therefore, casts some doubt on whether FFI is able to have a substantial effect on learners' communicative use of grammatical structures. However, the results reported above suggest that FFI can have a significant effect on the accuracy of use of grammatical structures, although the results also suggest that these gains are not inevitable and are contingent on a number of factors.

It is important to note that the research to date only provides evidence that FFI assists the acquisition of implicit knowledge in non-beginners. As noted above, the learners of all the studies in Table 1 were of intermediate level or higher. Thus whether FFI works for beginner learners remains to be tested. Until some means of measuring implicit knowledge in beginners can be found it is not clear how this can be accomplished. Also, N. Ellis' account of how implicit knowledge is developed suggests that FFI might not be effective for beginners as acquisition in the early stages is primarily a matter of extracting formulae and low-scope patterns from the input (see also Johnston's 1987 account of the processing operations that underlie early developmental stages).

Given the small number of studies that have investigated FFI in relation to free production, it is not possible to reach any firm conclusions regarding the variables that impact on success. Nevertheless, the analysis of the 11 studies is suggestive of what these variables might be. FFI was effective in all four studies involving young learners. However, this may reflect other characteristics of these studies rather than the learners' age.

In all four studies the treatment provided was extensive and in three of them the grammatical target was a relatively simple morphological feature. In the one study where the target structure was a complex syntactical feature (Day & Shapson, 1991), FFI had no effect on the learners' oral production, arguably a better measure of implicit knowledge as it is less amenable to monitoring using explicit knowledge.

Thus, the analysis suggests that the key factors are (1) the nature of the target structure and (2) the length of the treatment. FFI would seem to have a better chance of success if it is directed at simple morphological features (e.g., verb forms, articles or formulaic items) than at more complex syntactical structures involving permutations of word order (e.g., word order involving Spanish clitic pronouns and passive sentences). Possibly FFI succeeds for simple morphological features because it makes such forms salient to the learner and because they are processible; it is less successful in the case of complex syntactical features because these require more complex processing operations that can only be mastered sequentially over a long period of time, as proposed by Pienemann (1989) [6].

FFI involving extended treatment of the target structure is more likely to succeed than FFI with limited treatment. FFI where the instructional treatment is limited to one or two hours or less and is directed at complex syntactical features has no effect on learners' ability to produce the structures in free production (VanPatten & Sanz, 1995; Salaberry, 1997; Long, Inagaki & Ortega, 1997). This accords with N. Ellis' emphasis on frequency as the key determinant of acquisition. Nevertheless, extensive treatment does not guarantee success if the target structure is complex in nature (Williams & Evans, 1998).

There are times, however, when more limited instruction appears to be successful even if the target structure is complex in nature. Mackey's two studies show that at least some complex syntactical structures can be acquired through FFI. These studies addressed English question forms, a structure that other research has shown is amenable to instruction (e.g. White, Spada, Lightbown & Ranta, 1991). Murunoi's study found that a very short period of instruction was effective in promoting accurate use of English articles (a morphological feature but arguably complex). A possible explanation for these successes, despite the limited instruction they provided, may lie in the fact that the target structures are readily available to learners in their regular, non-instructional input. As Lightbown (1992) has noted, learners are likely to have regular exposure to questions forms and opportunities to produce them outside FFI. Thus, the learners in Mackey's and Murunoi's studies may have obtained the quantity of exposure required to learn the target structures through a combination of FFI and 'natural' input. The fact that both studies report that the effects of instruction were more evident in the delayed than the immediate post-tests lends support to such a hypothesis.

No conclusion regarding the relative effectiveness of focus-on-form and focus-on-forms instruction is possible from the analysis of the 11 studies. Focus-on-forms occurred in only two studies (VanPatten & Sanz, 1995; Salaberry, 1997) and in both cases the FFI was unsuccessful. However, in these studies the treatment was limited and the target structures were complex. In the five out of six studies involving focus-on-form that showed a clear effect for instruction (Harley, 1989; Lyster, 1994; Mackey & Philp, 1997; Mackey, 1999; Doughty & Varela, 1998) the FFI was extensive in nature. Thus it is not possible to conclude that it was the type rather than the extent of the instruction that was the crucial factor. In the one study where the focus-on-form instruction was limited (Long, Inagaki & Ortega, 1997), little effect was evident. What is needed is a comparison of focus-on-forms and focus-on-form instruction where both are extensive and both directed at a 'learnable' structure.

CONCLUSION

N. Ellis argues that much of language learning is implicit in nature as learners cannot be expected to develop awareness of the low-level distributional properties of the target language. However, he also argues that form-focused instruction has a role to play in forcing learners to attend to the structure of 'ambiguous sequences' and suggests, quoting Hulstijn and DeKeyser (1997), that it can 'narrow their hypothesis space'. Although he does not explicitly say so, N. Ellis is clearly of the view that instruction can aid the acquisition of implicit knowledge.

The analysis presented above lends broad support to this position. Taking performance in free production tasks (especially oral) as the measure of whether implicit knowledge has been acquired, the analysis demonstrates that at least sometimes FFI results in acquisition and that when it does the effects are durable. One caveat to this conclusion, however, is that the studies in question did not provide any information about the quality of the learners' free production. In particular, because there is no data on fluency (e.g. hesitation phenomena and reformulations), we cannot be certain that the learners were not monitoring their output. Free production tasks make it difficult for learners to perform on the basis of explicit knowledge but not impossible.

The analysis has examined a number of possible variables that impact on the success of the instruction — age, the target structure, the extent of the instruction and the type (focus-on-form vs. focus-on-forms). It suggests that the key variables may be the complexity of the target structure, the extent of the instruction and the availability of the target structure in non-instructional input. The challenge facing researchers is to identify the variables that make FFI work for implicit knowledge. If it is the 'language learner who counts', we need to know how to devise FFI that will help him/her do the counting.

A final comment is in order. In this chapter I have addressed whether FFI can have a direct effect on implicit knowledge. There is general agreement and strong empirical evidence to show that FFI can affect explicit knowledge. It seems reasonable to conclude that it is easier to teach explicit knowledge than implicit knowledge. Elsewhere (R. Ellis 1993a and 1997: see Chapters 10 and 11) I have argued that explicit knowledge can facilitate the subsequent acquisition of implicit knowledge (e.g. by helping to make forms salient to learners). This being the case another, possibly more tenable, route to implicit knowledge might be to use FFI to develop an explicit understanding of how problematic structures work and then allow the human categorization ability to build implicit knowledge through the input made available in unfocused tasks and 'natural' exposure. Perhaps we do not have to bother with trying to teach implicit knowledge directly.

Notes

[1] Studies that included a free production measure that could easily have been interpreted by the learners as a request to produce the target structure and thus might have encouraged the use of explicit knowledge were not included in the sample. Examples of studies excluded on these grounds were Harley (1998) and Nagata (1998).

[2] Two of the studies in Norris and Ortega's meta-analysis (Jourdenais *et al.*, 1995; Nagata, 1997) were not included in this study. Nagata's study was excluded because the production task required subjects 'to construct Japanese sentences using the target particles' and thus was considered unlikely to promote unplanned communicative use of the target structures. Jourdenais *et al.* was not available to the researcher.

[3] Norris and Ortega examined studies published in 1998 or earlier. The fact that it was possible to identify five further studies published since their review is indicative of the growing importance SLA researchers attach to including a measure of acquisition based on free production in their studies.

[4] The distinction between 'focus-on-form' and 'focus-on-forms' is not easy to operationalize (see Ellis, 2001 and Chapter 8 for a discussion of this distinction). Here 'focus-on-form' instruction was taken to include instruction that involved learners in using the target structure in the context of communicative activities. 'Focus-on-forms' instruction was operationalized as instruction where the majority of the activities involved text-manipulation rather than text-creation (Ellis, 1997).

[5] Interestingly, the effect size associated with metalingual judgements (k = 0.82) was much closer to that for free production.

[6] There is no mention whatsoever of Pienemann's work in N. Ellis' survey of SLA research — a somewhat surprising omission.

Chapter 6

Focusing on Form in the Communicative Classroom

SOME DEFINITIONS

Figure 1 displays the pedagogical options that gave shape to the study reported in this chapter. Language pedagogy can be accomplished by means of meaning-focused instruction or form-focused instruction. The latter can in turn consist of a focus-on-forms or a focus-on-form.

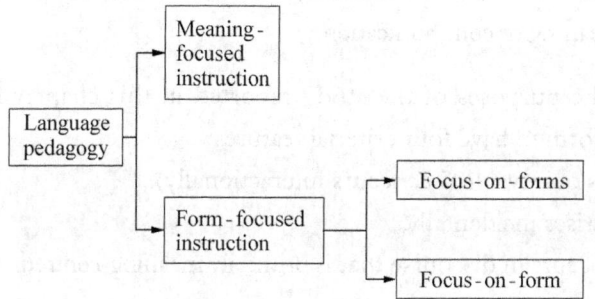

Figure 1: Some basic pedagogical options

It is common in both the pedagogic and the second language acquisition (SLA) literature to distinguish meaning-focused and form-focused instruction (Harmer, 1983; Doughty & Williams, 1998). The former refers to instruction directed at engaging learners in acts of communication where their attention is primarily directed at understanding and/or conveying message content (e.g. through task-based language teaching). The latter refers to instruction where the learner's attention is focused on linguistic forms and the semantic and pragmatic meanings these convey.

Form-focused instruction is of two basic types: (1) a planned attempt to intervene in interlanguage development and (2) incidental attempts to focus learners' attention onto forms in the course of instruction that is not explicitly designed to teach the forms. Somewhat confusingly, Long (1988; 1991) has labelled these two types of form-focused instruction 'focus on forms' and 'focus on form'. Focus on forms, according to Long (1988), consists of the teaching of discrete grammar points in accordance with a synthetic syllabus, such as a structural syllabus. Krashen (1982) refers to this as 'the structure-of-the-day' approach. The criterial features of focus-on-forms are (1) the pre-selection of a linguistic target for a lesson and (2) awareness on the part of the students of what the linguistic target for the lesson is.

Focus on form is defined by Long (1991, pp.45–46) as follows:

> Focus on form … overtly draws students' attention to linguistic elements as they rise incidentally in lessons whose overriding focus is on meaning or communication.

For the purposes of the study reported in this chapter I consider focus-on-form to have four criterial features:

1. It is observable (i.e. occurs interactionally).
2. It arises incidentally.
3. It occurs in discourse that is primarily meaning-centred.
4. It is transitory.

THE PSYCHOLINGUISTICS RATIONALE FOR FOCUS-ON-FORM

The psycholinguistic rationale for a focus-on-form draws on a number of claims:

1. Meaning-focused instruction, while effective in developing fluent oral communication skills, does not result in a high level of linguistic or sociolinguistic competence.

2. Form-focused instruction consisting of a focus-on-forms may not result in learners being able to restructure their interlanguages (see, for example, Chapters 2 and 3).

3. Form-focused instruction consisting of a focus-on-form can enable learners to develop fluency with accuracy because it creates the conditions for interlanguage restructuring to take place.

I will examine each of these claims.

There is plenty of evidence to demonstrate that learners are successful in learning how to communicate fluently and confidently as a result of content-based instruction (see, for example, reviews of the Canadian immersion studies in Genesee (1987) and Swain, 1985). Even in less favourable ESL or EFL learning contexts, instructional programmes designed to expose learners to the target language through communication of one kind or another have produced very favourable results. Lightbown (1992), for example, reports that eight-year children in New Brunswick, who participated in an experimental programme in which they worked entirely on their own for thirty minutes each day with various reading and listening materials designed to provide them with comprehensible input, demonstrated considerable oral ability at the end of the first year, greater in fact than that achieved by students taught through a traditional, focus-on-forms approach. Clearly, meaning-focused instruction that supplies learners with plentiful input that they can understand is effective in developing oral skills. However, there is also evidence to suggest that such instruction is not successful in enabling learners to achieve high levels of linguistic and sociolinguistic accuracy, suggesting, as claimed by Higgs and Clifford (1982), that there are limits to what can be achieved through 'natural' learning. French immersion students, for example, typically fail to learn marked verb forms. For example, they do not acquire the distinction between passé composé and imparfait (Harley, 1989) or conditional forms (Day & Shapson, 1991). They also fail to master sociolinguistic distinctions, such as that between *tu* and *vous* (Lyster, 1994).

Why do learners fail to learn basic tense and sociolinguistic distinctions even after hundreds of hours of meaning-focused instruction? One possibility is that they develop a high level of strategic competence that enables them to process input and output in the L2 without the need to attend closely to linguistic form. Indeed, the very nature of the instruction they experience, with its emphasis on processing language for meaning, may encourage the use of top-down strategies based on schematic knowledge and context at the expense of bottom-up strategies directed at decoding and encoding linguistic form. Schmidt (1990; 1994) has argued that acquisition cannot take place unless learners actually 'notice' linguistic forms in the input — a process that he suggests is necessarily conscious. Meaning-focused instruction does not encourage such noticing. Furthermore, it may actually inhibit it. VanPatten (1990) has suggested that learners, especially those with a low level of proficiency in the L2, have limited processing capacities, such that they cannot easily attend to both meaning and form at the same time and thus opt for whichever pays them the greater dividends. In the case of meaning-focused instruction this is obviously meaning. In short, what is good for developing the ability to process language for meaning in context may not be effective in developing advanced linguistic competence.

This has led researchers to look for ways of complementing meaning-focused instruction with some kind of form-focused instruction. One possibility is a focus-on-forms — to complement content-based or task-based instruction with planned form-focused lessons designed to address the particular linguistic features that have been found problematic to learners. The studies referred to above by Harley (1989), Day and Shapson (1991) and Lyster (1994) all testify to this possibility. These studies provide evidence to show that teaching learners forms (and, of course, the semantic and pragmatic meanings they realize) is, to some extent at least, successful, especially if the approach adopted is a 'functional' one (i.e. involves activities that teach form in relation to communicative activity).

Nevertheless, there are strong theoretical reasons, grounded on empirical studies (e.g. Pienemann 1989: see Chapter 3), to suggest that focusing on forms is problematic because learners follow their own built-in syllabus which only allows them to benefit from form-focused instruction directed at a specific form if they have established the prerequisite processing operations needed to acquire it. Several studies (e.g., Pica 1983; see Chapters 2 and 3) have shown that classroom learners follow the same order and sequence of acquisition as naturalistic learners, suggesting that interlanguage development may be impervious to direct intervention through instruction. These studies, however, have also shown that learners who have received form-focused instruction learn more rapidly and generally advance further along the interlanguage continuum than naturalistic learners. It would seem then that where rate and ultimate level of learning are concerned, a focus-on-forms may be of some benefit, especially if it is directed at linguistic features that they have already partially acquired. Nevertheless, whether a particular group of learners is ready to acquire a particular 'new' feature is bound to be a hit-or-miss affair. Also, focus-on-forms seems to work best when the instruction is intensive, involving repeated activities performed over a period of time, several weeks in the case of some of the studies referred to above. This necessarily limits the number of features that can be effectively treated. For these reasons, the other form-focused teaching option is worthy of consideration.

Focus-on-form is compatible with an information-processing theoretical view of L2 acquisition. As we have already noted, L2 learners experience problems in directing their attention simultaneously at meaning and form, opting for whatever focus is compatible with their immediate goals. A focus-on-form provides learners with the opportunity to take 'time-out' from focusing on message construction to pay attention to specific forms and the meanings they realise. It thus helps to alleviate the processing problems they experience. It also provides an antidote to the kind of top-down processing that L2 learners adopt to cope with communicative demands by forcing learners, from time to time, to engage in bottom-up processing. Furthermore, such an approach enables teacher and students to attend to features that are demonstrably problematic to learners (i.e. focus-on-form episodes are triggered either by something problematic in a learner utterance or by the learner's or teacher's wish to clarify understanding of a linguistic feature). In this way, focus-on-form is inherently remedial and, for that reason, pedagogically efficient.

A further rationale for focus-on-form can be found in the kind of skill-building theory advanced by Keith Johnson (1988; 1996). Johnson argues that skill-development occurs when learners obtain feedback. He suggests, however, that feedback is most effectively utilized by learners when it is provided under 'real operating conditions' (i.e. in natural contexts in which learners are trying to actually perform the skill). Such feedback enables learners to carry out a cognitive comparison between their own output, which reflects their current interlanguage system, and the negative evidence and models of target language forms provided through the feedback. In this way, learners have the opportunity to 'notice-the-gap' (Schmidt & Frota, 1986). Long (1996), drawing on Pinker (1989), however, argues that it is not sufficient to argue that negative evidence is a remedy to learners' linguistic problems but that it must be shown to (1) exist, (2) exist in a usable form, (3) be used by learners and (4) be necessary for successful acquisition. He presents theoretical and empirical reasons for believing that all these conditions can be met. Together, Johnson and Long offer a clear psycholinguistic rationale for focus-on-form; it provides learners with the negative evidence they need to develop their interlanguages in a manner that is usable.

Focus-on-form can also contribute to acquisition in another

way — it provides the impetus for what Swain (1985; 1995) has termed 'pushed output', i.e. output that stretches the learner's competence through the need to express an idea in language that is accurate and appropriate. When teachers respond to student errors through corrective feedback they potentially create conditions for students to attempt to produce the correct forms themselves (see Chapter 4). Doing so may help to foster the acquisition of these forms so that on subsequent occasions the students are able to use the correct forms without prompting.

CLASSROOM STUDIES OF FOCUS-ON-FORM

Studies of error treatment (see Chaudron (1987) for a review) indicate that it is an enormously complex process — a point evident in the elaborativeness of the discourse and category systems that have been developed to account for it. The research shows that some errors are more likely to be treated than others (e.g. lexical errors receive more attention than grammatical errors), although, of course, this is likely to vary considerably from teacher to teacher. The research also shows that there is considerable variation among teachers regarding the frequency with which errors are corrected and the preferred manner in which they are corrected. Teachers often simultaneously provide more than one kind of feedback on the same error. However, they do not correct all errors and are less likely to correct an error if it occurs frequently. Also on occasions teachers have been observed to correct 'errors' that have not in fact been made (Edmundson, 1985). Two general characteristics of teachers' error correction practices have been noted: imprecision and inconsistency. Imprecision is evident in the fact that teachers use the same overt behaviour (e.g. 'repetition') to both indicate that an error has been made and to reinforce a correct response. Nystrom (1983) commented: 'teachers typically are unable to sort though the feedback options available to them and arrive at an appropriate response'. Inconsistency arises when teachers respond variably to the same error made by different students in the same class, correcting some students and ignoring others. Such inconsistency is not necessarily detrimental, for, as Allwright (1975) has pointed out, it may reflect teachers' attempts to cater for individual differences among the students.

Recent studies of corrective feedback have sought to identify the frequency with which specific corrective categories are used. Lyster and Ranta (1997) found that of the various feedback types they identified in immersion classrooms, 'recasts' were the most common, accounting for some 55% of the total. The other types occurred with roughly equal frequency (i.e. between 14% for 'elicitation' and 5% for 'repetition'). They also examined student uptake in relation to the different types of teacher feedback. Interestingly, 'recasts', the most frequent type of feedback, resulted in the least amount of uptake (only 31%). 'Explicit correction' was also not very effective in this respect, leading to only 50% uptake. The most effective feedback types were 'elicitation' and 'clarification request', which resulted in 100% and 91% uptake respectively. When Lyster and Ranta looked at the kind of uptake (i.e. whether it was of the 'repair' or 'needs repair' type), they found that 'elicitation' was again the most effective, with 46% of uptake manifesting correction of the error, and 'clarification request' relatively ineffective, with only 28% of uptake in the 'repair' category. Lyster and Ranta conclude that 'the feedback-uptake sequence engages students more actively when ... the correct form is not provided to the students ... and when signals are provided to the learner that assist the reformulation of the erroneous utterance' (p.58). In a series of subsequent experimental studies (e.g. Lyster, 2004; Lyster & Mori, 2006) Lyster has provided evidence to support his view that feedback that prompts learners to self-correct results not just in more uptake with repair but also more acquisition than recasts.

Very little research has examined the effects of focus-on-form on acquisition in natural classrooms, Lightbown and Spada (1990) and Spada and Lightbown (1993) being notable exceptions. These studies examined intensive communicative ESL classes in Canada. The earlier study compared the accuracy with which students in four different classes performed several grammatical structures in an oral-communication task. Lightbown and Spada note that their teachers did not teach grammar lessons but rather reacted to errors as they occurred (i.e. practiced focus-on-form). They show that several of the structures (e.g. introducer forms with 'be', progressive -*ing* and possessive determiners) were performed more accurately by students in one of the classes than the others and suggest that this might have been because the teacher of this class gave more attention to form, although always in the context of the same communicative activities completed by the other classes. The second study reports an experimental investigation of form-focused instruction of the focus-on-forms kind (as I have defined this earlier). However, the results of interest here concern the control group, which experienced instruction that was primarily meaning-focused. Spada and Lightbown report that this group outperformed the experimental groups on the target structure (interrogatives). In order to explain this surprising finding they examined the actual interactions that took place in the experimental and control classrooms and found that the teacher in the control classroom asked many more questions than the teachers in the experimental classrooms. This teacher also corrected her students' errors in question formation far more frequently than one of the teachers of the experimental treatment, despite the fact that she was not trying to teach questions. The students in the control group also produced more spontaneous questions. Spada and Lightbown conclude that the success of the control group students in acquiring question forms derived from the focus-on-form that occurred over a period of several months. In effect, this study suggests that a focus-on-form can work as well as, if not better than, a focus-on-forms. More recent classroom studies that have investigated the effects of corrective feedback in communicative lessons (e.g. Ellis, Loewen & Erlam, 2006; Lyster, 2004; Sheen, 2006) also testify to the effectiveness of focus-on-form instruction in assisting L2 acquisition.

There have been a number of non-classroom experimental studies that claim to have investigated the effects of focus-on-form on acquisition. For example, Carroll and Swain (1993) examined the effects of different kinds of feedback on learners' learning of dative alternation [1]. This study showed that the group receiving explicit feedback involving metalinguistic comments outperformed both a control group and the other groups receiving different kinds of feedback (e.g. implicit correction in the form of recasts). Implicit correction also worked better than no correction. However, this study did not obtain measures of the students' ability to use the target structure in oral communication, arguably the best measure of acquisition (see Chapter 5). Carroll, Swain and Roberge (1992) investigated the effects of corrective feedback on learners' ability to distinguish French nouns ending in -*age* and -*ment*. They found that the treatment was effective with regard to the nouns actually taught but that it did not result in the learners' ability to generalize to new nouns. However, these studies, like more recent studies that have sought to teach specific grammatical features in a communicative context (e.g. Doughty & Varela, 1998; Williams & Evans, 1998), all involved planned form-focused instruction that was intensive (i.e. focused on a single linguistic feature) rather than incidental focus-on-form that is extensive (i.e. directed at a range of linguistic features).

It is, in fact, very difficult to investigate the effects of incidental focus-on-form on L2 acquisition as it is not possible to predict in advance which forms a teacher will focus on and thus impossible to establish whether students 'know' the forms prior to the lesson. A pre-test/ post-test study, then, is not feasible. Furthermore, focus-on-form is necessarily transitory, so it cannot be expected that a brief (and probably single) focusing on a specific form will have any immediate effect. Of course, acquisition may be fostered by repeated focusing on a specific form over several lessons. The effects of incidental focus-on-form on acquisition are likely to be accumulative and gradual. Indeed, such is the theoretical rationale for focus-on-form. It is unlikely, then, that any measurable 'effect' will be evident from a single lesson while it will also be very difficult to obtain reliable data regarding which forms are focused on over time. Lightbown and Spada's research, which involves post-hoc analyses of classroom process data over time, affords the most obvious way of studying the effects of focus-on-form but is necessarily time-consuming and laborious.

THE STUDY

Research Question

The study addressed the following general research question:

How did the participants focus on form during message-oriented exchanges in communicative classrooms?

Teaching Context

Two classes in a private English language school in Auckland were selected as the site for data collection. One of these classes was an intermediate class (Class 1) and the other a pre-intermediate class (Class 2). Each class had a different teacher and 12 students, although not all the students were present in every lesson observed.

The instruction was in two separate parts, divided by a break. In the first part, the teacher focused primarily on grammatical forms. The instruction in this part, therefore, was of the focus-on-forms kind. In the second part, after the break, the instruction was primarily communicative in that there was no pre-determined linguistic focus, although there was a general concern to provide opportunities for the students to practice the structure taught in the first part of the lesson. The focus-on-form episodes (FFEs) that were the focus of our study occurred in this second part of the lesson.

Participants

Each class consisted of 12 students, although attendance varied from day to day. In addition, the classes had open enrolment so some students left and new ones arrived during the course of the observations; however, the L1 composition of each class remained the same. In addition, the nationalities represented in the two classes were very similar with Class 1 consisting of 6 Japanese, 2 Koreans, 2 Swiss, 1 Thai and 1 Brazilian and Class 2 consisting of 4 Japanese, 3 Koreans, 3 Swiss, 1 Chinese, and 1 Brazilian.

Teacher One had taught full-time at the language school for four and a half years. She had completed the CELTA course at the school and had started teaching upon passing the course. She was concurrently finishing a Diploma course offered by the school, and saw herself pursuing a career in ESL. Teacher Two had also completed the CELTA course and had been teaching part-time at the language school for two years. Initially, she had seen teaching as a means of supporting other interests, but she had come to enjoy her work at the school and planned to remain indefinitely.

Data

The data comprised 14 hours of audio-recorded classroom talk from 10 ESL lessons (5 for each teacher). As previously noted, the recordings were all of lessons that occurred in the second part of a day's instruction (i.e. where the interaction was primarily message-focused). However, within these primarily communicative lessons, there was some explicit focus on forms. As a result, two hours of data were excluded from the analysis, leaving a total of 12 hours of message-oriented classroom discourse for analysis. (The remaining 12 hours were still evenly divided between the two classrooms.) In order to record whole class interaction as well as teacher interaction with individuals and small groups, a wireless, clip-on microphone was attached to the teacher in each class.

Identification of FFEs

The researcher who observed the lessons listened to the recordings in order to identify occasions where there was attention to linguistic form, i.e., grammar, vocabulary, spelling, discourse or pronunciation. Some of these sequences arose when one of the participants drew attention to a specific form (e.g. by asking a question about it) even though no linguistic problem had arisen in the discourse. Other sequences consisted of the participants' attempts to address an actual or perceived linguistic problem. It should be noted that occasions where a problem arose that was not related to linguistic form, occasions where there was a linguistic error with no attempt to address it, and occasions where an individual self-corrected an error without feedback were not considered. The researcher established each point in the recording where the attention to linguistic form started and the point where it ended. The end point occurred when either the topic changed back to a focus on meaning or to a focus on a different linguistic form.

Each FFE was then transcribed. The researcher subsequently listened to the recordings on several further occasions to check that (1) all FFEs had been identified, (2) the beginnings and endings of the FFEs had been correctly identified and (3) each FFE had been accurately transcribed. A broad transcription was used but pauses of any length were noted.

Analysis

Following identification and transcription of the FFEs, each FFE was repeatedly examined by a team of three researchers to establish a set of descriptive characteristics and categories to account for salient features. The main categories identified are described below.

Approach

In terms of the overall approach to focusing on form, the FFEs differed according to whether they were *responding FFEs* (RFFEs) or *initiating FFEs* (IFFEs). RFFEs are sequences which occur when a participant responds to an utterance produced by another participant that is perceived as problematic, either because its meaning is not clear or because it is seen as containing a linguistic error. RFFEs are therefore reactive. The research to date has addressed reactive focus on form and has paid little attention to proactive focus on form. The distinction is of potential importance for future research. Both approaches constitute ways of addressing gaps in the learners' knowledge system. However, they differ with regard to how this achieved. IFFEs typically supply learners with declarative and illustrative information about form. RFFEs have the potential to facilitate the kind of 'cognitive comparison' which some researchers have argued underlies the process of interlanguage restructuring (Tomasello & Herron, 1988; Ellis, 1994b). There is an obvious need to establish the relative effects of these two approaches on acquisition.

Instigator

This refers to the person responsible for bringing about a focus-on-form. In the case of RFFEs, the person who responds to the utterance containing a perceived problem is the instigator. In the case of IFFEs, the person who initiates the focus-on-form by raising a linguistic topic is the instigator. In both IFFEs and RFFEs the instigator may be a student or the teacher. There is a sound psycholinguistic reason for examining who is responsible for instigating a focus-on-form. A number of studies (see R. Ellis, 1998) have suggested that when learners have the opportunity to initiate discourse, opportunities for acquisition may be enhanced. Slimani (1989; 1992) has shown that learners are more likely to report learning new items from a lesson if the items occurred in sequences involving student topicalisation.

Linguistic Focus

The FFEs varied according to the linguistic focus. The following aspects of language received attention:

1. *grammar* — e.g. determiners, prepositions and pronouns, word order, tense, verb morphology,   auxiliaries and subject-verb agreement,

plurals, negation, question formation.

2. *vocabulary* — the meaning of open class lexical items including single word items and idioms.

3. *spelling* — the orthographic form of words.

4. *discourse* — textual relations, such as text cohesion and coherence, and pragmatics such as the appropriate use of specific forms according to social context.

5. *pronunciation* — supra-segmental and segmental aspects of the phonological system.

Timing

This characteristic refers to when the participants start attending discoursally to the linguistic form. When the participants start attending in the discourse adjacent to production (e.g. following on from production of an error in speaking) this is coded as 'immediate'. When the participants start attending after some intervening discourse (e.g. when an error is produced in writing and is only addressed subsequently) this is coded as 'delayed'. The distinction between immediate and delayed feedback is also of psycholinguistic interest. A recent review of the effects of corrective feedback on L2 learners' written compositions (Truscott, 1996) indicated that there is little effect on learners' acquisition of the forms corrected (i.e., learners subsequent use of these forms remains unchanged). In contrast, a number of studies of immediate corrective feedback in the context of classroom interaction (e.g. Lightbown & Spada, 1990; Ellis, Loewen & Erlam, 2006) suggest that such feedback can lead to improved accuracy. Coding FFEs for whether the feedback is immediate or delayed allows for the potential differential effect to be investigated.

Source

The problem source can be of two kinds, both triggering a focus on form. In some cases, the problem arises because a participant fails to comprehend something that another participant has said. In such cases, the source is coded as 'message'. Long (1983a) has coined the term 'negotiation of meaning' to refer to attempts by interlocutors to achieve understanding after a breakdown in understanding. It should be noted that such negotiation often arises because of some linguistic problem. However, this need not be the case, as on some occasions, negotiation of meaning occurs when the problem is one of content rather than language. In other cases, a focus on form arises when there is no problem in understanding what has been said. That is, a participant (usually the teacher) chooses to pay attention to a linguistic error in another participant's utterance even if he/she has understood the utterance. In such cases, the problem source is 'code'. The term 'negotiation of form' can be used to describe such episodes.

The distinction between FFEs involving the negotiation of meaning and the negotiation of form is of considerable theoretical importance. Long's Interaction Hypothesis, in both its original and more recent formulation (see Long, 1983a and 1996), is predicated on the claim that attention to form promotes acquisition when it arises in the negotiation of meaning. However, work by Swain (2000) provides a theoretical case for attention to form in the context of language related episodes which are triggered by a concern for form. In other words, Swain claims that negotiation of form can also benefit acquisition. Clearly, there is a need to distinguish between interactions involving negotiating meaning and form in order to investigate their relative impact on acquisition.

In many instances, the source of an FFE is clear, as the discoursal context shows whether a participant is negotiating meaning or form. However, FFEs involving lexical problems are more ambiguous. It is often not clear whether a teacher, for example, has elected to focus on a specific word because she failed to understand the student's message or because she wishes to take the opportunity to teach that word. This is because the treatment of lexical items in FFEs typically involves addressing their meaning. In the present study, we adopted the 'negotiation of meaning' as the default position. That is, an FFE was coded as 'code' only when the discourse context made it clear that a participant had understood the problem utterance.

The Reliability of the System

In order to determine the reliability of the descriptive system, two of the researchers independently coded a subset of the data. Initially 67 episodes (15%) were chosen randomly from the entire data set. In the case of differences, the two researchers discussed the coding discrepancies in order to reach agreement. A further 57 episodes were then recoded by both researchers. Inter-rater reliability was .89 or higher for all the categories.

RESULTS

Overall there were 448 FFEs in the 12 hours of lessons that we observed. This gives a rate of one FFE every 1.6 minutes. By way of comparison it can be noted that Lyster (1998) reports 558 responding FFEs in 1,100 minutes of immersion instruction, a rate of one FFE every 1.97 minutes. Lyster did not examine initiating FFEs. The rate observed in this study, then, can be considered comparable to that reported by Lyster. In both cases, the rate seems quite high. There were more FFEs in Class 2 (241) than in Class 1 (207).

Approach

Figures 2 and 3 below shows the proportion of responding and initiating FFEs overall and in the two classes separately. Overall, there was an almost equal number of both types (223 responding and 225 initiating). However, some differences were evident in the two classes, with Class 1 manifesting a majority of responding FFEs (52.2%) and Class 2 a majority of initiating FFEs (52.3%). It is notable, however, that a substantial proportion of the FFEs were initiating. This suggests a notable lacuna in the research to date, as this has examined reactive focus on form almost exclusively. The results of this study suggest the need to attend more carefully to proactive focus-on-form.

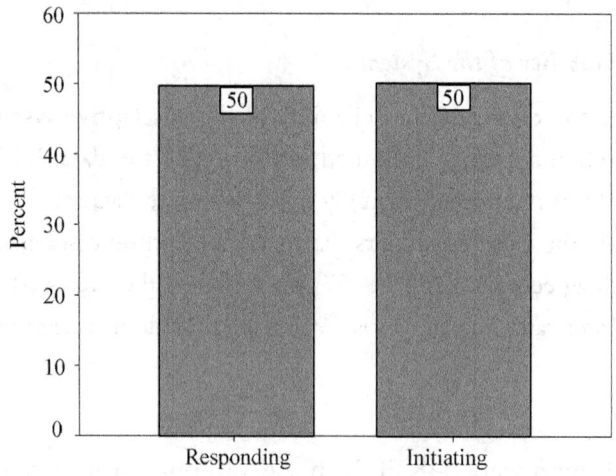

Figure 2: Approach Overall

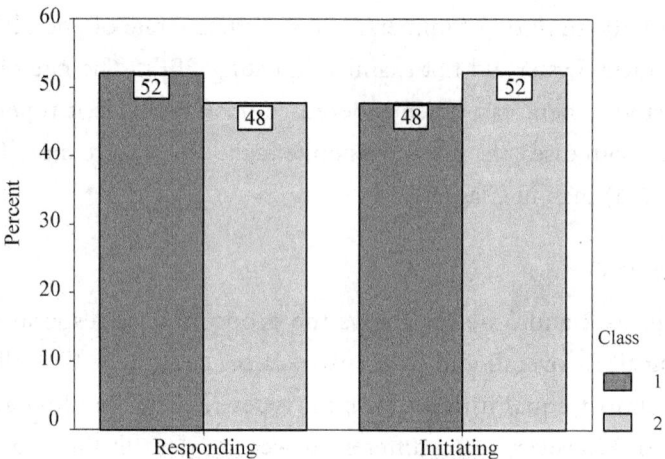

Figure 3: Approach by Class

Instigator

It might be expected that the vast majority of proactive FFEs were teacher-initiated. In fact, in the classrooms we investigated, this proved not to be the case (see Figure 4). Overall, the teacher initiated 268 FFEs and the students 180. Some differences were evident in the two classes (see Figure 5). In Class 1 the teacher initiated 62.3% whereas in Class 2 the teacher initiated somewhat less (57.7%). However, it is clear that in both classrooms the students were active in initiating FFEs.

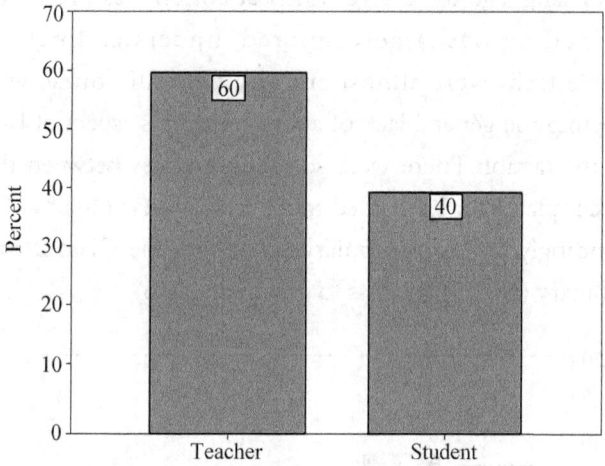

Figure 4: Instigator Overall

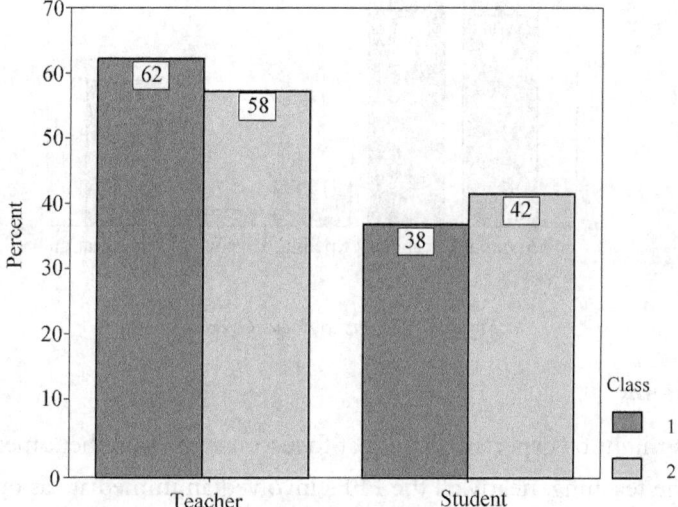

Figure 5: Instigator by Class

Linguistic Focus

The vast majority of the FFEs concerned grammar and vocabulary (see Figures 6 and 7). There was little difference between these two linguistic foci (Grammar 166 FFEs; Vocabulary 172 FFEs). The only other aspect of language to receive much attention was pronunciation (77 FFEs). Spelling was largely ignored, understandingly as the communicative tasks were almost entirely oral. Discourse was also ignored, reflecting the general lack of attention to this aspect of language in classroom interaction.There were some differences between the two classes. For example Class 1 attended more to grammar (40.6% of FFEs) and correspondingly less to vocabulary (36.2%) while Class 2 attended more to vocabulary (40.2%) and less to grammar (34%).

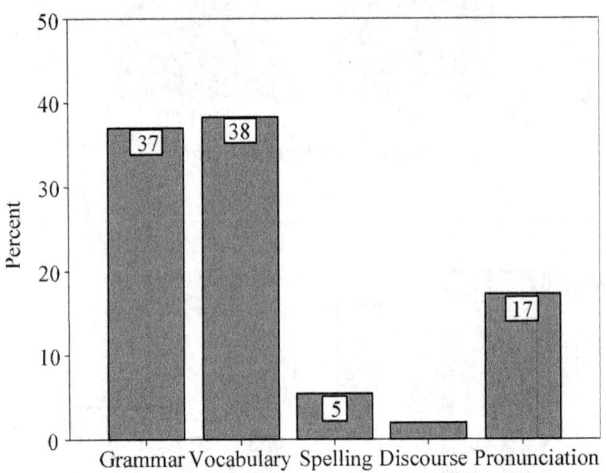

Figure 6: Linguistic Focus Overall

Timing

As might be expected given that focus-on-form is a phenomenon of real-time teaching, nearly all the FFEs involved an immediate as opposed to a delayed treatment of focus on form (411 FFEs versus 37) — Figure 8.

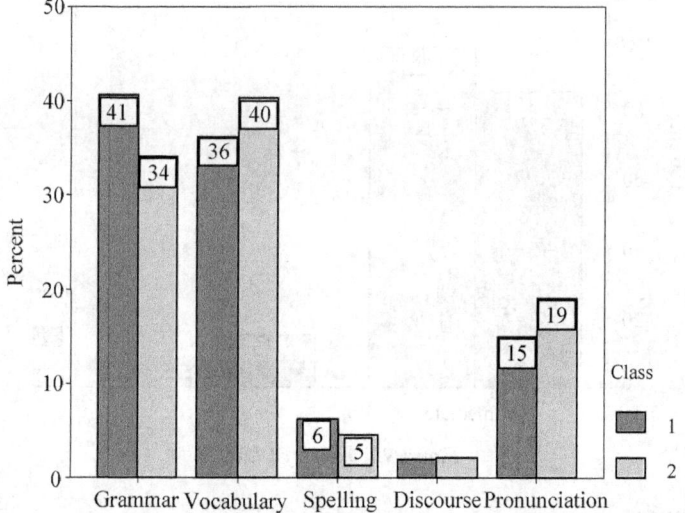

Figure 7: Linguistic Focus by Class

However, the two classes differed somewhat, with Class 1 accounting for 31 of the delayed FFEs (see Figure 9).

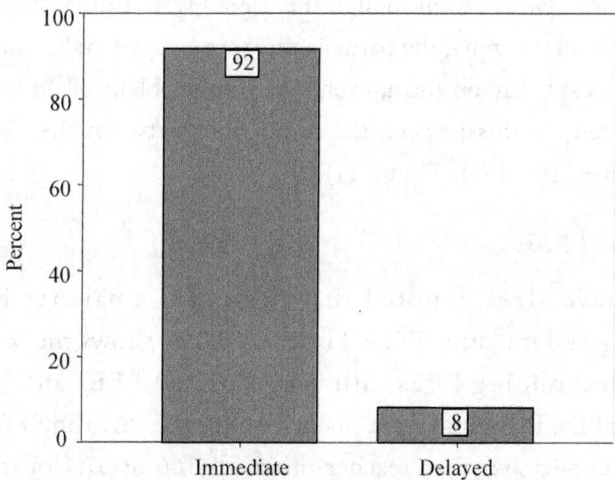

Figure 8: Timing Overall

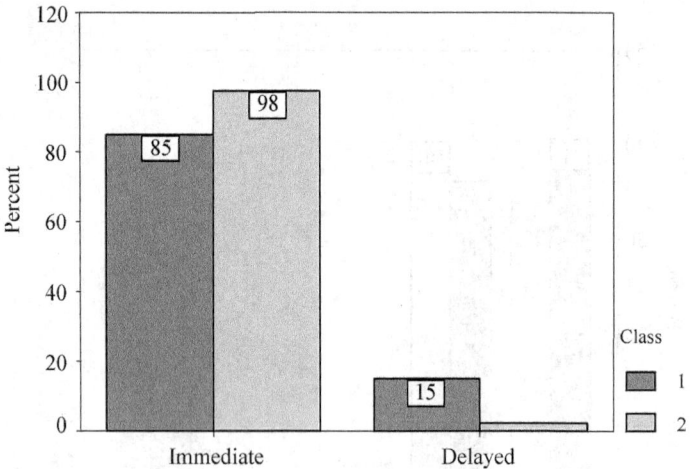

Figure 9: Timing by Class

Source

A finding of considerable interest is that most of the FFEs were code- rather than message-oriented (see Figure 10). Only 113 (25.2%) of the FFEs were directed at attention to form in the context of negotiating meaning; 335 (74.8%) occurred when the participants were negotiating form. In other words, even though the classes were primarily concerned with a focus on meaning, the participants were happy to take 'time out' to focus quite explicitly on form, even when no problem of understanding had occurred. In this respect, the differences between the two classes were relatively small (see Figure 11).

Types of FFE

We have already noted that there was a balance between responding and initiating FFEs. Figure 12 below shows the breakdown for the Responding FFEs, Student Initiated FFEs and Teacher-Initiated FFEs. Interestingly, it reveals that of the initiating FFEs, most were student- rather than teacher-initiated (166 or 37.1 of total FFEs as opposed to 59 or 13.2%). These results bear out the observation made earlier than in these particular classrooms, the students were

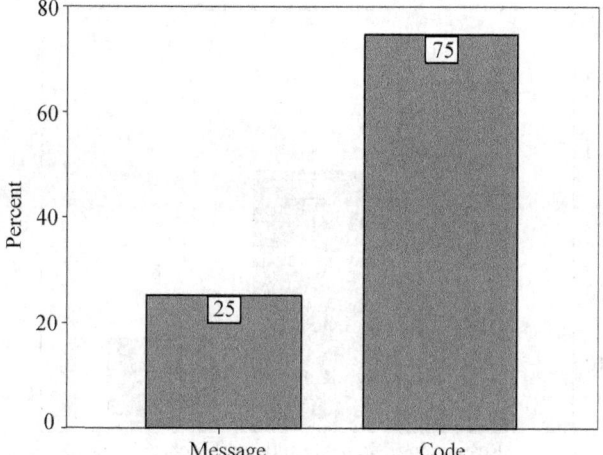

Figure 10: Source Overall

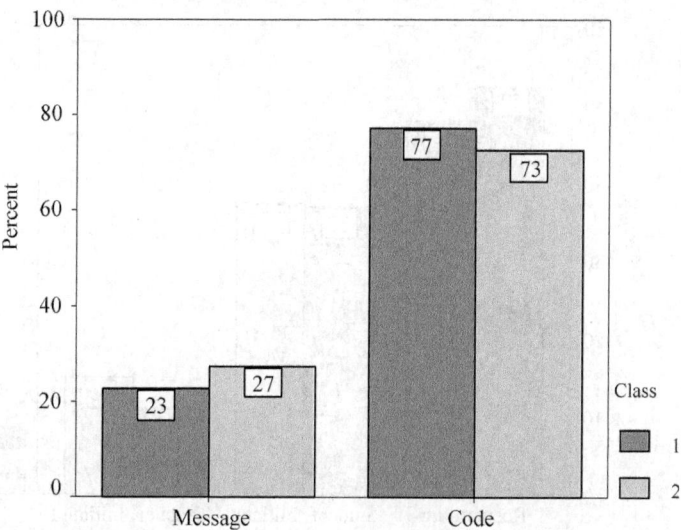

Figure 11: Source by Class

not hesitant to raise linguistic problems. The teachers' contribution to focus-on-form, in contrast, was primarily through Responding FFEs. Again, the differences between the two classes with regard to Types of FFEs were small (see Figure 13).

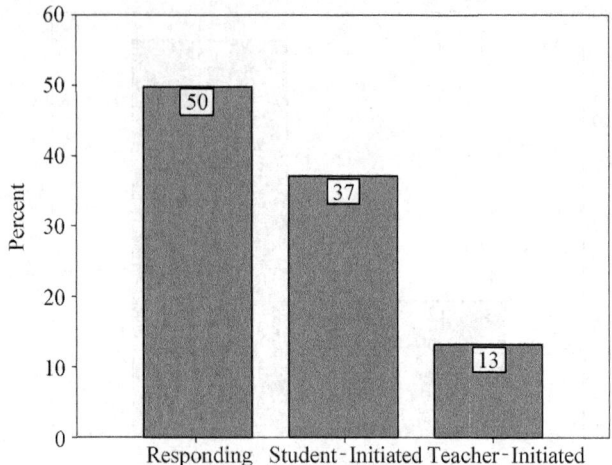

Figure 12: FFE Type Overal

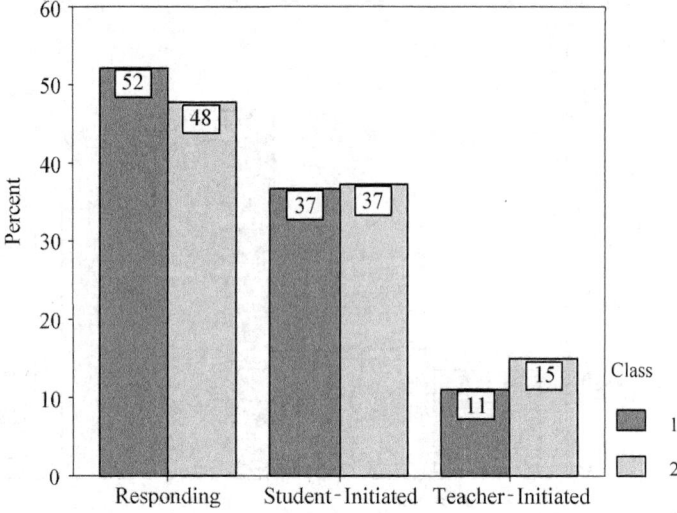

Figure 13: FFE Type by Class

SUMMARY

What general picture of how focus-on-form was accomplished in the two classrooms we studied do these results provide? First, we are struck by the sheer amount of attention to form that occurred in lessons that purported to be 'communicative' and, from our observations, were so. Second, it is clear that in these classes, a focus-on-form was not just a reactive phenomenon; it was also notably proactive. Third, it is clear that the students played a significant role in initiating a focus-on-form, with the teacher more evident in Responding FFEs. Fourth, in these classes, 'form' meant primarily 'grammar' and 'vocabulary'; other aspects of language did not get much of a look in. Fifth, much of the focus-on-form that arose was not triggered by a problem in communication but rather by a problem in using English correctly. That is to say, although the lessons were 'communicative', this did not prevent the participants paying regular attention to language for its own sake.

FURTHER RESEARCH

This study provides a description of how teachers and students handle attention to form while engaged in communicative activities. It provides a basis for investigating a number of further questions:

1. What factors influence students' successful uptake of a focus-on-form?

2. Does participation on focus-on-form episodes facilitate L2 acquisition?

3. To what extent do teachers' beliefs about language, language learning and language teaching impact on the quantity and quality of the focus-on-form that occurs in their classrooms?

4. To what extent do learners differ in their preparedness to initiate and to respond to a focus-on-form and what can explain the differences?

5. What affect does the nature of the communicative activity (i.e. the kind of task) have on opportunities to engage in focus-on-form?

6. What effect does teacher training/education have on teachers' preparedness and ability to provide a focus-on-form?

A number of these questions have already been investigated. Ellis,

Basturkmen and Lowen (2001) examined the extent to which learner uptake occurred in the different types of form-focused episodes. 'Uptake' is a student move that occurs as a reaction to some preceding move in which another participant (usually the teacher) either explicitly or implicitly provides information about a linguistic feature as a result of a perceived gap in the student's linguistic knowledge. Uptake is 'successful' when the student demonstrates the ability to use or understand the problematic feature. The study showed that in the classes observed student uptake was generally high and successful. It was more likely to be successful in reactive and student-initiated focus-on-form episodes than in teacher-initiated ones. The complexity of FFE also influenced whether the uptake was successful (i.e. it occurred more frequently in complex FFEs). Uptake is in itself not a measure of acquisition — although there are theoretical grounds for claiming that it can assist acquisition.

Loewen (2005) investigated to what extent focus on form episodes — and, in particular, uptake — impacted on L2 acquisition. Using a similar methodology to the one employed in this study, Loewen also administered tailor-made tests both the day after and two weeks later to learners who had participated in focus-on-form episodes. He reported that the learners were able to recall the linguistic information they received through the FFEs correctly nearly 60% of the time one day after and 50% two weeks later. He also reported that successful uptake was a significant predictor of correct test scores.

The third of the questions listed above was investigated by Basturkmen, Loewen and Ellis (2004). They conducted a study of teachers' beliefs about focus-on-form practices and found that their actual practice did not always correspond closely to their stated beliefs, in part because of a conflict in the beliefs the teachers held (e.g. they indicated a belief that communicative tasks should be directed at fluency rather than accuracy and that attention to form was therefore undesirable and yet felt obliged to provide linguistic information when asked to do so by their students).

Clearly, though, much more work is needed to explore how and when focus on form occurs in communicative lessons. For example, we know almost nothing about how individual learner differences influence learners' ability to participate and learn from focus-on-form episodes.

Focus on form is an important aspect of language teaching — especially communicative language teaching. It provides opportunities for incidental language acquisition. Arguably, incidental language acquisition is as important as intentional learning in the language classroom. It remains, however, poorly understood. By conducting studies of focus-on-form, we can increase our understanding of the conditions that foster incidental acquisition.

Note

[1] In English, some verbs like 'give' permit dative alternation (e.g. 'She gave Dave a present' and 'She gave a present to Dave') while other verbs like 'explain' do not (e.g. '* She explained Dave the problem').

Chapter 7

The Differential Effects of Corrective Feedback on Two Grammatical Structures

This chapter is based on Ellis, R. (2007). The differential effects of corrective feedback on two grammatical structures. In A. Mackey (Ed.). Conversational Interaction in Second Language Acquisition. Oxford: Oxford University Press.

INTRODUCTION: IMPLICIT AND EXPLICIT CORRECTIVE FEEDBACK

Studies of implicit and explicit corrective feedback demonstrate that both types of corrective feedback are effective in promoting acquisition of the grammatical structures targeted when the feedback is focused and intensive. A number of studies (for example, Carroll & Swain, 1993; Nagata, 1993; Carroll, 2001; Rosa & Leow, 2004) demonstrated that the explicit feedback was more effective than the implicit feedback. Ellis, Loewen and Erlam's (2006) study of the effects of recasts and metalinguistic feedback on the acquisition of English past tense *-ed* also found that the explicit type of feedback was more effective than the implicit type. However, a number of other studies (for example,

Kim & Mathes, 2001; Sanz, 2003) reported no difference. Only one study (Leeman, 2003) found implicit corrective feedback more effective than explicit feedback. However, in this case the explicit feedback took the form of 'source of problem indicated' (i.e. there was no positive or metalinguistic evidence provided), as this study was primarily concerned with investigating the relative effects of salient positive evidence and negative evidence on acquisition.

It is difficult to come to firm conclusions regarding the relative effectiveness of implicit and explicit corrective feedback on the basis of these studies for a number of reasons. First, the two types of feedback were not operationalized in the same way in all the studies. Implicit feedback was operationalized as recasts in most of the studies but recasts can vary enormously (see Ellis & Sheen, 2006). The explicit feedback also varied depending on whether it only indicated an error had been committed, provided a correction or included metalinguistic information or some combination of these strategies. In future research, it would seem sensible to 'bias for best' — that is, to operationalize the two types of feedback in such a way as to have the greatest potential effect on acquisition. Therefore, in the study reported below, implicit corrective feedback was operationalized as recasts that were partial, declarative, focused on a single error and involved a simple substitution and thus likely to be salient to the learners. Also, in accordance with Han's (2002) recommendation, the recasts focused intensively on a single grammatical structure. Explicit feedback was operationalized as source of problem indicated together with metalinguistic information (but no provision of the correct form).

A second reason why the results of previous studies are difficult to interpret is the method of operationalizing and testing acquisition. Most of the studies did not include measures of implicit knowledge, a general failing in form-focused instruction studies (Doughty, 2003a). The kinds of tests they typically employed (i.e. grammaticality judgment tests, sentence completion, picture prompt tests, translation tests) clearly favoured the use of explicit knowledge as they did not require learners to access their linguistic knowledge rapidly on-line and had no communicative purpose. It is, therefore, perhaps not so surprising that, on-balance, the studies found explicit corrective feedback to be the more effective. What is needed is a study that tests the effects of implicit and explicit feedback on both implicit and explicit L2 knowledge. The study reported below attempts this, using an oral imitation test to measure implicit knowledge and an untimed grammaticality judgment test and a metalinguistic knowledge test to measure explicit knowledge. The rationale for these measures is provided later in the method section.

Finally, the previous studies varied in their choice of target grammatical structure. Some of the studies investigated morphological features (for example, distinguishing nouns and verbs in Carroll (2001) or French grammatical gender in Lyster (2004)) while other studies examined syntactical features (for example, dative alternation in Carroll and Swain (1993) or clitic pronoun position in Spanish in Sanz (2003)). It is not unreasonable to suppose that the effectiveness of the corrective feedback treatment will depend on the choice of the target structure. Pienemann (1999), for example, proposes that the order in which grammatical structures are acquired as implicit knowledge depends on the processing operations they involve. Many of the target structures investigated to date involved complex processing operations that some of the learners may not have been developmentally ready for. The structures also differed considerably in how easy they were to learn as explicit knowledge. For example, Spanish noun-adjective agreement (Leeman, 2003) constitutes a relatively simple rule to understand whereas dative alternation is much more difficult. There is an obvious need to give careful consideration to the choice of target structure, bearing in mind both the developmental stage of the learners and the conceptual complexity of the structure chosen.

CHOICE OF TARGET STRUCTURE

One way of investigating what effect the choice of target structure has on acquisition is to conduct a study involving two different structures. However, experimental corrective feedback studies to date have generally focused on a single target structure. An exception is Nagata (1993). This computer-based study investigated the effects of two types of explicit correction ('source of problem indicated' and 'metalinguistic' explanation) on two different Japanese grammatical structures. The group receiving metalinguistic explanations made fewer errors in the post-test on one of the grammatical structures (particles) but there was no difference in the number of errors involving the other structure (verbal predicates) in a written achievement test. Nagata, however, was not primarily concerned with how feedback differentially affected the two structures and offered no discussion of the results pertaining to this.

In this section, therefore, I will consider a number of other experimental form-focused instruction studies that compared the effects of explicit/ implicit instruction on the acquisition of simple and complex structures. However, the basis for distinguishing the simple and complex structures differed greatly. DeKeyser (1995), for example, distinguished them in terms of whether the rules for the structures were categorical (simple) or 'fuzzy' and prototypical (complex) whereas Robinson (1996) relied on the judgments of a number of 'experts'. The operationalizations of implicit and explicit instruction in these studies also differed. In some cases explicit instruction consisted only of metalinguistic explanations (Scott, 1989) while in others it involved metalinguistic explanations accompanied by practice activities (de Graaf, 1997). Also, differences were evident in the instruments used to measure learning. In general, though, these were of the metalinguistic judgment and constrained constructed response type (Norris & Ortega, 2000). In fact, only one study (Scott, 1989) included an oral measure likely to tap implicit knowledge. Given these differences, care needs to be taken in synthesizing the results. The following is a tentative list of conclusions:

1. In general, explicit instruction is more effective with simple rules. However, this may simply reflect the fact that the testing instruments only provided measures of explicit knowledge.

2. For complex rules the picture is mixed. In three studies (DeKeyser, 1995; Robinson, 1996; Ayoun, 2001), the implicit instruction proved more effective. In two studies (Scott, 1989; De Graaf, 1997) the explicit instruction was more effective for learning complex structures.

3. In the one study that included an oral task more likely to tap implicit knowledge (Scott, 1989), no difference was found in the effects of the two types of instruction.

Taken together, these studies suggest that the choice of target structure does influence the effectiveness of the instruction. The studies also point to the need to provide clear and explicit grounds for distinguishing the target structures to be investigated and also to design testing instruments that measure both implicit and explicit knowledge.

The two structures chosen for the present study were regular past tense -*ed* and comparative -*er*. Brief descriptions of these two structures are provided below followed by an account of typical learner errors. Then, the rationale for the choice of the two structures is considered.

Regular Past Tense

Regular past tense is formed in English by adding /id/, /d/ or /t/ to the base form of the verb, depending on whether the final phoneme in the base is an alveolar stop, a voiced sound other than /d/ or a voiceless sound other than /t/. In the study, however, learners were credited with marking a verb for past tense providing they produced some identifiable form of the -*ed* inflection (i.e. accuracy of pronunciation was not an issue). In terms of Dulay, Burt and Krashen's (1982) surface structure taxonomy of L2 errors, typical learner errors in past tense -*ed* involve either omission or misformation. Omission is evident when learners use the verb's simple form (for example, 'ask') in place of the -*ed* form ('asked'). This is very common. Misformation occurs less frequently, as when learners substitute an alternative inflection for -*ed* (for example, 'asking').

Comparative Adjectives

The comparative structure investigated was:

noun X is (comparative adjective) than noun Y.

The form of the comparative adjective depends on prosody. A morphological form (-*er*) is chosen when the adjective is monosyllabic (for example, 'faster') or bisyllabic ending in -*y* (for example, 'happier') or -*er* (for example, 'cleverer'). A phrasal form (in the case of this study this was always 'more') is chosen otherwise (for example, 'more beautiful'). In a few cases both forms are possible (for example, 'oftener' and 'more often'). There are also a small number of suppletive forms (for example, 'better').

A variety of learner error types arise with the comparative — omission, double marking, regularization and misformation. Omission occurs when learners omit -*er* or 'more'(for example, 'simple' instead or 'simpler'; 'famous' instead of 'more famous'). Double marking arises when learners use both -*er* and 'more' with the same adjective (for example, 'more smarter'). Regularization is evident when learners overuse the morphological marker with adjectives that require a phrasal marker (for example, 'beautifuler'). Finally, misrepresentation is seen when learners substitute a phrasal comparative marker for the morphological marker (for example, 'more smart').

Learning Difficulty of the Two Structures

Past tense -*ed* and the comparative were chosen with two principal conditions in mind. First, both structures needed to be potentially learnable as a result of intensive corrective feedback provided over a relatively short period of time (one hour). To ensure this, the structures needed to be already evident in the learners' production but not to the point where they had already demonstrated mastery. Given that the participants in the study were classified as 'lower intermediate' (see the section on Participants below), it was reasonable to assume that this condition held. The results of the pre-test (reported later) supported this assumption. The second condition was that the two structures should be distinguishable in terms of their learning difficulty, i.e. one structure should be demonstrably easier than the other. The criteria used to establish this condition were as follows:

1. Grammatical domain

Whereas past tense *-ed* constitutes a purely morphological feature, the comparative is both morphological (i.e. there is phrasal or inflectional modification of the adjective) and syntactic (i.e. comparisons involve whole clause constructions).

2. Input frequency

While the input frequency of the two structures is likely to vary depending on the specific genres to which the learners are exposed, it is likely that overall past tense *-ed* occurs more frequently than comparative *-er*. This expectancy was borne out in an analysis of the 2 million word Corpus of Spoken Professional American English, which resulted in 10,175 past tense *-ed* items and 4,818 comparative forms, a ratio of more than 2 : 1 in favour of past tense *-ed* [1].

3. Learnability

According to Pienemann's (1999) Processability Theory, grammatical structures are acquired in an order that reflects a set of hierarchical processing operations. The two operations that govern past tense *-ed* and the comparative are, respectively, the category procedure and phrasal procedure. The category procedure differs from the phrasal procedure in that it does not involve any exchange of information from one sentence constituent to another. The *-ed* morphological marker of past time is attached to the verb in the learner's lexicon. That is, learners can access the past form of the verb without reference to any other constituent in the clause. The phrasal procedure allows diacritic features to be stored and unified between the head of a phrase and its modifiers. This procedure is required to enable learners to choose between the phrasal or morphological comparative adjective. In Pienemann's theory, the category procedure needs to be mastered before the phrasal procedure. For this reason, I hypothesize that past tense *-ed* will emerge before the comparative.

4. Explicit knowledge

The regular past tense rule is an easy rule to understand and thus learn as explicit knowledge; it states simply that *-ed* must be added to the simple form of the verb when referring to a completed action in the past. In contrast, the rule for the comparative is more complex as it must incorporate details of prosody (i.e. the syllabic structure of adjectives). Also, it requires explication of the syntactical patterns involving comparative sentences.

5. Scope

Hulstijn and de Graaf (1994) comment that 'the scope of a rule is said to be large or small when the rule covers more or fewer than 50 cases' (p.103). The scope of past tense *-ed* is clearly large. Ignoring morphophonemic variation, the *-ed* rule applies to every regular verb. The scope of the comparative is more difficult to assess. Clearly, both the morphological and phrasal markers occur in more than 50 cases but the numbers of suppletive and ambidextrous comparative adjectives are less than 50. Overall, the scope of the comparative rule can be said to be smaller than that of the past tense *-ed* rule.

6. Reliability

Hulstijn and de Graaf (1994) state that 'the reliability of a rule is said to be high or low when the rule applies in more or less than 90 per cent of all cases' (p.103). If 'cases' is taken to refer to 'all verbs' and 'all adjectives', then, clearly, neither the past tense *-ed* rule nor any of the comparative rules achieve the 90 per cent criterion. The *-ed* rule has low reliability because of the large number of irregular past tense forms in English. The rules for the use of the use of *-er* and 'more' each apply to less than 90 per cent of all adjectives. In addition, they both have a number of exceptions even when they are applied to the subset of adjectives they are relevant to. In this latter respect, they contrast with the past tense *-ed* rule.

7. Semantic/ formal redundancy

Both past tense *-ed* and the comparative are formal-semantic rules. That is, the morphological markers of these structures convey clear meanings. In both cases, the morphological markers are often redundant. Past time can be marked lexically by means of adverbs or can be inferred from context and frequently are in early L2 acquisition (Klein & Perdue, 1992). Morphological and phrasal markers of comparatives are also frequently redundant as the structure of a sentence frequently makes it clear that a comparison is intended.

These criteria afford a mixed picture with regard to the relative learning difficulty of the two structures. In terms of grammatical domain, input frequency, learnability, explicit knowledge and scope, past tense *-ed* emerges as easier than the comparative. However, in terms of reliability and semantic/formal complexity there is no obvious difference. Overall, however, these criteria do point to the comparative posing a greater learning burden than past tense *-ed*, but not to such an extent as to negate the first selection principle, namely that both structures are learnable by the intended participants in the study. Table 1 summarises the various claims made about the learning difficulty of the two structures.

Table 1: The learning difficulty of past tense -ed and the comparative

Criterion	Past tense- *ed*	Comparative
1. Grammatical domain	Morphological	Morphological and syntactic
2. Input frequency	Relatively frequent	Relatively less frequent
3. Learnability	Category procedure (lexical morphology)	Phrasal procedure (phrasal information)
4. Explicit knowledge	Easy	More difficult
5. Scope	Large	Smaller

(continued)

Criterion	Past tense- *ed*	Comparative
6. Reliability	Low	Low
7. Semantic/ formal redundancy	Often redundant	Often redundant
8. Experts' opinion	Easy	More difficult

THE STUDY

Research Questions

The study reported below was motivated by the mixed results of previous studies of the effects of implicit and explicit feedback on acquisition and by a paucity of studies that have examined whether the effect of corrective feedback differs according to target structure. To this end three research questions were formulated:

1. Do recasts have a differential effect on the acquisition of English past tense -*ed* and comparative?

2. Does metalinguistic feedback have a differential effect on the acquisition of English past tense -*ed* and comparative -*er*?

3. To what extent does the effect of corrective feedback on the different grammatical structures differ according to type of feedback?

Design

The effects of two types of oral corrective feedback (recasts and metalinguistic explanations) on the acquisition of two different grammatical structures (past tense -*ed* and comparative -*er*) were investigated in a quasi-experimental study involving two experimental groups and a control group, which followed a normal course of instruction (i.e. did not complete the instructional tasks and did not receive any feedback). The basic design of the study is shown in Table 2. The three groups completed a pre-test, post-test 1 (immediately after the treatment was completed) and post-test 2 (approximately two weeks after post-test 1). The testing involved three instruments: an Oral Imitation Test, an Untimed Grammaticality Judgement Test, and a Metalinguistic Knowledge Test.

Table 2: Design of the study

Group	Past tense *-ed*	Comparative
Group A (N=12)	Recasts	Metalinguistic explanation
Group B (N=12)	Metalinguistic explanation	Recasts
Group C (N=10)	No treatment	No treatment

Participants

The study was conducted in a private language school in New Zealand. Three classes of students (N=34) were involved. The school classified all the students as 'lower intermediate' according to scores in a placement or a previous class achievement test. Information obtained from a background questionnaire showed that the majority of the students (i.e., 77 per cent) were of East Asian origin. Most of them had spent less than a year in New Zealand; the mean length of time spent in New Zealand was just over six months. The mean age of all participants was 25 years. The students indicated that they had been formally engaged in studying English for anywhere from 8 months to 13 years with the average length of time being seven years. Around 44 per cent of participants indicated that their studies had been mainly formal (grammar-oriented) in nature, while 30 per cent had received mainly informal instruction and the rest a mixture of both formal and informal instruction.

The teaching approach adopted by the school placed emphasis on developing communicative skills in English. Students received between three and five hours of English language instruction a day, for which they were enrolled as part-time or full-time students. Classes were arbitrarily assigned to become one of the two treatment options or the control group.

Instructional Treatments

The instructional treatments for the two experimental groups lasted approximately one hour. They took the form of communicative tasks performed by the learners in a whole-class context. A researcher (acting as the teacher) provided corrective feedback either in the form of recasts or metalinguistic explanations whenever a participant made an error in a target structure. It is important to note that while the corrective feedback was directed at individual students, the tasks were designed to ensure that the attention of the whole class was focused as much as possible on the speaker at these times. The following description of the treatments will be in two parts; the tasks used to teach each grammatical structure and the corrective feedback provided.

Tasks

The tasks for past-tense -*ed* were as follows.

Task 1 (Day 1)

Students were assigned to four groups of three. Each group was given the same picture sequence which narrated a short story and one of four different versions of a written account of the same story. Each version differed in minor ways from the others. Students were told that they would have only a couple of minutes to read the written account of the story and that they needed to read it carefully because they would be asked to retell it in as much detail as possible. They were not allowed to make any written notes. The stories were removed and replaced with the following list of verbs that students were told they would need in order to retell the story.

visit   live   walk   turn   kill   want   follow   attack   laugh
point   stay   watch

Students were given about five minutes to plan the retelling of their story. They were told that they would not be able to use any prompts other than the picture sequence and verb list. The opening words of the story were written on the board, to clearly establish a context for past tense.

Yesterday, Joe and Bill . . .

Students were then asked to listen to each group's collective retelling of the story in order to identify what was different from their own story.

Task 2 (Day 2)

Students were once again assigned to groups of three. Each group was given a picture sequence depicting a 'day' in the life of one of two characters: Gavin or Peter. Each picture sequence was different. Pictures were chosen to depict actions that would require the use of verbs with regular past tense -*ed* forms. Students were given five minutes to prepare for recounting the day of either 'Gavin' or 'Peter'. Again, they were not allowed to take any written notes. Each group then gave an oral account to the rest of the class beginning with 'Yesterday Peter/ Gavin had a day off'. Students who were listening were provided with an empty grid and pictures which they had to place on the grid in the appropriate sequence. One picture card did not fit and students had to identify which card was remaining.

The tasks for comparative adjectives were as follows:

Task 1 (Day 1)

Students were told that they were going to complete an activity to find out if their teacher was sexist or not. The meaning of the word sexist was explained to them. Students were then asked to think of three words describing men and women and to use these words to write sentences comparing the two sexes using these models:

Men are _____ women

Women are _____ men

They took it in turn to say aloud their sentence (they were discouraged from reading) and to address it to their normal teacher whose reaction to the statement they would record in a table as being 'sexist' or 'not sexist'. They subsequently addressed the same statements to the researcher/teacher to ascertain who was the more sexist. When students had used up all their statements they were shown a number of one syllable adjectives and two syllable adjectives ending in -y and asked to make up further statements. When enough statements had been addressed to the researcher/teacher (i.e., 15) and consensus had been reached about how sexist they were, individual students' opinions were canvassed as to whether their normal teacher or the teacher/researcher was more sexist.

Task 2 (Day 2)

Students were told that they were going to play a game. They were asked to think of someone in the class and to write down three adjectives describing that person. The one syllable and two syllable adjectives ending in -y that were shown to them in Task 1 were written on the board as options for them to choose from. They were then told to think of three statements comparing themselves to that person using this model:

He/she is _____ me

Students then were asked to say their statements (without reading them) to the whole class. Their classmates had to guess who in the class was being described and compared to the speaker.

Corrective Feedback

A second researcher sat in all lessons and kept a pen-and-paper record of each time a student made an error and whether it was corrected by the researcher/teacher.

The students received corrective feedback while they performed the tasks, as follows:

Recasts:

The recasts were typically declarative and of the partial type and as such might be considered to lie at the explicit end of the implicit → explicit continuum for recasts (see Sheen, 2006). However, they intruded minimally into the flow of the discourse. For example:

Student:	... they saw and they follow follow follow him
Researcher:	Followed.
Student:	Followed him and attacked him.
Student:	Women are kind than men.
Researcher:	Kinder.
Student:	Kinder than women.

Metalinguistic feedback:

For the past tense, the instructor first repeated the error and then supplied metalinguistic information. For the comparative, the researcher only provided metalinguistic information as it was assumed it was clear which item this referred to. For example:

Student:	He kiss her.
Researcher:	Kiss — you need past tense.
Student:	He kissed.
Student:	Men are clever than women.
Researcher:	You need a comparative adjective.
Student:	Men are cleverer.

Testing Instruments and Scoring/ Coding Procedures

The immediate post-testing was completed the day following the second and last day of instruction and the delayed post-testing 12 days later. The tests were administered in the following order: Untimed Grammaticality Judgement Test, Metalinguistic Knowledge Test, Oral Imitation Test.

The Oral Imitation Test (Erlam, 2006) was intended to provide a measure of the learners' implicit knowledge, while the Untimed Grammaticality Judgement Test (ungrammatical sentences) and the Metalinguistic Test were designed to provide measures of learners' explicit knowledge. R. Ellis (2004; 2005) discusses the theoretical grounds for these claims. He argues that tests of implicit knowledge need to elicit use of language where the learners operate by 'feel', are pressured to perform in 'real time', are focused on meaning, and have little need to draw on metalinguistic knowledge. In contrast, tests of explicit knowledge need to elicit a test performance where the learners are encouraged to apply 'rules', are under no time pressure, are consciously focused on form, and have a need to apply metalinguistic knowledge. The Oral Imitation Test was designed to satisfy the criteria for tests of implicit knowledge while the Untimed Grammaticality Judgement Test and the Metalinguistic Test were designed to meet the criteria for tests of explicit knowledge. The tests are described in detail below.

1. Oral Imitation Test

This test consisted of a set of 36 belief statements. Statements were grammatically correct ($n=18$) or incorrect ($n=18$). They consisted of 12 statements targeting simple past tense -*ed* (six grammatical and six ungrammatical), 12 targeting comparative adjectives (six grammatical and six ungrammatical) and 12 distractor items. Examples of the past tense -*ed* items were:

Everyone liked the movie Star Wars.

* An American invent Microsoft Word

Examples of the comparative adjectives items were:

Life was easier fifty years ago than today.

* Asian people are tall than Americans

Examples of the distractor items were:

Young women like cigarettes and fast cars.

* People worry about their children future.

The sentences in the pilot test were extensively piloted with a view to establishing whether the length of the sentences and the procedures described below were effective in ensuring that learners were not able to simply rote memorize the sentences for reproduction. It was clear that the test achieved this objective. In audio recording the sentences care was also taken to ensure that the target featured (e.g. pat tense -*ed*) were clearly articulated and thus available to be heard by the learners.

Each statement was presented orally one at a time, on an audiotape, to test-takers who were required to first indicate on an answer sheet whether they agreed with, disagreed with or were not sure about the statement. They were then asked to repeat the statement orally in 'correct' English. Pre-test training presented students with both grammatical and ungrammatical statements (not involving past tense *-ed*) to practice with and they were given the correct responses to these items. Students' responses to all items were audio recorded. These were then analysed to establish whether obligatory occasions for use of the target structure had been established. Errors in structures other than the target structure were not considered. Each imitated statement was allocated a score of either 1 (i.e., the grammatically correct target structure was correctly imitated or the grammatically incorrect target structure was corrected) or 0 (the target structure was avoided/ the grammatically correct target structure was attempted but incorrectly imitated/ the grammatically incorrect target structure was imitated but not corrected). If a learner self-corrected, then only the initial incorrect production was scored as it was felt that this would provide the better measure of learners' implicit knowledge. Scores were expressed as percentage correct. Three versions of the test were created for use over the three testing sessions; in each the same statements were used but presented in a different order. Reliability (Cronbach's alpha) for the pre-test was .779. For more information about the theoretical rationale for this test and its design see Erlam (2006).

2. Untimed Grammaticality Judgement Test

This was a pen-and-paper test consisting of 45 sentences. Fifteen sentences targeted past tense *-ed*, and 15 sentences comparative adjectives and 15 sentences other structures. Of each set of 15 sentences, seven were grammatically correct and eight grammatically incorrect. Sentences were randomly scrambled in different ways to create three versions of the test. Test-takers were required to (1) indicate whether each sentence was grammatically correct or incorrect, (2) indicate the degree of certainty of their judgement (as proposed by Sorace, 1996) by typing in the box provided a score on a scale marked from 0 per cent to 100 per cent and (3) to self-report whether they used 'rule' or 'feel' for each sentence. Students were given six sentences to practice on before beginning the test. Each item was presented on a new page and test-takers were told that they were not allowed to turn back to look at any part of the test they had already completed. For past tense -ed, seven of the 15 statements presented the target structure in the context of new vocabulary and eight in the context of vocabulary included in the instruction. Learners' responses were scored as either correct (1 point) or incorrect (0 point). A total score was calculated and also separate scores for grammatical, ungrammatical test items. Reliability (Cronbach's alpha) for the pre-test was .63. Test-retest reliability (Pearson r) was calculated for the control group ($N=10$) only. For the pre-test and post-test 1 it was .65 ($p=.04$) and for the pre-test and post-test 2 it was .74 ($p = .01$).

3. Metalinguistic Knowledge Test

Students were presented with five sentences and told that they were ungrammatical. Two of the sentences contained errors in past tense -ed and three errors in comparative adjectives. The part of the sentence containing the error in each example was underlined. Students were asked to (1) correct the error, and (2) explain what was wrong with the sentence in English using their own words. They were shown two practice examples. As in the previous test each item was presented on a new page and test-takers were told that they were not allowed to turn back. Students were scored 1 point for correcting the error and 1 point for a correct explanation of the error. A percentage accuracy score was calculated for past tense -ed and for comparatives.

RESULTS

Table 3 shows the focused tasks elicited roughly equal numbers of attempted use of the two target structures (i.e. 196 for past tense -ed and 216 for the comparative). However, the participants produced more incorrect utterances for past tense -ed (79) than for the comparative (46).

In other words, the learners were more likely to get the comparative right than past tense -*ed*. Since feedback is contingent on learners' errors, the number of feedback moves directed at past tense -*ed* errors (67 for the Recasts and Metalinguistic Groups combined) exceeded that directed at the comparative (41). It should be noted, however, that the percentages of erroneous past tense and comparative errors corrected by the researcher were similar (85 per cent and 93 per cent respectively). A final observation of interest is that the Recast Group received more feedback than the Metalinguistic Group for both structures.

Table 3: Numbers of target forms elicited and feedback moves

Treatment groups	Past tense -*ed*			Comparative			Total
	Correct	Incorrect	Feedback	Correct	Incorrect	Feedback	Feedback
Recast (N=12)	45	49	42	74	24	22	66
Metalinguistic Knowledge (N=12)	72	30	25	96	22	19	44
Totals	117	79	67	170	46	41	110

Tables 4, 5 and 6 show the descriptive statistics (means and standard deviations) for the Oral Imitation Test, the Untimed Grammaticality Judgement Test and the Metalinguistic Knowledge Test. Scores for the grammatical and ungrammatical sentences in the Oral Imitation Test and the Untimed Grammaticality Judgment Test will be presented separately as the learners performed differently on these. Also, previous research (for example, Hedgcock, 1993; R. Ellis, 2005) has shown that learners apply different strategies with the two types of sentences. Specifically, the ungrammatical sentences in a grammaticality judgment test are more likely to tap learners' explicit knowledge. These statistics will be considered first for the Recast Groups and then the Metalinguistic Groups. Finally, the differential effect of the two types of corrective feedback will be examined.

Table 4: Descriptive statistics for the Oral Imitation Test

(a) Pre-test

Group	Past Tense -*ed*				Comparative -*er*			
	Grammatical		Ungrammatical		Grammatical		Ungrammatical	
	M	SD	M	SD	M	SD	M	SD
Recast	.278	.278	.194	.282	.751	.110	.264	.076
Meta	.444	.192	.333	.225	.505	.279	.140	.186
Control	.307	.207	.200	.253	.566	.238	.168	.193

(b) Post-test 1

Group	Past Tense -*ed*				Comparative -*er*			
	Grammatical		Ungrammatical		Grammatical		Ungrammatical	
	M	SD	M	SD	M	SD	M	SD
Recast	.403	.279	.319	.240	.813	.157	.472	.406
Meta	.618	.257	.375	.267	.751	.219	.583	.337
Control	.417	.317	.217	.209	.745	.225	.260	.193

(c) Post-test 2

Group	Past Tense -*ed*				Comparative -*er*			
	Grammatical		Ungrammatical		Grammatical		Ungrammatical	
	M	SD	M	SD	M	SD	M	SD
Recast	.514	.180	.375	.334	.848	.180	.639	.338
Meta	.736	.194	.653	.694	.831	.175	.639	.324
Control	.400	.211	.267	.196	.750	.179	.351	.264

Table 5: Descriptive statistics for the Untimed Grammaticality Judgment Test

(a) Pre-test

Group	Past Tense -*ed*				Comparative -*er*			
	Grammatical		Ungrammatical		Grammatical		Ungrammatical	
	M	SD	M	SD	M	SD	M	SD
Recast	.714	.122	.854	.129	.738	.210	.855	.159
Meta	.738	.134	.844	.108	.773	.156	.689	.265
Control	.586	.247	.788	.145	.713	.136	.840	.165

(continued)

(b) Post-test 1

Group	Past Tense -ed				Comparative -er			
	Grammatical		Ungrammatical		Grammatical		Ungrammatical	
	M	SD	M	SD	M	SD	M	SD
Recast	.833	.147	.844	.152	.964	.090	.969	.107
Meta	.929	.144	.833	.154	.845	.188	.918	.133
Control	.786	.181	.813	.189	.873	.216	.860	.165

(c) Post-test 2

Group	Past Tense -ed				Comparative -er			
	Grammatical		Ungrammatical		Grammatical		Ungrammatical	
	M	SD	M	SD	M	SD	M	SD
Recast	.784	.142	.813	.146	.929	.205	.918	.178
Meta	.941	.072	.844	.094	.894	.202	.968	.058
Control	.871	.142	.738	.190	.901	.097	.840	.203

Table 6: Descriptive statistics for the Metalinguistic Knowledge Test

(a) Pre-test

Group	Past Tense -ed		Comparative -er	
	M	SD	M	SD
Recast	.958	.144	.667	.201
Metalinguistic	.833	.246	.667	.284
Control	.850	.241	.667	.272

(b) Post-test 1

Group	Past Tense -ed		Comparative -er	
	M	SD	M	SD
Recast	.833	.326	.972	.096
Metalinguistic	.917	.194	.889	.296
Control	.900	.210	.667	.157

(continued)

(c) Post-test 2

Group	Past Tense -*ed*		Comparative -*er*	
	M	SD	M	SD
Recast	1.00	.000	.944	.130
Metalinguistic	.917	.194	1.0	.000
Control	.850	.337	.867	.172

Recast Groups

In the Oral Imitation Test scores for the comparative were considerably higher than those for past tense -*ed*. Grammatical and ungrammatical sentence scores for both structures showed an increase over time with the most marked increase evident in the ungrammatical scores for the comparative. To establish whether the grammatical and ungrammatical scores for the two structures were significantly different a split plot ANOVA (SPANOVA) was employed. No significant differences for time/group interaction were found for either grammatical sentences (df 2, $F=.792$, $p=.459$) or ungrammatical sentences (df 2, $F=1.026$, $p=.367$).

In the grammatical sentences in the Untimed Grammaticality Judgment Test, both Recast Groups showed an initial gain from pre-test to post-test 1 but a small subsequent decline in scores at post-test 2. This pattern was different for the ungrammatical sentences. Whereas the comparative Recast Group performed in much the same way as on the grammatical sentences, the past tense Recast Group showed a slight decline in scores from pre-test to post-test 1 and from post-test 1 to post-test 2. To establish whether the grammatical and ungrammatical post-test scores of the two structures were significantly different a SPANOVA was employed. No significant differences for time/group interaction were found for grammatical sentences (df 2, $F=1.976$, $p=.151$) or for ungrammatical sentences (df 2, $F=1.599$, $p=.214$).

In the Metalinguistic Knowledge Test, the past tense group scored higher than the comparative group overall. The comparative group's scores increased, mainly from pre-test to post-test 1. No statistical test was computed as scores for the past tense -*ed* were close to 1 on the pre-test.

Metalinguistic Groups

In the Oral Imitation Test, grammatical item scores increased for both past tense -*ed* and for the comparative from pre-test to post-test 1 and from post-test 1 to post-test 2. In the case of the ungrammatical items, however, the results were somewhat different for the two structures. As Figure 1 shows, the comparative scores showed a sharp increase from pre-test to post-test 1 whereas the past tense scores increased only moderately. In contrast, the past tense scores rose sharply from post-test 1 to post-test 2 whereas the comparative scores hardly increased at all. A SPANOVA found no statistically significant difference in the time/group interaction for the grammatical items (df 2, F=.210, p=.812) but did find one for the ungrammatical sentences (df 2, F=6.11, p=.005).

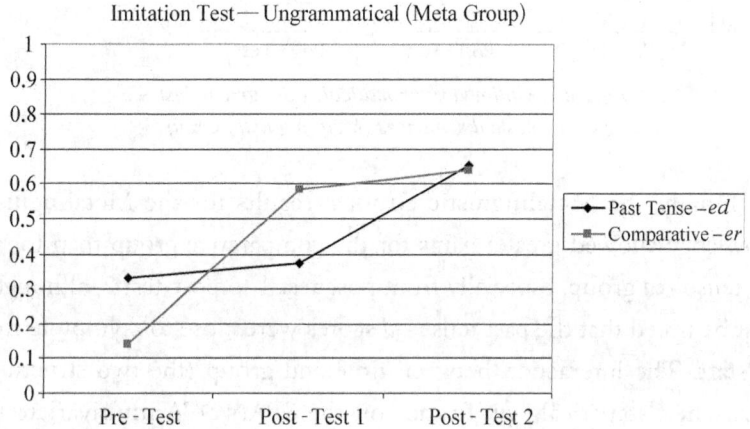

Figure 1: Oral Imitation Test — ungrammatical sentences (Metalinguistic Groups)

In the case of the grammatical sentences in the Untimed Grammaticality Judgment Test, the metalinguistic treatment benefited past tense -*ed* to a greater extent than the comparative. In particular, scores increased more strongly for past tense *-ed* from pre-test to post-test 1. Scores on the ungrammatical sentences showed a different pattern (see Figure 2) with the metalinguistic treatment having a stronger effect on the comparative. Indeed ungrammatical item scores for past tense *-ed* hardly changed. A SPANOVA found no significant time/ group interaction for the grammatical sentences (*df* 2, $F=1.699$, $p=.195$) but did find one for the ungrammatical items (*df* 2, $F=6.861$, $p=.003$).

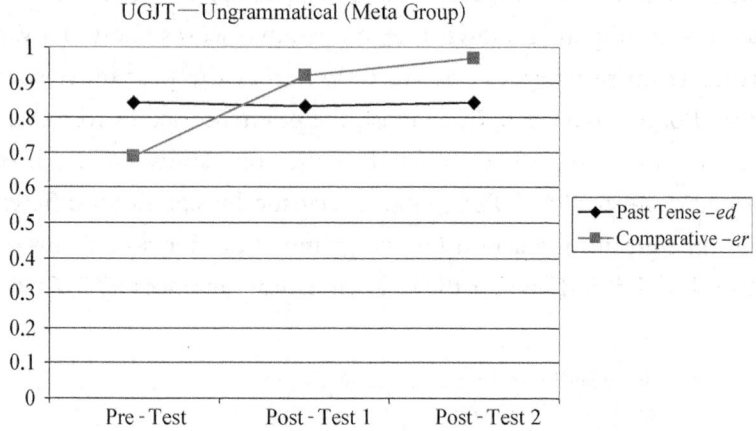

Figure 2: Untimed Grammaticality Judgment Test —
ungrammatical sentences (Metalinguistic Groups)

Finally, the Metalinguistic Groups' results for the Metalinguistic Knowledge showed greater gains for the comparative group than for the past tense *-ed* group, especially from post-test 1 to post-test 2, although it must be noted that the past tense *-ed* scores were close to asymptote from the start. The interaction between time and group (the two structures) approached statistical significance on the SPANOVA multivariate test ($F=3.23$, $p=.06$).

The Differential Effect of the Two Types of Corrective Feedback

Separate SPANOVAs (2 structures x 3 groups x 3 testing times) were computed separately for the grammatical and ungrammatical sentences in the Oral Imitation Test and the Untimed Grammaticality Judgment Test. Note that in this analysis the Control Group's scores were included. The tests of between subjects means for the two structures taken together showed that there were no significant group differences in the grammatical sentences in the Oral Imitation Test (df 2,$F = 2.247$, $p=.123$), in the grammatical sentences in the Untimed Grammaticality Judgment Test (df 3, $F=1.07$, $p=.355$) or in the ungrammatical sentences in the Untimed Grammaticality Judgment Test (df 2, $F=1.067$, $p=356$). However, the group difference for the ungrammatical sentences in the Oral Imitation Test (df 2, $F=4.431$, $p=.02$) was statistically significant. The post-hoc test (Least Significant Difference) showed that the Metalinguistic Groups outperformed the Control Group ($p=.006$) but that the differences between the Recasts Group and the Control Group ($p=.07$) and also between the experimental groups ($p=.256$) were not statistically significant.

The crucial statistic here, however, is the structure/ time/ group interaction. This addresses whether the effect of the two types of feedback differed according to structure over time. The results for the Multivariate Test show that the structure/ time/ group interaction was not statistically significant in the case of the Oral Imitation grammatical sentences (df2, $F=1.08$, $p=.405$) and in the case of both the Untimed Grammaticality Judgment Test grammatical sentences (df 2, $F=2.105$, $p=.091$) and ungrammatical sentences (df 2, $F=1.746$, $p=.151$) but that it was significant in the case of the Oral Imitation Test ungrammatical sentences (df2, $F=2.565, p=.047$).

To interpret these results it is necessary to reconsider the results reported for the effects of the two corrective feedback treatments on the two structures. These show that whereas the recast treatment had a very similar effect for both structures as measured by the Oral Imitation ungrammatical items, the metalinguistic treatment resulted in much larger initial gains (from pre-test to post-test 1) for the comparative but larger subsequent gains (from post-test 1 to post-test 2) for past tense -ed (see Figure1).

To sum up, only the metalinguistic feedback was found to be effective in promoting acquisition of both structures but its effect was somewhat different for each structure, with a statistically significant immediate effect evident for the comparative but only a delayed effect for past tense -*ed*. However, this effect was only evident on the ungrammatical sentences in the Oral Imitation Test.

DISCUSSION

In the introduction, I argued that the comparative presented greater learning difficulty than past tense -*ed*. However, the pre-test scores and the learners' performance in the treatments tasks do not entirely bear out this prediction. The lower intermediate-level learners investigated in this study achieved lower past-tense scores for the grammatical sentences in the Oral Imitation Test than for the comparative and performed the comparative more accurately in the instructional treatment. However, the metalinguistic and control groups' scores (but not the recast group's scores) for the ungrammatical items in the Oral Imitation Test were slightly higher for past-tense -*ed*. Taking the Oral Imitation Test as a test of implicit knowledge, the picture presented, therefore, is a mixed one; the pre-test scores do not convincingly demonstrate that past tense -*ed* was better acquired than comparative -*er*. Nor is the picture much clearer where the scores for the ungrammatical sentences of the Untimed Grammaticality Judgment are concerned; only in the case of metalinguistic group were the pre-test scores higher for past tense -*ed* than for comparative -*er*. However, in the case of the Metalinguistic Test, all three groups scored lower on the comparative than on the past tense.

The first research question concerned whether corrective feedback in the form of recasts had a differential effect on the acquisition of the two structures. The answer is clear. It did not. No statistically significant difference on any of the scores for the two structures was found. It is noticeable that the Recast Group's gains for both structures were only moderate. In the Oral Imitation Test grammatical and ungrammatical sentences the gains for past tense -ed from pre-test to post-test 2 were only .236 and .170 respectively. The gains for comparative were very low for the grammatical sentences (only .097) but higher for the ungrammatical sentences (.375). The gains for a control group (a group of ten learners that neither completed the communicative tasks nor received any feedback directed at the target structures) were .093 and .067 for the grammatical and ungrammatical past tense -ed sentences and .184 and .183 for the grammatical and ungrammatical comparative sentences. A similar picture emerges for the Untimed Grammaticality Judgment Test. The results of the SPANOVA showed that overall there was no difference between the performance of the Recasts Groups and the Control Group on the two structures.

The results of this study differ from those of previous studies (for example, Doughty & Varela, 1998; Han, 2002), which did find a positive effect for recasts on acquisition. The explanation for these different results may reside in the intensity and salience of the recasts. In the case of both Doughty and Varela and Han the recast treatment was provided over several weeks and it is likely that the recasts became salient to the learners. In the case of the present study, there were only 42 recasts directed at past tense -ed and 22 at the comparative, all in the course of one hour. Furthermore, the recasts were extremely brief (typically consisting of a single word) and may easily have been overlooked by learners who were likely to have been predominantly focused on meaning as they performed the tasks. If this line of argument is correct, it suggests that recasts will have only a limited effect on any grammatical structure unless they are intensive and salient.

The second research question concerned whether corrective feedback in the form of metalinguistic comments had a differential effect on the acquisition of the two structures. The results relevant to this question are summarised in Table 7. In this case, differential effects for the two structures were found. Overall, the metalinguistic feedback had a greater effect on the comparative. One possible explanation for this finding is that there were more metalinguistic feedback moves directed at the comparative but as Table 3 shows this was not the case (i.e. there were actually more feedback moves directed at past tense).

Table 7: Effects of metalinguistic feedback on the two structures

Test	Result
Oral Imitation — grammatical	No difference
Oral Imitation — ungrammatical	Different — greater initial gains on comparative but greater subsequent gains on past tense *-ed*.
Untimed Grammaticality Judgment Test — grammatical	No difference
Untimed Grammaticality Judgment Test — ungrammatical	Different — gains evident for comparative but not for past tense *-ed*.
Metalinguistic	Weak effect — gains greater for comparative.

Overall, the Metalinguistic Groups outperformed the Control Group (but not the Recasts Groups). In other words, the metalinguistic feedback, even when not intensive and prolonged, appeared to be salient enough to learners to assist acquisition. However, the metalinguistic feedback appears to have assisted the acquisition of the two structures in somewhat different ways. Whereas its effects on past-tense *-ed* were delayed those on the comparative were immediate. The obvious explanation for differences in the two Metalinguistic Groups' gains in explicit knowledge can be found in the different starting levels of explicit knowledge for the two structures. Pre-test scores on the Metalinguistic Knowledge Test (see Table 6) showed that the learners in this study already had well-developed explicit knowledge of past tense *-ed* at the start but not of the comparative. It is therefore hardly surprising that the results for the ungrammatical sentences in the Untimed Grammaticality

Judgement Test and those for the Metalinguistic Knowledge Test (both designed as tests of explicit knowledge) showed the metalinguistic feedback had a greater effect on the comparative. There was still room to develop explicit knowledge of this structure.

Of greater interest is the result for the ungrammatical sentences in the Oral Imitation Test, designed to measure implicit knowledge. Here, the metalinguistic feedback had a greater impact initially on the comparative but a greater delayed impact on past tense -ed. To explain this it is necessary to consider how explicit knowledge can facilitate the acquisition of implicit knowledge. N. Ellis (2005) proposes the following learning sequence:

> External scaffolded attention → internally motivated attention → explicit knowledge → explicit memory → implicit learning → implicit memory, automatization, and abstraction

In the case of the comparative, the metalinguistic feedback (constituting 'external scaffolded attention') induced 'internally motivated attention' and the enhancement of 'explicit knowledge' and 'explicit memory'. This had the immediate effect of enabling learners to notice the ungrammatical comparative constructions in the Oral Imitation Test and thus to correct them. Subsequently, the process of implicit learning continues but this is relatively slow as exposure to comparative forms was probably limited given their relative infrequency in input. In the case of past tense -ed, explicit knowledge and explicit memory are already well-established at the beginning of the study. The effect of the metalinguistic feedback, then, may have been simply that of 'freshening up' their explicit knowledge of this structure, enabling them to attend more closely to the instances of past tense -ed in the input they were exposed to between post-test 1 and post-test 2, which were likely to have been plentiful. As a result delayed implicit learning took place. If this explanation is correct, it follows that metalinguistic feedback may work in somewhat different ways for language acquisition depending on two factors; (1) how well-formed learners' existing explicit knowledge of a structure is and (2) the frequency with which learners are subsequently exposed to the structure.

The third research question concerned the differential effects of the two feedback treatments on the two structures. A differential effect was found only on the ungrammatical sentences of the Oral Imitation Test. Whereas the recast treatment resulted in a similar pattern of effect for both structures, the metalinguistic feedback produced varied effects. Again, this suggests that if recasts are not very salient to learners their effect on different structures will be much the same (i.e. they will have minimal effect on acquisition), while metalinguistic feedback, which is salient and provides explicit negative evidence, affects the acquisition of structures differently because of differences in the learners' pre-existing explicit knowledge and differences in the frequency with which the structures appear in subsequent input.

CONCLUSION

There is increasing evidence that corrective feedback contributes substantially to L2 acquisition. However, there have been almost no studies that have investigated the effects of different kinds of feedback on different grammatical structures. Yet, there is good reason to believe that the effects of feedback will vary according to the structure being targeted. The study reported in this chapter provides empirical evidence to suggest that this is the case. It found that while the effects of recasts were the same for the two structures investigated (possibly because they were not salient to the learners), the effects of metalinguistic feedback differed, favouring the comparative over the past tense -ed, especially in the immediate post-test. It would seem, therefore, that the extent to which learners are able to benefit from feedback depends, in part at least, on the structure being targeted and the nature of the feedback. It also suggests that metalinguistic feedback may work for acquisition differently depending on the target structure, sometimes producing immediate effects and sometimes delayed effects.

Metalinguistic feedback has been shown to be effective in promoting acquisition (see, for example, Ellis, Loewen & Erlam, 2006). However, it cannot be concluded that it will be equally effective for all grammatical structures. What is needed is further research to help us identify how linguistic factors determine when different kinds of feedback will work for acquisition. In the meantime, researchers would do well to take care not to generalize from studies that investigate the effects of only one type of feedback on a single target structure.

Note

[1] I would like to thank Michael Barlow for help with this analysis.

Chapter 8

Researching the Effects of Form-Focused Instruction on L2 Acquisition

This chapter is based on an article that first appeared in K. Bardovi-Harlig and Z. Dornyei (eds.) (2006). Themes in SLA Research. AILA Review 19. Amsterdam: John Benjamins.

INTRODUCTION

The purpose of this chapter is to set out a framework for conducting empirical studies that investigate the effects of instruction on second language (L2) acquisition. In a key article addressing definition and measurement in second language research (of which studies investigating form-focused instruction constitute a component), Norris and Ortega (2003) distinguished two general stages in the measurement process: *conceptualization* and *proceduralization*. The former is concerned with (i) construct definition, (ii) behavior identification and (iii) task specification, while the latter addresses (iv) behavior elicitation, (v) observation scoring and (vi) data analysis. My concern here is entirely with conceptualization and I will limit myself to considering construct definition and associated behavior identification (i.e. I will not attempt to specify the kinds of tasks that can be used to elicit data).Thus, the framework does not address methodological issues to do with the overall design of studies, important as these are (see Chaudron, 2003), nor is it concerned with the mechanisms for the elicitation, scoring and analysis of data.

Such a framework is needed as a basis for both evaluating and comparing the results of existing, published studies and for designing new ones. The framework will examine constructs related to three key areas of this research domain: (1) the type of instruction, (2) the target of the instruction, and (3) the definition and measurement of 'language acquisition'. It does not seek to prescribe (or proscribe) which constructs should be investigated but rather to specify which constructs are available for investigation. In short, the aim is to draw a conceptual map that can inform meta-analytical surveys of existing studies and the conceptualisation of new studies.

Ten representative and widely-cited studies of form-focused instruction (FFI) will be used to inform and illustrate the range of constructs to be considered. These studies are summarised in Table 1.

Table 1: Selected FFI studies

Study	Partici-pants	Instructional treatment	Target structure	Testing instruments
Harley (1989)	319 grade six learners in a French immersion pro-gramme	8 weeks of analytic-func-tional grammar instruc-tion. Explicit explanation followed by focused tasks involving corrective feed-back.	French *passe com-pose* and *imparfait.*	(1) oral interview (% error score); (2) rational cloze; (3) written compo-sitions (ratings of accuracy).
White *et al.* (1991)	82 grade 5 and 6 franco-phone ESL students in Canada	Explicit instruction followed by two hours of practice activities. Teachers were encouraged to provide cor-rective feedback.	English WH inter-rogatives.	(1) grammaticality judgement test; (2) preference task; (3) oral production task.

(continued)

Study	Partici-pants	Instructional treatment	Target structure	Testing instruments
Trahey and White (1993)	54 grade 5 franco-phone ESL students in Canada	Stories, games and exer-cises designed to expose learners to use of adverbs in a variety of positions (no production).	English adverb position.	(1) grammaticality judgement task; (2) preference task; (3) sentence manipu-lation task; (4) oral production task.
VanPatten and Cadierno (1993)	129 sec-ond-year univer-sity-level learners of L2 Spanish	Two instructional conditions: (1) traditional instruction (explanation + mechanical form-oriented practice; (2) input-processing instruction (explanation + structured-input activities).	Position of object clitic pro-nouns in Spanish.	(1) interpretation test — sentence-matching; (2) production test — picture-cued sentence comple-tion test.
DeKeyser (1995)	61univer-sity under-graduate/ graduate students	Computer delivered exposure to 124 Implexan sentences with illustrative pictures. Two instruction-al conditions: (1) explicit (rule explanation); (2) implicit (exposure only).	Miniature linguistic system (Implexan) involving categori-cal and allomorphic marking of plural nouns, of gender, of object and of plural verbs.	(1) Judgement tests — errors in vocabulary only (administered within treatment and at the end); (2) written production test in response to pictorial stimuli; (3) metalin-guistic test of ability to state rules (adminis-tered within and at end of the treatment).
Robin-son (1996)	104 predomi-nantly interme-diate-level Japanese ESL learn-ers.	Four instructional conditions:(1) Implicit condition (remembering sentences); (2) incidental condition (exposure in meaning-centred task); (3) rule-search condi-tion (identifying rules); (4) instructed condition (written explanations of rules).	(1) pseudo-clefts of location (hard rule); (2) subject-verb inversion following adverbial fronting (easy rule).	Grammaticality judgement test — measuring correct-ness of judgments and response times. Debriefing ques-tionnaire to measure awareness.

(continued)

Study	Participants	Instructional treatment	Target structure	Testing instruments
Doughty and Varela (1998)	34 middle school intermediate ESL students	Feedback in the context of oral and written science reports; feedback consisted of 'corrective recastings'.	English past tense.	Oral and written science reports; data analysed in terms of target like correctness and interlanguage development.
Rosa and O'Neill (1999)	64 fourth semester university-level learners of L2 Spanish	A multiple-choice jigsaw puzzle presented under four conditions: (1) rule explanation + rule search; (2) rule explanation + no rule search; (3) no rule explanation + rule search; (4) no rule explanation + no rule search.	Spanish contrary to fact conditional in the past (a complex structure).	Time-pressured multiple-choice recognition task. Think-aloud protocols to measure awareness.
Mackey (1999)	34 adult beginner/low-intermediate ESL students in Australia. The learners were classified as 'ready' and 'unready' to learn the target structure.	Various information-gap tasks performed under three conditions: (1) interactionally modified input directed at learners; (2) interactionally modified input just observed; (3) premodified input.	English interrogative forms.	Information-gap tasks similar to those used in the treatment.
Lyster (2004)	148 (grade 5) 10–11 years old in a French immersion program	Group 1 received form-focused instruction (FFI) + recasts; Group 2 FFI + prompts (including explicit feedback); Group 3 FFI only. The instruction involved typographically-enhanced texts, inductive rule-discovery tasks and practice activities involving both fluency and analysis tasks.	French grammatical gender (articles + nouns).	Four tests: (1) binary choice test; (2) text completion test (oral production task); (3) object identification test; (4) picture description test.

THE TYPE OF INSTRUCTION

Studies investigating the effects of form-focused instruction have been of two principal kinds: (1) non-interventional and (2) interventional. In non-interventional studies, researchers examine extant instructional settings that are presumed to have contained form-focused instruction. Early studies that sought to compare 'instructed learners' with 'naturalistic learners' (e.g. Pica, 1983; Pavesi, 1986) were of this kind. Such studies often provided very minimal accounts of the type of instruction for the simple reason that no or only limited evidence of what had transpired in the classroom in the name of instruction was available. The instruction was assumed to be form-focused, often of a fairly explicit or mechanistic kind, on the grounds that this was the pedagogic norm of the classrooms the learners were drawn from. Later non-interventional studies (e.g. Ellis, 1989), however, influenced by the recognition of the importance of collecting information about classroom processes (Allwright, 1988; Long, 1984) did attempt to obtain evidence about the nature of the instruction that transpired and provided more detailed accounts of it. In effect, in non-interventional studies, 'instruction' is conceived in terms of 'whatever transpires in the classroom investigated.' Such studies are important if the purpose of the research is to inform language pedagogy because they have high ecological validity but they are problematic for theory-building as the instruction is almost inevitably 'mixed', drawing eclectically on a variety of constructs, and thus making it difficult to interpret the effects of specific instructional constructs on acquisition. Nevertheless, there have been some successful attempts at *post hoc* analyses of these instructional processes. Lightbown and Spada (1990), for example, isolated one dimension of the instruction they investigated — corrective feedback — to explain why one of the classes in their study outperformed the others. The framework outlined below may serve as an aid in such *post hoc* analyses.

Increasingly, however, researchers have turned to interventional studies. In such studies, instruction is defined *a priori* in terms of an explicit set of constructs. These studies are directed at identifying the effects of specific types of instruction on acquisition, more often than not with a view to testing hypotheses drawn from some theory of L2 acquisition rather than to making pedagogical recommendations. The constructs that inform the definitions of instruction in these studies have been drawn from three principal sources: (1) established pedagogical techniques for teaching linguistic forms, (2) descriptive studies of the classroom processes involved in form-focused instruction and (3) SLA theory. A good example of (1) is 'PPP' (present-practice-produce) which is advocated in many teacher handbooks (e.g. Ur, 1996) as the preferred way of handling the teaching of grammatical structures. An example of (2) can be found in Lyster and Ranta's (1997) taxonomy of error correction strategies. This was based on descriptive data drawn from French immersion classrooms. Constructs taken from SLA theory include Long's (1991) distinction between 'focus-on-forms' and 'focus-on-form' and Van Patten's (1996) input-processing instruction.

This chapter will address the constructs that have informed interventional studies. Four general constructs will be examined:

1. focus-on-forms vs. focus-on-form
2. explicit vs. implicit instruction
3. input-based vs. output-based instruction
4. corrective feedback

Focus-on-Forms vs. Focus-on-Form Instruction

R. Ellis (2001) distinguished three broad types of instruction (see Table 2). This classification is based on (1) whether the primary focus of the instruction is on form or meaning and (2) how the instruction is distributed (i.e. whether the instruction aims at intensive attention to a single form or extensive attention to a variety of different forms). Thus, in the case of *focus-on-forms* instruction, the primary focus of the participants is on form and the distribution is intensive. In the case of *planned focus-*

on-form the primary focus is on meaning while the distribution is still intensive. In the case of *incidental focus-on-form* the primary focus is again on meaning but because there is no designated target structure the attention given to form is distributed across a range of linguistic features by means of either pre-emptive or reactive (corrective) form-focused episodes (Ellis, Basturkmen & Loewen, 2001: see also Chapter 6). In the case of incidental focus-on-form, then, there is no *a priori* planning of either the features to be targeted or the instructional techniques to be used to address form. For this reason, this type will not be considered any further. The constructs described below relate only to focus-on-forms instruction and to planned focus-on-form instruction. That is, they address the instructional options in intensive interventionist FFI.

Table 2: Types of FFI (R. Ellis, 2001)

Type of FFI	Primary Focus	Distribution
1. Focus-on-forms	Form	Intensive
2. Planned focus-on-form	Meaning	Intensive
3. Incidental focus-on-form	Meaning	Extensive

The dichotomous definition of focus-on-form and focus-on-forms types of instruction is controversial, however. In R. Ellis (2001), I chose to define these in terms of whether learners attend to form while they are primarily oriented towards message-comprehension/ production in order to achieve the outcome of some 'task' or whether they attend to form in activities whose principal goal is accurate language use (i.e. in 'exercises' of one kind of another). This corresponds closely to Long's original definition (Long, 1991; Long & Robinson, 1998). An alternative definition, favoured by some, is to view focus-on-form as instruction that is directed at establishing form-meaning mappings and focus-on-forms as instruction directed solely at formal accuracy by means of traditional, controlled exercises. For example, Doughty and Williams (1998) distinguish the two types as follows:

... a focus on form entails a focus on the formal elements of language, whereas focus on forms is limited to such a focus ... the fundamental assumption of focus-on-form instruction is that meaning and use must be evident to the learner at the time that attention is drawn to the linguistic apparatus needed to get the meaning across (p. 4).

Further, Doughty and Williams argue that the distinction between the two types constitutes a continuum rather than a dichotomy.

Some of the studies listed in Table 1 would be classified very differently on the basis of these different definitions. For example, Harley's (1989) study would constitute a focus-on-form study according to Doughty and William's definition, as the instructional treatment was largely 'functional' in nature, but according to R. Ellis (2001) it would be classified as a focus-on-forms study on the grounds that the instructional treatment required learners to orientate primarily towards the accurate use of the target structures.

I continue to argue for a dichotomy rather than for a continuum. I do so on the following grounds. First, it is crucially important to distinguish the context in which attention to form takes place. In the case of focus-on-forms, the context is shaped by instructional events and/ or rubrics that make it clear to the learners that the essential purpose of the activities they are engaging in is to focus on the processing/use of some specific linguistic feature. For example, if the practice activity is preceded by an explanation of the target feature (as in Harley's study), then, learners have been oriented towards accuracy and will realise that the purpose is to learn the feature. In the case of focus-on-form, the context is shaped by the teacher presenting the activity as an opportunity for practising communication, for example, by emphasising the outcome of the task. In such instruction attention to form is intended to be secondary to this overriding purpose. Second, it is not clear to me that any kind of instruction can be 'limited' to a 'focus on the formal elements of language', as Doughty and Williams suggest. Even very traditional focus-on-forms instruction (involving such non-functional activities as fill-in-the-gap exercises) is likely to entail some attention to the semantic meaning of the target feature. For example, an exercise which included sentences such as the following:

I _____ (live) in Zambia for eight years but now I live in England.

would surely be classified as focus-on-forms by Doughty and Williams but, in fact, requires learners to consider the meaning of the sentence in order to select the correct verb tense. In short, it is the overall context/purpose created by the instruction that determines what type it is and in this respect it is possible and theoretically necessary to distinguish between a 'communicative' and a 'learning' context. Of course, individual learners may always circumvent the intended context/purpose of the instruction (Batstone, 2002), but this is not relevant to the specification of constructs that can serve as a basis for external definitions of instruction; it merely suggests the need to investigate whether the way in which the learners orientate towards the instruction is in accordance with instructional intentions.

Explicit vs. Implicit Instruction

Interest in the distinction between explicit and implicit instruction has been motivated by a number of considerations. In the first place, these two types of instruction serve as the means for investigating explicit and implicit learning (i.e. learning that takes place with and without conscious awareness of what is being learned), as in the studies by Robinson (1996) and Rosa and O'Neill (1999) in Table 1. Second, they serve as one way of investigating whether L2 acquisition is dependent on negative or positive evidence and the relative effectiveness of these two types of evidence: explicit instruction can be viewed as providing one type of negative evidence (Long & Robinson, 1998) while implicit instruction constitutes a source of positive evidence (Trahey & White, 1993). The distinction has also figured in language pedagogy, where audio-lingual techniques have been viewed as implicit and grammar translation/ cognitive code techniques as explicit (Stern, 1983).

DeKeyser (1995) defines explicit instruction as involving 'some sort of rule being thought about during the learning process'. This definition, however, confounds instructional intention with learners' mental processing (which, as I have noted above, is always, to a degree, uncertain). A better definition might be 'instruction aimed at inducing learners to think consciously about some sort of rule'. Explicit instruction, so defined, can be deductive (i.e. the target feature is explained to the learners) or inductive (i.e. the learners are instructed to work out the rule for themselves). Both of these instructional options are reflected in the studies in Table 1. Several studies (e.g. White *et al.*, 1991; VanPatten & Cadierno, 1993) provided explicit deductive instruction. Two studies sought to compare the effects of deductive and inductive explicit instruction (Robinson, 1996; Rosa & O'Neill, 1999).

DeKeyser defines implicit instruction as involving learners memorizing instances or inferring rules without any awareness or intention. Thus, it is distinguished from explicit instruction by the absence of any attempt to make learners aware of the target structure. Operationalizing implicit instruction as 'memorizing instances' is the approach favoured in studies in psychology (e.g. Reber, 1976). Learners are provided with a list of sentences which serve as exemplars of the target structure (without being told this) and are asked to memorize them. This condition can be found in Robinson (1996). The alternative operationalization of implicit instruction involves providing learners with input data containing the target structure and/or with opportunities to produce the target structure, in both cases without any attempt to make them aware of what the target structure is. Thus, in this case, learners are expected to process input/output for message content. Trahey and White (1993), for example, flooded learners with input containing adverbs in different sentence positions. Likewise, one of DeKeyser's (1995) two instructional conditions involved exposure to sentences in a miniature language in a context where they could work out their meaning. However, VanPatten and Cadierno's (1993) input condition cannot be considered an example of implicit instruction as it was preceded by rule-presentation and also entailed directing learners' conscious attention to the target feature in the practice material.

Earlier, in R. Ellis (2001), I argued that both implicit and explicit instruction were sub-categories of focus-on-forms instruction. However, this is somewhat less clear to me now. If instruction involves rule-presentation or rule-discovery, then, clearly it requires a primary focus on form rather than meaning and so must constitute focus-on-forms. However, if rule-discovery involves consciousness-raising tasks (Fotos & Ellis, 1991; Fotos, 1994), the situation is a bit more complicated. Consciousness-raising tasks constitute a device for assisting learners to develop explicit knowledge of a specific feature and in this respect entail focus-on-forms. But they also serve as a device for stimulating communication (with language as the topic) and thus, in this respect, are meaning rather than form-focused. That is, they invite learners to communicate about language. Thus, CR tasks double up as a means for focusing on form and for creating opportunities for communication, as demonstrated in Fotos and Ellis (1991).

Now what about implicit instruction? This is directed at facilitating learning without awareness. However, if the implicit instruction requires learners to memorize sentences it cannot be said to involve a primary focus on meaning. Indeed, if the sentences have been derived from an artificial language (as in Reber's studies), then processing for meaning is not possible. This type of implicit instruction, then, seeks neither to direct learners' conscious attention to a specific form nor to require them to focus on meaning. Thus, this type of implicit instruction cannot be easily classified as belonging to either focus-on-forms or focus-on-form. In contrast, the other type of implicit instruction where learners are required to process input/output for meaning but without any awareness of what the target feature can be thought of as a type of focus-on-form. In short, then, whereas explicit instruction is clearly of the focus-on-forms type, implicit instruction cannot be so viewed.

This explication of the relationship between focus-on-forms/focus-on-form and implicit/explicit instruction differs from that of Norris and Ortega (2000) who provide examples of implicit and explicit procedures for both focus-on-forms and focus-on-form instruction. The main reason for this difference can be found in the fact that Norris and Ortega adhere to Doughty and Williams' much broader definition of focus-on-form than the definition I have argued for above.

Input-based vs. Output-based Instruction

The distinction between input- and output-based instruction derives from a computational model of L2 acquisition, which distinguishes (1) input, (2) intake (i.e. the processing of new forms in working memory), (3) acquisition (i.e. the incorporation of new forms into long-term memory), and (4) output. Thus, input-based instruction consists of activities that present learners with a stimulus and require them to respond non-verbally (e.g. by performing an action or identifying a picture) or, perhaps, with a minimal verbal response (e.g. 'yes' or 'no'). Output-based instruction consists of activities that require learners to produce sentences containing the target feature either orally or in writing.

Differing claims have been made for the roles of input and output in L2 acquisition. A number of SLA theorists (e.g. Krashen, 1981a; VanPatten, 1996) have argued that acquisition is primarily driven by input. VanPatten (2004), for example, while not dismissing a role for output, argues that using a form in output is not a 'direct route' to acquisition. Other researchers (e.g. Swain 1995; Skehan, 1998), however, have argued that output does contribute directly to acquisition in a number of ways. One way of evaluating these claims is to compare FFI instructional treatments that are input- and output-based, as in VanPatten and Cadierno (1993).

Input-based instruction is, however, a somewhat crude construct, as it can take a number of quite distinctive forms. As described in the discussion of implicit learning, it can simply involve the memorization of sentences or input flooding (i.e. exposing learners to texts that are rich in the target structure). Both of these instructional techniques can be classified as 'input without awareness-raising' (i.e. no attempt has been made to make learners conscious of what the learning target is). They contrast with other techniques that involve 'input with awareness' (i.e. where the input is presented in a manner designed to draw learners' conscious attention to the learning target). Two such techniques that have figured in FFI studies are 'enhanced input' and 'structured input'.

Enhanced input consists of oral and written texts which have been seeded with the target structure which is then highlighted in some way (e.g. by the use of emphatic stress or italics) in order to induce learners to notice it. None of the studies in Table 1 made use of enhanced input (White & Trahey's study constitutes an example of input-flooding). A good example of a study that did use this technique is Leeman *et al.* (1995). In this study, the input was enhanced by highlighting Spanish preterit and imperfect tenses in written input and by telling the students to pay special attention to how temporal relations were expressed in Spanish.

Structured input differs from enhanced input in that it presents learners with input in a context that requires them to demonstrate that they have correctly processed the target structure for meaning. The demonstration takes the form of a learner response to an input stimulus, with the response being either non-verbal (e.g. choosing the picture that matches the stimulus) or minimally verbal (e.g. indicating whether they agree/ disagree with some statement).

Input-with-awareness instructional techniques, therefore, aim to induce noticing of the target feature and the meaning it conveys either by simply making the target conspicuous in the input (enhanced input) or by requiring a response that demonstrates processing has taken place (structured input).

At this point, it is useful to consider VanPatten's 'input-processing instruction', as this makes use of the structured input construct, but cannot be simply equated with it. In the early input-processing studies (e.g. VanPatten & Cadierno, 1993), this type of instruction was operationalized as (1) explicit strategy training designed to assist learners in overcoming default interlanguage strategies such as the First Noun Principle, which states that learners tend to process the first noun or pronoun they encounter in the sentence as the subject/agent, and (2) structured-input activities. Thus, it involved two instructional constructs. Subsequently, VanPatten (VanPatten & Oikennon, 1996) redefined input-processing instruction as involving only structured-input (i.e. the explicit strategy training was no longer seen as an essential component). More crucially, he has recently also sought to redefine it in terms of the specific grammatical structures that are targeted (i.e. only those that are subject to learners' input-processing principles). From the point of view of identifying constructs that can inform FFI (my purpose in this section) this latter redefinition is not important — structured input is structured input — but from the point of view of the choice of target features for study (the focus of a later section) it is important. The essential point here is that 'structured input' and 'input-processing instruction' do not refer to exactly the same instructional phenomena.

Output-based instructional activities take a variety of forms. The constructs underlying such activities can be classified in terms of the distinction between focus-on-forms and focus-on-form and on one further distinction, text-manipulation vs. text-creation (Ellis, 1997), which is related to output-based practice of the focus-on-forms kind.

Focused tasks — also called 'structure-based production tasks' by Loschky and Bley-Vroman (1993) — are communicative tasks that have been designed to induce processing of some specific linguistic feature in production. The targeted feature, however, is not specified in the rubric of the task. Such tasks have two aims; (1) to stimulate communicative language use (as with unfocused tasks) and (2) to target the use of a particular, predetermined linguistic feature. They serve, therefore, as one of the principal ways in which focus-on-form instruction can be achieved. A number of studies in Table 1 employed such tasks — for example, Doughty and Varela (1998) used tasks relating to oral and written science reports to elicit use of English past tense while Mackey (1999) used a variety of information-gap tasks to provide opportunities for learners to produce question forms. A key issue is whether such tasks are successful in eliciting use of the target feature or, if the instruction incorporates corrective feedback (considered below), obligatory occasions for the use of the target feature. Both Doughty & Varela's and Mackey's studies were successful in this respect. However, they selected grammatical structures that can be considered easy to elicit. It is less clear that focused tasks can be successfully designed to elicit structures such as relative clauses, for which alternative forms are available and which therefore can be avoided by learners.

Text manipulation and text creation activities figure in focus-on-forms instruction. They differ from focused tasks in that the rubric specifies the learning target. Thus, the learners are made aware that the purpose of the activities is to learn the target feature. Text manipulation activities supply learners with the sentences they will be required to produce and ask them to operate on them in some limited way — e.g. fill in a blank, make a choice from items supplied, substitute an item, transform them into some other pattern etc. In contrast, text-creation activities require learners to produce their own sentences containing the target structure. They can involve the same materials as focused tasks but with the crucial difference that learners are told what feature they are supposed to use. The distinction between text-manipulation and text-creation activities is of both theoretical and pedagogical interest. Skill-building theories of L2 acquisition (e.g. DeKeyser, 1998) claim that explicit/declarative knowledge can be converted into implicit/procedural knowledge through practice. Such theories can be tested by examining whether an instructional sequence consisting of (1) explicit instruction → (2) text-manipulation practice → (3) text-creation practice does in fact result in implicit knowledge. Language pedagogy has traditionally made use of text-manipulation activities in the belief that they help learners improve accuracy. Currently, PPP, which involves the instructional sequence referred to above, is often advocated (e.g. Ur, 1996).

It should be clear from this analysis of input- and output-based instructional constructs that a straightforward comparison is not possible. The key question is *which* particular input-based option is to be compared with *which* output-based option. VanPatten and Cadierno (1993) sought to compare structured input with traditional instruction involving text manipulation. Arguably, this comparison is weighted in favour of structured input, given that this was designed to draw attention to form-function mapping, while the mechanical production exercises were not. A more convincing comparison would involve structured input and either focused tasks or text-creation activities, as all these types aim to induce learners' attention to the meaning realised by the target form. Erlam's (2003a) study involved this comparison. Interestingly, her results differed from those of the VanPatten studies, as she found that her output-based practice was somewhat more effective than input-based. Inconsistent results among studies may only be explicable after the instructional constructs on which they are based are carefully defined.

Corrective Feedback

Corrective feedback takes the form of responses to learner utterances containing an error. The responses can consist of (1) an indication that an error has been committed, or (2) provision of the correct target language form, or (3) metalinguistic information about the nature of the error, or any combination of these. Again, there has been considerable theoretical and pedagogical interest in corrective feedback. At the theoretical level, researchers have disputed whether it contributes to language acquisition. Researchers, such as Krashen (1982) and Schwartz (1993), argue that it plays no role whatsoever as acquisition is dependent on positive evidence and the negative evidence supplied by corrective feedback contributes only to the development of explicit knowledge. Other researchers have pointed out that certain types of corrective feedback provide positive evidence as well as negative evidence (see Ellis & Sheen, 2006). Finally, there is disagreement over what kind of corrective feedback benefits acquisition the most. Disagreements also arise in language pedagogy, where views about how best to conduct error correction have been informed more by tradition and received opinion than by hard evidence.

Corrective feedback differs in terms of how implicit or explicit it is. In the case of implicit feedback there is no overt indicator that an error has been committed, whereas in explicit feedback types there is. Implicit feedback often takes the form of *recasts*, defined by Long (2007) as 'a reformulation of all or part of a learner's immediately preceding utterance in which one or more non-target like (lexical, grammatical etc.) items are replaced by the corresponding target language form(s), and where, throughout the exchange, the focus of the interlocutors is on *meaning* not language as an object'. Recasts, therefore, provide positive evidence but, as Nicholas, Lightbown and Spada (2001) note, it is not clear whether they provide negative evidence, as learners may have no conscious awareness that the recast is intended to be corrective. Explicit feedback consists of either *explicit correction*, where the response clearly indicates that what the learner has said is incorrect (e.g. No, not 'goed' — 'went') and thus affords both positive and negative evidence, or of *metalinguistic feedback*, defined by Lyster and Ranta (1997) as 'comments, information or questions related to the well-formedness of the learner's utterance' (p.47), for example, 'You need past tense', which affords only negative evidence.

Corrective feedback can also be usefully distinguished in terms of whether it is directed at input (as in the case of recasts) or learner modification of their own output. Recasts may or may not result in modified output (i.e. reformulations of initially erroneous utterances). Indeed, descriptive research to date (e.g. Sheen, 2004) suggests that learners often do not bother to modify their output following recasts. In contrast, other forms of corrective feedback are much more likely to lead to modified output. *Clarification requests* (i.e. an indication to a learner that an utterance has been misunderstood) and *elicitation* (which involves techniques prompting learners to produce the correct form) have both been found to result in higher levels of modified output. Such corrective feedback strategies have been labelled 'prompts' by Lyster (2004).

Table 3 presents a classification of corrective feedback types. Such a classification affords theoretically interesting and pedagogically relevant comparisons for investigation (i.e. implicit vs. explicit; input-providing vs. output-pushing).

Table 3: A classification of corrective feedback constructs types

	Input-providing	Output-prompting (prompts)
Implicit	Recasts	Requests for clarification
Explicit	Direct corrections	Elicitations

Three of the studies in Table 1 investigated the effects of corrective feedback on acquisition. Doughty and Varela (1998) studied the effects of 'corrective recasting', which consisted of repetitions of learners' deviant utterances with the erroneous parts highlighted followed by recasts. Mackey (1999) investigated the effects of 'interactionally modified input' (i.e. corrective feedback that arose in the context of negotiation for meaning after a communication breakdown). Lyster (2004) compared the effects of recasts and prompts. However, Lyster (2004) included metalinguistic feedback under 'prompts' thus conflating implicit and explicit strategies under this heading. A study that separates out implicit and explicit strategies, reflecting current interest in the relative contributions of implicit and explicit feedback to acquisition, may be of greater theoretical interest.

Finally, it should be noted that all of the corrective feedback strategies can be used in both focus-on-form and focus-on-forms output-based instruction. Recent studies, however, have tended to investigate corrective feedback in the context of communicative language use (i.e. in focus-on-form instruction).

Summary

Table 4 shows the complete taxonomy of FFI constructs discussed in the previous sections. As reflected in the foregoing discussion, the distinction between focus-on-forms and focus-on-form instruction is seen as basic (see also other taxonomies of instructional options in Norris and Ortega (2000) and in Doughty and Williams (1998)). Thus I have indicated which of these two types the other instructional constructs relate to. It should be noted that while it may be possible to design instructional treatments involving a single construct (e.g. sentence-memorizing or input-flooding), it is more likely that treatments will involve a cluster of options. This is reflected in many of the studies in Table 1.

Table 4: A taxonomy of FFI constructs

Construct	Brief definition	Basic type
A. Explicit/ implicit instruction		
1. Explicit instruction a. deductive b. inductive	Instruction that seeks to develop explicit knowledge of a linguistic feature either by rule explanation (deductive) or rule discovery (inductive).	Focus-on-forms
2. Implicit instruction a. memorizing instances b. input-flooding	Instruction that seeks to cater to implicit learning by providing learners with data relating to a target feature without making them aware of what the feature is. The learners can be directed to just remember the input text (memorizing instances) or process it for meaning (input-flooding).	(a) Neither (b) Focus-on-form

(continued)

Construct	Brief definition	Basic type
B. Input- vs. out-based instruction 1. Input-based a. enhanced input b. structured input	Instruction that provides learners with data relating to a target feature and assists learners to notice this feature by either highlighting it (enhanced input) or requiring a response that draws conscious attention to it (structured input).	(a) Focus-on-form (b) Focus-on-form
2. Output-based a. focused tasks b. text-manipulation activities c. text-creation activities	Instruction that provides learners with opportunities to produce the target structure without informing them what the feature is (focused task) or by telling them, in which case the production practice can be mechanical (text-manipulation) or creative (text-creation).	(a) Focus-on-form (b) Focus-on-forms (c) Focus-on-forms
C. Corrective feedback 1. Implicit a. Input-providing b. Prompts	Corrective feedback that either provides learners with input containing the target (input-providing) feature or stimulates them to produce the target feature (prompts). In both cases, the corrective nature of the feedback is not made overt.	Either
2. Explicit	Corrective feedback that overtly indicates to learners that they have made an error.	Either

THE LINGUISTIC TARGET OF THE INSTRUCTION

The linguistic target of the instruction can be phonological, lexical, grammatical or pragmatic. Early FFI research focused on grammatical features but increasingly researchers are turning attention to features drawn from other levels of language. Rose and Kasper (2002), for example, offer a collection of studies that investigated the effect of instruction on the acquisition of pragmalinguistic features. For reasons of space, however, I will consider only grammatical features here. In all the studies in Table 1, the linguistic focus was grammatical.

A key criterion in selecting the target feature is problematicity (i.e. the feature chosen is, for one reason of another, seen as constituting a learning problem). Researchers need to be confident that the feature they have chosen has not yet been fully acquired by learners for the obvious reason that if learners already know the feature there is no need for any instruction. Problematicity, however, can be determined in different ways.

In some studies, the choice of the target feature is based on previous empirical findings that have demonstrated the feature is problematic to learners. In Harley's (1989) study, for example, French *passe compose* and *imparfait* were selected because earlier studies of immersion learners had shown that even after several years of content-based instruction Anglophone learners of L2 French were consistently failing to use these tenses accurately. Similarly, Lyster (2004) choose French grammatical gender because this was an attested problem in immersion learners. This approach to selecting the target feature might be labelled *remedial*.

Problematicity has also been defined in terms of some notion of grammatical complexity. The assumption here is that a feature that is grammatically complex can be predicted to be difficult to learn. There are, however, considerable problems in this approach, given that there is no convincing linguistic theory of grammatical complexity. DeKeyser's (1995) approach was to define complexity in terms of whether a specific grammatical rule was categorical or prototypical (i.e. whether a rule applied invariably or whether it applied probabilistically due to allomorphic variation). Because the target language was a miniature linguistic system (Implexan), it was possible for him to design target rules that were clearly distinguished in this way. In a natural language, however, it may be more difficult, as categorical rules are rare. Robinson's (1996) approach was to elicit the judgements of experts (experienced L2 teachers) as to whether specific grammatical features were 'simple' or 'complex'. Robinson argued that such an approach has a number of advantages; it is empirical, it is replicable, it has high face validity, and teachers are likely to employ criteria relating to information-processing load that are generally recognized as valid. It is interesting to note, however, that Robinson also felt the need to base final selection on whether a 'plausible explanation' could be found to confirm the easy/ hard rules identified by the experts.

There is a further problem in establishing a criterion of complexity as the basis for selecting a target feature. The relationship between grammatical complexity and learning difficulty is, of course, relative to the learners' general proficiency in the L2. This is less of a problem if learners are complete beginners (as, *de facto*, DeKeyser's learners were) but it is a problem if the learners are already proficient to some degree. With such learners, a feature may or may not constitute learning difficulty depending on their proficiency. In other words, grammatical complexity cannot be used as a basis for selection unless this question is addressed: 'What is easy/hard for the particular learners that will be the participants in the study?' Answering this question requires knowledge of the learners' stage of development and also some means of determining what is easy/ hard at different stages. It is for this reason that a number of researchers have sought to base their selection on what is currently known about acquisitional sequences.

Mackey (1999) based her choice of English question forms on a well-established sequence of development of this feature, i.e., Pienemann, Johnston and Brindley's (1988) account of the stages of acquisition that L2 learners traverse. She identified 5 developmental stages for questions, giving examples of specific interrogative forms for each stage. She then undertook to identify which stage each learner was at prior to the instructional treatment and thus was able to determine the effects of the treatment in terms of whether individual learners made any movement through the sequence. A similar approach was adopted by Spada and Lightbown (1999). In these studies, then, the choice of target feature was largely dictated by the availability of robust information about developmental sequences. Unfortunately, similar information is not available for many other features.

Other researchers have selected their target features in accordance with a theoretical account of L2 acquisition. Trahey and White's (1993) study was designed to investigate whether pre-emption operates in L2 acquisition, as it is claimed to do in L1 acquisition. That is, they wanted to examine whether positive L2 input was sufficient to induce parameter setting. Thus, they needed a target feature that would enable them to test this. The parameter they choose was Agreement (Agr), where there are differences between English and French, with, for example, English requiring the main verb to precede the adverb (weak Agr) and French not requiring this (strong Agr). They argued that French learners of English are likely to have difficulty expunging the SVAO order from their interlanguage because there was nothing in the input to demonstrate this order was disallowed. This study, however, was also based on empirical evidence that adverb position constituted a problematic feature for French learners of English.

Whereas Trahey and White based their selection of target feature on a linguistic theory (the parameter-setting model of UG), VanPatten drew on a psycholinguistic account of input-processing. As described in an earlier section, VanPatten argued that interlanguage is characterized by a number of default processing principles that guide learners' attention to linguistic forms in the input. His model 'attempts to capture under what conditions learners may or may not make connections between form in the input and a meaning and the processes they initially bring to the task of acquisition' (VanPatten, 2004, p.6). One such processing principle is the First Noun Principle, which states that 'learners tend to process the first noun or pronoun they encounter in a sentence as the subject of agent'. To investigate to what extent FFI can overcome such a principle it is necessary to identify a grammatical feature in a language which runs counter to the principle. It was this that motivated VanPatten and Cadierno's (1993) choice of feature — Spanish allows clitic object pronouns to appear sentence initially as in:

> La   sigue   el   senor
> Her-OBT   follows   the   man-SUBJ

thereby creating a learning problem. VanPatten has been critical of some studies that have purported to investigate input-processing instruction on the grounds that they have not selected features that clearly relate to his processing principles. However, given the way some of the principles are framed, it is not always easy to determine whether a specified grammatical feature does or does not relate to a principle. Over time VanPatten has sought to remedy this by offering increasingly more explicit and detailed definitions of the principles (see VanPatten, 2004).

Summary

The choice of target feature for a FFI study is obviously of crucial importance. The underlying criterion for selection is problematicity in terms of learning difficulty. There are a number of ways in which this can be established. These are summarised in Table 5. It should be noted that in many cases researchers base their selection on more than one method.

Table 5: Determining problematicity in the choice of target feature

Method	Comment
1. Remedial	Choice of target feature is based on previous empirical research which demonstrates that learners have difficulty in acquiring the feature.
2. Grammatical complexity	Choice is based on either some *a priori* notion of grammatical complexity or on expert's assessment of what constitutes an easy/hard to learn feature.

(continued)

Method	Comment
3. Acquisitional sequences	Choice is based on an attested acquisitional sequence, which allows researchers to define acquisition in terms of movement through the sequence.
4. Linguistic theory (e.g. the parameter-setting model of UG)	Choice is based on some linguistic theory that predicts that a given grammatical feature will be difficult to learn.
5. Psycholinguistic theory (e.g. VanPatten's input-processing principles).	Choice is based on a theory of input (or output) processing that predicts that a given grammatical feature will be difficult to learn.

DEFINING AND MEASURING ACQUISITION

How 'acquisition' is defined will influence how it is measured. Ellis (1997) and Bialystok and Sharwood Smith (1985) distinguished two senses of acquisition; (1) the internalization of completely new forms and (2) increased control over forms that have already been partially acquired. There is also a third way; (3) progress along a sequence of acquisition (i.e. movement from an early to later stage of development in an attested sequence). This third way of conceptualizing acquisition is important because it avoids the comparative fallacy (Bley-Vroman, 1983); that is, it avoids the need to base measurement on target language norms. In what ways, then, have researchers attempted to measure acquisition in these three different senses.

Acquisition as the Internalization of New Forms

One means of measuring acquisition as the internalization of new forms is in terms of whether learners demonstrate an ability to use a specified form which they could not use previously. How is this ability to be operationalized? Meisel *et al.* (1981) propose 'onset' — the first appearance of the form in a learner's spontaneous language production.

The problem here is that a form may first appear in a formulaic chunk and thus not be representative of true onset. This problem could be overcome if reliable procedures for distinguishing formulaic and creative language use were available. However, they are not. In her study, Mackey (1999) imposed a more stringent criterion — the presence of at least two examples of a structure in two different post-tests. In effect, she has redefined 'onset' as 'sustained development'. Given the difficulties of reliably determining onset this seems wise.

Acquisition as Increased Control

Most studies have measured acquisition in terms of increased control over the target form. As Norris and Ortega (2003) note, how such 'control' is operationalized depends on the theoretical framework of the study. They comment:

> Generative linguistic studies of SLA are likely to rely almost exclusively on the outcomes of grammaticality judgement tasks of various kinds, where *acquired* means native like levels of rejection of illegal exemplars of the target grammar ... Interactionist SLA researchers maintain that acquisition of L2 forms cannot be demonstrated until such forms are productively used in a variety of contexts in spontaneous performance; a multiplicity of performance data is therefore required to produce a complete picture of language development ... *Acquired* for emergentists, means fast accurate, and effortless performance attained along attested learning curves that reflect non-linear, exemplar-driven learning. (p.727-8).

However, Norris and Ortega's characterization of what counts as acquisition constitutes a somewhat idealized picture as researchers from all three theoretical paradigms have used a variety of measuring instruments.

What is common to studies in all three paradigms is a concern for accuracy. That is, instruction is said to have had an effect if learners demonstrate a statistically significant gain in accuracy over time (e.g. from pre-test to post-test). Measurements of accuracy involve a comparison between the learners' performance on some measuring instrument and either native-speakers' performance on the same instrument or the researcher's understanding of what constitutes target language norms. In making such a comparison, researchers assume that acquisition is a linear process. However, in part at least, L2 acquisition constitutes a curvilinear process involving a U-shaped pattern of development. In other words, taking accuracy as the criterion measure involves committing the comparative fallacy.

A variety of instruments have been used to measure accuracy. Norris and Ortega (2000) distinguish four types: (1) Metalinguistic judgments (i.e. learners evaluate the appropriateness or grammaticality of L2 target structures presented in a series of isolated sentences); (2) selected response (i.e. learners choose the correct response from a range of alternatives as in multiple-choice tests); (3) constrained constructed response (i.e. learners produce the target form within a highly controlled linguistic context as in fill-in-the-gap tests); (4) free constructed response (i.e. learners produce the target form in a task that involves meaningful communication).

Response times can also be calculated for (1), (2) and (3) but not easily for (4). Whereas (1) and (2) do not involve production of the target form, (3) and (4) do. (1), (2) and (3) provide scores derivable directly from the instruments used. In the case of (4), however, further analysis (e.g. obligatory occasion analysis) is needed to arrive at a score. Doughty (2003b) provides a very useful list of specific measures for each of Norris and Ortega's four types.

What is lacking in many studies that use these measures is any consideration of the construct validity of the instruments used (Douglas, 2001). That is, the studies do not specify what their measuring instruments are actually measuring. This is a serious omission given that learners' performance on different types of tests is highly variable (e.g.

gains in accuracy may be evident in constrained constructed response tests but not in free constructed response tasks). To guard against this, researchers often employ a variety of measuring instruments. The studies by White *et al.* (1991) and Lyster (2004) are good examples of this approach. Nevertheless, there is a need for a theoretical framework that can inform the choice of measurement instruments. R. Ellis (2005) suggests that a framework based on the distinction between implicit and explicit linguistic knowledge might serve as a basis for measuring what learners know about specific grammatical features. While these constructs are not easy to operationalize, the study reported in R. Ellis (2005) demonstrates that it may be possible to develop tests that provide relatively separate measures of the two types of knowledge. In a confirmatory factory analysis of scores from a battery of grammar tests, tests that involved a time-pressured response and/or a primary focus on meaning loaded on one factor (which was labelled 'implicit knowledge') while tests that involved judging sentences as ungrammatical or measured metalinguistic knowledge loaded on a second factor (labelled 'explicit knowledge'). If acquisition is to be characterized in terms of gains in implicit knowledge — the position adopted by all three of Norris and Ortega's theoretical paradigms — then clearly, researchers need to be confident that they are indeed measuring this type of knowledge. As Doughty (2003) rightly points out there has been a notable bias in favour of testing explicit knowledge.

Acquisition as Progress along an Acquisitional Sequence

Studies that have measured progress along an acquisitional sequence have typically been conducted within the interactionist paradigm and have involved the collection of samples of learner language by means of tasks that elicit communicative language use (i.e. free constructed responses). These samples are then submitted to what Ellis and Barkhuizen (2005) call 'frequency analysis' and Doughty and Varela (1998) call 'interlanguage analysis'. These involve identifying the different devices that a learner uses to perform the target feature and then calculating the frequency with which each device is used at different points in time (i.e. in the pre-test and post-tests). Stages of acquisition are determined by identifying which device is dominant at different points in time. Previous research is also consulted to establish the generality of the transitional constructions that constitute the sequence. Acquisition is said to have taken place if there is clear evidence that learners have shifted from the use of one device to another as a result of the instruction. For example, Doughty and Varela distinguished between (1) verbs with no past tense marking in obligatory contexts (e.g. *take*), (2) verbs that were marked for past tense but in non-target-like ways (e.g. *toke*) and (3) verbs that were marked for past tense in accordance with target language norms (e.g. *took*). They considered progress from (1) to (2) as evidence of acquisition as well as progress from (1) and (2) to (3).

There are advantages and disadvantages of measuring acquisition in this way. The most obvious advantage is that it avoids the comparative fallacy, by acknowledging that acquisition can take place even if learners fail to use the target language form. The disadvantages include the difficulty of eliciting obligatory occasions for some target features (a point discussed in an earlier section) and the time-consuming nature of the analyses involved. For these reasons, there have been relatively few studies that have employed this measure of acquisition.

The above discussion has considered the relationship between how acquisition is construed and how it is to be measured; that is, it has addressed the construct validity of testing instruments and procedures. Researchers also need to establish that their measures are reliable, for there can be no validity without reliability. In general, SLA researchers have failed to report the reliability of their measures (Douglas, 2001). Norris and Ortega's (2003) warning needs to be heeded:

> ... measurement error will continue to play an unknown role in most measurement-based SLA research until researchers begin to report appropriate reliability estimates and to consider the various sources of

error in their measures. (p.748)

Summary

Table 6 summarizes the main methods for measuring acquisition and the instruments involved. Although these approaches to measurement have been presented as alternatives, an approach involving multiple methods and instruments is likely to prove more informative. What is crucial, as Norris and Ortega (2003) emphasized, is that 'for all measures researchers should be able to demonstrate how a particular type and level of behavioural analysis enable construct-relevant interpretations to be made' (p. 738).

Table 6: Methods of measuring acquisition

Definition of acquisition	Method of measurement	Instruments
Internalization of a new linguistic feature	The presence of at least two exemplars of a structure that were not evident in the pre-test in two consecutive post-tests. This method requires production data.	The data for analysis can be collected by a variety of means but commonly a communicative task is chosen.
Increased control over use of a linguistic feature	Increased control is measured by means of a gain in accuracy from pre-test to post-test. This method employs both comprehension and production data.	A variety of instruments involving: 1. metalinguistic judgment; 2. selected response; 3. constrained selected response; 4. free constructed response.
Progress along an acquisitional sequence	Progress is measured in terms of changes in the frequency with which learners produce different constructions for performing the target variable. This method requires production data.	A communicative task that elicits a free constructed response.

CONCLUSION

Interventionist FFI studies that draw on theories of L2 acquisition or language pedagogy and research have been ongoing for the best part of 30 years. It is, perhaps, a sign of the growing maturity of this branch of SLA/language pedagogy, that there has been growing concern about the methodology of these studies. In the past few years a number of seminal articles have been published addressing different aspects of FFI research methodology, e.g. Douglas (2001), Ellis (1997), Norris and Ortega (2000; 2003), Doughty (2003a; 2003b). This chapter is intended as a contribution to this literature.

I have not attempted to outline a complete methodology for FFI studies nor to prescribe or proscribe what FFI researchers should do. Thus, I have not considered the overall design of FFI experiments. Nor have I argued that FFI researchers need to ground their studies in SLA theoretical constructs. In this respect, the position I have adopted differs from that of Doughty (2003a); I see much merit in researchers investigating purely pedagogical constructs if the purpose of the research is to inform pedagogy rather than SLA theory. Rather my aim has been to attempt to outline a framework that can inform the choices that researchers will need to make in three important areas of FFI research methodology — the type of instruction, the target structure and the measurement of acquisition. Of course, I have indicated my own preferences in my discussion of the options available to researchers in these three areas and I have emphasized the need to guard against certain methodological failings (such as the failure to report estimates of reliability). But there are few absolutes. What is important is that choices are made in accordance with the purpose of a study and with knowledge of the range of options available and of the pros and cons of selecting particular options. It is also important that researchers are able to present the choices they have made and their reasons for them in an explicit manner.

Section C
TEACHING GRAMMAR

Introduction

All the chapters in this section have a focus on the teaching of grammar. However, research is not ignored. My approach has always been to seek a warrant for any proposal about how to teach grammar in SLA theory and research. Thus, readers will find frequent reference to the results of research that has investigated the effects of form-focused instruction and the theories this research has supported. However, I would like to make clear my conviction that SLA research is only one type of evidence that can be used to advance proposals. Teachers' own experience of what 'works' for them in their own classroom also constitutes an important evidence base. Indeed, the proposals I advance in this section also draw on my own early experience of teaching grammar in Spain and in Zambia (see Chapter 1).

My ideas about how to teach grammar have evolved over time. Thus, readers should not expect to find a single 'position' in these chapters. However, there is consistency in my underlying approach to addressing the key question 'How can we teach grammar in a way that is compatible with how L2 learners learn it?' First, I acknowledge that learners have their own built-in syllabus — at least where the development of implicit knowledge is concerned — and that grammar instruction cannot subvert this syllabus. Thus the role of teaching is to facilitate the processes that are responsible for this syllabus, not to impose a syllabus on the learner. The role of instruction is to speed up the rate at which learners acquire the grammar of an L2. Second, I reject the view that there is just one 'correct' way to teach grammar. As a postmodernist, I view grammar teaching in terms of a range of methodological options that can help learners to achieve formal accuracy. Different options can assist learning in different ways. In this respect, I have been consistently misunderstood by my critics (e.g. Sheen, 2006), who have seen my advocacy of a particular option as representing how I think grammar should be taught. There is no single way to teach grammar.

I must admit, though, that I — along with many other SLA researchers — have been critical of present-practice-produce (PPP). This approach does have a warrant in SLA theory — in DeKeyser's (1998) skill-acquisition theory. This claims that grammar learning commences with declarative knowledge which is then converted into procedural knowledge through practice. 'Practice' is in fact a difficult and complex notion (see Chapter 9). It can involve both mechanical practice of the audiolingual kind and more meaning-based practice. DeKeyser argues that the latter type is needed if proceduralisation is to take place. The problem I have with skill-learning theory is that it is very unlikely that all grammar learning involves declarative knowledge as its starting point. This would seem to deny the possibility of incidental and implicit learning and the fact that much grammar is acquired without a basis in declarative knowledge. This theory is also problematic because it is forced to deny the learner's built-in syllabus. It assumes that instruction can dictate the route by which grammar is mastered. If form-focused instruction is powerless to alter the route of development — as several studies have shown — skill-learning theory is not tenable. However, PPP may still be of value in helping learners to improve the accuracy with which they perform grammatical features that they have already begun to acquire, i.e. to increase their control of features that they have already partially acquired. Much grammar teaching is so directed. But there are other ways of achieving this.

The options I discuss in the chapters in this section are based on a computational model of L2 acquisition. This claims that acquisition is dependent on the 'input' that learners are exposed to, which is processed internally, resulting in knowledge representations that are implicit in nature and that can be drawn on in 'output' (i.e. oral and written production). This model suggests that one way in which grammar can be taught is by assisting learners to process input by guiding them to 'notice' exemplars of grammatical features in the input (which left to their own devices they might ignore) and 'noticing-the-gap' between the input and their own output. This assistance, I suggest, can be achieved in three ways — by means of 'interpretation tasks', 'consciousness-raising tasks' and 'corrective feedback'. I will now briefly discuss each of these and point to chapters that deal with each.

Interpretation tasks (see Chapter 12) are input-based grammar activities that are designed to draw learners' attention to the target feature. They require the learner to (1) comprehend the input and (2) process the target feature in the input. The idea is to devise input that is rich in the target feature and that can only be comprehended if the meaning of the feature is processed. Comprehension and linguistic processing is demonstrated by the learner responding to the input non-verbally (e.g. by performing an action or selecting the appropriate picture that shows the meaning). The aim is to help learners construct form-function mappings (i.e. to link specific grammatical forms to specific semantic and functional meanings). In effect, then, interpretation tasks aim to teach grammar without the need for learners to actually produce the target feature. In promoting the use of such tasks, however, I am not claiming that production has no role in grammar learning — only that grammar learning can take place without the need to elicit production.

Consciousness-raising tasks (see Chapters 10 and 11) are intended to help learners construct explicit knowledge of grammatical forms and the meanings they convey. That is, they are directed at developing a declarative understanding of grammatical rules. Explicit knowledge can never be the final goal of grammar teaching which must be directed at developing the implicit knowledge that learners need to engage in communication effectively. Thus, the case for teaching explicit knowledge rests on the extent to which it facilitates the acquisition of implicit knowledge. I argue that it does this by helping learners to 'notice' and 'notice-the-gap'. When learners have explicit knowledge of a feature they are more likely to attend to the input to which they are exposed. Explicit knowledge can also play a role in the use of the L2 by enabling learners to monitor their output (i.e. they use their explicit knowledge to self-correct).Thus, explicit knowledge provides learners with 'crutches' that help them to walk until they have developed implicit knowledge. In promoting consciousness-raising tasks, I have argued that rather than teaching explicit knowledge directly as in traditional grammar teaching, it is better to encourage learners to work out grammar rules for themselves. Such tasks are called grammar discovery tasks.

The third option for grammar teaching is 'corrective feedback'. I use this term to refer to the feedback on errors that learners receive when engaged in some production task. Feedback in general is also important for the other two options. In the case of interpretation tasks, the learners need feedback on their non-verbal responses (i.e. they need to know whether they have processed the input correctly). In the case of consciousness-raising tasks, they need feedback on their attempts to formulate explicit grammar rules. Opportunities for corrective feedback on learner production arise in both controlled grammar exercises and in communicative tasks. Thus, it figures in both PPP and in task-based language teaching. My main interest has been in how corrective feedback is handled when learners perform communicative tasks. Such tasks can be 'focused' or 'unfocused'. Focused tasks (see Chapter 4) are designed to elicit the use of some specific grammatical feature in communication. In this case the corrective feedback will be directed solely (or perhaps mainly) at that feature — it will be intentional and intensive. Unfocused tasks are designed to elicit general communicative language use. In this case the corrective feedback will be incidental and extensive. That is, it will address whatever errors happen to arise as learners perform the task. There are a variety of ways in which corrective feedback can be executed and a key issue is which type if most likely to facilitate acquisition. My own research (see Chapters 4 and 7) suggests that corrective feedback is most effective when it is output-prompting (for example, when learners receive requests for clarification) and explicit (for example, when learners receive metalinguistic information about how to correct their errors). Corrective feedback, it should be noted, can occur in response to errors that learners make in both speech and writing. Chapter 16 outlines a taxonomy of written corrective feedback. I have come to believe that corrective feedback constitutes one of the main ways in which grammar teaching can assist acquisition.

To what are these options reflected in popular grammar teaching materials? I address this question in Chapter 14. Here I examined a number of grammar teaching textbooks in an attempt to identify which options are employed. My analysis showed that the favoured options are 'explicit explanation of grammar points' and 'controlled practice' — the options associated with PPP and which I think are the least effective. The analysis also showed that while consciousness-raising tasks do occur with some frequency, interpretation tasks figure only rarely. In this chapter, I discuss some of my own grammar teaching materials that embody different options.

In this section I have included two chapters of a general nature. Chapter 16 attempts to specify a number of general principles for instructed language learning by drawing on SLA research. This chapter covers more than just grammar teaching but I have included it because it suggests how grammar teaching fits into a broader instructional approach. Chapter 17 problematizes the whole concept of grammar teaching. It acknowledges that many issues are controversial and emphasizes that there are no simple formulas for ensuring its success. This chapter also articulates my view of the relationship between theory and practice (see Chapter 13). My proposals for grammar teaching are not intended as 'prescriptions' but rather as 'provisional specifications'. It is up to teachers to experiment with the different options in their own teaching context to seek evidence of what works for them and their learners.

Chapter 9

The Role of Practice in Classroom Learning

This chapter was based on an article that first appeared in AILA Review 5: 20–40.

INTRODUCTION

One of the advantages of the growth of empirical studies of classroom language learning is that cherished assumptions about language teaching can be subjected to scrutiny. In Ellis (1988a), I argued that this is the appropriate way to set about making use of the findings of second language acquisition (SLA) research. That is, what is needed is not research applied but applied research. The starting point in such an approach should not be the research itself but a pedagogical issue of importance. The research provides a means for examining whether the assumptions that lie implicit in pedagogic prescriptions are justified.

This is the approach that will be followed here. The pedagogical issue which is the focus of attention is 'practice'. This construct is an extremely slippery one, however, as it can mean different things to different people. I shall begin, therefore, by defining what I mean by 'practice'. Following this, various pedagogic claims for practice will be examined and a number of quantitative studies which have investigated the effect of practice on language learning will be considered. The results provided by these studies are inconsistent and conflicting. I will argue that a more qualitative approach — one that examines how 'practice' works out in actual classroom interaction — is needed to illuminate the nature of the relationship between practice and learning. Finally, a number of hypotheses, compatible with the available research, will be advanced regarding the role that practice plays in classroom language learning.

WHAT DO WE MEAN BY 'PRACTICE'?

Most methodologists distinguish two general stages in the teaching of linguistic knowledge; presentation and practice. These stages correspond to Rivers and Temperley's (1978) distinction between 'skill/ knowledge getting' and 'skill/knowledge using'.

In order to make sense of the term 'practice', therefore, we need to see it as in opposition to 'presentation'. The purpose of the presentation stage is to help the learner acquire new linguistic knowledge or to restructure knowledge that has been wrongly represented. The teacher's job in this stage of the lesson is described by Byrne (1986) in this way:

> At the presentation stage, your main task is to serve as a kind of informant. You know the language; you select the new material to be learned ... and you present this in such a way that the meaning of the new language is as clear and memorable as possible.

In the presentation stage it is the teacher who does the talking — provides input — while the learner listens and understands. Any production on the part of the learner is incidental, designed simply to introduce the new language into the memory store.

The 'practice' stage follows the 'presentation' stage. One of the assumptions of 'practice', therefore, is that the learner already knows the forms that are the target of the practice but needs to gain control over them. The purpose of practice is to activate the new knowledge to the point where it can be used automatically and correctly in normal communication. For this reason the learner is required to engage in extensive production of utterances containing the new structure. In contrast to the presentation stage, the emphasis is placed on learner participation, and the teacher needs a new role in order to accommodate this:

> You do the minimum amount of talking yourself. You are a skilful conductor of an orchestra, giving each performer a chance to participate and monitoring the performance to see it is satisfactory (Byrne, 1986).

Thus, practice is seen as something that learners need to do in order to make the transition from 'knowing' a feature to using it in real-life communication. A clear analogy exists with learning to play the piano; before the learner attempts to play a whole piece, she practices scales and short phrases.

Helping learners to achieve control over their knowledge requires different kinds of practice. A common distinction found in most training manuals is that between controlled and free practice. Controlled practice takes the form of various drills which require the mechanical production of specific linguistic forms. Free practice involves engaging in simulated communication which has been set up to provide opportunities for the use of those forms that have been presented and practiced in a controlled manner. Controlled and free practice are best viewed as the poles on a continuum. The continuum reflects the degree of focus required by the learner. In controlled practice the learner is required to focus more or less exclusively on the correct production of the target features. In free practice the learner is concerned with meaning rather than form. In between the two poles are other kinds of practice (e.g. guided and meaningful or contextualised practice).

It is possible to produce a fairly tight definition of controlled practice, as follows:

Controlled practice:

1. takes place when the learner has already internalised the specific feature which is the learning target;

2. involves production on the part of the learner;

3. involves the isolation of a specific linguistic feature;

4. requires the learner to focus attention on this linguistic feature;

5. requires the learner to carry out a mechanical operation that leads to correct production of the target feature;

6. involves the provision of teacher feedback regarding the accuracy of the learner's production of the target feature;

7. provides the learner with the opportunity to self-correct incorrect productions.

Although the list is an obvious one, it is important to be explicit, as only in this way is it possible to carry out a rigorous empirical investigation. Each defining characteristic of controlled practice represents, in fact, a largely untested assumption about the nature of language learning.

Free practice is not so easy to define. The problem lies in establishing clear criteria for distinguishing 'free practice' and 'communicative use'. One possible criterion is the purpose of the performance. It can be argued that when the learner is concerned with learning the L2, she engages in 'free practice', but when the learner is concerned with conveying a real message, she engages in 'communicative use'. A similar distinction might be made in the case of the pianist who plays a concerto in his studio as a preliminary to a full public performance. The distinction is not an easy one where the classroom language learner is concerned, however. For one thing, the learner may be engaged in both learning and communicating at the same time. That is, she may be entirely focused on meaning content but be fully aware that the real reason why she is taking part in the activity is to learn the language.

The whole idea of practice is, in fact, predicated upon a particular view of what language teaching consists of. Traditional methodology (the methodology we have been discussing to date) envisages a three-part process (see Brumfit, 1979):

| 1 | 2 | 3 |
| Present $\rightarrow$ | Controlled practice $\rightarrow$ | Free practice |

A communicative model of teaching presupposes a different process; 'communicative use' provides the basis for any focused language work:

| 1 | 2 | 3 |
| Communicative use $\rightarrow$ | Present $\rightarrow$ | Controlled practice |

However, an important question concerns whether any descriptive differences between learner output in free practice and communicative use will occur. If, in both cases, the performance is concerned with the exchange of meaningful messages, one might expect the same type of discourse to arise. Differences may arise if the learner spontaneously introduces the new features during free practice (i.e. without recourse to any conscious manipulation or editing of output). This, of course, is exactly what is intended by those who advocate the traditional methodology, but the everyday experience of teachers is that new material is frequently not reflected in free practice:

> ... students often seem to master a structure in drilling, but are then incapable of using it in other contexts (Haycraft, 1978, p.36).

Studies of the effects of form-focused instruction on SLA (e.g. Felix, 1981; Ellis, 1984a; Pienemann, 1984) support Haycraft's view. There are definite constraints on what is 'learnable' and, therefore, on what can be freely used.

It may be that we would do better not to try to draw any distinction between 'free practice' and 'communicative use', but to classify both as 'unfocused performance'. It would follow that the only real distinction is between focused and unfocused performance, as I have proposed elsewhere (Ellis, 1988b). Focused performance includes any kind of practice where the learner is consciously attending to the accurate production of specific target forms — irrespective of whether the language exercise is mechanical or meaningful (i.e. contextualised).

Unfocused performance occurs when the learner is oriented towards meaning exchange. Practice, according to this view, would correspond to focused performance and would be largely analogous with controlled practice, as described above.

All this may seem nothing more than semantic nit-picking, but it is in fact crucially important to come to a clear understanding of what is meant by 'practice'. The term is bandied about in a loose, ill-defined way with the result that precise research becomes very difficult and pedagogic prescriptions opaque.

THE PEDOAGIC CLAIMS FOR 'PRACTICE'

In considering the pedagogic claims we will restrict the discussion to 'controlled practice'. The term practice from now on will be used to refer exclusively to controlled practice.

In traditional methodology — as outlined in the previous section — practice has a clear purpose. Practice helps to make perfect by enabling the learner to gain control over new knowledge. This claim is closely associated with the precepts of behaviourist learning theory. Providing that the stimulus is carefully identified with a particular response and care is taken to ensure that the learner produces correct responses, 'habit strength' is built up. It is interesting to note that even in an age when behaviourist theory is largely discredited, the view that language consists of a set of habits which can be developed through concentrated practice does not die, as this quotation from Gowers and Walters (1983) indicates:

> Repetition practice helps to develop habits. However, in real life we are mostly able to choose which language to use and as we are largely non-mechanical beings this makes for a profoundly complex activity. Habit formation is a small, if essential, part of learning to communicate (p. 83).

For Gowers and Walters the 'small part' which habit formation comprises justifies some fifteen pages describing the teaching strategies needed for controlled practice. A quick survey of popular training manuals (e.g. Hubbard *et al.*, 1983; Harmer, 1983) reveals a similar firm commitment to controlled practice.

It is not necessary to invoke behaviourism in support of practice, however. Cognitive learning theory can also provide a rationale. Seliger (1977) suggests that the cognitive effects of practice counter what Ausubel (1971) refers to as 'obliterative subsumption', by which process new material is subsumed within existing networks so that its distinctive features are lost. Seliger gives the example of the learner who overgeneralizes the inverted word order of non-embedded questions in embedded questions:

> * I don't know how is he going to do it.

Practice serves to draw the learner's attention to the salient features of a new structure so that the essential attributes are not obliterated through overgeneralization or transfer. According to this view, therefore, practice has much the same function as 'presentation' — to develop awareness of linguistic form and in this way to overcome the effects of other, powerful cognitive processes. This is rather different from the kind of claim advanced by many methodologists, namely that practice aids control. Presumably a cognitive view places less emphasis on the need for sheer quantity of practice.

Most advocates of a communicative methodology are not prepared to abandon practice.

Littlewood (1981) justifies the inclusion of structural practice as 'a point of departure' for more communicative (i.e. meaning-focused) activities. He justifies his position like this:

> ... we are still too ignorant about the basic processes of language learning to be able to state dogmatically what can and cannot contribute to them. Structural practice may still be a useful tool, especially when

the teacher wishes to focus attention sharply and unambiguously on an important feature of the structural system (p. 9).

Littlewood's communicative approach does not really differ from the traditional approach in the sequence of teaching operations it proposes. The difference is only one of emphasis — free practice or communicative use is allocated more time with a corresponding reduction in controlled practice. Other proponents of a communicative methodology are more radical, advocating a re-ordering of the customary three steps of the teaching process, so that instruction commences with communicative use (cf. Brumfit's model, outlined above). Even here, however, a place is still provided for the controlled practice of those features of which the learner displays a lack in mastery.

There are, however, a number of 'natural' methods which reject any role whatsoever for practice. Prabhu (1987) proposes that grammatical competence can best be acquired if the learners engage throughout in meaning-focused activity. Prabhu set up the Communicational Teaching Project in South India to explore to what extent 'task based teaching' was feasible and whether it promoted the successful acquisition of grammar. Prabhu commented:

> Attempts to systematize input to the learner through a linguistically organised syllabus, or to maximize the practice of particular parts of language-structure through activities deliberately planned for that purpose were regarded as being unhelpful to the development of grammatical competence and detrimental to the desired preoccupation with meaning in the classroom (p. 1).

Thus Prabhu rejected controlled practice because he believed it obstructed the learner's engagement with meaning and so impeded learning. Instead, Prabhu and his aides developed a series of information-gap and reasoning-gap activities designed to stimulate meaning-focused interaction in the classroom.

To sum up, three different pedagogic positions regarding the role of practice are evident in the current literature:

1. Practice is necessary to ensure that learners develop correct language habits or to enable them to overcome 'obliterative subsumption'.

2. Practice is not necessary for language learning but is desirable either as a precursor to communicative language use or as a means of dealing with problems that arise in communicative language use.

3. Practice is neither necessary nor desirable for language learning and, in fact, can have a detrimental effect.

We can now turn to the available empirical research to see which of these positions it lends most support to.

EMPIRICAL STUDIES OF PRACTICE

We will begin by examining a number of quantitative studies. These provide conflicting results regarding the effectiveness of practice. We consider why this is and then go on to consider qualitative approaches.

Quantitative Studies

Quantitative approaches entail the collection of data relating to the practice opportunities afforded to different learners (the independent variable) and data relating to the learning outcomes of the same learners (the dependent variable). Scores on the independent variable are then correlated with scores on the dependent variable in order to establish whether there is any significant relationship between the two.

A number of such studies are summarised in Table 1. The results are extremely varied. Some studies (e.g. Seliger, 1977; Naiman *et al.*, 1978; Ellis & Rathbone, 1987) report positive relationships between the amount of practice and learning. One study (Ellis, 1984a: Chapter 2) reports a negative relationship; that is, those learners who received the most opportunities for practice displayed the smallest gains in acquisition. Other studies report either no relationship between practice and learning

(Day, 1984) or only a very weak relationship (Ely, 1986).

What explanation can be given for these mixed results? One of the problems is that different researchers work with different definitions of 'practice'. For Seliger (1977), for instance, practice consists of any speech act produced by a learner in the classroom. For Ellis (1984a) 'practice' consists of nominated opportunities for learners to produce utterances containing the target feature when presented with picture cues. Other researchers operationalize the construct in different ways. It is not always clear whether 'practice' — in the sense we have defined it above — is the target of study or whether it is participation in general. In the case of the latter, unfocused as well as focused production is included.

Another problem lies in the way that the dependent variable — learning — is measured. Three of the studies (Naiman *et al.*, 1978; Day, 1984; Ely, 1986) employed general measures of proficiency while the other three (Seliger, 1977; Ellis, 1984a; Ellis & Rathbone, 1987) obtained measures of the learners' knowledge of specific grammatical features. One possible explanation for the difference in the results obtained in the Seliger and Day studies (which followed similar designs) is the different way that learning was measured. It is also worth noting that in only two studies (Ellis, 1984a; Ellis & Rathbone, 1987) was any attempt made to relate practice in the production of a specific grammatical structure to the acquisition of that structure.

The main problem, however, lies in the difficulty of interpreting correlational statistics. A coefficient of correlation tells us only whether there is a significant relationship between two variables; it does not tell us about the direction of the relationship. All the studies in Table 1 were designed on the assumption that practice influences acquisition, either negatively or positively. Such an assumption may not be justified, however. It would be possible to argue that it is how much a learner knows that affects the amount of practice she receives. For example, learners perceived by the teacher as 'weak' might find themselves nominated to practice more frequently than strong learners. It would also be possible to argue that the relationship between practice and learning is interactional in nature; that is, the learner's proficiency influences the amount of practice which in turn affects the amount of learning. The diversity of results obtained suggests that a theoretical model in which practice is treated as a determinant of learning is far too simplistic. The whole relationship is much more complex, subject to the myriad variables that govern classroom behaviour.

The results of the Ellis and Rathbone (1987) study, in particular, give reason for querying whether the 'practice-causes-learning' model is tenable. They found that the amount of practice in the German word order rule V-END was not significantly related to the acquisition of V-END but was significantly (and positively) related to scores on a discrete-item test of grammatical proficiency. This test did not, in fact, include any items for V-END. In other words, practice in feature x was related more strongly to knowledge of features a, b ... n than to knowledge of feature x itself. Clearly a 'practice-causes-learning' explanation does not work here. However, a 'learning-causes-practice' explanation is possible. The learners' general knowledge of L2 German in some way governed the quantity of practice they took part in.

Table 1: Survey of quantitative studies of the role of practice in language learning

Study	Participants	Practice	Measures of learning	Results
Seliger (1977)	6 adults learning English	Amount of verbal interaction in the classroom; any student speech act counted as an interaction; initiations and responses scored separately	Cloze test; structure test; aural comprehension test	Total interaction scores correlated significantly with both structure and aural comprehension scores; percentage of initiations correlated significantly with aural comprehension.

(continued)

Study	Participants	Practice	Measures of learning	Results
Naiman et al. (1978)	Learners of L2 French in Grades 8, 10 and 12 of Anglophone schools in Canada	Various measures of classroom behaviour (e.g. student hand-raising; student complete/partial responses; student correct/incorrect response)	Comprehension test; imitation test	Positive significant correlations between hand-raising, complete responses, correct responses and students responding above 10 times and both measures of learning found; negative significant relationships existed between incorrect/partially correct responses and both learning measures.
Day (1984)	26 adult learners of L2 English in Hawaii; divided into high and low input generators	Responses to teacher general solicits; self-initiated turns	Oral proficiency (interviewer assessments of learners' grammatical, pragmatic and sociolinguistic competence); cloze test.	No significant correlations between classroom participation and oral proficiency or cloze test scores.
Ellis (1984a; Chapter 2)	13 children learning English as a L2 in Britain	Contextualised opportunities to produce WH Qs; number of practice exchanges per learner	Gains in the accuracy of production of WHEN Qs in an elicitation game played before and after instruction.	Children who had fewest opportunities for practice showed greatest gains.
Ely (1986)	72 first year adult learners of L2 Spanish at university in USA; half in first and half in second quarter	Number of self-initiated utterances in Spanish, i.e. volunteering a question or a response	Oral fluency in a story reproduction task (= absence of self-interrupted elements); oral correctness (based on error counts in stories); written correctness (based on final written examination).	No significant correlations reported.

(continued)

Study	Participants	Practice	Measures of learning	Results
Ellis and Rathbone (1987)	39 adult learners of L2 German; beginners	Number of occasions each learner attempted to produce a sentence with V-END in controlled practice; number of correct V-END sentences	Accuracy of V-END production in an oral narrative; discrete item test of general grammatical proficiency	Number of correct V-END sentences (but not total V-END practice) correlated significantly with V-END. Both correct and total practice of V-END correlated with general grammar proficiency. Relationship with general proficiency stronger than with V-END

The quantitative research into the role of practice which has been undertaken to date provides a salutary warning of the dangers of nomethetic studies of such a complex area as classroom language learning. Such research risks making assumptions about the nature of the relationship between instruction and learning which may not be warranted. In formulating researchable hypotheses, simplistic cause-effect models of teaching may be invoked — perhaps because such models are implicit in many pedagogic prescriptions — with consequent confusion in the results obtained. A wiser approach is to conduct careful qualitative studies first.

Qualitative Studies

Qualitative studies involve the careful analysis of interactional protocols. That is, the researcher examines what is actually said and done in the name of practice. Alternatively, qualitative studies may ask learners to introspect or retrospect on learning processes. Both kinds of research provide insights into a number of key aspects of practice:

1. The nature of the learner's contribution to practice sessions.
2. The nature of the teacher's contribution to practice sessions.

3. The factors determining the distribution of opportunities for practice.

We will briefly consider each of these.

Controlled practice results in three-phase interactional exchanges, in which the teacher initiates, the learner responds and the teacher supplies feedback. Three-phase exchanges are not restricted to controlled practice, however; they predominate in any teacher-dominated interaction where the pedagogic goal is to elicit a pre-determined response from the learner (Sinclair & Coulthard, 1975; Pica, 1987). What differentiates IRF exchanges in controlled practice from similar exchanges in more meaning-focused instruction is their interactional goal. In practice sessions the goal is to enable the learner to perform a specific linguistic feature correctly. This affects both the learner's and the teacher's contributions.

Studies of classroom interaction in which a learner is attempting to perform a new target structure reveal the difficulties which are often experienced. Ellis (1984b) provides the following protocol in which a 13-year-old Punjabi girl is struggling to perform a drill practising markers of plurality:

1. T: Now, what is this? (holds up pen)
2.   S: This is a pen.
3. T: What are these? (holds up two pens)
4.   S: This are a pen.
5. T: These are_____?
6.   S: Are pens.
7. T: What is this? (holds up a ruler)
8.   S: This is a ruler.
9. T: What are these? (holds up two rulers)
10.   S: This is ... are ... This are a rulers.
11. T: These are rulers. What are these?
12.   S: This are a rulers.

13. T: Not 'a'. These are_____?

14.   S: Rulers.

15. T: Rulers.

16.   S: Rulers.

The task requires the learner to encode a number of plural markers: (1) the plural demonstrative article ('these'), (2) the plural copula ('are'), (3) the zero article and (4) the plural noun form ('rulers', 'pencils' etc.). As Ellis observes, this learner fails to perform one or more of these markers in each attempt (see Table 2).

Table 2: Production of plurality markers by one learner in controlled practice

Utterance	Missing plural markers
4	(1), (3), (4)
6	(1)
10	(1), (3)
12	(1), (3)
14	(1), (2), (3)
16	(1), (2), (3)

One explanation for this is that the task of producing plural sentences is beyond this learner's competence. Although the learner probably 'knows' what is required of her, she is unable to comply because she has not reached the appropriate stage of development.

It is not certain what abilities a learner requires to perform a drill such as the one above successfully. Clearly, if the learner already controls the linguistic features which are the focus of the practice, correct production should pose no problem. In such a case, however, the practice is not achieving anything except allowing the learner to display knowledge that has already been thoroughly acquired.

What happens when the learner lacks the requisite control, as with the Punjabi girl? Hosenfeld (1976) set out to answer this question by asking learners to report on the strategies they used when performing drills. She concluded that what was being practiced were procedures for getting right answers rather than the grammatical items themselves. Correct responses merely indicate that the learner has accessed the appropriate cognitive strategies for reproducing the target structure; they do not show that learning is taking place. Qualitative studies, therefore, lead one to be sceptical whether any grammar-learning takes place in controlled practice.

Other qualitative studies have looked at the nature and consistency of the teacher's feedback — in particular what the teacher does when the learner's response contains an error. McTear (1975), for instance, found that teachers sometimes give up the task of correction and are often inconsistent, sometimes correcting an error and sometimes not. Allwright (1975) pointed out that teachers, in fact, may have a duty to be inconsistent as they need to respond to individual differences among the learners. Finally, it has been shown (Long, 1977) that the procedures that a teacher uses to correct an error may not always be explicit, so that learners have to interpret the teacher's treatment of error. The effectiveness of the treatment will depend on whether the learner is able to make the right interpretation. We can see many of these factors at work in the feedback provided by the Punjabi girl's teacher.

We now turn to consider the factors that influence the distribution of practice opportunities in a classroom. Ellis and Rathbone (1987) addressed this issue. They noted that practice may be volunteered or nominated and that this can influence the learner's production. For example, if responses are nominated in a predictable manner (e.g. alphabetically or line-by-line), learners are able to prepare in advance, whereas volunteered responses are likely to be more spontaneous.

One factor that influences who teachers nominate to respond in practice sessions is the learners' existing levels of competence. The protocol below shows what can happen:

1. T: Nun, erm, auf der nächsten
    Seite. Und warum sind sie
    imSchirmgeschaft? Mary.

2. S1: Erm, sie sind im Schirmgeschaft, weil, erm (.2.)

sie (.) möchten eine Schirm kaufen.

3. T: Was meinen die anderen? ist das richtig, was Mary sagt? (.3.) Roger, Sie schutteln den Kopf. Verstehen Sie? Sie schutteln den Kopf. Shaking your head. Wie sagen Sie es? Warum sind sie im Schirmgeschaft?

4. S2: Erm, weil sie einen Schirm kaufen möchten.

5. T: Weil Frau Meyer einen Schirm kaufen möchte. Und Mary sagte, weil Frau Meyer möchte einen Schirm kaufen.

The focus of the practice here is V-END. The teacher begins by nominating S1, who fails to produce a correct sentence. She then turns to S2, who has shown signs (i.e. by shaking his head) that he is both able and prepared to provide a correct answer. This he does. S2 functions as a kind of proxy teacher; he is called on to supply correct answers when other students make mistakes. It is not surprising, perhaps, that it is S2 who receives the most opportunities for practice in his class.

However, teachers probably vary considerably in the implicit principles they follow in deciding who to nominate for practice. Some may try to be egalitarian by ensuring that all students receive equal shares. Others may try to direct practice at those students who are most in need of it. Purely local factors can play a part. Thus, in the case of Ellis and Rathbone's study, the teachers tended to favour those learners who had elected to continue with German beyond the end of the year at the expense of those students who had decided to give it up. In short, a whole host of factors affect who gets nominated and how often they get nominated.

What factors govern volunteered responses? One factor is the learner's language ability.

Learners who already 'know' how to perform a structure are more likely to try their hand. Learners who are uncertain are more likely to hold back. This leads us back to the argument already advanced, namely that it may be acquisition that determines practice rather than vice versa. There are other factors, however. The nature of the practice activity can influence whether a learner is allowed to volunteer. In the Ellis and Rathbone study, volunteered responses occurred more frequently in freer practice activities (e.g. when students were allowed to compose their own sentences) than in text book exercises.

Even more important is the personal inclination of the individual learner. Some learners dislike being asked to perform in front of their peers and, therefore, rarely volunteer. Other learners are keen to try and feel no anxiety about risking themselves in public. Ely (1986), in the study referred to earlier, provides quantitative evidence of this; he found that risk-taking was a significant positive predictor of classroom participation, accounting for nearly 30% of learner variance. Ellis and Rathbone provide evidence from diary studies kept by some of the learners in their study to illustrate the marked difference in attitude to practice that learners hold. One learner dreads teachers' questions:

> I was really tense in this class when she was asking us questions ...
> As usual I was quite frightened when asked questions.
>
> I was quite frightened when asked questions again. I don't know why; the teacher does not frighten me but my mind is blocked when I'm asked questions. I fear lest I give the wrong answer ...

Another learner, however, has no qualms about making mistakes and welcomes the opportunity to take part in productive practice:

Again today, volunteers were asked to read a passage. I find it irritating that no-one seems to want to volunteer apart from one or two people. I'd rather volunteer and make an idiot of myself ... I think this is important because I want to learn really quickly.

Quite apart from their general attitudes towards practice, learners can vary in the extent to which they willingly participate on a day-to-day basis, as a result of purely personal factors or even the time of the day. A host of potentially interacting factors determine to what extent and when a learner volunteers answers in class.

These qualitative studies lead us to see controlled practice in a very different light from that shed by the quantitative, pseudo-experimental studies. Practice comes to be seen as a social event involving personal investment on the part of the learner. Practice consists of a particular kind of interaction which is negotiated by the participants in accordance with the social and personal factors that prevail in a given teaching context. Once practice is seen in this way, it becomes difficult to seek a direct, causative link between practice and learning. There are simply too many intervening variables. Thus, even practice that meets clear definitional criteria will be implemented variably and have different outcomes.

DISCUSSION

So far I have considered the pedagogical arguments for controlled practice and reviewed the empirical research which has examined the role that practice plays in language learning. We observed that mainstream pedagogy — for both traditional and communicative language teaching — affords a definite place for controlled practice. The empirical research, however, suggests that the relationship between controlled practice and learning is far more complex than is presupposed in most methodological prescriptions and that there is no clear evidence that controlled practice does in fact promote SLA. Although it would be difficult to come to any firm conclusion on the basis of the limited research that has been conducted to date, it is clear that controlled practice can mean very different things in different classrooms depending on the social and personal relationships that prevail between the teacher and the learners. In other words, it is a mistake to treat even controlled practice as a monolithic phenomenon.

In this section I will consider a number of other points that bear on the role of controlled practice, drawing more generally on the results of SLA research. First, the nature of the linguistic feature which is the instructional target may influence whether the practice works or not. Meisel, Clahsen and Pienemann (1981) distinguish developmental and variational features of SLA. Developmental features are features that are constrained by strategies of language processing. They are acquired sequentially because the development of each feature can only take place when the necessary processing strategies have been activated. Pienemann (1984) has shown that formal instruction is powerless to change the sequence of acquisition of developmental features such as German word order rules (see also Chapter 3). He found that only those learners who were ready to learn INVERSION (i.e. were at the immediately preceding stage) benefitted from instruction; learners who were not ready showed no improvement and some even regressed. Variational features are features that are not constrained by language-processing strategies and, theoretically therefore, can be acquired at any time. Johnston (undated) argues that because variational features are 'computationally simple' they are teachable. He reports the results of a study designed to teach immigrant German children the copula. This showed that they responded quite positively, with the rate of omission of copula dropping by over 50% in some cases after a week of targeted teaching of various kinds. Practice, therefore, may have differential success depending on the structure that is the focus of the instruction.

The second point concerns how controlled practice is viewed. In the preceding sections I have treated it as a kind of 'focused instruction' in accordance with a pedagogical perspective. However, controlled practice can be viewed simply as 'input'. That is, in the course of engaging in controlled practice the learner is exposed to a variety of L2 features, not just the specific feature which is the instructional target. For example, a lesson planned to practice markers of plurality (as in the protocol considered earlier) also exposes the learners to input in the use of the copula:

> What is this?
> This is a pen. etc.

It is possible that such input — although not the focus of the lesson — will facilitate the acquisition of developmental features the learner is ready for or variational features such as copula. It is also possible that because drills model specific L2 features with high frequency (e.g. Verb -*ing*) over-learning will take place (Lightbown, 1983). If we view controlled practice as 'input' we have to recognize that what is learnt may not be the same as what is taught; the lesson may have been designed to teach feature x, but the learners do not acquire x, although they do acquire y. Researchers and methodologists may not be comfortable with this possibility, as, once again, it is potentially threatening to the value that is traditionally placed on practice. Also, if we view practice as 'input', we are forced into asking whether the input provided in this way is of equal quality for the purposes of facilitating SLA as input provided through meaning-focused communication.

The third point concerns the temporal relationship between practice and acquisition. The assumption that underlies pedagogic statements about controlled practice is that the relationship is an immediate one; that is, as a result of engaging in controlled practice, acquisition (at least in the form of the strengthening or automatizing of knowledge) takes place then and there. It is possible, however, that practice has a delayed effect. Figure 1 suggests how this might arise.

Controlled practice contributes directly to explicit (i.e. declarative) knowledge, but not to implicit (i.e. procedural) knowledge. Implicit

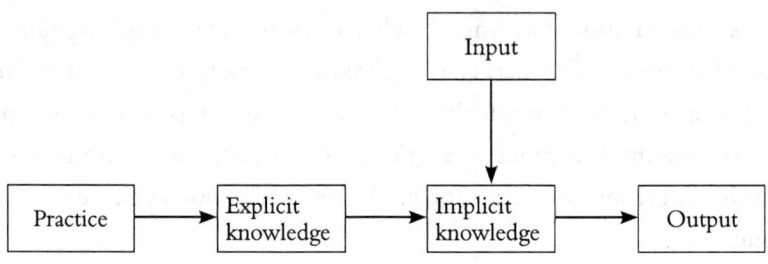

Figure 1: The delayed effect of practice

knowledge is dependent on meaning-focused input which the learner processes in accordance with the current state of her interlanguage. Communicative output draws predominantly on implicit knowledge.

However, controlled practice contributes indirectly to implicit knowledge as explicit knowledge can sensitize the learner to the occurrence of specific features in the input which otherwise would not be attended to. According to this view of classroom SLA, therefore, controlled practice has a delayed effect. The real value of such practice is in enabling learners to formulate declarative knowledge and, possibly, in the input that also feeds into implicit knowledge. If this is so, however, we need to ask whether controlled practice is the best way of raising consciousness about the formal properties of a language. Controlled practice is designed to automatize rather than to sensitize and for this reason is time-consuming. There may be more efficient ways (such as problem-solving tasks) of helping learners develop useful explicit knowledge.

The points discussed in this section constitute hypotheses that are grounded in current SLA research and theory but clearly need further testing. They all lead in the same direction—namely, to question the conventional pedagogic arguments advanced in support of controlled practice.

SUMMARY AND CONCLUSION

One of the functions of applied linguistics is to submit pedagogical assumptions to close scrutiny. In this chapter I have used both the results of empirical SLA research and SLA theoretical perspectives to examine the pedagogic claims that are frequently made for controlled practice.

The following is a summary of the main points that have been raised:

1. A model of teaching in which practice is seen as determining learning (the 'practice-causes-acquisition' model) is simplistic and not tenable. Controlled practice is a form of classroom interaction and, as such, is a varied phenomenon influenced by a host of social and personal factors. It is probably for this reason that quantitative studies of practice have produced conflicting results.

2. Frequently, it is acquisition that determines practice, rather than vice-versa. That is, how much of the L2 a learner already knows controls how much practice she gets, as qualitative studies of practice have shown. Frequently the way practice is conducted by the teacher reflects her assessment of the proficiency attained by individual learners. In this way, practice may simply serve to reinforce the learners' and the teacher's preconceptions about who is succeeding and who is not succeeding. That is, a kind of self-fulfilling prophecy may be acted out through practice.

3. Controlled practice is designed to automatize items that are already part of the learner's interlanguage; qualitative studies suggest that it does not achieve this. Frequently learners fail to produce correct exemplars of the target structure and the teacher connives at this. Controlled practice may do little more than develop the strategies needed for reproductive competence.

4. Even if controlled practice is credited with causing learning, there are strong theoretical grounds for believing that only some grammatical features (i.e. variational features) can be influenced easily by practice. Controlled practice will only facilitate the acquisition of developmental features if the necessary processing prerequisites have been established.

5. Controlled practice is a source of input; the learner may select from this input what she is ready and prepared to process, irrespective of

what structure is the target of the practice.

6. The real role of controlled practice may be to raise the learner's consciousness about language form. This consciousness may not be convertible into implicit knowledge directly but may facilitate it in the long term. There may be better ways of raising the learner's consciousness than controlled practice, however (see Chapter 10).

We are led to conclude that where controlled practice is involved the old axiom 'practice makes perfect' may not apply to language learning or, at least, not in the way that many teachers and methodologists think it does. It is possible, however, that communicative practice (i.e. practice that is meaning-focused in nature) may have a direct effect on acquisition.

Grammar Teaching — Practice or Consciousness-Raising?

This chapter is based on R. Ellis (ed.). Second Language Acquisition and Second Language Pedagogy. Clevedon: Multilingual Matters.

INTRODUCTION

Two major questions need to be considered with regard to grammar teaching in second language (L2) pedagogy:

1. Should we teach grammar at all?
2. If we should teach grammar, how should we teach it?

The first question has been answered in the negative by some applied linguists. Krashen (1982), for instance, has argued that formal instruction in grammar will not contribute to the development of 'acquired' knowledge—the knowledge needed to participate in authentic communication. Prabhu (1987) has tried to show, with some success, that classroom learners can acquire an L2 grammar naturalistically by participating in meaning-focused tasks. Others, however, including myself, have argued that grammar teaching does aid L2 acquisition, although not necessarily in the way teachers often think it does. My principal contention is that formal grammar teaching has a delayed rather than instant effect.

The focus of this chapter is the second question. I am going to assume that we should teach grammar (for evidence of the effectiveness of grammar teaching see the chapters in Section 2 of this book) and turn my attention to how we should set about doing so. Specifically, I want to consider two approaches, which I shall refer to as 'practice' and 'consciousness-raising'. I shall begin by defining these. I will then briefly consider the case for practice and argue that the available evidence suggests that it may not be as effective as is generally believed. I will then present a number of arguments in support of consciousness-raising and conclude with an example of a 'CR-task'.

DEFINING PRACTICE AND CONSCIOUSNESS-RAISING

For most teachers, the main idea of grammar teaching is to help learners internalize the structures taught in such a way that they can be used in everyday communication. To this end, the learners are provided with opportunities to practice the structures, first under controlled conditions, and then under more normal communicative conditions. Ur (1988, p. 7) describes the practice stage of a grammar lesson in these terms: 'The practice stage consists of a series of exercises . . . whose aim is to cause the learners to absorb the structure thoroughly; or to put it another way, to transfer what they know from short-term to long-term memory'.

It is common to distinguish a number of different types of practice activities — mechanical practice, contextualised practice, and communicative practice. Mechanical practice consists of various types of rigidly controlled activities, such as substitution exercises. Contextualized practice is still controlled, but involves an attempt to encourage learners to relate form to meaning by showing how structures are used in real-life situations. Communicative practice entails various kinds of 'gap' activities which require the learners to engage in authentic communication while at the same time 'keeping an eye, as it were, on the structures that are being manipulated in the process' (Ur, 1988, p. 9).

Irrespective of whether the practice is controlled, contextualized, or communicative, it will have the following characteristics:

1. There is some attempt to isolate a specific grammatical feature for focused attention.

2. The learners are required to produce sentences containing the targeted feature.

3. The learners will be provided with opportunities for repetition of the targeted feature.

4. It is expected that the learners will perform the grammatical feature correctly. In general, therefore, practice activities are 'success-oriented' (Ur, 1988, p. 13).

5. The learners receive feedback on whether their performance of the grammatical structure is correct or not. This feedback may be immediate or delayed.

These five characteristics provide a definition of what most methodologists mean by practice. It should be noticed that each characteristic constitutes an assumption about how grammar is learnt. By and large, though, these assumptions go unchallenged and have become part of the mythology of language teaching.

Consciousness-raising, as I use the term, involves an attempt to equip the learner with an understanding of a specific grammatical feature — to develop declarative rather than procedural knowledge of it. The main characteristics of consciousness-raising activities are the following:

1. There is an attempt to isolate a specific linguistic feature for focused attention.

2. The learners are provided with data which illustrate the targeted feature and they may also be supplied with an explicit rule describing or

explaining the feature.

3. The learners are expected to utilize intellectual effort to understand the targeted feature.

4. Misunderstanding or incomplete understanding of the grammatical structure by the learners leads to clarification in the form of further data and description or explanation.

5. Learners may be required (although this is not obligatory) to articulate the rule describing the grammatical structure.

It should be clear from this list that the main purpose of consciousness-raising is to develop explicit knowledge of grammar. I want to emphasize, however, that this is not the same as metalingual knowledge. It is perfectly possible to develop an explicit understanding of how a grammatical structure works without learning much in the way of grammatical terminology. Grammar can be explained, and, therefore, understood in everyday language. It may be, however, that access to some metalanguage will facilitate the development of explicit knowledge.

A comparison of the characteristics of consciousness-raising with those listed for practice shows that the main difference is that consciousness-raising does not involve the learner in repeated production. This is because the aim of this kind of grammar teaching is not to enable the learner to perform a structure correctly but simply to help her to 'know about it'. Here is how Rutherford and Sharwood Smith (1985) put it:

> CR is considered as a potential facilitator for the acquisition of linguistic competence and has nothing directly to do with the use of that competence for the achievement of specific communicative objectives, or with the achievement of fluency.

Whereas practice is primarily behavioural, consciousness-raising is essentially concept-forming in orientation.

The two types of grammar work are not mutually exclusive, however. Thus, grammar teaching can involve a combination of practice and consciousness-raising and, indeed, traditionally does so. Thus many methodologists recommend that practice work be preceded by a presentation stage, to ensure that the learners have a clear idea about what the targeted structure consists of. This presentation stage may involve an inductive or deductive treatment of the structure. Also, practice can be rounded off with a formal explanation of the structure. Even strict audiolingualists such as Brooks (1960) recognized the value of formal explanations of patterns as 'summaries' once the practice activities had been completed. Indeed, it is arguable that no grammar teaching can take place without some consciousness-raising occurring. Even if the practice is directed at the implicit learning of the structure and no formal explanation is provided, learners (particularly, adults) are likely to try to construct some kind of explicit representation of the rule.

Nevertheless, the distinction is a real and important one. Whereas practice work cannot take place without some degree of consciousness-raising (even if this is not its primary purpose), the obverse is not the case; consciousness-raising can occur without practice. Thus, it is perfectly possible to teach grammar in the sense of helping learners to understand and explain grammatical phenomena without having them engage in activities that require repeated production of the structures concerned. One way this occurs is by presenting learners with rules for memorization — teaching about grammar. This is what occurred in the grammar translation method. Such an approach has been discredited on a number of grounds, and it is not my intention to advocate its reintroduction. There are other ways of raising consciousness that are compatible with contemporary educational principles, however. Before considering them, I want to consider the extent to which the faith methodologists have in practice is justified.

DOES PRACTICE WORK

A number of empirical studies have investigated whether practice contributes to L2 acquisition (see Chapter 9). These studies are of two kinds: those that seek to relate the amount of practice achieved by individual learners with general increases in proficiency (e.g., Seliger, 1977; Day, 1984) and those that have examined whether practising a specific linguistic structure results in its acquisition (e.g., Ellis, 1984a).

The results of both types of research are not encouraging for supporters of practice. Correlational studies (i.e., the first kind just referred to) have produced mixed results. Some studies have found a relationship between amount of practice and gains in proficiency, but others have failed to do so. Even when a study does show a strong relationship, it does not warrant claiming that practice causes learning. In order to say something about cause and effect, we have to interpret a correlational relationship. It is perfectly possible to argue that it is the learners' proficiency that influences practice, rather than vice versa. Teachers may direct more practice opportunities at those learners who they think are able to supply correct answers — thus, the more proficient receive more practice. Indeed, one of the requirements of practice — that it be success-oriented — would lead us to predict that this will happen. The detailed analysis of classroom interactions that result from practice activities supports such an interpretation.

Studies which have investigated whether practising a specific structure results in its acquisition provide evidence to suggest that practice often does not result in the autonomous ability to use the structure. In other words, practising a grammatical structure under controlled conditions does not seem to enable the learner to use the structure freely. I carried out a study (Ellis, 1984a; see Chapter 2) to see whether practising 'when' questions enabled learners to acquire this structure. It did not. Ellis and Rathbone (1987; see Chapter 3) investigated whether practising a difficult word-order rule with learners of L2 German resulted in its acquisition. Again, it did not. There are also doubts whether learners are able to transfer knowledge from controlled to communicative practice. Once learners move into a meaning-focused activity, they seem to fall back on their own resources and ignore the linguistic material they have practiced previously in form-focused activity.

There are, of course, problems with such studies as these, and it would be unwise to claim that they conclusively demonstrate that practice does not work. It may be that the practice was of the wrong kind, that it was poorly executed, or that there was not enough of it. It may be that practice only works with some kinds of learners. Nevertheless, the studies cast doubts on the claims methodologists make about practice.

There are also strong theoretical grounds for questioning the effectiveness of practice. Pienemann (1985) has proposed that some structures are developmental in the sense that they are acquired in a defined sequence. It is impossible for the learner to acquire a developmental structure until the psycholinguistic processing operations associated with easier structures in the acquisitional sequence have been acquired. According to Pienemann's Teachability Hypothesis, a structure cannot be successfully taught (in the sense that it will be used correctly and spontaneously in communication) unless the learner is developmentally ready to acquire it. In other words, the teaching syllabus has to match the learner's developmental syllabus. For practice to work, then, the teacher will have to find out what stage of development the learners have reached. Although it is technically possible for the teacher to do this, it is impractical in most teaching situations.

Of course, it does not follow from these arguments that practice is without any value at all. Practice probably does help where pronunciation is concerned — it gives learners opportunities to get their tongues around new words and phrases. Also, practice may be quite effective in helping learners to remember new lexical material, including formulaic chunks such as 'How do you do?', 'Can I have a . . . ?', and 'I don't understand'. Some learners — extroverts who enjoy speaking in the classroom, for example — may respond positively to practice activities. For these reasons, practice will always have a place in the classroom. It needs to be recognized, however, that practice will often not lead to immediate procedural knowledge of grammatical rules, irrespective of its quantity and quality.

To sum up, there are strong grounds — empirical and theoretical — which lead us to doubt the efficacy of practice. 'Practice' is essentially a pedagogical construct. It assumes that the acquisition of grammatical structures involves a gradual automatization of production from controlled to automatic. It ignores the very real constraints that exist on the ability of the teacher to influence what goes on inside the learner's head. Practice may have limited psycholinguistic validity.

THE CASE FOR CONSCIOUSNESS-RAISING

We have seen that the goal of practice activities is to develop the kind of automatic control of grammatical structures that will enable learners to use them productively and spontaneously. We have also seen that there are reasons to believe that this may not be achievable. The problem lies in assuming that we can teach grammar for use in communication. If we lower our sights and instead aim to develop the learner's awareness of what is correct but without any expectancy that we can bring the learner to the point where she can use this knowledge in normal communication, then the main theoretical objections raised against practice disappear. Consciousness-raising is predicated on this lesser goal.

Practice is directed at the acquisition of implicit knowledge of a grammatical structure — the kind of tacit knowledge needed to use the structure effortlessly for communication. Consciousness-raising is directed at the formation of explicit knowledge — the kind of intellectual knowledge which we are able to gather about any subject, if we so choose. Of course, the construction of explicit representations of grammatical structures is of limited use in itself. It may help the learner to perform successfully in certain kinds of discrete-item language tests. It may also help to improve her performance in planning her discourse, as when we monitor our output in order to improve it for public perusal. But, crucially, it will not be of much use in the normal, everyday uses of language. Explicit knowledge is not much use when it comes to communicating in everyday situations. For this, we need implicit knowledge.

We need to ask, therefore, whether the more limited goal of consciousness-raising — to teach explicit knowledge — has any value. Ultimately, consciousness-raising can only be justified if it can be shown that it contributes to the learner's ability to communicate. I want to argue that, although consciousness-raising does not contribute directly to the acquisition of implicit knowledge, it does so indirectly. In other words, consciousness-raising facilitates the acquisition of the grammatical knowledge needed for communication.

The acquisition of implicit knowledge involves three processes:

1. Noticing (the learner becomes conscious of the presence of a linguistic feature in the input, whereas previously she had ignored it).

2. Comparing (the learner compares the linguistic feature noticed in the input with her own mental grammar, registering to what extent there is a 'gap' between the input and her grammar).

3. Integrating (the learner integrates a representation of the new linguistic feature into her mental grammar).

The first two processes involve conscious attention to language; the third process takes place at a very 'deep' level, of which the learner is generally not aware. Noticing and comparing can take place at any time; they are not developmentally regulated. But integration of new linguistic material into the store of implicit knowledge is subject to the kinds of psycholinguistic constraints discussed earlier.

How, then, does consciousness-raising contribute to the acquisition of implicit knowledge? I would like to suggest that it does so in two major ways:

1. It contributes to the processes of noticing and comparing and, therefore, prepares the grounds for the integration of new linguistic material. However, it will not bring about integration. This process is controlled by the learner and will take place only when the learner is developmentally ready.

2. It results in explicit knowledge. Thus, even if the learner is unable to integrate the new feature as implicit knowledge, she can construct an alternative explicit representation which can be stored separately and subsequently accessed when the learner is developmentally primed to handle it. Furthermore, explicit knowledge serves to help the learner to continue to notice the feature in the input, thereby facilitating its subsequent acquisition.

Consciousness-raising, then, is unlikely to result in immediate acquisition. More likely, it will have a delayed effect.

There are also educational reasons that can be advanced for grammar teaching as consciousness-raising. The inclusion of foreign languages in the school curriculum is not motivated entirely by the desire to foster communication between speakers of different languages, although this has become the most prominent aim in recent years. This inclusion has, and always has had, a more general goal — that of fostering intellectual development. 'Grammar' embodies a body of knowledge the study of which can be expected to contribute to students' analytical skills. It constitutes a serious content and, as such, contrasts with the trivial content of many modern textbooks.

It is not my intention, however, to advocate a return to 'teaching about grammar', or, at least, not in the form that this was carried out in the past. The arguments that I have presented in favour of consciousness-raising do not justify giving lectures on grammar. Such a transmission-oriented approach runs contrary to progressive educational principles. What I have in mind is a task-based approach that emphasizes discovery learning by asking learners to solve problems about grammar. The following is an example of this approach.

AN EXAMPLE OF A CONSCIOUSNESS-RAISING TASK

Consciousness-raising tasks can be inductive or deductive. In the case of the former, the learner is provided with data and asked to construct an explicit rule to describe the grammatical feature which the data illustrate. In the case of the latter, the learner is supplied with a rule which is then used to carry out some task. We do not know, as yet, which type results in the more efficient learning of explicit knowledge — probably both will prove useful.

Table 1 provides a simple example of an inductive task designed to raise learners' awareness about the grammatical differences between 'for' and 'since'. This problem has been designed with a number of points in mind. First, the intention is to focus on a known source of difficulty; learners frequently fail to distinguish 'for' and 'since'. Second, the data provided must be adequate to enable the learners to discover the rule that governs the usage of these prepositions in time expressions. In the case of this task, the data include both grammatical and ungrammatical sentences. Third, the task requires minimal production on the part of the learners; instead, emphasis is placed on developing an 'idea' of when the two forms are used. Fourth, there is an opportunity to apply the rule in the construction of personalized statements. This is not intended to 'practice' the rule but to promote its storage as explicit knowledge; production, therefore, is restricted to two sentences and there is no insistence on automatic processing. Such tasks as these can be designed with varying formats. They can make use of situational information, diagram, charts, tables, and so on. They can also be used in both lockstep teaching (i.e., when the teacher works through a problem with the whole class) or small-group work.

Table 1. An example of a CR problem-solving task

1. Here is some information about when three people joined the company they now work for and how long they have been working there.		
Name	Date Joined	Length of Time
Ms Regan	1945	45 yrs
Mr Bush	1970	20 yrs
Ms Thatcher	1989	9 mths
Mr Baker	1990 (Feb)	10 days

2. Study these sentences about these people. When is 'for' used and when is 'since' used?
   a. Ms Regan has been working for her company for most of her life.
   b. Mr Bush has been working for his company since 1970.
   c. Ms Thatcher has been working for her company for 9 months.
   d. Mr Baker has been working for his company since February.

3. Which of the following sentences are ungrammatical? Why?
   a. Ms Regan has been working for her company for 1945.
   b. Mr Bush has been working for his company for 20 years.
   c. Ms Thatcher has been working for her company since 1989.
   d. Mr Baker has been working for his company since 10 days.
4. Try and make up a rule to explain when 'for' and 'since' are used.

5. Make up one sentence about when you started to learn English and one sentence about how long you have been studying English. Use 'for' and 'since'.

CONCLUSION

In this chapter I have argued the case for grammar teaching as consciousness-raising. In one respect, this does not constitute a radical departure from what teachers have always done. Many teachers have felt the need to provide formal explanations of grammatical points. But in another respect, it does represent a real alternative in that it removes from grammar teaching the need to provide learners with repeated opportunities to produce the target structure. So much effort has gone into devising ingenious ways of eliciting and shaping learners' responses, more often to little or no avail as learners do not acquire the structures they have practiced. Consciousness-raising constitutes an approach to grammar teaching which is compatible with current thinking about how learners acquire L2 grammar. It also constitutes an approach that accords with progressive views about education as a process of discovery through problem-solving tasks.

There are, of course, limitations to consciousness-raising. It may not be appropriate for young learners. Some learners (e.g., those who like to learn by 'doing' rather than 'studying') may dislike it. It can only be used with beginners if the learners' first language is used as the medium for solving the tasks. However, the alternative in such situations is not practice. Rather, it is to provide opportunities for meaning-focused language use, for communicating in the L2, initially perhaps in the form of listening tasks. All learners, even those who are suited to a consciousness-raising approach, will need plenty of such opportunities. Consciousness-raising is not an alternative to communication activities, but a supplement.

Chapter 11

The Structural Syllabus and Second Language Acquisition

This chapter is based on an article that first appeared in TESOL Quarterly, Vol. 27, pp. 91–113.

INTRODUCTION

A structural syllabus consists of a list of grammatical items, usually arranged in the order in which they are to be taught. This kind of syllabus is probably still the most common in language teaching today. Yalden (1983) describes it as 'traditional' on the grounds that it is the basis of the grammar translation and audiolingual methods. However, it also serves as a basis for more 'modern' methods — Total Physical Response (Asher, 1977) and The Silent Way (Gattegno, 1972), for example. The move towards a communicative approach to language pedagogy in the 1970s and 1980s resulted in alternative syllabuses (in particular, the notional-functional syllabus (Wilkins, 1976), the task-based or procedural syllabus (Prabhu, 1987), and the process syllabus (Breen, 1984). These syllabuses continue to attract a lot of attention, but they have never totally replaced the structural syllabus.

The problems of a structural syllabus, discussed in detail in numerous publications during the 1970s and 1980s (see Krahnke, 1987), have not disappeared, however. The principal problem is that of learnability, the extent to which it is possible for learners to learn the structures they are taught. This problem has always been recognized by language teaching methodologists (see Palmer, 1917), but it has been given additional weight by research which has shown that the acquisition of specific grammatical features is constrained developmentally. Corder (1967) suggested that learners possess a 'built-in syllabus', which regulates when it is possible for them to acquire each grammatical feature. Subsequent studies of naturalistic language learning (see Hatch, 1978b; Meisel, Clahsen, & Pienemann, 1981; Wode, 1980) have given empirical support to this claim. Also, studies designed to investigate whether learners succeed in learning the structures they are taught (e.g., Ellis, 1984a; 1989; Felix, 1981; Pienemann, 1984; 1989) suggest that often they are unable to internalize new structural knowledge in a manner that enables them to use it productively in communication unless they are ready to do so. For example, Pienemann (1984) has provided evidence that learners of German as a second language only acquire a feature such as inversion if they have previously acquired word order structures that are easier to process. In other words, in order to acquire Feature D, learners must already have acquired Features A, B, and C. Learnability, therefore, remains a central problem in syllabus design. How can the content of a syllabus be selected and graded in a way that is compatible with the learner's ability to learn? This is a problem for any syllabus but it becomes acute when the content is specified in grammatical terms.

The main purpose of this chapter is to address this problem and to present a proposal for how it might be overcome. The chapter will begin with a brief discussion of the difference between two types of linguistic knowledge — implicit and explicit knowledge. This distinction underlies much of the discussion in the rest of the chapter. It will also consider the relationship between these two types of knowledge. There follows a detailed discussion of structural syllabuses in relation to each type of knowledge. The main argument of this chapter is that the structural syllabus is a valid device for raising learners' consciousness about grammar; this role is discussed in the concluding section.

IMPLICIT AND EXPLICIT KNOWLEDGE OF AN L2

It has been hypothesized that the learner internalizes two types of knowledge — implicit and explicit knowledge. As Bialystok pointed out, this distinction is common in cognitive psychology. Explicit knowledge refers to knowledge that is analyzed (in the sense that it can be described and classified), abstract (in the sense that it takes the form of some underlying generalization of actual linguistic behavior), and explanatory (in the sense that it can provide a reasonably objective account of how grammar is used in actual communication). Explicit knowledge is available to the learner as a conscious representation, but it is not the same as 'articulated knowledge' (i.e., spoken or written accounts of the knowledge). A learner may have constructed a conscious abstract representation of a grammatical rule (e.g., have formulated an idea that *-s* on the end of a noun signals more than one) and yet not be able to put this idea into words. Often, however, explicit knowledge is developed together with metalinguistic knowledge (e.g., terms such as plural), and this helps the learner to articulate it.

Two kinds of implicit knowledge can be identified; formulaic knowledge and rule-based knowledge. Formulaic knowledge consists of ready-made chunks of language — whole utterances, such as I don't know or utterance frames with one or more empty slots, such as *Can I have a ___*? Rule-based knowledge consists of generalized and abstract structures which have been internalized. In both cases, the knowledge is intuitive. Native speakers know a large number of formulas which they have learned as unanalyzed units (see Pawley & Syder, 1983). They also know rules that enable them to understand and produce novel sentences without conscious effort. Implicit knowledge of rules is largely hidden and we know relatively little about how they are represented in the mind. It is doubtful, however, whether the manner of their representation corresponds closely to the way they are represented as explicit knowledge, one of the reasons why published grammars generally do not claim that the rules they describe have psychological validity.

Because implicit knowledge becomes manifest only in actual performance (both comprehension and production), it is, perhaps, not surprising to find that there is disagreement concerning the nature of the mechanisms responsible for its acquisition, particularly where rules are involved. Whereas some researchers (e.g., White, 1987) view rules in both native speaker and learner grammars as primarily linguistic in nature, others (e.g., Clahsen, 1984; McLaughlin, 1978) see them as cognitive (i.e., involving the same general mechanisms that underlie other kinds of learning). Although much of the research into developmental sequences does not specify which type of knowledge is involved, it is clear that it is implicit knowledge that the researchers have in mind. For example, Wode's (1980) account of how German children progress through a series of stages in acquiring English negatives and interrogatives assumes that the knowledge they are slowly constructing is implicit rather than explicit.

Another distinction from cognitive psychology that is often referred to in L2 acquisition research is declarative and procedural knowledge. These terms were used initially by Ryle (1949) and subsequently taken up by cognitive psychologists like Anderson (1983) to distinguish knowledge as a set of facts (declarative knowledge) and knowledge about how to do things (procedural knowledge). An example may make this clearer. Knowledge of the rules of the highway code (e.g., 'Always signal before overtaking') would constitute declarative knowledge while knowledge of how to drive a car in accordance with these rules would be procedural. Anderson characterizes classroom L2 learning as beginning with declarative knowledge of grammatical rules (usually supplied by the teacher), which is gradually proceduralized, resulting in the ability to use the foreign language without thinking.

The explicit/implicit and declarative/procedural distinctions may appear to be very similar, but in fact, they are not, as Figure 1 shows. Whereas the terms explicit/ implicit label the type of knowledge learners possess in terms of whether it is conscious or intuitive, the terms declarative/procedural concern the degree of control over L2 knowledge the learner has, distinguishing knowledge that can be used only with effort through controlled processing from knowledge that can be used effortlessly through automatic processing. (Bialystok, 1982, also depicts linguistic knowledge as two intersecting continua, which she labels +/– analyzed and +/– automatic. The former relates to the implicit/ explicit dimension and the latter to the declarative/procedural dimension.)

Table 1: The difference between explicit/implicit and declarative/procedural Knowledge

	Declarative	Procedural
Explicit	*Type A* Conscious knowledge of L2 items	*Type B* Conscious knowledge of learning, production, and communication strategies. The learner can use explicit knowledge easily and rapidly.
Implicit	*Type C* Intuitive knowledge of L2 items	*Type D* Ability to employ learning, production, and communication strategies automatically. The learner can use intuitive knowledge fluently.

Thus, explicit/implicit refer to a knowledge dimension, whereas declarative/procedural refer to a process dimension. The key point to note is that the two distinctions intersect; we can talk about both explicit and implicit knowledge as existing in declarative and procedural form. Although the distinction between explicit and implicit knowledge is not itself controversial, the relationship between the two is. The main point of debate is whether explicit L2 knowledge can convert into implicit L2 knowledge. One of the assumptions of traditional language teaching methods based on a structural syllabus is that explicit knowledge can become implicit knowledge through practice. According to this view, learners automatize or proceduralize knowledge that is initially explicit by doing grammar activities. In terms of Figure 1, this is tantamount to claiming that practice enables learners to move from Type A knowledge to Type D, the goal of most language programs. The notion of automatizing or proceduralizing explicit knowledge so that it becomes implicit is a somewhat confused one. It derives from the failure to clearly distinguish explicit/implicit knowledge from declarative/procedural knowledge. Thus, whereas it is legitimate to talk about the proceduralization of declarative knowledge, it is not legitimate to equate this with the conversion of explicit into implicit knowledge.

The key issue — and it is here that we run up against the learnability question — is whether we can manipulate the process by which a learner moves from Type A to Type D knowledge. Two positions can be distinguished — a non-interface and an interface position. According to the former, it is impossible to lead learners from Type A to Type D knowledge through practicing declarative explicit knowledge (as shown in Figure 2a). This position sees Type D knowledge as deriving from proceduralizing Type C knowledge. Practicing explicit knowledge (Type A) may result in greater facility in using this knowledge (Type B) but will still involve accessing conscious L2 knowledge.

The interface position comes in a strong and a weak form. According to the strong version, Type A knowledge can be converted into Type D knowledge through practice and there are no constraints on this taking place (see Figure 2b). According to the weak version, Type A knowledge may develop into Type C knowledge providing learners are ready to accommodate the new knowledge into their interlanguage systems. Opportunities for formally practicing the new knowledge or for communicating naturally in contexts that call for its use will be needed before Type D knowledge develops (see Figure 2c).

Krashen (1981a) has argued strongly in favor of a non-interface position. He argues that explicit knowledge may assist learners in certain kinds of language performance in the form of monitoring but that it does not help them to acquire implicit knowledge. Others (e.g., Gregg, 1984; McLaughlin, 1978; Sharwood Smith, 1981) have opted for a strong interface position, according to which explicit knowledge can change into implicit knowledge as a result of practice.

It is my contention that the evidence available from research into the effects of grammar instruction on L2 learning (see Ellis, 1990; Larsen-Freeman & Long, 1991, for recent reviews of the literature) is compatible only with a weak interface position. This research suggests the following conclusions:

1. Grammar instruction results in faster learning and in higher levels of L2 grammatical accuracy (see Long, 1983a; Pica, 1983).

2. Grammar instruction directed at a grammatical feature that learners are not ready to acquire as implicit knowledge does not succeed (see Felix, 1981; Pienemann, 1984; 1989).

3. Grammar instruction directed at a grammatical feature that learners are ready to acquire as implicit knowledge is successful (see Harley, 1989; Pienemann, 1984; 1989).

The first conclusion cannot be easily explained by a non-interface theory. The second conclusion contradicts a strong interface theory. All three conclusions are compatible with a weak interface theory.

Figure 3 provides a model of L2 acquisition that incorporates a weak interface position. The model distinguishes input, intake, and implicit L2 knowledge. Input refers to the samples of the L2 that the learner is exposed to as a result of contact with the language in communication (oral and written). Formal instruction can also provide input (i.e., general exposure to the L2), although its raison d'etre is to teach specific grammatical items. Intake refers to the linguistic properties in the input

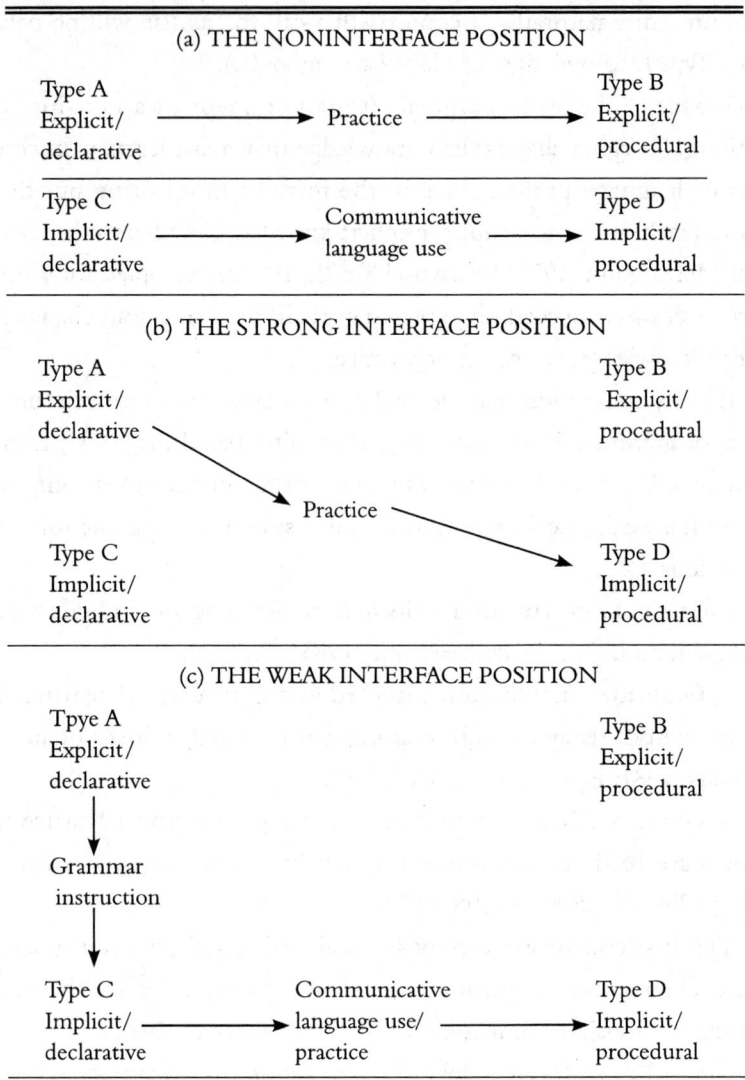

Figure 2: The non-interface and the strong and weak interface positions

that the learner attends to. Not all of these properties will be immediately incorporated into the learner's interlanguage system; only those features that are finally incorporated become implicit knowledge of the L2.

The model shows that implicit knowledge can be internalized in two

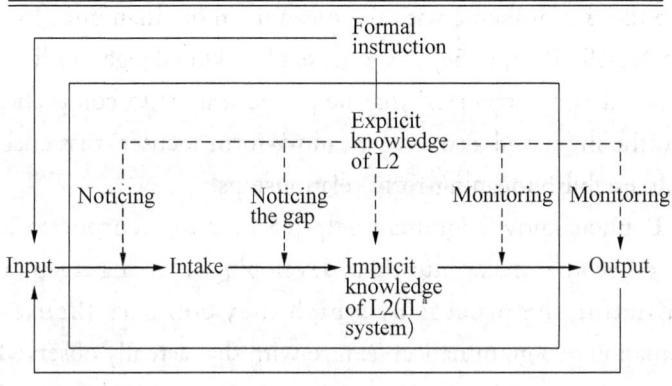

ᵃIL=interlanguage.

Figure 3: A model of L2 acquisition incorporating a weak interface position

ways. The main way is by deriving intake from the input. A secondary way is directly from the explicit knowledge that is learned through formal instruction. This way is considered secondary for two reasons; first, the amount of new grammatical knowledge derived in this way is likely to be limited because only a small portion of the total grammatical properties of a language can be consciously learned (see Krashen, 1982), and second, explicit knowledge can only feed directly into implicit knowledge if learners are developmentally ready to incorporate it (hence the dotted line).

The model posits a number of other uses of explicit knowledge, however:

1. Explicit knowledge is also available for use in monitoring (as proposed by Krashen, 1982). Monitoring can occur before an utterance is produced or after. Monitored output constitutes one source of input. As Terrell (1991) puts it, 'monitoring can apparently interact with acquisition, resulting in learners acquiring their own output' (p. 61).

2. Explicit knowledge can help learners to notice features in the input and also to notice the meanings that they realize. For example, if learners know that plural nouns have an -s, they are more likely to notice the -s on the ends of nouns they hear or read in input and also more likely to

associate the -*s* morpheme with the meaning 'more than one'. In a sense, then, as Terrell (1991, p. 58) suggests, explicit knowledge can function as a kind of 'advance organizer' that helps the learner to comprehend and segment the input and also as a 'meaning-form focuser' that enables the learner to establish meaning-form relationships.

3. Explicit knowledge may help learners to incorporate features that have become intake into their developing interlanguage grammars by facilitating the process by which they compare their existing representation of a grammatical feature with that actually observed in the input. For example, if learners know that plural nouns have an -*s*, they are better equipped to notice the difference between this feature in the input and its omission in their own output.

Monitoring, noticing, and noticing-the-gap are all mental processes and hence are shown inside the 'black box' in Figure 3. Because the availability of relevant explicit knowledge does not guarantee their operation, all three processes are represented by dotted lines.

A key aspect of this model is the role that explicit knowledge is hypothesized to play in noticing and noticing-the-gap. According to Schmidt (1990), the process of noticing is frequently (and perhaps necessarily) a conscious one. He defines it operationally as availability for verbal report. A variety of factors can induce learners to notice features in the input — the demands of a task, the high frequency of an item in the input, the unusual nature of a feature, the inherent salience of a feature, and interaction that highlights a feature. Noticing-the-gap (Schmidt & Frota, 1986) occurs when learners make the effort to establish in what ways a new feature, which they have heeded in the input, is different from their existing interlanguage representation. This entails some form of comparison between what learners typically do in their output and what is present in the input. Learners may notice a feature but not bother to notice the gap. Neither noticing nor noticing-the-gap guarantees that the new feature will be incorporated into the learner's interlanguage system, as in many cases this will be constrained by the learner's stage of development.

This model, then, envisages that explicit knowledge can convert directly into implicit knowledge under certain, fairly stringent conditions related to the learner's stage of development. It also allows for explicit knowledge to have an indirect effect on acquisition by helping to facilitate the processes of noticing and noticing-the-gap. It is hypothesized that learners who know about a grammatical feature because they have learned about it through grammar instruction are in a better position to heed this feature when it subsequently occurs in the input and also are better able to notice the difference between the input and their own production. Empirical evidence in support of the claim that explicit knowledge facilitates subsequent noticing can be found in Fotos (1992). Explicit knowledge functions as a kind of 'acquisition facilitator' (Seliger, 1979) by providing 'hooks' on which to hang subsequent acquisition (Lightbown, 1985b).

THE STRUCTURAL SYLLABUS AND L2 ACQUISITION

A structural syllabus employs a synthetic teaching strategy, defined by Wilkins (1976) as 'one in which the different parts of the language are taught separately and step-by-step so that acquisition is a process of gradual accumulation of the parts until the whole of the language has been built up' (p. 2). The execution of this teaching strategy involves the course designer in making principled decisions regarding which parts of the language to teach (i.e., selection) and which order to teach them in (i.e., grading). However, as Wilkins points out, the job of synthesizing the items which have been presented in small pieces is left to the learner.

A structural syllabus can serve as a basis for the development of either implicit or explicit knowledge. In the case of the former, the aim of the syllabus is the development of the kind of intuitive knowledge that is required to communicate in the L2. In the case of the latter, the aim is knowledge about the language — some kind of conscious representation of the 'rules' that makeup the language. The structural syllabuses used in the audiolingual and oral-situational methods are directed at implicit knowledge, whereas the grammar-translation method is directed at explicit knowledge.

The Structural Syllabus and Implicit Knowledge

In the case of a structural syllabus for implicit knowledge, the aim is to 'teach the language, not about the language' (Moulton, 1961). The term teaching the language can refer to both the comprehension and the production of grammatical items. It is possible to teach a structure only for comprehension, but in most methods that employ a structural syllabus, the aim is to enable the learners to produce the items correctly. As we will see, it is this insistence on production that creates many of the problems. A possible solution to the difficulties of a structural syllabus might be to settle for the lesser but still worthwhile goal of teaching grammar for comprehension.

When production is the goal, another distinction is important. Whereas some structural syllabuses (e.g., those underlying strict audiolingual courses) are based on the idea that each item will be fully mastered before another item is introduced, others (e.g., those underlying more modern approaches to grammar teaching such as that described in Ur, 1988) recognize that mastery occurs only in the long term and that each item will probably only be partially acquired before another is introduced. These two views of structural syllabuses will be referred to as immediate mastery and gradual mastery. The problems of both will now be examined.

STRUCTURAL SYLLABUSES FOR IMMEDIATE MASTERY

Ultimately a structural syllabus directed at immediate mastery will only work if the order in which the grammatical items are taught corresponds to the order in which the learners can learn them. In other words, the syllabus must satisfy the criterion of learnability. Designers of structural syllabuses have always acknowledged this, and learnability has always figured as one of the criteria of selection and grading. Mackey (1965), for instance, identified five factors that contributed to learnability: similarity (i.e., between the target language and the native language), clarity, brevity, regularity, and learning load. The notion of learnability that underlies these factors is a rational rather than a psycholinguistic (or empirical) one. It reflects an external account of what ought to be learnable.

To what extent does the ordering of items derived from these external criteria conform with the learner's 'built-in syllabus'? One way of answering this question is to compare the order of items in sample structural syllabuses with the natural order of acquisition reported in studies of L2 acquisition. If it can be shown that the orders do not match, the solution is simple — devise a syllabus where they do. It is doubtful whether such a solution is possible, however. L2 acquisition research has not investigated all the features that the learner will need to be taught, so there is only information relating to the acquisition of a fairly small number of grammatical items currently available. Also, there is uncertainty regarding research that has investigated the 'natural order' of acquisition. For example, a number of studies produced evidence that learners of different ages and with different first languages follow the same order of acquisition of a set of English grammatical morphemes (Krashen, 1977), but this research has been challenged on a number of grounds (see Hatch, 1978c). In particular, it is difficult to maintain the view that L2 acquisition involves the systematic mastery of discrete grammatical items, as this research appears to assume.

Another problem is that the grammatical items found in a structural syllabus do not have psycholinguistic validity. Bley-Vroman (1983) has argued convincingly that the categories of a descriptive grammar, from which the items of a structural syllabus are derived, bear no relation to the mental categories which learners construct in the process of learning a language. Learners appear to construct their own rules, many of which are transitional and hence do not correspond to any of the rules found in a reference grammar of the target language. For example, the sequence of acquisition for German word order rules (see Meisel, Clahsen, & Pienemann, 1981) contains a stage where adverb preposing occurs, as in Sentence 1.

1. *Heute wir gehen ins Kino.* (Today we go to the cinema.) Such a rule represents an advance on the previous stage during which adverbs, if used, only occur at the ends of utterances. However, the adverb-preposing rule results in an error because in the target language it obligates the application of a further rule, inversion:

2. *Heute gehen wir ins Kino.* (Today go we to the cinema.) This is a rule which the learner does not yet know.

This sentence illustrates how acquisition involves the construction of rules not found in the target language (i.e., adverb-preposing without inversion) and shows that progress can actually result in errors not evident at an earlier stage.

A third problem is that structural syllabuses treat each item as discrete and separate. It has been shown, however, that the acquisition of a new form can affect the organization of the learner's entire mental grammar (see Huebner, 1983). The rules that make up this grammar are interrelated in complex ways, so any change may involve not just an addition of a new form but the restructuring of the whole system (McLaughlin, 1990). This reorganization may not necessarily take place in accordance with the way the target language grammar is constructed. If the implicit knowledge system that a learner builds is viewed as a form-function network (Ellis, 1985; Rutherford, 1987), then the acquisition of a new form leads the learner not just to assign it a certain functional value but also to reassess the functional values assigned to forms previously acquired. It follows that the nature of the form-function system constructed at any one stage of development will be unique until the learner finally arrives at the target language grammar.

In short, it is difficult to see how a structural syllabus directed at the immediate mastery of grammatical items (defined as the ability to use the items accurately in production) can cope with these learnability issues.

STRUCTURAL SYLLABUSES FOR GRADUAL MASTERY

A case might still be made for the use of structural syllabuses as a basis for teaching implicit knowledge for use in production if it can be shown they are compatible with a view of acquisition as a process of gradual mastery. The structural syllabuses associated with the oral-situation approach were, in fact, based on this view of L2 acquisition. Palmer (1917), for example, distinguishes conscious and subconscious learning and clearly sees the former as a precursor of the latter, at least where adult learners are concerned. Palmer opposes a purely 'natural' method that caters to subconscious learning on the grounds that it is inefficient. He argues for 'conscious study of the microcosm' through the graded presentation of linguistic items. He believes it possible to guide the learner through a series of general stages involving (a) receiving knowledge, (b) fixing the knowledge in memory, and (c) developing the ability to use the knowledge as skill. In other words, Palmer adheres to a view of language learning similar to that of proponents of a strong interface theory. It is probably true to say that views close to those of Palmer underlie the continued use of structural syllabuses for teaching implicit knowledge today (see Ur, 1988).

How can a structural syllabus reflect the process by which learners achieve gradual mastery of linguistic features? Clearly a simple linear syllabus cannot do so. Learners may be able to receive a new feature and perhaps also fix the knowledge in memory, but it is unlikely that a single treatment will result in their developing the ability to use the knowledge as skill. One way around this problem might be to design a spiral syllabus. Howatt (1974) suggests that such a syllabus accords better with the natural process of learning because learners have their attention directed at the same items on several occasions but in different combinations and with different meanings. It is possible, therefore, that a spiral syllabus can cater to implicit knowledge.

The key question, however, is whether it is possible to guide the process by which explicit knowledge becomes implicit knowledge by means of a cyclical representation of grammatical items. According to the model of L2 acquisition shown in Figure 3, this is only possible if the presentation of an item coincides with the learner's readiness to acquire it. A spiral syllabus may increase the likelihood of this occurring, but it is still a hit-or-miss affair. The only way to guarantee the effectiveness of a structural syllabus directed at implicit knowledge is by ensuring it is compatible with the learner's internal syllabus, and this, as we have already seen, is problematic.

STRUCTURAL SYLLABUSES FOR COMPREHENSION

It is possible, however, that the problems of the structural syllabus directed at implicit knowledge can be overcome if the goal of the syllabus is to enable learners to comprehend rather than to produce the items within it. In this case, the teaching materials based on the syllabus would provide activities that enable learners to (a) hear sentences containing the structures listed in the syllabus and (b) identify the specific functions performed by the features (i.e., to establish form-meaning relationships). For example, to help learners comprehend the meaning of plural -*s*, they might be asked to listen to sentences such as *He put the books on the table* and *He gave his friend the pen* and to choose which pictures from a set of pictures correspond to the meanings of the sentences. The pictures for each sentence would include distracters (e.g., one showing a man putting a single book on the table or giving his friend two pens) as well as accurate representations of the sentences actually said. Such activities would be directed at helping the learner to notice new grammatical features in the input and the grammatical meanings they realize. Like traditional grammar materials, they would be specially contrived to focus the learner's attention on specific items, but they would differ from them in that they would not require the learner to produce sentences containing the items.

Pienemann's (1985) distinction between *input for comprehension* and *input for production* provides a rationale for such a syllabus. Pienemann argues that the developmental sequence through which learners pass reflects the gradual mastery of a series of processing operations responsible for language production. His own proposal regarding syllabus design is as follows:

1. Do not demand a learning process which is impossible at a given stage (i.e. order teaching objectives in line with stages of acquisition).

2. But do not introduce deviant forms.

3. The general input may contain structures which were not introduced for production. (p. 63)

This constitutes a serious attempt to suggest how a structural syllabus can take account of learnability, but it runs up against a number of objections — our knowledge of developmental sequences remains patchy and relates primarily to formal features of the language (i.e., little is known about how learners build form-function networks). It is not clear how teachers are supposed to identify the developmental stages which individual learners have reached or whether this can be practically achieved, and it requires teachers to construct teaching programs tailored to the psycholinguistic needs of individual learners, which, as Lightbown (1985b) has pointed out, may be unrealistic in many teaching situations [1]. These objections all arise because Pienemann views the primary goal of a structural syllabus as that of providing input for production. They do not appear to apply if the syllabus is directed at providing input for comprehension. Pienemann suggests that such input can be allowed to arise naturally in the course of communication, but he does not consider the possibility that it might be contrived through formal instruction.

It is possible, however, to envisage an approach where input for comprehension is carefully planned and structured to ensure that the learner is systematically exposed to specific grammatical features. This proposal is a modest one in the sense that the goal is no longer the development of full implicit knowledge of the L2 but only the facilitation of intake. Although this constitutes a substantially reduced goal for structural syllabuses, it is nevertheless still a significant one. Chaudron (1985) has argued that intake 'has important status in second language research' (p. 1), and a similar position can be adopted with regard to its importance for language pedagogy. There is a need, as Chaudron emphasizes, for investigating precisely which factors influence intake. One way in which this can be undertaken is through studies of how formal instruction affects learners' ability to notice and comprehend specific grammatical items (see VanPatten & Cadierno, 1991, for an example of such a study).

SUMMARY

We have considered two views of the structural syllabus — one that sees it as a basis for teaching accurate production and the other that sees it as a basis for facilitating intake through the comprehension of specific grammatical items. In the case of the former, the structural syllabus can serve as a device for bringing about the immediate mastery of grammatical items. We have seen that such a view is not compatible with what is known about the way learners acquire an L2. It can also serve as a device for ensuring the gradual mastery of items. We have seen that this view also runs up against the problem of learnability, even if the syllabus recycles the items. In both cases the difficulties arise as a result of treating the structural syllabus as an instrument for teaching learners to produce grammatical items correctly. It has been suggested that these difficulties might be overcome if the goal becomes the comprehension rather than the production of grammatical items.

In this case, the goal of the syllabus is intake facilitation rather than the full development of implicit knowledge.

The Structural Syllabus and Explicit Knowledge

Another way in which the problem of learnability can be side-stepped is by making the goal of a structural syllabus explicit rather than implicit knowledge. In other words, the syllabus serves as a basis for developing a conscious rather than intuitive understanding of grammatical rules, and there is no expectancy that learners will be able to use the knowledge they have learned in fluent production. This amounts to a reversal of Moulton's slogan, cited above — we should teach about the language, not the language.

This proposal rests on two principal assumptions:

1. The acquisition of explicit knowledge contributes to the development of L2 proficiency.

2. The acquisition of explicit knowledge can take place as an accumulation of discrete entities.

Assumption 1 derives from and is supported by the weak-interface model discussed earlier. Assumption 2 is justified if it is accepted that explicit knowledge consists of a body of conscious knowledge about isolated grammatical items and rules, a view adopted by many learners, as this quotation from Moore (1989) illustrates:

> As a learner I have two major problems to overcome — accumulating a large number of partial entities, whether they be lexical items, grammatical rules, or whatever; secondly, finding opportunities to try out combinations of them, in both structured and unstructured situations. Once I have acquired, say, two thousand partial entities, I am better placed to communicate than if I have acquired only a hundred. (p.157)

As Moore recognizes, accumulating the 'facts of language' is not the whole of acquisition, but it can help to get the learner started.

There are educational as well as psycholinguistic arguments in favour of teaching grammatical facts. Breen (1985) addresses the question of what is authentic for the social situation of the classroom and argues that because the *raison d'etre* of this situation is language learning, the content of the teaching program should be drawn from the 'culture of the classroom'. Breen's idea is that the communicative and social aspects of learning should serve as content for language work. One source of such content is the linguistic and pragmatic systems of the language. A syllabus that isolates various formal and functional features with a view to making these the topics of learning activities might accord with the expectations of many learners. Grammar constitutes a serious and intellectually challenging content.

What will a syllabus for explicit knowledge consist of? On what basis should the selection and grading of the grammatical content proceed? We will consider somewhat briefly a number of possibilities.

Perhaps the most obvious one is to make use of the criteria which have been traditionally used. Widdowson (1968) identifies two general principles that syllabus designers have drawn on: (a) relative difficulty and (b) usefulness (i.e., the coverage value of an item and the classroom value of the item). However, as Widdowson points out, these two principles are often in conflict as what is useful is often not relatively simple. It is not clear, therefore, to what extent they can be applied in a systematic manner and Halliday, McIntosh, and Strevens (1964) are probably right in claiming that it is 'practical teaching experience' that often serves as a basis for selection and grading, although this rather begs the question as to what this actually consists of. Certainly, there is considerable agreement regarding both what structures to teach (at least in general courses) and in what order they should be taught (see Yalden, 1983).

One way in which these traditional criteria might be sharpened is by using the insights obtained from the study of linguistic markedness [2] in language learning. This constitutes the second possibility. The notion of markedness is not itself new — adherents of structural grading have long worked with a similar notion to that underlying much current discussion of the concept (see Mackey's, 1965, discussion of 'regularity', for example), but recent studies do give greater precision to the concept. For example, the NP + PP pattern after dative verbs such as give in sentences like *Bob gave a gift to Isabel* can be considered less marked than the NP + NP pattern after the same verbs in sentences like *Bob gave Isabel a gift* on a number of grounds. The latter sentence is more transparent, the integrity of the verb and the direct object is maintained, and it is more regular (i.e., just about all dative verbs permit the NP + PP pattern, but only some permit the NP + NP pattern). This kind of information can be used to make decisions regarding which linguistic feature to introduce early and which late. But it is not yet clear how this information should be used. It can be argued that learners generally find it easier to handle unmarked features, so these should be introduced first, but it has also been suggested that learners will be able to project their knowledge of marked features to associated unmarked features (see Eckman, 1985), which constitutes an argument in favor of focusing attention on marked features. Also, unmarked features may be learned by most learners naturally and, therefore, do not require explicit attention. In contrast, marked features are often not acquired (see Bardovi-Harlig & Bofman, 1989; Long, 1988) unless the learners' conscious attention is directed at them. On balance, the arguments favor the selection of marked rather than unmarked features in a syllabus for explicit knowledge.

A third alternative for organizing the content of a structural syllabus is derived from another old idea — that of remedial teaching. The content of a remedial language program is established through the identification and description of learners' errors. It rests on the simple idea that formal language teaching will be more efficient if it concentrates on what the learner has not learned rather than on teaching the whole grammar. However, as Corder (1981) has noted, there is no reason why remedial teaching should work any better than initial teaching unless the psycholinguistic causes of errors are taken into account. Once again, then, we seem to come up against the learnability problem. In the case of a structural syllabus designed to teach explicit knowledge, this problem is side-stepped, however, if, as we have argued, it only arises where implicit knowledge is involved. A remedial syllabus might consist of a list of structures which have been shown to be problematic to either learners in general or, better still, to the particular group of learners for whom the syllabus is intended. This constitutes a record of the potential deviations and serves, therefore, as a checklist. Armed with this list, the teacher would need to observe the learners' errors in order to establish whether the potential deviations actually occur in their production and, if so, when. The teacher would then devise activities to draw the learners' attention to errors and help them compare the errors to the correct target language forms.

To sum up, the aim of a structural syllabus for explicit knowledge is to raise learners' consciousness about how the target language grammar works. As Larsen-Freeman (1991) has pointed out, this will involve (a) drawing attention to how grammatical forms are formed, (b) developing an understanding of how particular grammatical forms signal particular grammatical meanings, and (c) helping learners realize what constitutes appropriate use of the forms in context. The rationale for this use of a structural syllabus is that explicit knowledge may help learners to notice features in the input that they might otherwise ignore and also to notice the gap between the input and their own interlanguage productions. The content of such a syllabus might be determined on the basis of traditional criteria for the selection and grading of grammatical structures, by the principled selection of marked linguistic features, or remedially, by identifying gaps in the learners' implicit knowledge through error analysis.

CONCLUSION: CONSCIOUSNESS-RAISING AND THE STRUCTURAL SYLLABUS

This chapter has sought to present a new rationale for the structural syllabus. The need for this has arisen from the recognition that the traditional rationale, which derives from behaviorist learning theory, is inadequate because it cannot provide a satisfactory solution to the learnability problem. The new rationale rests on the claim that grammar teaching should be directed at consciousness-raising rather than practice (see Fotos & Ellis, 1991). Consciousness-raising refers to a deliberate attempt on the part of the teacher to make the learners aware of specific features of the L2; it entails an attempt to instil an understanding of the formal and functional properties of these features by helping the learners develop a cognitive representation of them. *Practice*, on the other hand, involves an attempt to supply the learner with plentiful opportunities for producing targeted structures in controlled and free language use in order to develop fully proceduralized implicit knowledge. It is not intended, however, to suggest that practice has no role at all in language teaching. Practice may still be important as a means of helping learners gain control over formulaic knowledge, and it probably also has some place in the teaching of pronunciation.

What is being challenged here is the traditional role it has played in the teaching of grammatical items.

In accordance with the preceding discussion, two kinds of consciousness-raising can be identified. In the case of *consciousness-raising for comprehension*, the aim is to focus the learners' attention on the meaning (s) performed by specific grammatical properties. It has been suggested that this is tantamount to helping the learner to intake — a necessary (but not sufficient) step for internalization of the feature as implicit knowledge. This type of consciousness-raising will be achieved by means of activities that induce a learner to notice and understand the feature in the input (i.e., activities that require reception rather than production in the L2).

In the case of *consciousness-raising for explicit knowledge*, the aim is to help the learner learn about a particular grammatical feature by developing an explicit representation of how it works in the target language. In many cases, this will involve teaching the learner the metalanguage needed to talk about grammatical rules. It has been hypothesized that explicit knowledge also aids the process of intake formation by facilitating noticing and noticing-the-gap. This type of consciousness-raising can be achieved by means of traditional grammar explanation of the kind found in the grammar-translation method. Another way, however, is to make use of problem-solving tasks that supply the learners with the data they need to discover the rule for themselves. An example of such a task is provided in Fotos and Ellis (1991). If such tasks are carried out in the target language, they serve the double purpose of raising learners' consciousness about a specific grammatical item while providing opportunities for communicating in the target language — the learners will be communicating about grammar.

Traditionally, a structural syllabus has been used as the basis for designing a complete language course. This was possible because the goal was procedural implicit knowledge, which underlies the actual ability to use the L2 in communication. However, if the goal of a structural syllabus is the lesser one of consciousness-raising, it can no longer serve as a complete course, as the ultimate goal of most courses will continue to be the ability to use the L2 in production. It follows that the structural syllabus can only provide part of a course. It will need to be complemented by other kinds of syllabuses that are based on the provision of input of the kind that has been hypothesized to promote implicit knowledge — a functional or a task-based syllabus, for example (see Long & Crookes, 1991). The precise relationship between the structural component and these other components of an overall syllabus remains to be decided. In restating the case for a structural syllabus, therefore, we have also acknowledged its reduced value. The new structural syllabus will serve as a facilitator rather than as a prime mover of L2 acquisition.

Finally, it needs to be acknowledged that many of the claims of both the model of L2 acquisition shown in Figure 3 and the pedagogical arguments based on it have only limited support from existing empirical research. Clearly, there is a need to demonstrate that the various claims that have been made regarding consciousness-raising are valid. However, I am assuming here that it is legitimate to advance pedagogical proposals without waiting for the necessary empirical support to be collected. Indeed, empirical L2 studies provide only one way of validating such proposals. The other, which may well be more important, is the well-established method of trying them out in the classroom and using practical experience as a basis for rejecting, accepting, or refining them. At the moment, the best that can be said is that these claims are compatible with the L2 research that has been carried out to date. The essential points are (a) that it is premature to dismiss the structural syllabus as a basis for L2 acquisition and (b) that considerable modification of the role traditionally given to such a syllabus is likely to be needed.

ACKNOWLEDGMENTS

I would like to thank two anonymous TESOL Quarterly readers, whose constructive comments helped me greatly to sharpen my arguments.

Notes

[1] Currently, Pienemann and his associates have developed sophisticated computer software to facilitate diagnosis. It is not clear to me how practical this will be in many teaching situations, as it necessitates teachers' obtaining reliable data regarding the structures learners are able to perform at any one stage of development — a painstaking and time-consuming process.

[2] Markedness is not an altogether clear notion as it has been defined in different ways. In one definition a feature is considered marked if it can be shown to be less common in the world's languages than some other, related feature (i.e., typological markedness). In another definition, a feature is considered marked if its use is in some way more restricted than another related feature (e. g., an is more marked than a because it occurs only before nouns and adjectives that begin with a vowel). Universal Grammar supplies yet another definition of markedness. The concept of markedness is perhaps best considered at this point in time as of potential rather than realized value to the designer of a structural course.

Chapter 12

Interpretation Tasks for Grammar Teaching

This chapter is based on article that appeared in *TESOL Quarterly, Vol. 29, pp.87–105.*

INTRODUCTION

Although applied linguists now largely agree that L2 classroom acquisition occurs when learners participate in interaction that affords comprehensible input and output (Krashen, 1985; Long, 1983b; Pica, 1992; Swain, 1985), they have also recognized that higher levels of grammatical competence require direct intervention in interlanguage development. A case has been made for supplementing activities designed to focus learners' attention on message conveyance with activities that also require a focus on form (R. Ellis, 1993a; VanPatten, 1993; White, 1987). How, then, should this be done? What kinds of grammar teaching will work best for acquisition?

Traditionally, grammar teaching has been conducted by means of activities that give learners opportunities to produce sentences containing the targeted structure. These activities can consist of mechanical pattern-practice drills of the kind found in the audiolingual method or situational grammar exercises in which the target structure is contextualized in terms of some real or imaginary situation (see Ur, 1988, for examples). The underlying assumption of both types of activity is that having learners produce the structure correctly and repeatedly helps them learn it.

This traditional approach faces a number of problems. First, second language acquisition (SLA) research (e.g., Ellis, 1989; Pienemann, 1984) has shown that learners pass through a number of stages on route to acquiring the ability to produce a target language structure and that grammar teaching often does not alter this sequence. Teaching learners to produce a target structure that they are not ready to produce may not work. Second, asking learners to produce grammatical structures they find difficult and then correcting them when they make mistakes may increase their anxiety and result in a psycho-affective block to learning anything (Krashen, 1982).

An alternative approach to grammar teaching is to design activities that focus learners' attention on a targeted structure in the input and that enable them to identify and comprehend the meaning(s) of this structure. This approach emphasizes input processing for comprehension rather than output processing for production and requires the use of what I have termed interpretation tasks to replace traditional production tasks (R. Ellis, 1993b).

This chapter describes and illustrates interpretation tasks for grammar teaching. I will begin, however, with a brief examination of the psycholinguistic rationale for a comprehension-based approach to grammar teaching.

A PSYCHOLINGUISTIC RATIONALE

Figure 1 presents a model of L2 acquisition (see R. Ellis, 1990; 1993a). This model, designed to address the role of formal instruction in acquisition, is based on a distinction between implicit and explicit L2

Figure 1: A Model of L2 Acquisition Incorporating a Weak Interface Position

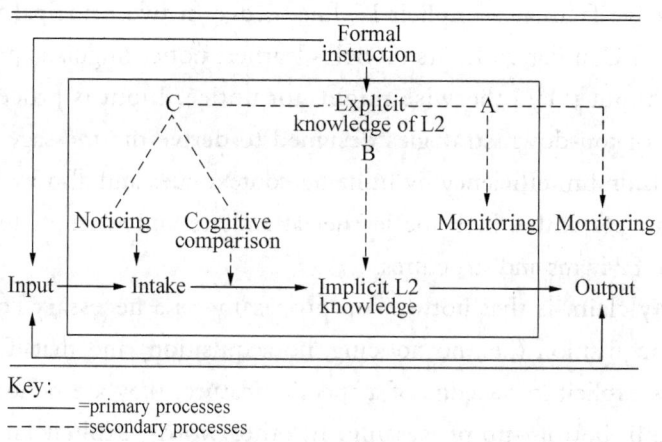

Key:
————— =primary processes
– – – – =secondary processes

knowledge. Implicit knowledge is typically manifest in some form of naturally occurring language behavior (e.g., a conversation). It is intuitive and, therefore, exists in unanalyzed form. It can be abstract and structured (i.e., rule based) or chunk-like (i.e., formulaic). Explicit knowledge typically manifests itself in some form of problem-solving activity (e.g., a sentence transformation exercise), but it can also be accessed in natural language use that allows time for monitoring, as represented by A in Figure 1. Explicit knowledge is held consciously and is stored in analyzed form. Unlike implicit knowledge, therefore, it is reportable.

The model is a weak-interface model. That is, it hypothesizes that explicit knowledge of L2 items and structures may convert directly into implicit L2 knowledge (see B in Figure 1) but, as the dotted lines are intended to suggest, usually does not. This position is grounded in research which indicates that learners do not bypass developmental sequences (which I assume to reflect implicit knowledge) as a result of practicing target structures (Ellis, 1989; Pienemann, 1984; 1989; Schumann, 1978b).

In addition to this direct relationship between explicit and implicit L2 knowledge, the model hypothesizes an indirect relationship, and it is this that is most important. The model proposes that explicit L2 knowledge facilitates implicit L2 knowledge in two principal ways, as shown in C in Figure 1. First, it helps learners notice linguistic properties of the input they otherwise might not notice. Input is processed by means of top-down strategies designed to derive the message content with maximum efficiency by utilizing context cues and also by bottom-up strategies with which the learner attends to and attempts to decode specific L2 items and structures.

My claim is that bottom-up processing is a necessary condition of L2 acquisition (i.e., no noticing, no acquisition) and that if learners possess explicit knowledge of a specific feature, they are better able to engage in bottom-up processing. In other words, explicit knowledge helps learners obtain intake (i.e., to process grammatical information for short-term and maybe medium-term memory). This hypothesis owes much to Faerch and Kasper's (1986) views concerning the importance of bottom-up processing for acquisition and to Schmidt's (1990;1994) ideas about the role of consciousness in language learning. Faerch and Kasper (1986) suggest that whereas effective listening involves the use of top-down processes, where learners utilize contextual information and existing knowledge to understand what is said, the acquisition of new linguistic forms may require the use of bottom-up processing, where learners pay attention to forms that are problematic to them. Schmidt argues that no learning is possible without some degree of consciousness. He distinguishes between intentionality and attention, arguing that 'while the intention to learn is not always crucial to learning, attention (voluntary or involuntary) to the material to be learned is' (Schmidt, 1992, p. 209). Neither Faerch and Kasper nor Schmidt are suggesting that learners attend consistently to form when they are communicating. Clearly that is not possible if communication is to proceed smoothly. At certain points, however, their attention may be directed away from comprehending for meaning to attending to and subjectively noticing specific language forms.

Second, intake is also enhanced when learners carry out a second operation-comparing what they have noticed in the input with what they currently produce in their own output. This kind of cognitive comparison [1] is hypothesized to help learners identify what it is that they still need to learn. It can serve two functions: It can help learners 'notice the gap' (Schmidt & Frota, 1986, p. 310) between the input and their own output, and it can give the learner evidence that an existing hypothesis regarding a target language structure is the correct one. In other words, cognitive comparisons serve as a mechanism for disconfirming or confirming hypotheses in implicit knowledge.

This model allows us to identify a number of processes [2] involved in learning and using grammatical features.

• *Interpretation*

This is the process by which learners endeavor to comprehend input and in so doing pay attention to specific linguistic features and their meanings. It involves noticing and cognitive comparison and results in intake.

• *Integration*

Integration occurs when learners are able to incorporate intake into their developing interlanguage systems (i.e., their implicit knowledge). Not all intake is so accommodated, as learners are only able to incorporate features for which they are ready [3]. Integration may also be accompanied by restructuring (McLaughlin, 1990). That is, the incorporation of new linguistic material may cause learners to reorganize the information in their existing interlanguage systems.

• *Production*

Production typically relies on implicit knowledge (cf. Krashen's Monitor Model), but this can be supplemented by explicit knowledge through monitoring (see A in Figure 1). Production does not serve as the primary means for acquiring new linguistic knowledge although it may help learners to gain mastery over features that have already entered their interlanguage (i.e., it can lead to greater accuracy).

One implication of this model for pedagogy is that grammar teaching might usefully focus on interpretation. As VanPatten (1993) puts it:

> Given the important role of input and input processing in second language acquisition, it is reasonable to wonder whether or not explicit instruction in grammar that involves a focus on input is more appropriate than traditional approaches to grammar instruction where learners are engaged in production.

Although the model also affords other roles for grammar teaching (e.g., consciousness raising to develop learners' explicit knowledge and production practice to help learners use already learned features more accurately), it suggests that teachers might profitably try to focus learners' attention on noticing and understanding specific grammatical features in input, as it is by this means that the acquisition of new features gets started. Before we consider how this might be done, however, we will briefly examine what empirical evidence there is in favor of interpretation-based grammar teaching.

SOME EMPIRICAL EVIDENCE

Empirical support for an input-based approach to teaching grammar can be found in the early studies of the comprehension approach (see Winitz, 1981). A general finding of these studies was that beginning learners who were exposed to input they were required to comprehend but not asked to produce outperformed learners following a more traditional, production-based program in tests of listening and reading comprehension (as might be expected) and did as well and often better in tests of speaking and writing.

A good example of a comprehension-based approach is Total Physical Response (TPR) (see Asher, 1977). This method follows a structural syllabus but does not involve production practice, at least in the early stages. Instead learners are asked to perform actions to demonstrate their understanding of commands that have been specially contrived to teach the structures. Asher has conducted a number of studies (e.g., Asher, Kusudo, & de la Torre, 1974), involving both children and adults, to evaluate the effectiveness of TPR in comparison to other, production-based methods, in particular, the audiolingual method. The results he reports demonstrate that TPR leads not only to better comprehension and production but also to enhanced motivation and greater persistence in language learning [4]. In a review of comprehension-based approaches,Gary (1978) identifies four main advantages: (a) a cognitive advantage (i.e., better L2 learning), (b) an affective advantage (i.e., the avoidance of the stress and embarrassment that often accompanies trying to produce sentences in front of others), (c) an efficiency advantage (i.e., a comprehension-based approach works equally well with low and high aptitude learners), and (d) a utility advantage (i.e., teaching listening skills helps a learner become functional in using the L2 and also enables a learner to continue their language study independently of the teacher).

Although evaluation studies of comprehension-based approaches to language teaching demonstrate their effectiveness in promoting overall L2 proficiency, they do not show (or try to show) that comprehending input enables learners to acquire specific grammatical features. A number of recent studies, however, provide evidence of just this. Doughty (1991) investigated the effects of instruction on adult learners' acquisition of relative clauses. The instruction took the form of a computer-assisted reading lesson, based on a text specially designed to include examples of the target structure. One group received help in understanding the text by means of expansions or clarifications of sentences containing relative clauses. A second group received explicit instruction on relative clauses. A third control group just read the sentences. Doughty found that the first and second groups improved in their ability to produce relative clauses to a significantly greater extent than the control group. She also found that the first group outperformed both the second and third groups in a test that measured overall comprehension of the passage. In other words, the meaning-oriented instruction directed at making sentences containing the target structure comprehensible seemed to work best because it led to both acquisition of the target structure and to better overall comprehension.

VanPatten and Cadierno (1993) compared traditional production-oriented practice with listening practice that required learners to process, specially contrived input. The study involved university-level Spanish learners and focused on object-verb-subject word order and clitic object pronouns in Spanish. They found that the learners who were asked to process input by means of interpretation-based grammar tasks outperformed those taught by means of production-based practice on a test that measured comprehension of the target structures and, more surprisingly, did just as well on a test that measured ability to produce the target structures accurately. These results were repeated in follow-up tests administered 1 month later. VanPatten and Cadierno suggest that whereas the production-based instruction only contributed to explicit knowledge, the comprehension-based instruction created intake which the learners were able to integrate into their interlanguage systems (i.e., it led to implicit knowledge).

A somewhat similar study was carried out by Tuz (1992) on Japanese university students studying general English. In this case the target structure was word order with psychological verbs such as like, attract, and disgust (see next section). Both groups made use of a set of pictures depicting events involving psychological verbs, similar to those found in Activity 1 of the materials provided in the Appendix. In the case of the control group, the pictures were used as stimuli for sentence production, whereas in the experimental group, they were used to practice comprehension of sentences containing psychological verbs. The results of this study were even more striking than those of VanPatten and Cadierno. Again, the learners receiving the comprehension-based instruction outperformed those receiving the production-based instruction on a comprehension test of the structure, but, in addition, they also outperformed them on a production test. The interpretation tasks used in this study enabled the learners to develop the kind of knowledge needed to both comprehend and produce the target structure and did so to a much greater extent than the production tasks. Unfortunately, the study had no follow-up test, so it is not possible to say to what extent this advantage was maintained over time.

The research to date, therefore, suggests that comprehension-based instruction not only results in greater overall proficiency but is also more effective in enabling learners to acquire specific grammatical structures.

One caveat is in order, however. The tests used in both the early studies of comprehension-based language teaching and in the later studies investigating specific grammatical structures were of the kind that allowed for the use of explicit L2 knowledge through monitoring. VanPatten and Cadierno's (1993) claim that comprehension-based instruction results in implicit L2 knowledge is speculative, therefore. Before we can be sure of this, we need to investigate whether the knowledge obtained through comprehension-based instruction can be used in spontaneous communication, where there is little opportunity to employ explicit knowledge through monitoring.

DESIGNING INTERPRETATION TASKS

Interpretation tasks have the following goals:

1. To enable learners to identify the meaning(s) realized by a specific grammatical feature (i.e., to help them carry out a form-function mapping). In this case, the goal is grammar comprehension, to be distinguished from what might be termed message comprehension, which can take place without the learner having to attend to the grammatical form. For example, on hearing the sentence:

I'd like three bottles please.

a learner may be able to understand that bottles is plural in meaning without noticing the -s morpheme or understanding its function.

2. To enhance input (Sharwood Smith, 1993) in such a way that learners are induced to notice a grammatical feature that otherwise they might ignore. In other words, interpretation tasks are designed to facilitate noticing.

3. To enable learners to carry out the kind of cognitive comparison that has been hypothesized to be important for interlanguage development.

Learners need to be encouraged to notice the gap between the way a particular form works to convey meaning in the input and how they are using the same form or, alternatively, how they convey the meaning realized by the form when they communicate. One way of fostering this is to draw learners' attention to the kinds of errors that learners typically make.

Interpretation tasks can be devised as sequences of activities that reflect these three operations. That is, in the first instance, learners are required to comprehend input that has been specially contrived to induce learners to attend to the meaning of a specific grammatical structure, followed by a task that induces learners to pay careful attention to the important properties of the target feature, and finally by a task that encourages the kind of cognitive comparison learners will have to perform ultimately on their own output. This proposal is, in fact, not so different from an earlier proposal of Ingram, Nord and Dragt (1975). They suggested that the development of listening fluency required learners to pass through three phases: (a) the Decoding Phase, when learners were invited to respond to stimuli by selecting from alternative answers, (b) the Auditory-Response Phase, where learners were required to anticipate what was going to be said, and (c) the Self-Monitoring Phase, where learners were asked to identify errors or incongruities. (a) and (c) resemble the processes of noticing and error-identification. However, (b) appears to involve the kind of top-down processing involved in message comprehension rather than the bottom-up processing needed for grammar comprehension.

Two factors are important in selecting target structures — problematicity and learnability. Problematicity can be determined by examining samples of the learners' output in order to determine (a) which grammatical structures are not yet being used (i.e., the forms have not been acquired) and, also, more crucially, (b) the forms that are being used but incorrectly because their target function(s) has not yet been acquired. This will call for some kind of error analysis (Corder, 1974).

The problems so identified become candidates for instruction, the final selection of which will need to take account of learnability. This concerns whether the learner is able to integrate new grammatical information into the interlanguage system. In the case of problems resulting from lack of knowledge of target forms it will be very difficult to decide when a particular group of learners are ready to acquire a specific new form. However, if the new learning required is that of assigning a different function to an already acquired form, learnability may be less of a problem. The best candidates for interpretation tasks, therefore, may be structures for which the form is known but the meaning(s) realized by the form is not [5]. Many learners, for example, will be familiar with the simple form of regular verbs (e.g., come/comes) but not yet use this form to express general truths (e.g., *Iron rusts if it gets wet* .) or futurity (e.g., *I fly to Tokyo next week*.).

A good example of a problematic structure for many intermediate learners is what Burt (1975) has referred to as psychological predicate constructions. Tuz's (1992) study demonstrated that Japanese learners do have considerable difficulty in both comprehending and producing sentences with such verbs. Burt's article suggests that this difficulty may be one that learners with other L1s also experience. A psychological verb (e.g., love, prefer, bore, and worry) is one that refers to some affective state. These typically occur in transitive constructions in which one noun phrase functions as experiencer and the other as a stimulus. The following might be considered the unmarked order:

Experiencer + verb + stimulus

(e.g., *Mary loves cats.*)

whereas the more marked order[6] is:

Stimulus + verb + experiencer
(e.g., *Mary worries her mother.*)

The learning problem arises in the marked order. Learners overgeneralize the unmarked pattern, thus misunderstanding sentences that take the marked order. The above sentence, for example, may be understood as Mary worries about her mother. It can also result in production errors, as when a learner says:

* He doesn't worry the cat.

when intending to say *The cat doesn't worry him.*

Burt suggests that psychological predicate constructions are an example of global grammar in that they affect overall sentence organization and seriously interfere with communication. As such, they are prime candidates for instruction. To overcome the problem that they pose, learners need to (a) recognize that psychological verbs fall into two classes according to the order of the noun phrases that function as experiencer and stimulus and (b) discover which verbs belong to which class. Given that intermediate learners will already have acquired a knowledge of transitive constructions and will already be using many psychological verbs, the problem can be considered to be primarily one of function rather than form.

An interpretation task for teaching marked psychological verbs is included in the Appendix. This begins with an activity designed to practice students' comprehension of sentences containing a number of psychological verbs, some common and some not so common. In this activity, students are required to assess the truthfulness of a set of sentences in relation to pictures. The input is oral. For example, the students hear a sentence such as:

She loved his hairstyle.

and evaluate it in relation to a picture which shows a woman looking admiringly at a young man with an exotic hairdo. The sentences are contrived in such a way that there are pronominal clues as to the correct meaning. For example, the pronoun 'his' in the above sentence indicates that the sentence is about a man's hairstyle, not a woman's. In this way, students can arrive at the correct interpretation of sentences even if they are not sure of which group a particular verb falls in.

Another feature of Activity 1 is that learners are allowed to request repetition of sentences. This is to encourage the process of negotiating input, which a number of researchers (e.g., Long, 1983b) have hypothesized is important for comprehension and acquisition. This activity is designed to have students grapple initially with meaning while encouraging them to pay attention to the syntactic relations between words.

The second activity is more analytic. It focuses students' attention on the experience in sentences containing both unmarked and marked psychological verbs. In this case the input is written so as to allow time for students to reflect on the sentences. They are asked to draw arrows to show who or what experiences the feeling described by the verb. For example if the verb is 'like' the arrow will need to go from the subject of the sentence to the verb:

Sometimes people like dogs.

whereas if the verb is 'disgust', the arrow will need to go from the object of the sentence to the verb:

Sometimes people disgust dogs.

This activity has a consciousness-raising function. That is, it seeks to make students aware of the grammatical difference between psychological verbs such as 'like' and 'disgust'. It can be extended by other consciousness-raising activities (see Ellis, 1994c). For example, students might be asked to classify the verbs in the sentences they are exposed to into two groups according to whether the experience is the grammatical subject or object. The teacher might also like to provide an explicit explanation of the difference between the two verb groups.

The third activity requires attention to both the target form and the meaning of a set of sentences. VanPatten (1993) distinguishes between referential and affective or learner-centered activities. The former call for an objective interpretation of sentences, whereas the latter ask for a more personalized response. Thus, although Activities 1 and 2 are referential in nature, Activity 3 is learner-centered. The students, for example, are asked to reveal something about their personal responses to attributes of women and men. If they read a sentence such as:

> *Tall women frighten me.*

and evaluate it as true, partly true, or not true for them. If time permits, the teacher can use the students' responses in this activity to carry out a survey of what types of men/women the students feel positive and negative about.

The final activity — Activity 4 — focuses students' attention on the difference between the correct way of using marked psychological verbs and the incorrect way. This is done by means of a dialogue which the students listen to. They hear an imaginary language learner (Koji) attempt to explain his reaction to different types of women to a native-speaking friend. However, he has not yet learned that with marked psychological verbs the experience is the grammatical object rather than the subject. The result is that he produces such sentences as:

> * *I frighten tall women.*

when he means to say:

> *Tall women frighten me.*

His friend helps him by rephrasing the sentences correctly. The students' task is to identify the incorrect sentences Koji produces and work out what he should have said.[7]

This task illustrates a number of general principles for the design of interpretation tasks in general. These are:

1. Learners should be required to process the target structure, not to produce it.

2. An interpretation activity consists of a stimulus to which learners must make some kind of response.

3. The stimulus can take the form of spoken or written input.

4. The response can take various forms (e.g., indicate true-false, check a box, select the correct picture, draw a diagram, perform an action) but in each case the response will be either completely nonverbal or minimally verbal.

5. The activities in the task can be sequenced to require first attention to meaning, then noticing the form and function of the grammatical structure, and finally error identification.

6. As a result of completing the task, the learners should have arrived at an understanding of how the target form is used to perform a particular function or functions in communication (i.e., they must have undertaken a form-function mapping).

7. Learners can benefit from the opportunity to negotiate the input they hear or read.

8. Interpretation tasks should require learners to make a personal response (i.e., relate the input to their own lives) as well as a referential response.

9. As a result of completing the task, learners should have been made aware of common learner errors involving the target structure as well as correct usage.

10. Interpretation grammar teaching requires the provision of immediate and explicit feedback on the correctness of the students' responses.

However, the extent to which each principle is essential in the sense that it contributes to task-effectiveness or affects learning outcomes remains to be seen.

CONCLUSION

A number of applied linguists (e.g., Krashen, 1982; Prabhu, 1987) have argued in favor of what I term a zero position where grammar teaching is concerned.[8] That is, they have proposed that attempts to teach grammar should be abandoned and learners allowed to develop their interlanguages naturally by engaging in communication in the L2. This position is motivated by research showing that learners progress along a natural sequence of development for grammatical structures, which direct instruction is unable to circumvent. This chapter has proposed an approach to grammar teaching that is compatible with how learners learn grammar. Interlanguage development can be more readily influenced by manipulating input than output, an approach that requires interpretation tasks that cause learners to attend to specific grammatical properties in the input, to identify and understand the meanings they convey, and to compare the form-function mappings of the target language with those that characterize the interim stages of learners' own interlanguage development.

Interpretation tasks offer teachers the chance to intervene directly in interlanguage development. But they do not guarantee that their intervention will be successful because intake may not become part of implicit L2 knowledge. Nor is it the case that all grammar teaching should be comprehension-based. There may be a role for other forms of grammar teaching, such as consciousness-raising (Ellis, 1994c) and perhaps, also, production-based instruction as a way of improving learners' accuracy in the use of target language grammatical forms they have already acquired. Interpretation tasks are proposed as just one — albeit a highly promising one — of several ways of tackling grammar instruction.

Finally, the emphasis this chapter has placed on grammar teaching is not meant to suggest that there is no room for tasks that invite learners to make a free selection from whatever current linguistic resources are available to them (e.g., information-gap tasks). A complete language program will include a variety of tasks that invite both a focus on form and a focus on message conveyance.

Notes

[1] The term cognitive comparison replaces the term noticing the gap used in previously published versions of this model (see R. Ellis, 1993a). This is because this term better captures the fact that learners need to notice when their own output is the same as the input as well as when it is different.

[2] VanPatten (1993) has identified a very similar set of processes. He refers to them as input processing, accommodation and restructuring, and monitoring, access, retrieval, speech accommodation.

[3] There are various ways of explicating what is meant by readiness. Pienemann and Johnston (1987), for example, suggest that the acquisition of developmental grammatical features is only possible if learners have developed the prerequisite processing operations.

[4] Asher's studies evaluating TPR should be treated with some caution. They only examined beginning learners and typically did not include follow-up tests. It is not certain, therefore, whether TPR is equally effective with more advanced learners or whether the advantages are long term.

[5] It may not be necessary to totally exclude problems resulting from ignorance of form, however, if the instructional aim is not to effect a change in the learner's interlanguage (i.e., long-term L2 memory) but the lesser one of facilitating intake (i.e. short-term memory). In this case, learnability may not be an issue and the choice of target structures can be determined solely on the grounds of problematicity. It remains to be seen, however, whether learnability is only an issue where integration is concerned (as I suspect) or whether it also applies to noticing and comprehending.

[6] The grounds for considering experiencer + verb + stimulus unmarked are (a) some of the most common psychological verbs in English function in this way (e.g., like, enjoy, want), and (b) these verbs do not easily permit the alternative pattern (e.g., *The book was wanted by Mary*). However, psychological verbs that permit the stimulus + verb + experiencer pattern also

easily permit the alternative pattern (e.g., *Mary worries John - John worries about Mary*).

[7] It can be argued that learners will need subsequent opportunities to try to use psychological verbs in communicative production tasks (e.g., information-gap tasks). This is when they need to be encouraged to pay close attention to their own output. One way in which this might be achieved is through focused communication tasks (see Chapter 4).

[8] Krashen (1982) does allow for some grammar teaching — for what he terms subject matter. This, however, has a very limited place and is only for students who 'are interested in the study of language per se' (p.119).

APPENDIX

Activity 1: Comprehending

Listen to the sentences and decide whether they describe the pictures below. If you think they describe the picture put a check in the blank next to the picture. If you think they do not, put a cross. If you like you can ask the teacher to repeat a sentence.

1. She appreciated his singing.

_____

2. His present offended her.

_____

3. Her driving impressed him.

_____

4. He deplored her laziness.

_____

Activity 2: Paying Attention

Draw arrows to show who or what experiences the feeling described by the verb in these sentences. Use a dictionary to check the meanings of any verbs you do not know.

Examples: Sometimes people like dogs.

Sometimes people disgust dogs.

1. Mary worries her mother.

2. Cats bother Mary.

3. John prefers dogs.

4. Few politicians impress people.

5. Jane loves smart men.

6. Poor people envy rich people.

7. Sometimes teachers amuse their students.

8. Rabbits like children.

9. Sometimes men disappoint women.

10. Dolores mourns her father.

Activity 3: Responding Personally

Respond to each of these sentences with:

True

Partly true

Not true

1. Tall women frighten me.

2. Women who can cook impress me.

3. Smartly dressed women impress me.

4. Very clever women overwhelm me.

5. Quiet women interest me.

6. Talkative women bore me.

7. Argumentative women confuse me.

8. Women with a sense of humor charm me.

Activity 4: What's the Difference?

Listen to Randy talk to his Japanese friend Koji. Can you work out what Koji should have said?

Listening text:

Randy: You know something. I don't really like tall women. I get a bit scared by them.

Koji: Yeah, I am the same. I frighten tall women.

Randy: Sorry?

Koji: I frighten tall women.

Randy: Oh, you mean you get frightened by tall women.

Koji: Yeah. And clever women too. I overwhelm clever women.

Randy: I know what you mean. They overwhelm me too.

Koji: But the worst are argumentative women. I confuse them.

Randy: They confuss you?

Koji: Uh? I mean I get confused by them.

Randy: They don't worry me. I like a good argument.

Koji: And the next worst is talkative women.I bore them.

Randy: You bore them. Or they bore you. I think you mean they bore you.

Koji: Yeah, they bore me.

Chapter 13

Teaching and Research:
Options in Grammar Teaching

This chapter is based on article that first appeared in TESOL Quarterly Vol. 32, pp. 39–60.

This chapter addresses the relationship between language teaching and research. It also examines what current second language acquisition (SLA) research has to say about the effectiveness of different ways of teaching grammar. These two purposes are related. An account of instructional options serves as a basis for proposing how SLA research and teaching might best inform each other.

The social worlds of the teacher and the researcher are often very different (Crookes, 1997). Teachers operate in classrooms where they need to make instantaneous decisions regarding what and how to teach. Researchers, more often than not, work in universities, where a system of rewards prizes rigorous contributions to a theoretical understanding of issues. Teachers require and seek to develop practical knowledge; researchers endeavor to advance technical knowledge. This distinction, then, encapsulates the divide that often exists between the two.

PRACTICAL VERSUS TECHNICAL PROFESSIONAL KNOWLEDGE

The distinction between technical and practical knowledge [1] is common in the literature dealing with the practice of professionals such as doctors, lawyers, and teachers (see Calderhead, 1988; Eraut, 1994). Technical knowledge is explicit; that is, it exists in a declarative form that has been codified. For these reasons it can be examined analytically and disputed systematically. Technical knowledge is acquired deliberately either by reflecting deeply about the object of enquiry or by investigating it empirically, involving the use of a well-defined set of procedures for ensuring the validity and reliability of the knowledge obtained. Technical knowledge is general in nature; that is, it takes the form of statements that can be applied to many particular cases. For this reason, it cannot easily be applied off-the-shelf in the kind of rapid decision-making needed in day-to-day living.

Over the years, SLA research has provided a substantial body of technical knowledge about how people learn an L2. This is reflected in the ever-growing set of technical terms used to label this knowledge — for example, overgeneralization and transfer errors, fossilization, order and sequence of acquisition, input and intake, noticing, negative and positive evidence (see the glossary in Ellis, 1994a). This technical knowledge and the terms that label it constitute goods that are constantly being produced by SLA researchers.

In contrast, practical knowledge is implicit and intuitive. Individuals are generally not aware of what they practically know. For example, I know how to tie my shoelace, but I have little awareness of the sequence of actions I must perform to do this and could certainly not describe them very well. Practical knowledge is acquired through actual experience by means of procedures that are only poorly understood. Similarly, it is fully expressible only in practice, although it may be possible, through reflection, to codify aspects of it. The great advantage of practical knowledge is that it is proceduralized and thus can be drawn on rapidly and efficiently to handle particular cases.

Practicing professionals are primarily concerned with action involving particular cases, and for this reason they draw extensively on practical knowledge in their work. Freidson (1977), for example, describes how medical practitioners operate:

> One whose work requires practical application to concrete cases simply cannot maintain the same frame of mind as the scholar or scientist: he cannot suspend action in the absence of incontrovertible evidence or be skeptical of himself, his experience, his work and its fruit. ... Dealing with individual cases, he cannot rely solely on probabilities or on general concepts or principles: he must also rely on his own senses. By the nature of his work the clinician must assume responsibility for practical action, and in so doing he must rely on his concrete, clinical experience. (as cited in Eraut, 1994, p. 53)

Similarly, teachers, in the act of teaching, rely to a large extent on their practical knowledge (Calderhead, 1988).

Of course, teachers do make use of technical knowledge in planning lessons, choosing and writing teaching materials and tests, and deciding what methodological procedures to utilize. This corresponds to what van Lier (1991) has referred to as the planned aspect of teaching. However, there is also an improvised side. To accomplish a lesson, teachers are faced with the need to make countless unplanned decisions about what and how to teach. As van Lier describes it, 'In any lesson, planned and improvised actions and interactions may be tightly interwoven' (p.47).

Teachers, however, often experience difficulty in integrating technical and practical knowledge. Pennington and Richards (1997), for example, report on the failure of five novice Cantonese teachers of English in Hong Kong to implement in their classroom teaching the communicative teaching principles and practices they were taught during a BA course. They suggest that one reason for this failure was the teachers' preexisting schema for teaching based on their learning experiences as students in the Hong Kong school system. In other words, faced with the need to survive in the classroom, these teachers rejected their technical knowledge and instead relied on their practical knowledge. More experienced teachers may be more successful in interweaving the two types of knowledge but, as the literature on professional activity makes clear, this is no easy task [2].

The crucial issue, then, is the nature of the relationship between technical and practical knowledge. To what extent and in what ways can the technical knowledge derived from research influence actual teaching? How can technical knowledge be utilized in the creation of the kind of practical knowledge with which teachers must necessarily work when they improvise lessons? Can practical knowledge contribute to technical knowledge? How? Before turning to these questions, I examine research that has addressed the effects of form-focused instruction on L2 acquisition. I have chosen this area because it is one of obvious potential relevance to language teaching.

OPTIONS IN FORM-FOCUSED INSTRUCTION

Early focus-on-form studies (e.g., Ellis, 1984a; Pienemann, 1984) were primarily concerned with finding out whether form-focused instruction worked (i.e., whether it enabled learners to acquire the structures they had been taught). These early studies did not distinguish different kinds of form-focused instruction. Instead, they tended to treat focus on form as a generic phenomenon to be contrasted with focus on meaning. Subsequently, however, researchers have turned their attention to another question — What kind of form-focused instruction works best? — that accords more closely, perhaps, with the teacher's perspective. It is this question that motivates the following survey of research.

One way of characterizing differences in instruction is in terms of options. Stern (1992) sees the identification of options as a way of proceeding beyond the concept of method, which is now generally recognized as too crude a concept on which to base either research or teaching (Kumaravadivelu, 1994). One set of options Stern considers is what he refers to as teaching strategies. It is possible to describe a number of such strategies for form-focused instruction based on what is known about how learners acquire an L2.

The particular model of L2 acquisition that will serve as a basis for identifying these options is derived from a computational metaphor. There are, of course, other metaphors, which doubtlessly suggest other instructional options. However, the computational metaphor is currently dominant in SLA (see Lantolf, 1996, for a discussion). According to this metaphor, L2 learners are viewed as intelligent machines that process input in a mental black box. This contains wired-in or previously acquired mechanisms that enable learners to internalize new knowledge for use in output tasks. The particular computational model that informs the discussion of options below is shown in Figure 1.

The model indicates a number of points where form-focused instruction can intervene in interlanguage development. In the case of Point A, instruction is directed at input (i.e., attempts are made to contrive oral or written texts in such a way that learners are induced to notice specific target features as they try to comprehend the texts). Following VanPatten (1993), this option will be referred to as structured input. Point B involves explicit instruction (i.e., attempts to develop learners' explicit understanding of L2 rules — to help them learn about a linguistic feature). Point C entails production practice (i.e., creating opportunities for learners to practice producing a specific target structure). Point D consists of negative feedback, showing learners when they have failed to produce a structure correctly. Whereas Point A provides learners with positive evidence (i.e., examples of how a particular grammatical structure works), Point D offers negative evidence (i.e., indications of erroneous use and perhaps also corrections).

Two general comments are in order. The first is that form-focused lessons typically involve combinations of these options. For example, explicit instruction, production practice, and negative feedback are often combined. This makes good sense from the teacher's point of view as it optimizes the potential effect of the instruction. However, it is problematic from the researcher's point of view because it is difficult to determine which specific option is responsible for any learning that takes place.

The second general point is to emphasize that these four options constitute macro-options. Each one can be broken down into more delicate micro-options. For example, there are many ways of delivering production practice depending on whether the pedagogic aim is to carefully control learners' output or to provide opportunities for relatively free production using the targeted structure. Both teachers and researchers have to decide what micro-options to use. The problem is that although the choice of macro-options can be theoretically motivated by the kind of computational model shown in Figure 1, there is often no theoretical basis in SLA for selecting micro-options. For example, structured input can require students to demonstrate their understanding by matching sentences to pictures or by responding to commands through actions, but there is no obvious rationale in SLA for preferring one micro-option over the other. Such options have a pedagogical status but no obvious psycholinguistic justification.

Below the macro-options are illustrated with sample teaching materials, and recent research relating to each option is reviewed. In the case of the structured-input option, a fairly comprehensive review is included as this is an area that has attracted considerable interest from SLA researchers and that also offers an innovative alternative to traditional grammar teaching. Research directed at the other options is examined more selectively, for reasons of space. One of the purposes of this review is to demonstrate some of the problems teachers may have in making use of the technical knowledge provided by the research.

The Structured-Input Option

This option asks learners to process input that has been specially contrived to induce comprehension of the target structure. Learners are required to listen to or read texts consisting of discrete sentences or continuous discourse and to indicate their understanding of them, for example, by carrying out a command, drawing a picture, ticking a box, or indicating agreement or disagreement. The learners' responses to the input stimuli are nonverbal or minimally verbal; they do not involve actually producing the structure.

Here is an example of a grammar task that makes use of this option. The target structure is predicate adjectives (e.g., the distinction between boring and bored). L2 learners have been observed to confuse these, producing sentences such as *I am boring with you (Burt, 1975). In this task, the learners have to simply indicate whether they agree or disagree with a series of statements.

An Example of a Structured-Input Task

Do you agree or disagree with these statements?
1. Quiet people are boring.
2. I am bored when someone tells a joke.
3. People who gossip a lot are very irritating.
4. I get irritated with small talk.
5. It is interesting to talk about yourself.
6. I am interested in people who always talk about themselves.
   [etc.]

The psycholinguistic rationale for the structured-input option is that acquisition occurs when learners attend to the new structure in input rather than when they try to produce it. A number of recent studies have investigated the relative effects of structured input and production practice on the acquisition of specific linguistic features. In interpreting the results of these studies it is important to consider the kinds of tests used to measure the learning outcomes. All the studies examined below used both comprehension-based tests, which favor the structured-input group, and production tests, which favor the production-practice group.

However, most of the studies to date have not incorporated any test of the learners' ability to use the target structure in communicative speech. A further issue in this research is whether the instruction included explicit explanation of the target feature in addition to practice involving structured-input or production activities.

VanPatten and Cadierno (1993) compared traditional production-oriented practice with oral structured-input practice directed at groups of university students. Both groups also received explicit instruction in the target structure. The focus of this study was the positioning of object clitic pronouns in Spanish (e.g., *Te invito para el sábado*). The subjects were tested by means of a discrete-item listening test and a discrete-item written production test. The results showed that the structured-input group outperformed the production-practice group on the listening comprehension test and did just as well on the written production test. These results were repeated in follow-up tests administered 1 month later. VanPatten and Cadierno suggest that whereas the production-based instruction only contributed to explicit knowledge, the comprehension-based instruction created intake that led to implicit knowledge. Cadierno (1995) reports almost identical results in a study that focused on a morphological feature (Spanish past tense forms).

Similar results were also obtained by Tanaka (1996), who compared the relative effects of structured input and production practice on the acquisition of English relative clauses by 123 high school students in Japan. In this study, both groups again received explicit instruction relating to the target structure but were given different kinds of practice.

A comprehension test and a controlled production test were administered before the treatment, 5 days after the treatment, and again 2 months later. On both the immediate and the delayed comprehension post-test, the structured-input group outperformed the production-practice group. In fact, the production-practice group showed hardly any improvement on pre-test scores. On the production tests, both groups showed gains on their pre-test scores. The production-practice group obtained significantly higher scores than the structured-input group on the immediate post-test but not on the delayed post-test. This suggests that structured input in conjunction with explicit instruction resulted in durable learning that was available for use in both comprehension and production tasks. In contrast, production-based instruction in conjunction with explicit information resulted in learning that was available for use only in production and that atrophied markedly over time.

A limitation of these studies was the kinds of tests used to measure production. The discrete-point tests they used do not show convincingly that the comprehension treatment was effective in developing the implicit knowledge needed for communication. To address this issue, VanPatten and Sanz (1995) compared a group receiving explanation of object clitic pronouns followed by structured-input practice with a control group that received no instruction directed at the target structure. This study incorporated a number of different tests (e.g., sentence completion and video narration) in written and oral versions. The structured-input group significantly improved their accuracy in producing the target structure (clitic pronouns in L2 Spanish) on all the written tests, outperforming the control group, which showed no improvement. This confirmed the results of the earlier study. However, no statistically significant difference was found between the structured-input group and the control group on the oral video narration test — an integrative test involving unplanned production and, therefore, arguably a measure of implicit knowledge. The study thus does not provide convincing evidence that input-processing instruction led to changes in implicit knowledge.

In all of these studies, the instruction involved two focus-on-form macro-options — explicit explanation combined with structured input. A question of some importance, then, is whether the advantage found for the input-processing groups in these studies was due to explicit explanation, structured input, or a combination of the two. VanPatten and Oikkenon (1996) set out to investigate this using fourth-semester high school students. The focus was again object pronoun placement in Spanish. There were three experimental groups: Group 1 received a grammatical explanation together with structured-input practice, as in the earlier studies, Group 2 received just explicit instruction, and Group 3 received just structured-input practice. On a discrete-item comprehension test, Groups 1 and 3 both performed better than Group 2, but there was no difference between Groups 1 and 3. On the production test, Group 1 but not Group 3 performed better than Group 2, but the difference between Groups 1 and 3 was not statistically significant. VanPatten and Oikkenon conclude that 'significant improvement on the interpretation test is due to the presence of structured-input activities and not to explicit information' and that even on the production test 'the effects of explicit information are negligible' (p.508). Note, however, that explicit instruction did lead to better performance on both tests and also that the tests used in this study did not include a measure of communicative performance.

Two other studies have produced very different results. Salaberry (1997) set out to replicate the VanPatten and Cadierno (1993) study with similar subjects and the same grammatical focus (clitic pronouns in Spanish). He used three tests — a comprehension test, a discrete-item production test, and a free-narration test based on a video. These tests were administered before the instruction, immediately after the instruction, and 1 month later. Both experimental groups improved on the comprehension tests with the production-practice group performing as well as the structured-input group. No improvement in either group was evident on the discrete-item production tests, but Salaberry acknowledges that this may have been because all the subjects achieved high scores on the pre-test, thus leaving little room for improvement. Also, as in VanPatten and Sanz's (1995) study, the two groups did not differ on the free-narration test, although Salaberry notes that this test produced few obligatory occasions for object clitic pronouns.

Finally, the results of DeKeyser and Sokalski's (1996) study also failed to show an advantage for structured input. The grammatical focus was clitic pronouns (as in the previous VanPatten studies) and the conditional form of the verb in Spanish, a structure that the researchers argue is easy to perceive but difficult to produce. In the case of object clitic pronouns, the immediate post-tests (which were highly controlled in nature) showed that the structured-input group did better on the comprehension test whereas the production-practice group did better on the production test. However, on the delayed post-test no difference between the groups on either test was evident. For the conditional, production practice resulted in better scores on both the comprehension and the production tests, but again there was no difference between the groups on the delayed test. However, the pre-test scores for both structures were high, leaving little room for further learning. It is not easy to reach firm conclusions based on these studies as (a) the results of the different studies are not in agreement, (b) there are obvious design differences in the studies (e.g., in the level of knowledge of the target structures displayed by the subjects in pre-tests), and (c) to date the research has not shown that structured input has any effect on unplanned language use. Thus, the technical knowledge afforded by the research on structured input is ambivalent. Perhaps the most that can be said is that it suggests that structured-input practice may provide a useful alternative to production practice [3].

Explicit Instruction

The principal choice regarding explicit instruction is whether to teach explicit rules directly or to develop activities that enable learners to discover the rules for themselves. Direct explicit instruction takes the form of oral or written explanations of grammatical phenomena. They can stand by themselves or can be accompanied by exercises in which learners attempt to apply the rule they have learned. In indirect explicit instruction, learners complete consciousness-raising tasks in which they analyze data illustrating the workings of a specific grammatical rule. Here is an example of a consciousness-raising task directed at helping learners discover when to use 'at', 'in', and 'on' in adverbial time phrases.

An Example of a Conscious-Raising Task

1. Underline the time expressions in this passage.

I made an appointment to see Mr. Bean at 3 o'clock on Tuesday the 11th of February to discuss my application for a job. Unfortunately, he was involved in a car accident in the morning and rang to cancel the appointment. I made another appointment to see him at 10 o'clock on Friday the 21st of February. However, when I got to his office, his secretary told me that his wife had died at 2 o'clock in the night and that he was not coming into the office that day. She suggested I reschedule for sometime in March. So I made a third appointment to see Mr. Bean at 1 o'clock on Monday the 10th of March. This time I actually got to see him. However, he informed me that they had now filled all the vacancies and suggested I contact him again in 1998. I assured him that he would not be seeing me in either this or the next century.

2. Write the time phrases into this table.

at	in	on
at 3 o'clock		

3. Make up a rule to explain when to use at, in, and on in time expressions.

Fotos and Ellis (1991) investigated the relative advantages of direct and indirect consciousness-raising. We found that both options resulted in statistically significant gains in understanding the rule for dative alternation in two groups of college-level Japanese students. In one group, direct explicit instruction resulted in higher scores on a grammaticality judgement test, but in the other the consciousness-raising task proved equally effective. In a more elaborate follow-up study, Fotos (1994) found that indirect instruction worked as well as direct instruction in teaching explicit knowledge of three different structures (adverb placement, dative alternation, and relative clauses) to 160 Japanese university students.

There are a number of reasons for favoring the indirect option. An invitation to discover rules for themselves may be more motivating to learners than simply giving them the rules. Also, if consciousness-raising tasks are performed in groups and the target language is used as the medium for solving the problems they pose, the tasks double as communicative tasks. Learners can as well talk about grammar as talk about any other topic.

Other research has investigated the relative effects of teaching grammar deductively by means of direct explanation versus teaching it inductively through controlled production practice. This comparison underlay the global method studies of the 1960s (e.g., Scherer & Wertheimer, 1964; Smith, 1970), which failed to demonstrate whether one method (e.g., the grammar-translation or the audiolingual method) was better than another. Early small-scale studies (e.g., Hammerley, 1975; Seliger, 1975), however, found some advantage for explicit instruction, particularly when the target structure was relatively simple.

A number of recent experimental studies, based on studies in cognitive psychology using artificial languages (see Reber, 1989) confirm these early results. For example,Robinson (1996) investigated 104 adult students of English (mainly Japanese) learning both an easy rule (subject-verb inversion after an adverbial of location as in Into the house ran John) and a complex rule (pseudo-clefting as in *Where Mary and John live is in Chicago not New York*). The subjects viewed the sentences on a computer screen under varying conditions. One group (labelled the implicit group) was simply asked to remember the sentences. A second group (called the incidental group) was given comprehension questions about the sentences, to which they answered yes or no. A third group (the rule-search group) was asked to identify the rules illustrated by the sentences, and the fourth group (the instructed group) first received direct explanations of the rules and then tried to apply them to the sentences. The group receiving explicit explanations outperformed all the other groups on a grammaticality judgement test administered immediately after the treatment. Other recent studies (e.g., DeKeyser, 1994, 1995; N. Ellis, 1993) have produced similar results in favor of explicit instruction.

However, there are obvious problems in applying the results of these studies to language pedagogy. One is that the studies often did not include a delayed test. It is not clear, for example, whether the advantage Robinson (1996) found for the group that received explicit instruction was maintained over time. More seriously, the studies did not include tests of communicative behaviour. For example, it can be argued that the grammaticality judgement test in Robinson's study favored the explicit instruction group because it could be answered using explicit knowledge.

Once again, then, the results of the research do not afford conclusions that can be readily applied to language pedagogy. Fotos' (1994) research suggests that if explicit knowledge is the goal, it may be effectively taught via consciousness-raising tasks. However, there is no clear evidence to date that explicit instruction of any kind leads to greater grammatical accuracy in communicative language use.

Production Practice

Devices for eliciting production of target structures range on a continuum from highly controlled text-manipulation exercises (e.g., a substitution drill) to much freer text-creation tasks, in which learners are guided into producing their own sentences using the target structure (see the example below). A well-established methodological principle in current grammar teaching is to begin with text-manipulation and then move to text-creation activities. In this way teachers hope to push the learner from controlled to automatic use of the target structure.

Examples of Production-Practice Tasks

A. *Text manipulation*

Fill in the blanks in these sentences.

1. Mr. Short was born ___ 1944 ___ a Tuesday ___ May ___two o'clock ___ the morning.
2. Mr. Long was born ___ 1955 ___ a Saturday ___ November ___five o'clock ___ the afternoon.
   [etc.]

> B. *Text creation*
>
> Find three people who know
> • the year they were born
> • the day they were born
> • the time of day they were born
> Complete this table about the three people.
>
> Name Year Day Time
> 1.
> 2.
> 3.
> Now tell the class about the three people you talked to.

Learners require time to integrate new grammatical structures into their interlanguage systems. Many structures involve learners passing through a series of transitional stages before they arrive at the target language rule (see Ellis, 1994a, chapter 3). It is uncertain, then, whether production practice directed at such structures in the course of a lesson, or even a series of lessons, can enable learners to construct the kind of knowledge needed for communication. Furthermore, learners have their own built-in syllabus (Corder, 1967), according to which they acquire some structures before others. If the production practice is directed at a structure the learners are not yet ready to acquire, it is likely to fail (Pienemann, 1984) or to result in some misrepresentation of the rule (Eubank, 1987). It was problems such as these that led Krashen (1982) to reject any major role for form-focused instruction in L2 acquisition.

There may still be a place for production practice, however. Schmidt (1994) notes that there is a skill aspect as well as a knowledge aspect to L2 learning. Thus, although production practice may not enable learners to integrate entirely new grammatical structures into their interlanguages, it may help them use partially acquired structures more fluently and more accurately. Indeed, the results of the DeKeyser and Sokalski (1996) study discussed earlier could be interpreted as demonstrating precisely this. Other focus-on-form studies (e.g., Harley, 1989; Spada & Lightbown,

1993; White, Spada, Lightbown & Ranta, 1991), which have included plentiful production practice (albeit in conjunction with other macro-options), have also shown that clear and sometimes durable gains in knowledge can occur.

An interesting question is whether production practice based on text manipulation or on text creation is best suited to improving learners' control over structures. Castagnaro (1991) examined the effects of two kinds of production practice on Japanese college students' ability to produce complex noun phrases. A control group was given a picture of a kitchen and simply practiced labelling the objects in it. One experimental group took part in a repetition and blank-filling exercise based on the same picture and designed to practice complex noun phrases. The second experimental group was asked to work in pairs to produce their own sentences describing the various kitchen objects. The learners in this group did best in a post-test that measured their ability to produce complex noun phrases.

The results of the studies reviewed in this section suggest that it would be premature to abandon approaches to teaching grammar that emphasize production practice. The task facing teachers is to decide when production practice can assist their students and when it is not likely to succeed — a task that calls for considerable technical knowledge. Teachers also need to consider what kind of production practice to provide. To date, there is insufficient evidence to show that one kind of practice (e.g., free practice) works better than another (e.g., controlled practice).

Negative Feedback

Negative feedback shows learners that an utterance they have just produced is incorrect. It serves, therefore, to help learners notice the gap between their own deviant productions and grammatically correct productions. Negative feedback often occurs in conjunction with production practice. However, there are reasons for believing that it may prove more effective if it takes place in the context of activities in which the primary focus is on meaning rather than on form. Keith Johnson (1988) has argued that 'learners need to see for themselves what has gone wrong, in the operating conditions in which they went wrong' (p.93). Below is an example of the kind of correction that arises naturally in communication.

Negative Feedback as a Recast

A: I born on 1944.
B: Oh, you were born in 1944.
A: Yeah, in 1944.

This type of correction is known as a recast. It involves an interlocutor (such as the teacher) reformulating a learner's utterance or part of an utterance in accordance with target-language norms. Lyster and Ranta (1997) found that recasts were the most common form of correction in French immersion lessons. They also identified five other types of feedback: (a) explicit correction, in which the teacher provides the correct form; (b) clarification requests, in which the teacher indicates an utterance has not been understood; (c) metalinguistic feedback, in which the teacher uses technical language to refer to an error (e.g., 'It's feminine'); (d) elicitation, in which the teacher attempts to elicit the correct form from the student; and (e) repetition, in which the teacher simply indicates an error has been made by repeating all or part of a learner's utterance. A question of obvious interest to teachers is which of these types of feedback is most effective. One way of answering this is by examining learners' uptake (i.e., learners' attempts to repair their own errors). Lyster and Ranta found that recasts were the least likely type of feedback to elicit student repair. Elicitation led to the most uptake, evenly divided between successful (i.e., the student repaired the error) and unsuccessful. Metalinguistic feedback produced slightly less overall uptake but had a similar success rate.

Of course, uptake does not show that students have learned the correct feature. To demonstrate this, it is necessary to find out whether students avoid making the same error on subsequent occasions. Here, the results of the research are mixed. In a review of research into the effects of corrective feedback on learners' written compositions, Truscott (1996) concluded that feedback did not help learners eliminate errors from their subsequent written work. However, a number of recent classroom studies suggest that negative feedback in the context of communicative activities may promote interlanguage development. Lightbown and Spada (1990) report that when teachers corrected learners' errors during communicative lessons, the frequency of at least some errors (e.g., it has ... instead of the correct there is ...) was reduced.

Doughty and Varela (1995) investigated the effects of negative feedback on learners' communicative output. Sixth- to eighth-grade ESL learners were given negative feedback (in the form of recasts) focusing on past tense errors in their oral and written lab reports of scientific experiments. Doughty and Varela report that over a 6-week period the learners given this feedback showed gains in terms of both their use of correct target language forms and their use of various interlanguage forms used to mark pastness (e.g., they used the incorrect 'toke' where before they had used 'take'). These gains were evident in both their oral and written lab reports. In contrast, a control group showed gains only in the use of interlanguage markers of pastness in their written lab reports (i.e., there were no overall gains in the use of target forms and no gains in the use of interlanguage past forms in their oral production). This research demonstrates that negative feedback directed at errors made in communication can accelerate interlanguage development.

There remains considerable uncertainty regarding the value of negative feedback. According to some theorists (e.g., Krashen, 1982), correction does not contribute to interlanguage development. However, as we have seen, there is growing evidence that negative feedback can contribute to the kind of implicit knowledge used in communication. Yet very little is known about which kind of feedback is most effective.

Here is an area, then, where teachers have no choice but to rely on their practical knowledge. Indeed, given that error correction involves attending to a variety of social and affective factors (see Allwright, 1975), technical knowledge about what works best for language acquisition can never provide a complete basis for correcting errors.

BRIDGING THE GAP

The preceding brief discussion of four macro-options for delivering form-focused instruction together with examples of recent research provides a basis for examining more closely the relationship between research and teaching. How can the gap between technical and practical knowledge be bridged?

Is the Gap Worth Bridging?

Educational researchers are committed to establishing a solid knowledge base through research that is valid, reliable, and trustworthy. The assumption is that this knowledge base can inform and improve language pedagogy. There are problems with such a view, however, concerning both the quality of the research and the nature of the relationship between researcher and teacher.

The research examined in this paper is fairly typical of the kind of focus-on-form investigations currently being undertaken. The studies generally demonstrate a sophisticated awareness of the requirements of experimental research (e.g., the importance of pre-testing and the need for control groups). Nevertheless, there are reasons for exercising caution about the findings. There are methodological problems. For example, not all the studies used random sampling, a standard requirement of experimental research, for the simple reason that it is often not possible or ethical in educational research. Also, many of the studies investigated combinations of instructional options, making it difficult to determine which option was responsible for the effects observed. But even if these methodological problems were to be overcome, doubts about the generalizability of the research would remain. It does not follow that the results obtained for a specific group of learners being taught a specific grammatical structure apply to all the individuals in a group, to other groups, or to other grammatical structures. Given the enormous complexity of both teaching-learning situations and L2 acquisition, it is simply not possible to advocate general solutions on the basis of 1, 2, or even 20 studies. Furthermore, the conflicting nature of the results so far obtained, itself a reflection of the complexity referred to above, precludes firm proposals.

The assumption that research can provide a knowledge base for making pedagogical decisions is also dangerous because it commonly implies a particular power relationship between researcher and teacher. It places researchers at the top of a social hierarchy, giving them the responsibility for making decisions, and teachers at the bottom, consigned to implementing research-driven curricula, a state of affairs commonly criticized in the educational literature (e.g., Carr & Kemmis, 1986). Clarke (1994) has inveighed against such a state of affairs in TESOL, arguing that communication becomes dysfunctional when teachers are placed in a position of receiving 'proclamations' from researchers. He argues teachers should 'keep their own counsel regarding what works and does not work' (p.23).

It might be argued, therefore, that if the research cannot afford general solutions and if the utilization of research findings implies an inequitable relationship between researcher and teacher, teachers might do better to rely on their own practical knowledge, as Clarke (1994) advocates. Yet this conclusion is not warranted. It derives from a failure to address how practical knowledge and technical knowledge can interact.

Models for Relating Research to Teachers' Practice

Weiss (1977) outlines three models for relating research-based knowledge to professional activity. According to the decision-driven model, the starting point for research is not a theory of L2 acquisition or a previous piece of research but rather some practical issue of direct concern to teachers. The form-focused research examined in this chapter was theoretically driven, but it was also motivated by issues of practical importance to teachers. How best to teach grammar is a question that many teachers feel the need to address. Investigating different options is a better way of tackling the problem of grammar teaching than simply abandoning it in favor of communicative language teaching, as some have suggested (e.g., Krashen, 1982). Williams (1995) points out that the current research suggests ways in which a focus on form can be incorporated into communicative activities. However, research findings do not provide a basis for proclaiming solutions to practical problems. Rather, as Cronbach (1980) has argued, such findings should be used interpretatively rather than applicatively.

Weiss's second model is the knowledge-driven model, in which the primary goal of research is to advance the knowledge base of a discipline by constructing and testing explicit theories or by developing research methodology. The research on options in grammar teaching was partly undertaken with this function in mind. The specific options that have been studied were based on theoretical accounts of how learners acquire an L2. The research on structured input, for example, is premised on the hypothesis that interlanguage development occurs as a result of processing input, not output. Krashen (1983) has argued that it is not research *per se* that should be used to address pedagogical issues but rather the theory derived from the research. Theory, he claims, provides teachers with 'an underlying rationale for methodology in general' (p.261) and thus helps them to adapt to different situations.

The knowledge-driven model has been a major influence in the development of teacher education programs in TESOL. Stern (1983), for example, has argued the case for developing a foundation of knowledge in applied linguistics, which includes SLA. He argues commonsensically that judgements that are based on 'sound theoretical foundations' (p.2) will produce better results than those that are not. Most teacher educators, myself included, would concur. Thus, teachers who are familiar with the research on options are better equipped to develop valid theories of their own (Williams, 1995) and, therefore, are more likely to become effective teachers of grammar. There is, however, a major problem. The knowledge-driven model assumes that teachers will be consumers of research-based knowledge but does not address how this consumption will take place. How can/do teachers make use of the research on form-focused options?

The third of Weiss's (1977) models — the interactive model — addresses this crucial issue. Here technical and practical knowledge are interrelated through the performance of some professional activity. The way in which this achieved is highly complex. One way of facilitating this process is for teachers to treat the results of research they find interesting as provisional specifications to be tested out in their own classrooms. As Stenhouse (1975) has put it:

> The crucial point is that the proposal (from research) is not to be regarded as an unqualified recommendation but rather as a provisional specification claiming no more than to be worth putting to the test of practice. Such proposals claim to be intelligent rather than correct. (p. 25)

In a sense, then, the research serves as a heuristic to guide teachers' experimentation in their own classrooms.

An example of a provisional specification is the finding that the structured-input option for teaching grammar may result in deeper and more durable learning than traditional production practice. To date, however, the research on this option has investigated only a few populations of learners and only three or four grammatical structures. Are the findings of this research applicable to other groups of students and other structures? Accepting that the findings of such research are no more than provisional obviates the problems of generalizing research findings, referred to earlier. Teachers can investigate the relevance of research findings to their own classroom either informally by simply trying out new ideas or systematically through action research, using their own practical knowledge of teaching to operationalize technical constructs (such as structured input). The case for using action research in this way in our field has been made by, among others, Crookes (1993), Nunan (1990), Widdowson (1990), and Williams (1995). Action research is seen both as a way of improving teaching and as a way of overcoming the 'dysfunctions of the theory/practice discourse' that Clarke (1994) objects to.

A second way of interrelating the two kinds of knowledge is for researchers and teachers to work collaboratively. However, collaboration often takes the form of researchers co-opting teachers into working on questions derived from theory or previous research. In other words, it is the researcher's perspective that is paramount, which reinforces the hierarchical divide between researchers and teachers. However, there are other forms of collaboration. Louden (1992) describes a longitudinal project he undertook with Joanna, an elementary school teacher. Louden's goal was 'to understand from the inside how reflection contributes to the action teachers take in their own classroom' (p.178). He sought to blur the distinction between himself as researcher and his subject as teacher. Thus, although he drew on his technical knowledge to propose solutions to problems that arose in the course of teaching, it was Joanna who decided what to accept and what to reject. Louden's work provides an example of how Weiss's (1977) interactive model might be effectively implemented. It suggests a profitable line for applied focus-on-form research.

CONCLUSION

In this chapter, I have suggested that the notion of options provides a basis for both researching and conducting form-focused instruction. However, the identification of a common framework for research and teaching does not ensure their symbiosis. To achieve this, it is necessary to consider what kinds of research are most likely to lead to interdependence.

I have discussed three types of research. One is theoretical-pedagogical research, in which the goal is to develop technical knowledge by addressing theoretical issues of potential practical relevance to teachers. This type of research is researcher-led (although it may also involve teachers). It is manifest in all the studies of form-focused instruction referred to in this chapter. Such research is of value to teachers in that it is a source (although not the only one) of provisional specifications that individual teachers can test out informally through their own teaching. The second type of research is action research, in which teachers take responsibility for identifying their own research questions and conducting their own investigations. Action research provides a more systematic means by which teachers can investigate the provisional specifications provided by theoretical-pedagogical research. Finally, there is participatory research, in which a researcher and a teacher collaborate inside the teacher's classroom, pooling their expertise in a manner that gives the teacher control over decision-making.

Surprisingly, very little research has explored how teachers arrive at decisions about what grammar to teach and when and how to teach it, a notable exception being Borg (this issue). That study documents the personal pedagogical system evident in one teacher's teaching of grammar. This system was derived in part from his training as a language teacher and in part from his own experience as a language learner and teacher. Such studies can also illuminate in what ways teachers interpret and personalize research findings in their teaching. For, as Eraut (1994) points out, teachers do not simply act on technical knowledge but transform it through action. Very little is known about how this takes place in the grammar class.

Notes

[1] The distinction between technical and practical knowledge, found in discussions of professional expertise, is analogous with the distinctions between explicit and implicit L2 knowledge and between declarative and procedural L2 knowledge, both of which are common in the SLA literature.

[2] However, other practitioners of language pedagogy (e.g., syllabus designers, test constructors, and materials writers) may find it less problematic to integrate technical and practical knowledge than do classroom teachers, as those practitioners' activities rely more on planning than on improvisation.

[3] It is also worth noting that, to date, no study has investigated whether combining structured input and production practice results in better learning than using these options separately.

Chapter 14

Methodological Options in Grammar Teaching Materials

This chapter is based on a chapter that appeared in E. Hinkel and S. Fotos (Eds.) *New Perspectives on Grammar Teaching in Second Language Classrooms.* *Mahwah, NJ.: Lawrence Erlbaum.*

INTRODUCTION

There are a large number of published grammar practice books for teachers to select from. Key questions are: What methodology for teaching grammar do these books employ? What is the empirical/ theoretical basis for the chosen methodology? [1] The first question can be answered by undertaking a careful analysis of the methodological features of a selection of the available books. The second can be answered by examining the explicit comments of the authors of the book (e.g. in the introductory sections) or by inferring the guiding principles from the types of activities employed. In this chapter I shall address both questions.

There have been relatively few attempts to conduct a methodological analysis of the instructional options incorporated into grammar practice books. Fortune (1998), in a survey review of six widely used grammar books for EFL, identified a number of primary features. He referred to the 'gang of three': (1) isolated, decontextualized sentences, (2) sentence completion involving the adaptation of an unmarked lexical item (often a verb) presented in brackets and (3) gap-filling. He then discusses a number of 'significant developments' in pedagogy, in particular consciousness-raising activities directed at (4) 'noticing' how specific grammatical structures are used and (5) understanding how the structures work. Fortune's features provide a basis for carrying out a methodological analysis. It will be elaborated on in the following section.

There have been rather more attempts to address the question of how grammar should be taught, both from an empirical and a theoretical standpoint. For example, a number of recent studies have investigated the effectiveness of 'implicit' as opposed to 'explicit' grammar teaching (e.g. Robinson, 1996; DeKeyser, 1997) and also, more relevant to my concerns here, of production-based as opposed to input-based grammar teaching (e.g. VanPatten & Cadierno, 1993; Salaberry, 1997). There is, of course, no shortage of theorizing about grammar teaching on the basis of models of second language (L2) acquisition (e.g. Krashen, 1982; R. Ellis, 1993a: Chapter 11; Long, 1988).

The main purpose of this chapter is to develop a framework that can be used to describe and design materials for teaching grammar. I will proceed as follows. First, I will examine the instructional options typically selected by authors of some popular grammar teaching books. This provides a picture of how grammar teaching is currently conceptualized. Second, I will review theoretical and empirical research that has addressed a number of options that have been neglected in grammar teaching. Third, I will consider some materials for teaching grammar that incorporate these options.

AN ANLYSIS OF THE METHODOLOGICAL OPTIONS IN GRAMMAR PRACTICE BOOKS

Elsewhere I have outlined a system of options for teaching grammar based on a pyscholinguistic model of language acquisition (see Chapter 13). Here I would like to try to develop a parallel system of options based on a sampling of grammar practice teaching materials. These options differ from the psycholinguistic options in that they are *methodological* in nature, reflecting the practice of grammar teaching as this is represented in published textbooks. As might be expected the two sets of options do not match exactly, although, as we will see, there are some noteworthy correspondences.

The methodological options described below were derived from inspecting a number of ESL/EFL grammar practice books (see Table 1 for a list). I looked at one unit of materials from each book, choosing the unit dealing with the Present Continuous Tense as this grammar point figured in all the books [2]. I read through each unit making a note of the options that were used. I then attempted to codify the options (to build a system) by classifying them into general categories with subdivisions. The system that I arrived at is shown in Figure 1. The terms used in this system are intended to be entirely descriptive (i.e. not evaluative). For example, the terms 'authentic' or 'contrived' are not intended to convey either positive or negative views about their value in grammar teaching.

Three sets of options were identified related to general aspects of the materials; **explicit description**, **data**, and **operations**. These aspects may or may not all be present in any one grammar practice book. As we will see below, all the books I examined used options relating to explicit description and to operations but only some included a data option. It is also possible to envisage a grammar practice book that does not include any explicit description (i.e. one based on audiolingual principles). The only obligatory options, it would seem are those concerning operations as these relate to the *practice* function of the books. A grammar *reference* book, in contrast, would obligatorily provide explicit descriptions but probably would not offer any operations for the reader to perform.

Explicit description refers to whether the materials either provide learners with an explanation of the grammar point (i.e.**supplied**) or whether they require learners to develop their own explanation (**discover**). Other more detailed methodological options relating to this general distinction can be identified but are not included in Figure 1. For example, in the case of explicit descriptions that are supplied a distinction might be drawn between 'verbal' and 'diagrammatic' descriptions.

The data options involve the provision of text containing exemplars of the target structure. To count as 'data' this text must be independent of any text associated with operations. For example, complete dialogues illustrating the target structure constitute 'data' but gapped dialogues requiring students to fill in the missing words were classified under 'operations'. Data options were subdivided in terms of **source**, **text size**, and **medium**. Source refers to whether the data provided consisted of **authentic** materials (i.e. texts for which there was a real-life not just a pedagogic context) or **contrived** materials (i.e. the author of the grammar practice book had devised the sentences him- or herself to illustrate the grammar point). Text size concerns whether the text comprising the data consist of **discrete sentences** (one of Fortune's 'gang of three') or are **continuous**. Finally, the text comprising the data can be **written** or **oral**. There is the potential for these options to combine in different ways. For example, the data could consist of text that was authentic, discrete sentences and oral or contrived, continuous and written. As we will shortly see, the actual combinations evident in the materials were very restricted.

The operations evident in the materials were classified according to whether they involved **production** (i.e. the students were required to produce sentences containing the target structure), **reception** (i.e.

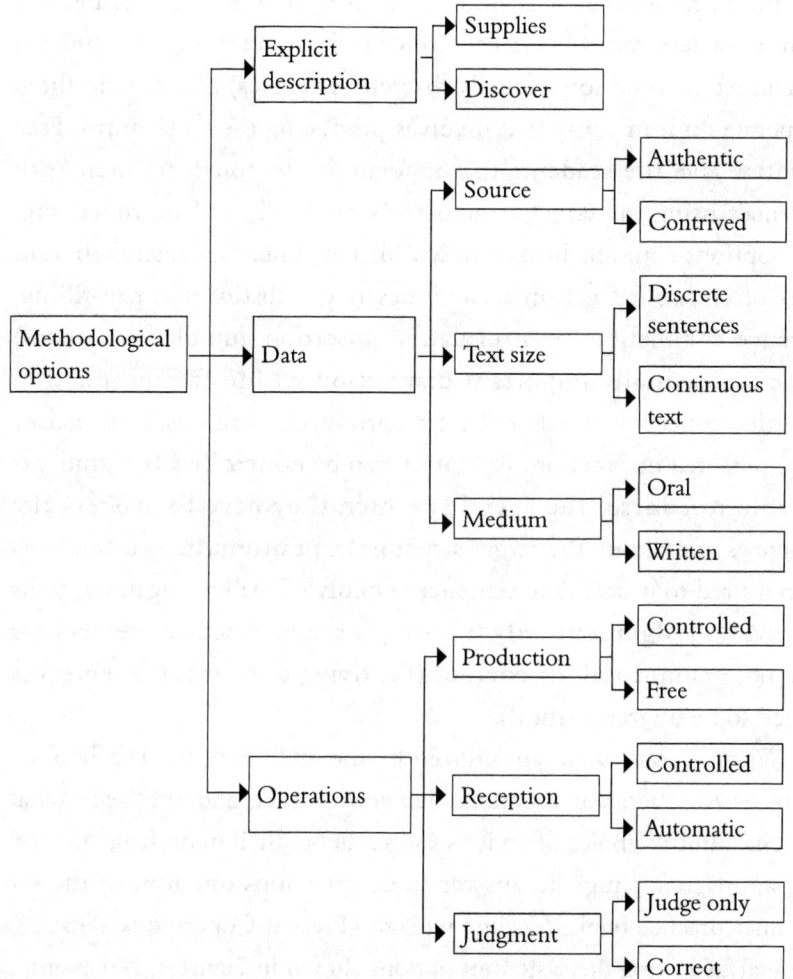

Figure 1: A system of methodological options employed in grammar practice books

the students were required to perform some activity to demonstrate they had understood sentences containing the target structure) or **judgement** (i.e. the students were required to identify whether sentences containing the target structure were grammatical or ungrammatical). Each of these options is further broken down. Production can be **controlled** or **free**. This distinction reflects a continuum rather than a dichotomy. That is, production activities can be more or less controlled/free. Controlled activities provide students with a text of some sort (usually discrete sentences) and require them to operate on it in a way that involves producing the target form. Free activities give the students the opportunity to construct their own sentences using the target structure. Again, both the 'controlled' and 'free' options could be broken down further. There are many different types of controlled grammar activities (e.g. substitution, gap-filling, sentence completion, transformation, insertion, jumbled sentences) while a potentially important distinction within free production activities concerns whether the text produced is representational or more personal in function. Reception can be **controlled** (i.e. students are able to control the speed at which they have to process the sentences containing the target structure) or **automatic** (i.e. students are required to process the sentences rapidly). Finally, judgement tasks can involve **judgement only** (i.e. simply stating whether a sentence is or is not grammatical) or **correct** (i.e. trying to correct the sentences judged to be ungrammatical).

What options, then, are utilized by the authors of the text books I sampled? Are there some options that appear to be underutilized? What does the author's choice of options suggest about their underlying 'theory' of grammar teaching? To answer these questions one unit of the six grammar practice books (dealing with the Present Continuous Tense [2]) was analyzed using the system of options shown in Figure 1. No attempt was made to determine the frequency with which each author used the different options. Instead, I sought to simply ascertain whether a particular option was evident at any point in a unit. The results of the analysis are shown in Table 1.

It is clear that two features are predominant; explicit description supplied and controlled production. Only one of the grammar practice books (Jones, 1992) failed to provide any grammatical explanation; all the books provided opportunities for controlled production practice.

Table 1: Analysis of methodological features in six grammar practice books

Books	1	2	3	4	5	6	Totals
Methodological features							
A. Explicit description							
1. Supplied	*	*	*		*	*	5
2. Discover				*		*	2
B. Data							
1. Source							
a. Authentic							0
b. Contrived			*			*	2
2. Text size							
c. Discrete sentences							0
d. Continuous			*			*	2
3. Medium							
a. Oral						*	1
b. Written			*			*	2
C. Operations							
1. Production							
a. Controlled	*	*	*	*	*	*	6
b. Free	*		*	*		*	4
2. Reception							
a. Controlled	*					*	2
b. Automatic						*	1
3. Judgements							
a. Judge only							
b. Correct	*					*	2
Total features per book	5	2	6	3	2	11	

Key: 1. Badalamenti and Henner-Stanchina (1993)
   2. Eastwood (1992)
   3. Elbaum (1996)
   4. Jones (1992)
   5. Murphy (1994)
   6. Schoenberg (1994)

In this respect then, the grammar practice books of today are probably not so different from those of previous decades. Grammar teaching is still characterized predominantly as (1) explaining/describing grammar points and (2) providing opportunities for controlled production practice. However, most of the books do also cater for free production practice. Usually, this takes the form of contextualized grammar activities (sometimes rather misleadingly labelled 'communicative') but occasionally there are also information-gap activities.

It is also revealing to note which features are not common in these books. Only two of the books, Jones (1992) and Schoenberg (1994), provide any opportunity for students to discover how a grammar point works for themselves. In fact, even these two books provide very few grammar discovery tasks and the actual tasks offer little in the way of guidance to the student. Also rather rare are data options. Of course most of the other books do provide examples of usage as part of the explicit description and all the books provide examples in the context of the production activities. However, only Elbaum (1996) and Schoenberg (1994) offer the learners independent data illustrating the use of the Present Continuous Tense. In both cases the data are contrived rather than authentic and involve continuous text. In Schoenberg, the data are provided in both an oral and a written form. This is the only book to be accompanied with an audio cassette. Finally, there is conspicuous paucity of receptive practice activities or activities involving grammatical judgements. Students have little opportunity to process these structures in oral or written texts without some form of accompanying production activity.

The books also vary in the number of different features they incorporate. Two of the books, Eastwood (1992) and Murphy (1994), both best-sellers, are most limited in this respect; they make use of only two features — supplied explicit description and controlled production practice. Such materials have the virtue of simplicity but they offer a rather impoverished view of grammar teaching. In contrast, Schoenberg (1994) manifests 11 different methodological features. This book provides a rich and varied approach to grammar teaching. One of the 'costs', however, is that each unit is rather long, the one on the Present Continuous Tense running to 22 pages (compared with 2 pages in Eastwood or Murphy).

The predominant 'theory' of grammar teaching that emerges from this analysis is a very traditional one. Grammar constitutes a 'content' that can be transmitted to students via explicit descriptions and a 'skill' that is developed through controlled practice — an amalgamation of the beliefs underlying the grammar translation and audiolingual methods. However, there are also signs that this predominant philosophy is being rethought by some authors. In particular, the need to encourage learners to discover grammar rules for themselves, to provide them with data where they can 'notice' how grammatical features are used and to teach grammar through options involving reception rather than through production practice are evident in some of the materials. In the sections that follow we will examine the theoretical rationale for such options and also consider some of the empirical research that has investigated them.

DISCOVERING ABOUT GRAMMAR

The first neglected option I would like to consider is discovering about grammar — enabling the students to build their own mini-grammars by helping them to investigate how specific points of grammar work. In effect, this requires students to function in much the same way as field linguists [3] do when they set about constructing descriptions of languages (see Bloomfield, 1933). There are two key theoretical issues that relate to this option; the role of **explicit knowledge** in L2 acquisition and the value of **discovery** as a general method of learning.

Current theories of L2 acquisition distinguish implicit and explicit knowledge. Implicit knowledge is knowledge of grammar. It refers to that knowledge that is intuitive and automatic (i.e. it can be rapidly accessed for use in unplanned language use). For example, native speakers of English 'know' that a nonce form like 'flacate' is a verb that does not permit dative alternation (i.e. cannot be used in sentences like * Mary flacated John the cake). However, they would be unable to tell you why (i.e., their knowledge of the underlying rule is entirely implicit) [4]. Probably the bulk of a native speaker's grammatical competence is comprised of implicit knowledge. Explicit knowledge is knowledge about grammar. It refers to knowledge that is conscious and can be accessed only slowly. It is typically used in what I have elsewhere termed 'secondary processes' of language use (e.g. monitoring output derived initially from implicit knowledge or translating sentences constructed in the learner's first language — see Ellis (1984b)). Explicit knowledge is, therefore, *analyzed*. However, it exists independently of learners' ability to verbalize it and thus cannot be equated with metalanguage. Native speakers draw on explicit knowledge in certain contexts, especially those that call for a careful style. This distinction between implicit and explicit knowledge is widely recognized in both cognitive psychology (e.g. Reber, 1989; Paradis, 1994) and in SLA (e.g. Bialystok, 1991; Schmidt, 1990). As Schmidt (1994) points out, it is separate from and should not be confused with the distinction between implicit and explicit *learning*. That is, whether a person is able to learn a language without consciousness, a matter of controversy, needs to be considered independently of the kind of knowledge they develop.

It would seem reasonable that writers of grammar practice materials should make clear what kind of grammatical knowledge they are aiming at. In fact, though, they rarely do so. Eastwood (1992), for example, says in the 'Introduction' to his book that 'special attention is given to those points which are often a problem for learners' (p.8) but does not explain what he means by 'problem'. Does he mean a 'problem in understanding' (i.e. explicit knowledge) or a 'problem in using a grammatical structure in unplanned language use' (i.e. implicit knowledge)? Probably the latter but there is no way of being sure. Murphy (1994) is a little clearer. He tells us the book 'concentrates on those structures which intermediate students want to use but which often cause difficulty' (p.viii). Presumably, then,

Murphy has implicit knowledge in mind. This would seem to be also the case with the other books listed in Table 1.

There is, however, a major problem in trying to teach implicit knowledge. This is that learners have been shown to acquire grammatical structures in a particular order and also to learn each structure very gradually, manifesting sequences of acquisition that include transitional structures (see Ellis, 1994a, Chapter 3, for an account of the natural order and sequence of acquisition). This has led to what Pienemann (1986) calls the Teachability Hypothesis which predicts that 'instruction can only promote language acquisition if the interlanguage is close to the point when the structure to be taught is acquired in the natural setting' (p. 37). In other words, learners have their own built-in syllabus (Corder, 1967) which they follow no matter what order grammatical structures are taught in. Mostly, writers of grammar practice books simply ignore this problem. That is, they present and practice grammatical structures in accordance with notions of 'difficulty' that have been passed down from one generation of writers to another without asking whether these notions have any psycholinguistic basis. Where writers do recognize the problem of teaching learners grammatical structures for unplanned language use (i.e. implicit knowledge), the solution is to ensure that 'students practice new structures in a variety of contexts to help them internalize and master them' (Schoenberg, 1994, p. xii) and, in particular, to ensure that there are plenty of opportunities to use the structure in communicative activities (see Larsen-Freeman's 'Introduction' to Badalamenti and Henner-Stanchina (1993)). This faith in production practice seems to reflect an unacknowledged adherence to behaviourist theories of language learning, now discredited. In fact, the available evidence is clear — grammar practice, even when it is 'communicative', does not allow learners to sidestep the natural processes of grammar learning (see Chapter 9 for a review of studies that have investigated the effects of grammar production practice). In short, then, teaching implicit knowledge through production practice is unlikely to work unless it so happens that the instruction coincides with the learner's state of readiness to acquire the specific grammatical structure that is the target of a lesson. Teachers spend a lot of time grouping learners according to ability but it is unlikely that they can precisely identify when they are ready to acquire a specific structure [5].

One solution to this problem is to make explicit knowledge rather than implicit knowledge of grammar the target of the teaching materials. This is what I have proposed in a series of publications (e.g. R. Ellis, 1993a, 1994b, 1997; see Chapters 11 and 13). This solution is based on four assumptions. The first is that the constraints that govern the teaching of implicit knowledge do not apply to the teaching of explicit knowledge. That is, the notions of 'order' and 'sequence' do not apply where explicit knowledge is concerned. In this respect, I would argue that explicit knowledge of grammar is not dissimilar to explicit knowledge of dates in history; it can be learned in any order, and one piece of information can be added to another incrementally. The second is that L2 learners (at least adolescent and adult learners) are capable of mastering quite sophisticated explicit knowledge. In this respect, I differ from Krashen (1982), who believes that learners are only able to learn simple and portable rules like the 3rd person -*s* rule, and follow instead Green and Hecht (1992), who demonstrated empirically that the learners in their study (high school and university level German learners of English) could demonstrate a good understanding of complex rules. The third assumption is that explicit knowledge, although not necessary for developing implicit knowledge, can assist the processes involved in its use and acquisition. I have argued that this occurs because explicit knowledge serves to (1) monitor language use and, thereby, to improve accuracy in output, (2) facilitate 'noticing' of new forms and new form-function mappings in the input and (3) make possible 'noticing-the-gap' (i.e. comparing what is noticed in the input with what learners are producing themselves). In other words, teachers may be able to facilitate the development of implicit knowledge indirectly by helping learners develop explicit knowledge. The fourth assumption is that grammar teaching, directed at explicit knowledge, should not seek to have an immediate effect on learners' ability to use a grammatical structure accurately in communication. Instead, it should accept that any effect is likely to be delayed.

If it is accepted that explicit knowledge constitutes a valid instructional goal, the next question concerns how such knowledge can best be taught. There are two basic options here. It can be taught directly or indirectly (see Ellis, 1997). Direct instruction takes the form of explicit descriptions/explanations of grammar points given to the learners. As we have seen, this is the preferred approach in the grammar practice books analyzed in Table 1. Indirect instruction involves helping learners to discover about grammatical rules for themselves. It implies a problem-solving approach where students are given data illustrating a specific grammatical structure which they are then helped to analyze in order to extract the underlying rule. As we have seen, this approach was rare in the grammar practice books we examined [6].

A discovery-based approach to teaching explicit knowledge has much to recommend it. First, it is potentially more motivating than simply being told a grammatical rule and, for this reason, students may be more likely to remember what they learn. Second, it can encourage students to form and test hypotheses about the grammar of the L2, processes that are believed to be central to ultimate acquisition (Corder, 1967). Third, it can lead to powerful insights about the grammar of a language that cannot be found in any published descriptions. As Hawkins (1984) points out, there is a great deal that linguists do not know about the grammar of a language and an exploratory approach can lead students to insights not to be found in any published description. Related to this point, a discovery-based approach enables learners to recognize that grammar is conventional rather than logical. As Faerch (1985) puts it, 'students have to learn that grammar and vocabulary do not always operate on the basis of what they consider to be normal, relative to their knowledge of other languages (primarily the L1), nor on the basis of what appears to be logical' (p. 190). In contrast, a direct approach may foster the false belief in learners that grammar is inherently logical. Fourth, and perhaps most important, discovery grammar tasks have a learning-training function. They help to develop the skills that learners need to investigate language autonomously — to become field linguists. Armed with these skills, students can carry out their own analyses of how the L2 grammar works, an activity that studies of the good language learner (e.g. Naiman *et al.* 1978) suggest may be important for successful language learning. Finally, if students carry out the discovery tasks by talking in the L2, they are in fact 'communicating'; grammar can serve as a content for talk. For some learners at least, talking about grammar may be more meaningful than talking about the kinds of general topics often found in communicative language courses.

Of course, to justify an indirect approach it is necessary to demonstrate that it is at least as effective as a direct approach in developing accurate explicit knowledge of L2 grammar in students. This is what Fotos set out to investigate. Fotos and Ellis (1991) reported a study designed to investigate the relative effectiveness of direct and indirect explicit grammar instruction. We found that both options resulted in statistically significant gains in understanding the rule for dative alternation in two groups of college-level Japanese students. In one group, direct explicit instruction resulted in higher scores on a grammaticality judgement test [7] but in the other indirect explicit instruction proved equally effective. In a more elaborate follow-up study, Fotos (1994) found indirect instruction worked as well as direct instruction in teaching explicit knowledge of three different structures (adverb-placement, dative alternation and relative clauses). Fotos (1993) was also able to demonstrate that the explicit knowledge that the learners gained from the discovery tasks helped to promote noticing of the target structures in subsequent message-oriented input. Caution must be exercised in generalizing from these studies as they investigated only one type of learner (Japanese university-level students taking general English classes), but they suggest that at least in some teaching contexts indirect teaching of explicit knowledge can be as effective as direct teaching.

NOTICING GRAMMATICAL FEATURES

The data options were also poorly represented in the grammar practice books analyzed in Table 1. That is, there were relatively few activities exposing students to what Sharwood Smith (1993) has called 'enhanced input' and requiring them to pay attention to the specific grammatical structure(s) targeted in this input. The exception was Schoenberg (1994). This book typically begins each section with a dialogue specially written to contain many examples of the target structure (e.g. Present Continuous Tense). The students are asked 'to listen and read' this text and then to answer some surface comprehension questions of a general nature.

A computational model of L2 acquisition, of the kind advocated by Krashen (1985) or Ellis (1994b), views acquisition as originating in input [8]. Learners acquire new grammatical structures when they encounter them in input, intake them and incorporate them into their existing interlanguage system. Such a model lends theoretical support to activities that expose learners to input rich in specific grammatical structures. However, exposure alone may not be enough for acquisition to take place. Learners may also need to pay conscious attention to (i.e. to **notice**) the grammatical structures in the input (Schmidt, 1990, 1994). Noticing may be the necessary condition for input to become intake. There are a number of ways in which such noticing can be brought about. One is by requesting students to identify the examples of the target structure in the data (e.g. 'Underline all the verbs in the Present Continuous Tense'). Another is to highlight the examples in some way, for example by italicizing them. A question of some importance, then, is which type of input data is most effective in promoting noticing and acquisition.

In fact, there have been relatively few studies examining what effect different ways of enriching input has on noticing and acquisition. Jourdenais *et al.*(1995) found that learners exposed to texts in which the preterit and imperfect verb forms in Spanish were typographically highlighted in texts were more likely to subsequently use these past tense forms than learners who read texts where the same verbs forms were not highlighted. Trahey and White (1993) and Trahey (1996) showed that input that is enriched but not enhanced (i.e. no attempt was made to focus learners' attention on the target feature) resulted in the learners acquiring a new rule for adverb positioning in English but not for eliminating a non-target rule that was part of the learners' current interlanguage. Leeman *et al.* (1995) found that instruction consisting of highlighting Spanish preterit and imperfect verb forms in written input, telling the students to pay special attention to them and correcting learner errors led to students supplying the target forms more frequently in comparison to students who received no such instruction. However, it is not possible in this study to distinguish what effect each of these different options had. Two other studies have reported that enriched input has little effect on acquisition. White (1995) failed to find any effect for either enriched input or explicit instruction on Japanese and francophone learners' mastery of reflexive binding in English, although this may have been because of problems with the test used in this study. Alanen (1995) also found that enriched input had little effect on beginner learners' acquisition of Finnish locative expressions and consonant gradation although he did note that input containing typographically enhanced forms led to the learners using a greater a variety of suffix forms, albeit ungrammatical. The amount of enriched input in this study was very small.

It is likely that we will see further research directed at identifying the kinds of enriched input that work best for noticing and acquisition. Ideally, such studies should be theoretically-based (i.e. there should be some principled selection of the input features that are chosen for investigation). Also there is a need to find ways of measuring the effects on noticing and acquisition separately.

Research investigating the data options shown in Table 1 is desirable. Various claims have been made for using authentic data in language teaching materials (see, for example, Harmer, 1983, p.150) but, to my knowledge, there has been no research testing whether such data enhances acquisition. Indeed, there are strong arguments to be found in both SLA (e.g. Krashen, 1981a) and language pedagogy (e.g. Tickoo, 1993) in support of simplified texts. Also, a number of studies have found that simplified input aids comprehension (Parker & Chaudron, 1987) and some (e.g. Ellis, 1995a) that it also facilitates acquisition. There is also widespread support in language pedagogy for the use of continuous text as opposed to discrete sentences but a complete absence of research investigating this belief. Neither has there been any research examining the relative advantages of presenting data in oral or written form. Oral data requires learners to process the target structure 'on-line' (i.e., as the input is received); in contrast, written data typically allows learners the opportunity to process the data more slowly and deliberately [9]. This difference may be important. The development of implicit knowledge may benefit from opportunities for on-line processing of input. In contrast, controlled processing may be more likely to result in explicit knowledge. It is possible, therefore, that oral data are more likely to promote real interlanguage change than written data. Such an argument suggests that teaching grammar through listening may prove especially effective, but, like the other options, it has not been empirically tested [10].

Several studies have compared two instructional options — enriched input and direct explicit instruction — on acquisition. These studies show a clear advantage for direct explicit instruction. Alanen (1995), for example, found that the group of learners receiving explicit instruction outperformed the groups receiving different kinds of enriched input. Robinson (1996) also found that learners given explicit instruction in both an easy grammatical rule (adverbial preposing as in 'Into the house ran John') and a difficult rule (pseudo-clefting as in 'Where Mary and

John live is Chicago') outperformed learners who just received input (referred to as the 'implicit' condition by Robinson) on a grammaticality judgement test. Studies by DeKeyser (1995) and N. Ellis (1993) have also found in favour of explicit instruction. However, the method of testing in these studies (usually a grammaticality judgement test) favoured the explicit group. It is possible that enriched input will work better than explicit instruction if acquisition is measured by means of a test that requires on-line processing of the target structures.

Also, from a materials development point of view it may make little sense to juxtapose data options and explicit instruction options in this way, as they can be easily combined, both contributing to the development of awareness in learners. Explicit instruction that is based on discovery tasks of the kind discussed above involve both data options and explicit rule formation. Students are presented with structured data which they analyze in order to extract the underlying rule for the target structure. The relationship between the two options, then, is as follows:

> data (analyzing) → explicit rule

An alternative arrangement might be to begin by providing an explicit rule and then to follow-up with noticing activities, where students are asked to identify the target structure in data:

> explicit rule → data (noticing)

A more complicated sequence might consist of:

> data (analyzing) → explicit rule → data (noticing)

as in Fotos (1994). Materials illustrating this type of sequence are discussed in a later section.

INPUT-PROCESSING INSTRUCTION

Closely connected to the data options associated with 'noticing' are the reception-based options referred to under 'operations' in Table 1. While it is technically feasible to envisage an approach to grammar teaching based solely on exposing learners to data rich in the targeted structures (sometimes referred to as 'input-flooding'), a more likely approach is one that combines data options with some kind of task designed to promote input-processing.

VanPatten (1996) defines input-processing instruction as 'a type of grammar instruction whose purpose is to affect the ways in which learners attend to input data' (p. 2). He emphasizes that 'it does not mean that any old input activity is viable' (p. 8) but involves attempts to alter the way learners actually process input. In other words, VanPatten envisages that learners will receive strategy training relating to how to set about paying attention to form in the input. Such training is intended to help students move from the 'default strategies' that they typically employ and that give rise to the transitional constructions found in interlanguage. For example, learners typically operate a 'first-noun strategy' according to which they assign the role of subject or agent to the first noun in an input string. Such a strategy leads to incorrect processing in strings where the first noun phrase is not the agent, as for example in passive sentences in English:

The committee was given a prize by Marcia.

As part of input-processing instruction students can be told to pay careful attention to the first noun to see whether it really is functioning as agent/subject and to look for linguistic clues (such as passive verb forms) to help them decide. Another example involves morphological marking of verbs. L2 learners frequently ignore these, relying instead on adverbial markers of time and aspect. In such a case, strategy training consists of pointing out to students the necessity of attending to tense/aspect markers in sentences that do not contain an adverbial. Such training, then, is designed to overcome the natural processes of 'simplification' found in L2 acquisition.

Input-processing also involves eliciting non-verbal (or, perhaps, minimally verbal) responses from learners that show whether they have been successful in processing the target structure in the input. This can be achieved in a variety of ways; performing an action (as in Total Physical Response), matching sentences with pictures, indicating whether statements are true or false, filling in the gaps in a written text by listening to an oral version of the text, choosing the correct L1 translation of an L2 sentence, agreeing/disagreeing with statements etc. The kinds of input-processing responses required by such tasks depend on the learners having comprehended the input but they involve more than just comprehension; they entail processing the specific linguistic forms they have noticed for meaning. In this respect, input-processing instruction differs from general listening/reading instruction, which encourages learners to make extensive use of contextual information and background knowledge (i.e. to engage in top-down processing). Input-processing instruction induces learners to attend to linguistic form (i.e. it forces bottom-up processing).

Both VanPatten (1996) and myself (Ellis, 1995b) have suggested guidelines for developing input-processing teaching materials. VanPatten suggests the following principles:

1. Teach only one thing at a time.

2. Keep meaning in focus.

3. Learners must do something with the input.

4. Use both oral and written input.

5. Move from sentences to connected discourse.

6. Keep the psycholinguistic processing strategies in mind.

I have suggested that the activities in input-processing instruction might be sequenced to require first attention to meaning (i.e. learners are invited to comprehend the message content of the input), then to noticing the target form and the meaning it conveys in the input, and finally to noticing-the-gap (i.e. spotting the kinds of typical errors that learners make when using the target structure). These guidelines are reflected in the materials discussed in the following section.

A number of studies (e.g. VanPatten & Cadierno, 1993; VanPatten & Sanz, 1995; VanPatten & Oikkenon, 1996; Tanaka, 1996; DeKeyser & Sokalski, 1996; Salaberry, 1997) have investigated the effectiveness of input-processing instruction, usually in terms of a comparison with production-based instruction. In Ellis (1999a), I have summarized the results and proposed the following conclusions. Input-processing instruction in conjunction with explicit instruction leads to gains in learners' ability to comprehend the target structures. Furthermore, it works better in this respect than production-based instruction. Input-processing instruction also results in gains in learners' ability to produce the target structures but in this respect it is not superior to production-based instruction. However, the gains in production that result from input-processing instruction may be more durable than those obtained from production-based instruction. That is, improvement in learners' ability to produce the target structures accurately tends to disappear in the case of production-based instruction but to persist in the case of input-processing instruction. However, research has failed to demonstrate that input-processing instruction results in learners' ability to immediately use the target structures in unplanned language use. Thus, it remains to be seen whether input-processing instruction affects interlanguage development (implicit knowledge) or whether it just serves to raise awareness (noticing and understanding). This is a key issue that needs to be further studied.

In general, the theoretical rationale and the results of research to date are sufficiently supportive of input-processing instruction for writers to incorporate tasks requiring reception-based operations in their materials. Input-processing operations, of course, can be combined with other options, including explicit instruction and production-practice. In the next section we discuss some materials that illustrate how this might be achieved.

SOME ILLUSTRATIVE TEACHING MATERIALS

The main thesis of this chapter is that materials writers have typically neglected a number of methodological options which SLA theory and research suggest may be effective in promoting L2 acquisition. What then might materials that incorporate these neglected options look like? We will briefly consider some examples from Rutherford (1987) and Ellis and Gaies (1998).

Rutherford suggests two kinds of instruments for raising learners' consciousness about grammar: (1) those involving learner judgement or discrimination and (2) those posing a task to be performed or a problem to be solved. The examples below are taken from Rutherford (1987, p.160–167). The first type includes both conventional grammaticality judgement tasks, as in this example directed at helping learners recognize that English needs a formal subject:

(A)   Decide whether each sentence is correct or incorrect. Identify the errors and correct them.

1. In Lake Maracaibo was discovered the oil.

2. After a few minutes the guests arrived.

3. In my country does not appear to exist any constraint on women's rights.

and semantic discrimination tasks that explore learners' ability to process particular grammatical constructions, such as complex noun phrases, as in this example:

(B)   Which of the statements can be inferred from the text provided?

The passing of the bill has given rise to further bitterness among the various linguistic communities in the province.

1. The various linguistic communities are bitter.

2. Bitterness caused the bill to be passed.

3. The province is bitter at the linguistic community.

Task completion/problem-solving tasks also involve judgement on the part of the learner, but, in addition, they require learners to act on their intuitions (i.e. they involve a degree of production as well as reflection). Here is an example of a task that requires learners to use dummy 'it' and the appropriate verb complementizer (e.g. 'Many

Canadians find <u>it</u> important to learn English'.

(C)   Rewrite each of the sentences below incorporating the sentence in brackets into the main sentence.

1. Many French Canadians find [They learn English] important.

2. Quebec makes [Quebec preserves its French-speaking identity] a rule.

3. Quebec takes [French is to be given priority over English] for granted.

It should be noted that in such a production activity the aim is not so much to 'practice' the target structure as to develop the learners' understanding of it. As Rutherford's examples make clear, production tasks can serve a consciousness-raising function.

Like Rutherford's activities, the materials in Ellis and Gaies (1998) are remedial in nature; that is, they focus on grammatical problems that L2 learners are known to experience. The materials have already been described in Chapter One. Here is an example of one unit. The activities are sequenced as suggested in Chapter 12 — they begin with general comprehension of the text, then prompt noticing (and rule discovery) and finally address noticing-the-gap. There is also an opportunity for students to experiment with using the target structure in their own sentences. Table 2 provides an analysis of the methodological options used in this unit.

LEVEL♦♦♦♦♦   SUBJECT-VERB AGREEMENT WITH SIMPLE PRESENT TENSE

18

Movie Listings

Have you seen a movie recently?
What was it about?

ERROR BOX

✗ Gwyneth Paltrow play Emma.

✗ Three former college friends plan revenge.

LISTENING TO COMPREHEND

Listen to the movie listings. Complete this table.

	Film	Type	Subject
1.	Grace of My Heart	_____	singing carreer of Edna Buxton
2.	_____	bittersweet comedy	_____
3.	Hoop Drems	documentaty	_____
4.	The Long Kiss Goodnight	_____	a woman's search for her identity

LISTENING TO NOTICE

Listen again. Choose the correct form of the verb in parentheses [ ].

WORD BOX
* a career
* a drama
* amnesia
* a comedy
* a professional
* a documentary
* an action thriller

1. Grace of My Heart

This drama **follows** the singing carreer of Edna
<small>1 (follow/follows)</small>
Buxton as she _____ through the pop music
<small>2 (move/moves)</small>
world of the late '50s and '60s.

2. Big Night

This bittersweet comedy tells the story of two Italian immigrants who

_____ a restaurant in New Jersey. But their American Dream
<small>3 (open/opens)</small>

_____ sour and things end up badly.
<small>4 (turn/turns)</small>

3. Hoop Dreams

This documentary follows four years in the lives of 14-year-olds Arthur

Agee and William Gates, two exceptionally talented basketball players.

They _____ up poor in downtown Chicago and _____ of
<small>5 (grow/grow)</small>   <small>6 (dream/dreams)</small>

careers as highly paid professionals.

4. The Long Kiss Goodnight

This action thriller stars Geena Davis playing a school teacher who

_____ from amnesia. She hires a detective, played by Samuel L.
7 (suffer/suffers)

Jackson, and together they _____ for her past and true identity.
8 (search/searches)

UNDERSTANDING THE GRAMMAR POINT

1. Complete this table. Use the information in the movie listings.

	Subject	Verb
1.	*drama*	*follows*
2.	*she*	
3.	*who (two Italians)*	
4.		
5.		
6.		
7.		
8.		

2. Which form of the verb is used with singular subjects?
Which form of the verb is used with plural subjects?

CHECKING

Choose the correct form of the verb to complete these movie listings.

1. The Relic

Penelope Ann Miller and Tom Sizemore ___star___ in this thriller. They
1 (star)

_____ partners when a number of murders _____ place in the
2 (become) 3 (take)

museum where biologist Margo Green _____.
4 (work)

2. Romeo and Juliet

Leonardo DiCaprio and Clare Danes _____ in this remake of
5 (star)

Shakespeare's classic story of two doomed lovers. The action takes place in a gang-filled Los Angeles neighborhood. A rockin sound-track

_____ the action moving.
6 *(keep)*

TRYING IT

Think of a movie you have seen

LANGUAGE NOTE
Use the simple present tense

recently. Write your own listing describing the movie.

_____

_____

_____

_____

Table 2: Analysis of methodological features in Ellis and Gaies (1998)

Methodological features	
A. Explicit description	
1. Supplied	*
2. Discover	*
B. Data	
1. Source	
a. Authentic	
b. Contrived	*
2. Text size	
c. Discrete sentences	
d. Continuous	*
3. Medium	
a. Oral	*
b. Written	*
C. Operations	
1. Production	
a. Controlled	
b. Free	*
2. Reception	
a. Controlled	
b. Automatic	*
3. Judgements	
a. Judge only	*
b. Correct	*
Total features	10

CONCLUSION

The design of grammar teaching materials needs to draw on the accumulated experience of teachers. By analyzing the methodological options in a number of popular grammar practice books I have attempted to show that there is a clear tradition evident in such materials. This emphasises two predominant methodological features: the provision of descriptions of grammatical points and controlled production exercises.

Tradition, however, also needs to be challenged. One way of doing so is by drawing on SLA theory and research. Over the last 25 years this has been directed primarily at describing and explaining how learners acquire the grammar of an L2 and has led to a number of insights and possibilities that can be incorporated into teaching materials. In particular, SLA suggests that grammar practice materials might include discovery-type grammar tasks for raising learners' consciousness about grammar, data in the form of structured input to induce 'noticing' of target structures and input-processing tasks. I have given examples of materials that include these options. I have tried to show in this chapter how SLA can guide the development of teaching materials.

Of course, I do not wish to claim that because such materials have the support of SLA theory and research they are more valid than materials based on teachers' accumulated experience. This would be not only presumptuous but also wrong. For a start, SLA researchers and theorists are not in total agreement as to what constitute the optimal conditions for grammar acquisition [11]. Also, countless learners have successfully learned from traditional grammar teaching materials. It would, therefore, be very mistaken to argue that all such materials should include grammar discovery, noticing and input-processing tasks. Rather, as I have argued elsewhere (see Ellis, 1997), SLA should be seen as one source of 'provisional specifications' (Stenhouse, 1975) that teachers need to experiment with through their own day-to-day teaching and through 'insider research' (Widdowson, 1990). Teaching materials have an important mediating role in this process. They constitute a means of operationalizing research or theory-based specifications about teaching. In this respect, grammar practice materials can serve as an important source of innovation in language teaching.

Notes

[1] There are, of course, other important questions concerning grammar teaching — in particular, what grammar points should be taught? However, my concern in this chapter is entirely with the methodology of grammar teaching, not with its content.

[2] There was no unit dealing with the Present Continuous Tense in Jones (1992). However, as my aim was to include a representative sample of current grammar practice books, I felt it important to include Jones' book, as it represented a more 'functional' approach to grammar teaching than the other books. I selected the unit dealing with Past Continuous and Present Perfect Continuous.

[3] This is not a new idea. Jespersen (1904) advocated what he called 'Inventional Grammar' which was created by students themselves as they gained insight into the grammar of the language they were studying.

[4] Roughly speaking, the rule is that if the verb is two syllables or longer, as in the case of verbs of Latin origin, they do not permit dative alternation but that if the verb is one syllable and of Anglo-Saxon origin it does.

[5] The impracticality of basing grammar syllabuses on the natural order and sequence of acquisition derives primarily from the fact that grammar structures cannot be taught as 'accumulated entities' (Rutherford, 1987) but rather need to be integrated into highly complex interlanguage systems. This involves not just the 'addition' of new features but also the 'restructuring' of existing knowledge (McLaughlin, 1990), a process that is highly complex and necessarily gradual.

[6] There are some books that adopt a discovery-based approach to grammar, notably Bolitho and Tomlinson's *Discover Grammar* (1980) designed for trainees teachers of a second/foreign language who need to develop an explicit knowledge of grammar.

[7] The explanation that Fotos and Ellis (1991) offer for the superiority of the direct instruction with one of the groups they studied was that the instructor did not ensure that the discovery grammar task was carried out properly. This, of course, may reflect an inherent limitation of such tasks — namely, that they

require considerable expertise and care on the part of the instructor to ensure they work.

[8] In some versions of the computational model of L2 acquisition, output also has a role to play (see, for example, Swain, 1995; Skehan, 1998). However, even in these versions, output works primarily in terms of either securing quality input or creating the psycholinguistic conditions that promote input.

[9] It would, of course, be possible to induce rapid, less controlled processing of written data if the learners are required to read the texts at speed, as in faster reading exercises.

[10] A body of research that could be interpreted as lending support to teaching grammar through listening is that conducted by Asher and his associates (see Asher, 1977) comparing Total Physical Response (TPR) and other language teaching methods (e.g. grammar translation and audiolingualism). TPR is a method that teaches grammatical structures through oral commands. Asher's research regularly found that this method proved superior to other methods for beginner-level learners. However, Asher did not compare the relative advantages of using oral or written commands, as in TPR the commands are primarily oral.

[11] DeKeyser and Sokalski (1996), for example, argue on the basis of skill-learning theory that production and receptive activities are beneficial, contributing respectively to learners' ability to comprehend and produce the target structures.

Chapter 15

Principles of Instructed Language Learning

This chapter is based on an article that first appeared in System Vol. 33: 209–224.

INTRODUCTION

Second Language Acquisition (SLA), as a sub-discipline of applied linguistics, is still a very young field of study. While it may not be possible to identify its precise starting point, many researchers would agree that the late sixties marked the onset of an intense period of empirical and theoretical interest in how second languages are acquired. Much of this research has been directed at understanding and contributing to more effective instructed language learning. In addition to the numerous studies that have investigated the effects of instruction on learning (Norris and Ortega's meta-analysis published in 2000 identified 79 studies), much of the theorizing about L2 instruction has been specifically undertaken with language pedagogy in mind, for example Krashen's Monitor Model (Krashen, 1981a), Long's Interaction Hypothesis (Long, 1996), DeKeyser's skill-learning theory (DeKeyser, 1998), VanPatten's input processing theory (VanPatten, 1996, 2002) and my own theory of instructed language learning (Ellis, 1994b) all address the role of instruction in L2 acquisition.

However, the research and theory do not afford a uniform account of how instruction can best facilitate language learning. There is considerable controversy (see Chapter 17). In particular, there is no agreement as to whether instruction should be based on a traditional focus-on-forms approach, involving the systematic teaching of grammatical features in accordance with a structural syllabus, or a focus-on-form approach, involving attention to linguistic features in the context of communicative activities derived from a task-based syllabus or some kind of combination of the two. Nor is there agreement about the efficacy of teaching explicit knowledge or about what type of corrective feedback to provide or even when explicit grammar teaching should commence. These controversies reflect both the complexity of the object of enquiry (instructed language acquisition) and also the fact that SLA is still in its infancy.

Given these controversies, it might be thought unwise to attempt to formulate a set of general principles of instructed language acquisition. Hatch's (1978d) warning — 'apply with caution' — is as pertinent today as it was some thirty years ago. Nevertheless, I think there is a need to try to draw together a set of generalisations that might serve as the basis for language teacher education, and I am not alone in this, for Lightbown (1985a, 2000) has felt and responded to a similar need. If SLA is to offer teachers guidance there is a need to bite the bullet and proffer advice, so long as this advice does not masquerade as prescriptions or proscriptions (and there is always a danger that advice will be so construed) and so long as it is tentative, in the form of what Stenhouse (1975) called 'provisional specifications'. I have chosen to present my own provisional specifications in the form of 'principles'. I do not expect that all SLA researchers or all language teachers will agree with them. I hope, though, that they will provide a basis for argument and for reflection.

PRINCIPLE 1: INSTRUCTION NEEDS TO ENSURE THAT LEARNERS DEVELOP BOTH A RICH REPERTOIRE OF FORMULAIC EXPRESSIONS AND A RULE-BASED COMPETENCE

Proficiency in an L2 requires that learners acquire both a rich repertoire of formulaic expressions, which caters to fluency, and a rule-based competence consisting of knowledge of specific grammatical rules, which cater to complexity and accuracy (Skehan, 1998). There is now widespread acceptance of the importance played by formulaic expressions in language use. Native speakers have been shown to use a much larger number of formulaic expressions than even advanced L2 learners (Foster, 2001). Formulaic expressions may also serve as a basis for the later development of a rule-based competence. N. Ellis (1996), for example, has suggested that learners bootstrap their way to grammar by first internalising and then analyzing fixed sequences. Classroom studies by R. Ellis (1984a), Myles, Mitchell & Hooper (1998; 1999) and Myles (2004) demonstrate that learners often internalize rote-learned material as chunks, breaking them down for analysis later on.

Traditionally, language instruction has been directed at developing rule-based competence (i.e. knowledge of specific grammatical rules) through the systematic teaching of pre-selected structures — what Long (1991) has referred to as a focus-on-forms approach. While such an approach certainly receives support from the research that has investigated direct intervention in interlanguage development, curriculum designers and teachers need to recognize that this type of instruction is as likely to result in students learning rote-memorized patterns as in internalizing abstract rules (Myles, 2004). This need not be seen as an instructional failure, however, as such patterns are clearly of value to the learner. It points instead to an acknowledgement of what can be realistically achieved by a focus-on-forms approach, especially with young, beginner learners.

If formulaic chunks play a large role in early language acquisition, it may pay to focus on these initially, delaying the teaching of grammar until later, as I have proposed in E. Ellis (2002c). A notional-functional approach lends itself perfectly to the teaching of prefabricated patterns and routines and may provide an ideal foundation for direct intervention in the early stages. Clearly, though, a complete language curriculum needs to ensure that it caters to the development of both formulaic expressions and rule-based knowledge.

PRINCIPLE 2: INSTRUCTION NEEDS TO ENSURE THAT LEARNERS FOCUS PREDOMINANTLY ON MEANING

The term 'focus on meaning' is somewhat ambiguous. It is necessary to distinguish two different senses of this term. The first refers to the idea of semantic meaning (i.e. the meanings of lexical items or of specific grammatical structures). The second sense of focus on meaning relates to pragmatic meaning (i.e. the highly contextualized meanings that arise in acts of communication). To provide opportunities for students to attend to and perform pragmatic meaning a task-based (or, at least, a task-supported) approach to language teaching is required. It is clearly important that instruction ensures opportunities for learners to focus on both types of meaning but, arguably, it is pragmatic meaning that is crucial to language learning.

There is an important difference in the instructional approaches needed for semantic and pragmatic meaning. In the case of semantic meaning, the teacher and the students can treat language as an object and function as pedagogues and learners. But in the case of pragmatic meaning, they need to view the L2 as a tool for communicating and to function as communicators [1]. In effect, this involves two entirely different orientations to teaching and learning.

The opportunity to focus on pragmatic meaning is important for a number of reasons:

1. In the eyes of many theorists (e.g. Prabhu, 1987; Long, 1996), only when learners are engaged in decoding and encoding messages in the context of actual acts of communication are the conditions created for acquisition to take place.

2. To develop true fluency in an L2, learners must have opportunities to create pragmatic meaning (DeKeyser, 1998).

3. Engaging learners in activities where they are focused on creating pragmatic meaning is intrinsically motivating.

In arguing the need for a focus on pragmatic meaning, theorists do so not just because they see this as a means of activating the linguistic resources that have been developed by other means but because they see it as the principal means by which the linguistic resources themselves are created. This is the theoretical position that has informed many highly successful immersion education programmes around the world (see Johnson & Swain, 1997). However, in advocating this principle, I do not wish to suggest that instruction needs to be directed exclusively at providing learners with opportunities to create pragmatic meaning, only that, to be effective, instruction must include such opportunities and that, ideally, over an entire curriculum, they should be predominant.

PRINCIPLE THREE: INSTRUCTION NEEDS TO ENSURE THAT LEARNERS ALSO FOCUS ON FORM

There is now a widespread acceptance that acquisition also requires that learners attend to form. Indeed, according to some theories of L2 acquisition, such attention is necessary for acquisition to take place. Schmidt (1994), for example, has argued that there is no learning without conscious attention to form [2].

Again, though, the term 'focus on form' is capable of more than one interpretation. First, it might refer to a general orientation to language as form. Schmidt (2001) dismisses this global attention hypothesis, arguing that learners need to attend to specific forms. Second, it might be taken to suggest that learners need to attend only to the graphic or phonetic instantiations of linguistic forms. However, theorists such as Schmidt and Long are insistent that focus on form refers to form-function mapping (i.e. the correlation between a particular form and the meaning(s) it realises in communication). Third, 'focus on form' might be assumed to refer to awareness of some underlying, abstract rule. Schmidt, however, is careful to argue that attention to form refers to the noticing of specific linguistic items, as they occur in the input to which learners are exposed, not to an awareness of grammatical rules.

Instruction can cater to a focus on form in a number of ways:

1. Through grammar lessons designed to teach specific grammatical features by means of input- or output-processing. An inductive approach to grammar teaching is designed to encourage 'noticing' of pre-selected forms; a deductive approach seeks to establish an awareness of the grammatical rule.

2. Through focused tasks (i.e. tasks that require learners to comprehend and process specific grammatical structures in the input, and/or to produce the structures in the performance of the task).

3. By means of methodological options that induce attention to form in the context of performing a task. Two methodological options that have received considerable attention from researchers are (a) the provision of time for strategic and on-line planning (Yuan & Ellis, 2003; Foster & Skehan, 1996) and (b) corrective feedback (Lyster, 2004).

Instruction can seek to provide an <u>intensive</u> focus on pre-selected linguistic forms (as in a focus-on-forms approach or in a lesson built around a focused task) or it can offer incidental and <u>extensive</u> attention to form through corrective feedback in task-based lessons. There are pros and cons for both intensive and extensive grammar instruction. Some structures may not be mastered without the opportunity for repeated practice. Harley (1989), for example, found that Anglophone learners of L2 French failed to acquire the distinction between the preterit and imparfait past tenses after hours of exposure (and presumably some corrective feedback) in an immersion programme but were able to improve their accuracy in the use of these two tenses after intensive instruction. However, intensive instruction is time-consuming (in Harley's study the targeted structures were taught over an 8 week period!) and thus there will be constraints on how many structures can be addressed. Extensive grammar instruction, on the other hand, affords the opportunity for large numbers of grammatical structures to be addressed. Also, more likely than not, many of the structures will be attended to repeatedly over a period of time. Further, because this kind of instruction involves a response to the errors each learner makes it is individualized and affords the skilled teacher on-line opportunities for the kind of contextual analysis that Celce-Murcia (2002) recommends as a basis for grammar teaching. Ellis *et al.* (2001) reported that extensive instruction occurred relatively frequently in communicative adult ESL lessons through both pre-emptive (i.e. teacher or student-initiated) and reactive (i.e. corrective feedback) attention to form. Loewen (2002) showed that learners who experienced such momentary form-focused episodes demonstrated subsequent learning of the forms addressed in both immediate and delayed tests. However, it is not possible to attend to those structures that learners do not attempt to use (i.e. extensive instruction cannot deal with avoidance). Also, of course, it does not provide the in-depth practice that some structures may require before they can be fully acquired. Arguably, then, instruction needs to be conceived of in terms of both approaches.

PRINCIPLE 4: INSTRUCTION NEEDS TO BE PREDOMINANTLY DIRECTED AT DEVELOPING IMPLICIT KNOWLEDGE OF THE L2 WHILE NOT NEGLECTING EXPLICIT

Implicit knowledge is procedural, is held unconsciously and can only be verbalized if it is made explicit. It is accessed rapidly and easily and thus is available for use in rapid, fluent communication. In the view of most researchers, competence in an L2 is primarily a matter of implicit knowledge.Explicit knowledge 'is the declarative and often anomalous knowledge of the phonological, lexical, grammatical, pragmatic and socio-critical features of an L2 together with the metalanguage for labelling this knowledge' (Ellis, 2004). It is held consciously, is learnable and verbalizable and is typically accessed through controlled processing when learners experience some kind of linguistic difficulty in the use of the L2. A distinction needs to be drawn between explicit knowledge as analysed knowledge and as metalingual explanation. The former entails a conscious awareness of how a structural feature works while the latter consists of knowledge of grammatical metalanguage and the ability to understand explanations of rules.

Given that it is implicit knowledge that underlies the ability to communicate fluently and confidently in an L2, it is this type of knowledge that should be the ultimate goal of any instructional programme. How then can it be developed? There are conflicting theories regarding this. According to skill-building theory (DeKeyser, 1998), implicit knowledge arises out of explicit knowledge, when the latter is proceduralized through practice. In contrast, emergentist theories (Krashen, 1981a; N. Ellis, 1998) see implicit knowledge as developing naturally out of meaning-focused communication, aided, perhaps, by some focus on form. Irrespective of these different theoretical positions, there is consensus that learners need the opportunity to participate in communicative activity to develop implicit knowledge. Thus, communicative tasks need to play a central role in instruction directed at implicit knowledge.

The value in teaching explicit knowledge of grammar has been and remains today one of the most controversial issues in language pedagogy. In order to make sense of the different positions relating to the teaching of explicit knowledge it is necessary to consider two separate questions:

1. Is explicit knowledge of any value in and of itself?
2. Is explicit knowledge of value in facilitating the development of implicit knowledge?

Explicit knowledge is arguably only of value if it can be shown that learners are able to utilize this type of knowledge in actual performance. Again, there is controversy. One position is that this is very limited. Krashen (1982) argues that learners can only use explicit knowledge when they 'monitor' and that this requires that they are focused on form (as opposed to meaning) and have sufficient time to access the knowledge. Other positions are possible. It can be argued that explicit knowledge is used in both the process of formulating messages as well as in monitoring and that many learners are adroit in accessing their explicit memories for these purposes, especially if the rules are, to a degree, automatized. However, this does require time. Yuan and Ellis (2003) showed that learners' grammatical accuracy improved significantly if they had time for 'on-line planning' while performing a narrative task, a result most readily explained in terms of their accessing explicit knowledge.

Irrespective of whether explicit knowledge has any value in and of itself, it may assist language development by facilitating the development of implicit knowledge. This involves a consideration of what has become known as **interface hypothesis**, which addresses whether explicit knowledge plays a role in L2 acquisition. Three positions can be identified. According to the non-interface position (Krashen, 1981a), explicit and implicit knowledge are entirely distinct with the result that explicit knowledge cannot be converted into implicit knowledge. This position is supported by research that suggests that explicit and implicit memories are neurologically separate (Paradis, 1994). The interface position argues the exact opposite. Drawing on skill-learning theory (DeKeyser, 1998), it argues that explicit knowledge becomes implicit knowledge if learners have the opportunity for plentiful communicative practice. The weak interface position (R. Ellis, 1993a) claims that explicit knowledge primes a number of key acquisitional processes, in particular 'noticing' and 'noticing the gap' (Schmidt, 1994). That is, explicit knowledge of a grammatical structure makes it more likely learners will attend to the structure in the input and carry out the cognitive comparison between what they observe in the input and their own output. These positions continue to be argued at a theoretical level.

The three positions support very different approaches to language teaching. The non-interface position leads to a 'zero grammar' approach, i.e. one that prioritizes meaning-centred approaches such as task-based teaching. The interface position supports PPP — the idea that a grammatical structure should be first presented explicitly and then practiced until it is fully proceduralized. The weak interface position has been used to provide a basis for consciousness-raising tasks (Ellis, 1991) that require learners to derive their own explicit grammar rules from data they are provided with.

This principle, then, asserts that instruction needs to be directed at developing both implicit and explicit knowledge, giving priority to the former. However, teachers should not assume that explicit knowledge can be converted into implicit knowledge, as the extent to which this is possible remains controversial.

PRINCIPLE 5: INSTRUCTION NEEDS TO TAKE ACCOUNT OF THE LEARNER'S 'BUILT-IN SYLLABUS'

Early research into naturalistic L2 acquisition showed that learners follow a 'natural' order and sequence of acquisition (i.e. they master different grammatical structures in a relatively fixed and universal order and they pass through a sequence of stages of acquisition on route to mastering each grammatical structure). This led researchers like Corder (1967) to suggest that learners had their own 'built-in syllabus' for learning grammar as implicit knowledge. Krashen (1981a) famously argued that grammar instruction played no role in the development of implicit knowledge (what he called 'acquisition'), a view based on the conviction that learners (including classroom learners) would automatically proceed along their built-in syllabus as long as they had access to comprehensible input and were sufficiently motivated. Grammar instruction could contribute only to explicit knowledge ('learning').

   There followed a number of empirical studies designed to (1) compare the order of acquisition of instructed and naturalistic learners (e.g. Pica, 1983), (2) compare the success of instructed and naturalistic learners (Long, 1983a) and (3) examine whether attempts to teach specific grammatical structures resulted in their acquisition (Ellis, 1984a; Chapter 2). These studies showed that, by and large, the order and sequence of acquisition was the same for instructed and naturalistic learners, a finding supported by later research (e.g. Ellis, 1989 — Chapter 3; Pienemann, 1989); that instructed learners generally achieved higher levels of grammatical competence than naturalistic learners and that instruction was no guarantee that learners would acquire what they had been taught. This led to the conclusion that it was beneficial to teach grammar but that it was necessary to ensure it was taught in a way that was compatible with the natural processes of acquisition.

   How, then, can instruction take account of the learner's built-in syllabus? There are a number of possibilities:

   1. Adopt a zero grammar approach, as proposed by Krashen. That is, employ a task-based approach that makes no attempt to predetermine the linguistic content of a lesson.
   2. Ensure that learners are developmentally ready to acquire a specific target feature. However, this is probably impractical as teachers have no easy way of determining where individual students have reached and it would necessitate a highly individualized approach to cater for differences in developmental level among the students. Also, as we noted earlier, such fine-tuning may not be necessary. While instruction in a target feature may not enable learners to 'beat' the built-in syllabus it may serve to push them along it as long as the target structure is not too far ahead of their

developmental stage.

3. Focus the instruction on explicit rather than implicit knowledge as explicit knowledge is not subject to the same developmental constraints as implicit knowledge. While it is probably true that some declarative facts about language are easier to master than others, this is likely to reflect their cognitive rather than their developmental complexity, which can more easily be taken into account in deciding the order of instruction. Traditional structural syllabuses, in fact, are graded on the basis of cognitive complexity [3].

PRINCIPLE 6: SUCCESSFUL INSTRUCTED LANGUAGE LEARNING REQUIRES EXTENSIVE L2 INPUT

Language learning, whether it occurs in a naturalistic or an instructed context, is a slow and laborious process. Children acquiring their L1 take between two and five years to achieve full grammatical competence, during which time they are exposed to massive amounts of input. Ellis and Wells (1980) demonstrated that a substantial portion of the variance in speed of acquisition of children can be accounted for by the amount and the quality of input they receive. The same is undoubtedly true of L2 acquisition. If learners do not receive exposure to the target language they cannot acquire it. In general, the more exposure they receive, the more and the faster they will learn. Krashen (1981a, 1994) has adopted a very strong position on the importance of input. He points to studies that have shown that length of residence in the country where the language is spoken is related to language proficiency and other studies that that have found positive correlations between the amount of reading reported and proficiency/literacy. For Krashen, however, the input must be made 'comprehensible' either by modifying it or by means of contextual props. Researchers may disagree with Krashen's claim that comprehensible input (together with motivation) is all that is required for successful acquisition, arguing that learner output is also important (see Principle 7 below) but they agree about the importance of input for developing the highly connected implicit knowledge that is needed to become an effective communicator in the L2.

How can teachers ensure their students have access to extensive input? In a 'second' language teaching context, learners can be expected to gain access to plentiful input outside the classroom, although, as Tanaka (2004) has shown in a study of adult Japanese students learning English in Auckland, not all such learners are successful in achieving this. In a 'foreign' language teaching context (as when French or Japanese is taught in schools in the United Kingdom or United States), there are far fewer opportunities for extensive input. To ensure adequate access, teachers need to:

1. Maximise use of the L2 inside the classroom. Ideally, this means that the L2 needs to become the medium as well as the object of instruction. A study by Kim and Elder (2005) revealed that foreign language teachers of French, German, Japanese and Korean in Auckland secondary schools varied enormously in the extent to which they employed the L2 in the classroom (i.e. between 88 and 22 percent of the total input).

2. Create opportunities for students to receive input outside the classroom. This can be achieved most easily be providing extensive reading programmes based on carefully selected graded readers, suited to the level of the students, as recommended by Krashen (1989). Elley (1991) reviewed studies that showed that L2 learners can benefit from both reading and from being read to. Also, ideally, if more resources are available, schools need to establish self-access centres which students can use outside class time. Successful FL learners seek out opportunities to experience the language outside class time. Many students are unlikely to make the effort unless teachers (a) make resources available and (b) provide learner-training in how to make effective use of the resources.

It can be claimed with confidence that, if the only input students receive is in the context of a limited number of weekly lessons based on some coursebook, they are unlikely to achieve high levels of L2 proficiency.

PRINCIPLE 7: SUCCESSFUL INSTRUCTED LANGUAGE LEARNING ALSO REQUIRES OPPORTUNITIES FOR OUTPUT

Contrary to Krashen's insistence that acquisition is dependent entirely on comprehensible input, most researchers now acknowledge that learner output also plays a part. Skehan (1998) drawing on Swain (1995) summarises the contributions that output can make:

1. production serves to generate better input through the feedback that learners' efforts at production elicit;
2. it forces syntactic processing (i.e. obliges learners to pay attention to grammar);
3. it allows learners to test out hypotheses about the target language grammar;
4. it helps to automatize existing knowledge;
5. it provides opportunities for learners to develop discourse skills, for example by producing 'long turns';
6. it is important for helping learners to develop a 'personal voice' by steering conversation on to topics they are interested in contributing to.

Ellis (2003) adds one other contribution of output:

7. it provides the learner with 'auto-input' (i.e. learners can attend to the 'input' provided by their own productions).

The importance of creating opportunities for output, including what Swain (1985) has called pushed output (i.e. output where the learner is stretched to express messages clearly and explicitly), constitutes one of the main reasons for incorporating tasks into a language programme. Controlled practice exercises typically result in output that is limited in terms of length and complexity. They do not afford students opportunities for the kind of sustained output that theorists argue is necessary for interlanguage development. Research (e.g. Allen *et al.*, 1990) has shown that extended talk of a clause or more in a classroom context is more likely to occur when students initiate interactions in the classroom and when they have to find their own words. This is best achieved by asking learners to perform oral and written tasks.

PRINCIPLE 8: THE OPPORTUNITY TO INTERACT IN THE L2 IS CENTRAL TO DEVELOPING L2 PROFICIENCY

While it is useful to consider the relative contributions of input and output to acquisition, it is also important to acknowledge that both co-occur in oral interaction and that both computational and sociocultural theories of L2 acquisition have viewed social interaction as the matrix in which acquisition takes place. As Hatch (1978a) famously put it, 'one learns how to do conversation, one learns how to interact verbally, and out of the interaction syntactic structures are developed' (p.404). Thus, interaction is not just a means of automatizing existing linguistic resources but also of creating new resources. According to the Interaction Hypothesis (Long, 1996), interaction fosters acquisition when a communication problem arises and learners are engaged in negotiating for meaning. The interactional modifications arising help to make input comprehensible, provide corrective feedback, and push learners to modify their own output in uptake. According to the sociocultural theory of mind, interaction serves as a form of mediation, enabling learners to construct new forms and perform new functions collaboratively (Lantolf, 2000). From this perspective, learning occurs first on the social plane and only later on the psychological plane. In both theories, while social interaction may not be viewed as necessary for acquisition, it is viewed as a primary source of learning.

What then are the characteristics of interaction that are deemed important for acquisition? In general terms, opportunities for negotiating meaning and plenty of scaffolding are needed. Karen Johnson (1995) identifies four key requirements for interaction to create an acquisition-rich classroom:

1. Creating contexts of language use where students have a reason to

attend to language.

2. Providing opportunities for learners to use the language to express their own personal meanings.

3. Helping students to participate in language-related activities that are beyond their current level of proficiency.

4. Offering a full range of contexts that cater for a 'full performance' in the language.

Johnson suggests that these are more likely to occur when the academic task structure (i.e. how the subject matter is sequenced in a lesson) and the social participation structure (i.e. how the allocation of interactional rights and obligations shapes the discourse) are less rigid. Once again, this is more likely to be provided through 'tasks' than through exercises. Ellis (1999b) suggests that a key to ensuring interaction beneficial to acquisition is giving control of the discourse topic to the students. This, of course, is not easily achieved, given that teachers have a duty to ensure that classroom discourse is orderly, which, in turn, is most easily achieved by taking control of the discourse topic by means of IRF (teacher initiate – student respond – teacher feedback) exchanges. Thus creating the right kind of interaction for acquisition constitutes a major challenge for teachers. One solution is to incorporate small group work into a lesson. When students interact amongst themselves, acquisition-rich discourse is more likely to ensue. However, there are a number of dangers in group work which may militate against this (e.g. excessive use of the L1 in monolingual groups).

PRINCIPLE 9: INSTRUCTION NEEDS TO TAKE ACCOUNT OF INDIVIDUAL DIFFERENCES IN LEARNERS

While there are identifiable universal aspects of L2 acquisition, there is also considerable variability in the rate of learning and in the ultimate level of achievement. In particular, learning will be more successful when:

1. The instruction is matched to students' particular aptitude for learning.

2. The students are motivated.

It is probably beyond the abilities of most teachers to design lessons involving the kind of matching instruction employed in Wesche's (1981) study, which used language aptitudes tests to identify different learning styles and then sought to match the kind of instruction provided to the learners' preferred approach to learning. However, teachers can cater to variation in the nature of their students' aptitude by adopting a flexible teaching approach involving a variety of learning activities. They can also make use of simple learner-training materials (e.g. G. Ellis & Sinclair, 1989) designed to make students more aware of their own approaches to learning and to develop awareness of alternative approaches. Good language learner studies (e.g. Naiman *et al.*, 1978) suggest that successful language learning requires a flexible approach to learning. Thus, increasing the range of learning strategies at learners' disposal is one way in which teachers can help them to learn. Such strategy training needs to foster an understanding that language learning requires both an experiential and an analytical approach and to demonstrate the kinds of strategies related to both approaches. School-based students often tend to adopt an analytical approach to learning (even if this does not accord with their natural aptitude) as this is the kind of approach generally fostered in schools (Sternberg, 2002). They may have greater difficulty in adopting the kind of experiential approach required in task-based language teaching. Some learner-training, therefore, may be essential if learners are to perform tasks effectively [4].

Dornyei's research has shown the kinds of teaching strategies that teachers can employ to develop and maintain their students' intrinsic motivation. Dornyei (2001) also makes the obvious point that 'the best motivational intervention is simply to improve the quality of our teaching' (p. 26). He points in particular to the need for 'instructional clarity' and refers to Wlodkowski's (1986) checklist for achieving this. This includes such obvious recipes as 'explain things simply' and 'teach at a pace that is not too fast and not too slow'. Teachers also need to accept that it is their responsibility to ensure that their students are motivated and stay motivated and not bewail the fact that students do not bring any motivation to learn the L2 to the classroom. While it is probably true that teachers can do little to influence students' extrinsic motivation, there is a lot they can do to enhance their intrinsic motivation.

PRINCIPLE 10: IN ASSESSING LEARNERS' L2 PROFICIENCY IT IS IMPORTANT TO EXAMINE FREE AS WELL AS CONTROLLED PRODUCTION

Norris and Ortega's (2000) meta-analysis of studies investigating form-focused instruction demonstrated that the extent of the effectiveness of instruction is contingent on the way in which it is measured. They distinguished four types of measurement:

1. metalinguistic judgement (e.g. a grammaticality judgment test).
2. selected response (e.g. multiple choice).
3. constrained constructed response (e.g. gap filling exercises).
4. free constructed response (e.g. a communicative task).

They found that the magnitude of the instruction's effect was greatest in the case of (2) and (3) and least in (4). Yet, arguably, it is (4) that constitutes the best measure of learners' L2 proficiency, as it is this that corresponds most closely to the kind of language use found outside the classroom. The ability to get a multiple choice question right amounts to very little if the student is unable to use the target feature in actual communication.

Free constructed responses are best elicited by means of tasks. Performance elicited by means of tasks can be assessed in three ways (Ellis, 2003): (1) a direct assessment of task outcomes, (2) discourse analytic measures and (3) external ratings. (2) is not practical for busy classroom teachers as it requires transcribing speech and then painstakingly calculating such measures as number of error-free clauses and clause complexity. (3) is practical but it requires considerable expertise to ensure that the ratings of learner performance are valid and reliable. (1) holds out the most promise. However, it is only possible with closed tasks (an i.e. task for which there is a single correct outcome). An example would be a Spot the Difference Task where learners are asked to interact in order to find a specified number of differences in two similar pictures. In this task, assessment would consist of establishing whether they were able to successfully identify the differences. In other words, assessment is not based on what the language learners produce but rather whether they have been able to use the L2 to achieve a successful outcome of a task.

CONCLUSION

These general principles have been derived from my understanding of SLA. I have drawn on a variety of theoretical perspectives, although predominantly from what Lantolf (1996) refers to as the computational model of L2 learning. I am aware that this model has its limitations and is open to criticism, in particular that it is not socially sensitive because it fails to acknowledge the importance of social context and social relations in the language learning process (see Block (2003) for an extended critique along these lines). It would be clearly useful to attempt to formulate a set of principles based on the broader conceptualisation of SLA of the kind advocated by Block and others but this was not my aim here. There will always be a need for a psycholinguistic account of how learners internalize new linguistic forms and how they restructure their linguistic knowledge in the process of acquisition. Language use is not language acquisition, only a means to it. To my mind, the computational model provides a solid foundation for developing a set of principles that articulate the relationship between language use and acquisition. It also constitutes a metaphor that teachers can easily relate to.

Notes

[1] It is also possible to teach pragmatic meaning as an 'object'. That is, specific pragmatic meanings (e.g. requesting or apologizing) can be identified and instructional materials developed to teach learners the linguistic means

for performing these strategies. See Kasper and Rose (2002) for examples of studies that have investigated the effectiveness of this approach. Such an approach constitutes a version of 'focus on forms'. Here, however, I wish to emphasise the need to create materials that allow students to create their own pragmatic meanings through communication.

[2] The extent to which attention to form is necessary for learning remains controversial however. A number of researchers (e.g. Williams, 2005) have provided evidence to demonstrate that some learning takes place without awareness. Schmidt (2001) has modified his position somewhat to allow for the possibility of non-conscious registration of linguistic form, arguing only that 'more attention results in more learning' (p. 30).

[3] A good example of where 'cognitive complexity' and 'developmental complexity' can be distinguished is subject-verb agreement in English. This is typically introduced very early in structural courses but it is invariably only mastered at a very advanced stage of development.

[4] Foster (1998) reports that the adult ESL learners she investigated engaged in very little negotiation of meaning when performing tasks because they failed to take them seriously. They viewed them as 'games' and eschewed negotiation because it would detract from the 'fun'.

Chapter 16

A Typology of Written Corrective Feedback Types

This chapter is based on article that appeared in *English Language Teaching Journal*, Vol. 63: 97–107.

INTRODUCTION

How teachers correct second language (L2) students' writing is a topic that has attracted enormous interest from researchers and teachers alike. However, as a recent review of feedback on L2 students' writing (Hyland & Hyland, 2006) makes clear, despite all the research there are still no clear answers to the questions researchers have addressed. Hyland and Hyland observed:

> … while feedback is a central aspect of L2 writing programs across the world, the research literature has not been equivocally positive about its role in L2 development, and teachers often have a sense they are not making use of its full potential (p. 83).

Guenette (2007) pointed out that one of the reasons for the

uncertainty lies in the failure to design corrective feedback (CF) studies that systematically investigate different types of written CF and control for external variables that are likely to impact on how effective the CF is. One way forward, then, might be for researchers and teachers to systematically identify the various options available for correcting students' writing as a basis for both designing future studies and for pedagogical decision-making.

I would like to make a start on this agenda by examining the various options (both familiar and less familiar) for correcting students' written work. I will focus on just one kind of correction — the correction of linguistic errors — and consider studies that have examined the different options by way of illustrating how they have been investigated and the limitations in the research to date. I will argue that identifying the options in a systematic way is essential for both determining whether written corrective feedback is effective and, if it is, what kind of corrective feedback is most effective.

A TYPOLOGY OF OPTIONS FOR CORRECTING LINGUISTIC ERRORS

Table 1 presents a typology of teacher options for correcting linguistic errors in students' written work [1]. These options have been identified by inspecting both teacher handbooks (e.g. Ur 1996) and published empirical studies of written feedback (e.g. Robb *et al.*, 1986; Chandler, 2003; Ferris, 2006).

A basic distinction needs to be made between the options involved in (1) the teacher's provision of corrective feedback and (2) the students' response to this feedback. Clearly, corrective feedback can only have an impact if students attend to it. Thus, any account of corrective feedback must consider both aspects.

Table 1: Types of teacher written corrective feedback

Type of CF	Description	Studies
A. Strategies for providing corrective feedback		
1. Direct CF	The teacher provides the student with the correct form.	(e.g.Lalande, 1982; Robb *et al.*, 1986).
2. Indirect CF	The teacher indicates that an error exists but does not provide the correction.	
a. indicating + locating the error	This takes the form of underlining and use of cursors to show omissions in the student's text.	Various studies have employed indirect correction of this kind (e.g. Ashwell 2000; Ferris & Roberts, 2001;Chandler, 2003).
b. indication only	This takes the form of an indication in the margin that an error or errors have taken place in a line of text.	Fewer studies have employed this method (e.g. Robb *et al.*, 1986).
3. Metalinguistic CF	The teacher provides some kind of metalinguistic clue as to the nature of the error.	
a. Use of error code	Teacher writes codes in the margin (e.g. ww = wrong word; art = article).	Various studies have examined the effects of using error codes (e.g. Lalande, 1982; Ferris & Roberts, 2001;Chandler, 2003).
b. Brief grammatical descriptions	Teacher numbers errors in text and writes a grammatical description for each numbered error at the bottom of the text.	Sheen (2007) compared the effects of direct CF and direct CF + metalinguistic CF.
4. The focus of the feedback	This concerns whether the teacher attempts to correct all (or most) of the students' errors or selects one or two specific types of errors to correct. This distinction can be applied to each of the above options.	Most studies have investigated unfocused CF (e.g.Chandler, 2003; Ferris, 2006). Sheen (2007), drawing on traditions in SLA studies of CF, investigated focused CF.
a. Unfocused CF	Unfocused CF is extensive.	
b. Focused CF	Focused CF is intensive.	

(continued)

Type of CF	Description	Studies
5. Electronic feedback	The teacher enters indicates an error and provides a hyperlink to a concordance file that provides examples of correct usage.	Milton (2006).
6. Reformulation	This consists of a native speaker's reworking of the students' entire text to make the language seem as native-like as possible while keeping the content or the original intact.	Sachs and Polio (2007) compared the effects of direct correction and reformulation on students' revisions of their text.
B. Students' response to feedback	For feedback to work for either redrafting or language learning learners need to attend to the corrections. Various alternatives exist for achieving this.	
1. Revisions required		A number of studies have examined the effect of requiring students to edit their errors (e.g. Ashwell, 2000; Ferris & Roberts, 2001; Chandler, 2003).
2. No revisions required a. students asked to study corrections b. students just given back corrected text		Sheen (2007) asked students to study corrections. A number of studies have examined what students do when just given back their text with revisions (e.g. Cohen & Cavalcanti, 1990; Sachs & Polio, 2007). No study has systematically investigated different approaches to revision.

Strategies for Providing Corrective Feedback

Five basic strategies for providing written corrective feedback can be identified, with a number of options associated with some of them.

1. Direct CF

In the case of *direct CF* the teacher provides the student with the correct form. As Ferris (2006) notes, this can take a number of different forms — crossing out an unnecessary word, phrase or morpheme, inserting a missing word or morpheme, and writing the correct form above or near to the erroneous form. Example 1 illustrates direct correction.

Example 1:

> a   a   the
> A dog stole ^ bone from ^ butcher. He escaped with having ^ bone. When the
>   over   a   a   saw   a
> dog was going through ^ bridge over the river he found ^ dog in the river.

Direct CF has the advantage that it provides learners with explicit guidance about how to correct their errors. This is clearly desirable if learners do not know what the correct form is (i.e. are not capable of self-correcting the error themselves). Ferris and Roberts (2001) suggest direct CF is probably better than indirect CF with student writers of low levels of proficiency. However, a disadvantage is that it requires minimal processing on the part of the learner and thus, although it might help them to produce the correct form when they revise their writing, it may not contribute to long-term learning. However, a recent study by Sheen (2007) suggests that direct CF can be effective in promoting acquisition of specific grammatical features.

2. Indirect CF

Indirect CF involves indicating that the student has made an error without actually correcting it. This can be done by underlining the errors or using cursors to show omissions in the students text or by placing a cross in the margin next to the line containing the error (as in the example below) . In effect, this involves deciding whether or not to show the precise location of the error.

Example 2:

> A dog stole X bone from X butcher. He escaped with X having X   X bone. When the dog was going X through X   X bridge over   X the X   river he found   X dog
>
> in the river.
> X = missing word
> X _ X = wrong word

As already noted, indirect feedback is often preferred to direct feedback on the grounds that it caters to 'guided learning and problem solving' (Lalande, 1982) and encourages students to reflect about linguistic forms. For these reasons, it is considered more likely to lead to long-term learning (Ferris & Roberts, 2001). The results of studies that have investigated this claim, however, are very mixed. Some studies (e.g. Lalande, 1982) suggest that indirect feedback is indeed more effective in enabling students to correct their errors but others (e.g. Ferris and Robert's own study) found no difference between direct and indirect CF. No study to date has compared the effects of these two types of CF on whether they have any effect on accuracy in new pieces of writing.

In accordance with Ferris and Roberts' general line of argument, it might be claimed that indirect feedback where the exact location of errors is not shown might be more effective than indirect feedback where the location of the errors is shown (as illustrated in example 2) as students would have to engage in deeper processing. Robb *et al.* (1986) investigated four types of feedback including direct feedback and indirect feedback where the number of errors was given in each line of text. They reported no significant difference. Lee (1997), however, specifically compared the two types of indirect correction and found that learners were better able to correct errors that were indicated and located than errors that were just indicated by a check in the margin. However, Lee did not consider long-term gains.

3. Metalinguistic CF [2]

Metalinguistic CF involves providing learners with some form of explicit comment about the nature of the errors they have made. The explicit comment can take two forms. By far the most common is the use of error codes. These consist of abbreviated labels for different kinds of errors. The labels can be placed over the location of the error in the text or in the margin. In the latter case, the exact location of the error may or may not be shown. In the former, the student has to work out the correction needed from the clue provided while in the latter the student needs to first locate the error and then work out the correction. Examples of both are provided below. A major issue in error codes is how delicate the categories should be. For example, should there be a single category for 'articles' (as in the examples below) or should there be separate categories for 'definite' and 'indefinite articles'? Most of the error codes used in research and language pedagogy employ relatively broad categories.

A number of studies have compared using error codes with other types of written CF. Lalande (1982) reported that a group of learners of L2 German that received correction using error codes improved in accuracy in subsequent writing whereas a group receiving direct correction made more errors. However, the difference between the two groups was not statistically significant. Robb *et al.* (1986) included an error codes treatment in their study but found it no more effective than any of the other three types of CF they investigated (i.e. direct feedback and two kinds of indirect feedback). Ferris (2006) reported that error codes helped students to improve their accuracy over time in only two of the four categories of error she investigated. Longitudinal comparisons between the number of errors in students first and fourth compositions showed improvement in total errors and verb errors but not in noun errors, article errors, lexical errors or sentence errors. Ferris and Roberts (2001) found that error codes did assist the students to self-edit their writing but no more so than indirect feedback. Overall, then, there is very limited evidence to show that error codes help writers to achieve greater accuracy over time and it would also seem that they are no more effective than other types of CF in assisting self-editing.

Example 3:

> art.   art.   WW
> A dog stole bone from butcher. He escaped with having bone. When the dog was
>   prep.   art.   art
> going through bridge over the river he found dog in the river.
>
> art. = article error
> WW = wrong word

Example 4:

> Art. x 3; WW   A dog stole bone from butcher. He escaped with having bone.
> Prep.; art.   When the dog was going through bridge over the river he
> Art.   found dog in the river.

The second type of metalinguistic CF consists of providing students with metalinguistic explanations of their errors. An example is provided below. This is far less common, perhaps because it is much more time-consuming than using error codes and also because it calls for the teacher to possess sufficient metalinguistic knowledge to be able to write clear and accurate explanations for a variety of errors. Sheen (2007) compared direct and metalinguistic CF, finding that both were effective in increasing accuracy in the students' use of articles in subsequent writing completed immediately after the CF treatment. Interestingly, the metalinguistic CF also proved more effective than the direct CF in the long term (i.e. in a new piece of writing completed two weeks after the treatment).

Example 5:

>   (1)   (2)   (3)
> A dog stole bone from butcher. He escaped with having bone. When the dog was
>   (4)   (5)   (6)
> going through bridge over the river he found dog in the river.
> (1), (2), (5) and (6) — *you need 'a' before the noun when a person or thing is mentioned for the first time.*
> (3) — *you need 'the' before the noun when the person or thing has been mentioned previously*
> (4) — *you need 'over' when you go across the surface of something; you use 'though' when you go inside something (e.g. 'go through the forest').*

4. Focused versus unfocused CF

Teachers can elect to correct all (or most) of the students' errors, in which case the CF is unfocused. Alternatively they can select specific error types for correction. For example, in the above examples the teacher could have chosen to correct just article errors. The distinction between unfocused and focused CF applies to all of the previously discussed options.

Processing corrections is likely to be more difficult in unfocused CF as the learner is required to attend to a variety of errors and thus is unlikely to be able to reflect much on each error. In this respect, focused CF may prove more effective as the learner is able to examine multiple corrections of a single error and thus obtain the rich evidence they need to both understand why what they wrote was erroneous and to acquire the correct form. If learning is dependent on attention to form then it is reasonable to assume that the more intensive the attention, the more likely the correction is to lead to learning. Focused metalinguistic CF may be especially helpful in this respect as it promotes not just attention but also understanding of the nature of the error. However, unfocused CF has the advantage of addressing a range of errors, so while it might not be as effective in assisting learners to acquire specific features as focused CF in the short term, it may prove superior in the long run.

The bulk of the CF studies completed to date have investigated unfocused CF. In Sheen's (2007) study, the CF was of the focused kind (i.e. it addressed errors in the use of articles for first and second mention) and, as already noted, that proved effective in promoting more accurate language use of this feature. However, to date, there have been no studies comparing the relative effects of focused and unfocused CF. This is clearly a distinction in need of further study.

5. Electronic feedback

Extensive corpora of written English (either carefully constructed or simply available via search engines such as Google) can be exploited to provide students with assistance in their writing. This assistance can be accessed by means of software programmes while students write or it can be utilized as a form of feedback. I am concerned only with the latter here. Electronic resources provide learners with the means where they can appropriate the usage of more experienced writers.

Milton (2006) describes an approach based on a software programme called 'Mark My Words'. This provides teachers with an electronic store of approximately 100 recurrent lexico-grammatical and style errors that he found occurred frequently in the writing of Chinese students. The store also provides a brief comment on each error and with links to resources showing the correct form. The programme enables the teacher to use the electronic store to insert brief metalinguistic comments into a student's text. The text is then returned to the student who then consults the electronic resources to compare his/her usage with that illustrated in the samples of language made available. This assists the student to self-correct. The same programme also generates an error log for each piece of writing, thus drawing students' attention to recurrent linguistic problems. Milton does not report a study of the effectiveness of this method of correcting student errors but provides anecdotal evidence that it can work. He describes receiving a 10-page document from a student, identifying 100 errors using 'Mark My Words' and then asking the student to consult the electronic resources and revise the text himself. Milton reported that the students' revisions were successful.

There are some obvious advantages of this option. One is that it removes the need for the teacher to be the arbiter of what constitutes a correct form. Teachers' intuitions about grammatical correctness are often fallible; arguably, a usage-based approach is more reliable. It can also be argued that the key to effective error correction is identifying the learner's textual intention. While the approach advocated by Milton still lays the onus on the teacher to identify errors, it allows the learners to locate the corrections that are most appropriate for their own textual intentions and so encourages student independence.

6. Reformulation

The final option we will consider is similar to the use of

concordances in that it aims to provide learners with a resource that they can use to correct their errors but places the responsibility for the final decision about whether and how to correct on the students themselves.

A standard procedure in error analysis is reconstruction. That is, in order to identify an error the analyst (and the teacher) needs to construct a native-speaker version of that part of the text containing an error. The idea for reformulation as a technique for providing feedback to learners grew out of this procedure. It involves an expert writer rewriting the student's text in such a way as 'to preserve as many of the writer's ideas as possible, while expressing them in his/her own words so as to make the piece sound native-like' (Cohen, 1989, p.4). The writer then revises by deciding which of the expert writer's reconstructions to accept. In essence, then, reformulation involves two options 'direct correction' + 'revision' but it differs from how these options are typically executed in that the whole of the student's text is reformulated thus laying the burden on the learner to identify the specific changes that have been made.

Sachs and Polio (2007) report an interesting study that compared reformulation with direct error correction. The main difference between these two options was 'a matter of presentation and task demands and was not related to the kinds of errors that were corrected'. The difference in presentation is illustrated in the extract from a complete reformulation below.

Example 6 (from Sachs & Polio, 2007, p. 78):

Original version: As he was jogging, his tammy was shaked.

Reformulation: As he was jogging, his tummy was shaking.

                                   tummy   shaking
Error correction: As he was jogging his <u>tammy</u> was <u>shaked</u>.

The students were shown their reformulated/corrected stories and asked to study them for 20 minutes and take notes if they wanted. Then, one day later, they were given a clean sheet of paper and asked to revise their stories but without access to either the reformulated/corrected texts or the notes they had taken. Both the groups that received reformulation and corrections outperformed a control group. However, the corrections group produced more accurate revisions than the reformulation group. As Sachs and Polio point out, reformulation is a technique that is not restricted to assisting students with their surface level linguistic errors; it is also designed to draw attention to higher order stylistic and organizational errors. Thus, their study should not be used to dismiss the use of reformulation as a technique for teaching written composition. Nevertheless, it would seem from this study that it does not constitute the most effective way of assisting students to eliminate linguistic errors when they revise.

The Student's Response to the Feedback

An essential feature of corrective feedback is how the student responds to the corrections provided. The various options are also shown in Table 1.

The student's response frequently takes the form of revision of the initial draft — an important stage in process writing. Much of the research that has investigated written CF (e.g. Ferris & Roberts, 2001) has centred on whether students are able to make use the feedback they receive when they revise.

One approach has been to describe and classify the types of revisions that students make. Ferris (2006), for example, identified a number of revision categories in the re-drafts of 146 ESL students' essays. Her taxonomy is reproduced in Table 2. Overall, Ferris found that 80.4% of the errors subject to corrective feedback were eliminated in the redrafted compositions either by correcting the error or by deleting the text containing the error or by making a correct substitution. 9.9% of the errors were incorrectly revised while in a further 9.9% no change was made.

This study (along with a number of others) suggests that corrective feedback is effective in helping students to eliminate errors in redrafts of their writing. However, from the perspective of L2 learning, such research is of limited interest, as Truscott (1996) pointed out, as showing that CF helps students to correct their errors in second drafts tells us nothing about whether they are able to use them in new pieces of writing.

Table 2: Student revision analysis categories (from Ferris, 2006)

Label	Description
Error corrected	Error corrected per teacher's marking.
Incorrect change	Change was made but incorrect.
No change	No response to the correction was apparent.
Deleted text	Student deleted marked text rather than attempting correction
Substitution, correct	Student invented a correction that was not suggested by the teacher's marking.
Substitution, incorrect	Student incorrectly made a change that was not suggested by teacher's marking.
Teacher-induced error	Incomplete or misleading teacher marking caused student error
Averted erroneous teacher marking	Student corrected error despite incomplete or erroneous teacher marking

Revision can also be viewed as part of written CF (i.e. as another option). That is to say, students may or may not be given the opportunity to revise their writing following one of the other types of feedback. It then becomes possible to investigate whether providing the opportunity to revise assists learning. In a carefully designed study, Chandler (2003) compared indirect CF plus the opportunity to revise with indirect CF where there was no opportunity to revise. Chandler reported that accuracy improved from the first to the fifth piece of writing significantly more in the group that was required to correct their errors than in the group that just received indication of their errors. Also, this increase in accuracy was not accompanied by any decrease in fluency (e.g. the learners' texts did not reduce in length as accuracy increased) . Chandler noted that 'what seems to be a crucial factor ... is having the students do something with the error correction besides simply receiving it' (p.293). However, this study had no control group and thus did not address whether revising errors leads to acquisition of the correct forms.

There is also the issue of what students actually do with the corrections when they are not required to carry out any revisions. Students may be simply given back their corrected texts (and then simply ignore the corrections) or they may be required to pay close attention to them. In the Chandler study, the no-revision group was simply handed back their corrected writing. It is possible, however, that if they had been asked to carefully examine the corrections, they would have shown similar improvements in accuracy to the group that revised following the CF. Clearly, corrections can only work if writers notice and process them. Fazio's (2001) study of primary level children is a reminder that some learners often fail to attend to linguistic corrections. In this longitudinal study, the pupils became less accurate in a number of grammatical areas over time!

The question of whether to require students to simply attend to the corrections or to revise based on them raises an interesting theoretical issue. Is it the additional 'input' that the corrections afford or the 'output' that occurs when students revise that is important for learning. Guenette (2007) argued that students 'have to notice the feedback and be given ample opportunities to apply the corrections' (p.52). But students may succeed in noticing corrections even if they are not required to revise their writing. Here again there is no research that has addressed this issue.

USING THE TYPOLOGY

There is an obvious need for carefully designed studies to further investigate the effects of written CF in general and of different types of CF. A typology such as the one outlined in this article provides a classification of one of the key variables in written CF studies — the type of CF. It makes it possible for researchers to conduct research that systematically examines the effect of distinct types and combinations of CF. Of course the type of CF is only one of several variables influencing the effectiveness of written CF. Other variables identified by Guenette (2007) are the nature of the population being studied (in particular the nature of the learners' L2 proficiency), the nature of the writing activities that the students undertake, the kinds of errors that are corrected, and whether or not there is any incentive for the students to write accurately.

The typology is not only valuable for the design of experimental studies. It can also assist descriptive research. Such research examines such issues as how teachers carry out CF and how students respond to corrections. While descriptive studies are typically data-driven, they can benefit from examining to what extent the categories in the typology accurately reflect actual practice. They can also serve to refine the categories.

Like Guenette I want to emphasize that there is no 'corrective feedback recipe'. Given the complexity of CF it is unlikely that even better designed studies will provide clear-cut answers to the kinds of questions raised in the introduction to this article. The search for the 'best' way to do written CF may in fact be fundamentally mistaken if it is accepted that CF needs to take account of the specific institutional, classroom and task contexts. As Hyland and Hyland (2006) commented, 'it may be … that what is effective feedback for one student in one setting is less so in another' (p.88). Indeed, a sociocultural perspective on CF would emphasise the need to adjust the type of feedback offered to learners to suit their stage of development although how this can be achieved practically remains unclear in the case of written CF where there is often limited opportunity to negotiate the feedback with individual learners.

The typology might also be of assistance to teachers. Teacher handbooks such as Ur's (1996) wisely do not attempt to prescribe how teachers should do written CF. Instead, they invite teachers to develop their own correction policy by raising a number of key issues. What is important, however, is for teachers to have a clear and explicit account of the options available to them, an understanding of the rationale for each option and some knowledge of the research findings (uncertain as these are). The typology provides teachers with a basis for examining the options and for systematically experimenting with them in their own teaching.

Notes

[1] I have chosen to focus on the teacher's role in corrective feedback. Thus, I have not included in my typology options involving peer feedback. This should not be construed as suggesting that teacher feedback is to be preferred to peer feedback.

[2] There is an obvious difference between simply indicating an error (how I have chosen to define indirect CF) and providing students with metalinguistic information about their errors. Lumping 'indicating errors' and 'error codes' into a single category, as some researchers have done, is misleading and unhelpful.

Chapter 17

Current Issues in the Teaching of Grammar: An SLA Perspective

This chapter is based on an article that first appeared in TESOL Quarterly 83 Vol. 40: 83–107.

SOME PROBLEMS

In this chapter, I will identify and discuss a number of key issues relating to the teaching of grammar in a second language (L2) and, by drawing on theory and research in SLA, suggest ways in which these problems might be addressed. I will point to a number of alternative solutions to each problem, indicating that more often than not there are no clear solutions currently available. The aim, therefore, is not to identify new solutions to existing controversies, nor even to present new controversies. Rather it seeks to address within the compass of a single article a whole range of issues related to grammar teaching, to problematize these issues, and by so doing to provide a counter-weight to the advocacy of specific, but also quite limited, proposals for teaching grammar that have originated in some SLA quarters. However, I will conclude with a statement of my own position on these issues.

The questions that will be addressed are:

1. Should we teach grammar or should we simply create the conditions by which learners learn naturally?
2. What grammar should we teach?
3. When should we teach grammar? Is it best to teach grammar when learners first start to learn an L2 or to wait until later when learners have already acquired some linguistic competence?
4. Should grammar instruction be massed (i.e. the available teaching time be concentrated into a short period) or distributed (i.e. the available teaching time spread over a longer period)?
5. Should grammar instruction be intensive (e.g. cover a single grammatical structure in a single lesson) or extensive (e.g. cover many grammatical structures in a single lesson)?
6. Is there any value in teaching explicit grammatical knowledge?
7. Is there a best way to teach grammar for implicit knowledge?
8. Should grammar be taught in separate lessons or integrated into communicative activities?

DEFINING 'GRAMMAR TEACHING'

Traditionally, grammar teaching is viewed as the presentation and practice of discrete grammatical structures. This is the view promulgated in teacher handbooks.Ur (1996), for example, in her chapter on 'Teaching Grammar' has sections on 'presenting and explaining grammar' and 'grammar practice activities'. Hedge (2000) in her chapter on 'Grammar' similarly only considers 'presenting grammar' and 'practicing grammar'. This constitutes an overly narrow definition of grammar teaching. It is certainly true that grammar teaching can consist of the presentation and practice of grammatical items. But, as will become apparent in the subsequent discussion of the above questions, it need not. First, some grammar lessons might consist of presentation by itself (i.e. without any practice), while others might entail only practice (i.e. no presentation). Second, grammar teaching can involve learners in discovering grammatical rules for themselves (i.e. no presentation and no practice). Third, grammar teaching can be conducted simply by exposing learners to input contrived to provide multiple exemplars of the target structure. Here, too, there is no presentation and no practice, at least in the sense of eliciting production of the structure. Finally, grammar teaching can be conducted by means of corrective feedback on learner errors when these arise in the context of performing some communicative task.

The definition of grammar teaching that informs this article is a broad one:

> Grammar teaching involves any instructional technique that draws learners' attention to some specific grammatical form in such a way that it helps them to either understand it metalinguistically and/or process it in comprehension and/or production so that they can internalize it.

SHOULD WE TEACH GRAMMAR?

This question was motivated by early research into naturalistic L2 acquisition, which showed that learners appeared to follow a 'natural' order and sequence of acquisition (i.e. they mastered different grammatical structures in a relatively fixed and universal order and they passed through a sequence of stages of acquisition on route to mastering each grammatical structure). This led researchers like Corder (1967) to suggest that learners had their own built-in syllabus for learning grammar. In line with this, Krashen (1981a) argued that grammar instruction played no role in 'acquisition', a view based on the conviction that learners (including classroom learners) would automatically proceed along their built-in syllabus as long as they had access to 'comprehensible input' and were sufficiently motivated. Grammar instruction could contribute to 'learning' but this was of limited value as communicative ability was dependent on 'acquisition'.

There followed a number of empirical studies designed to (1) compare the order of acquisition of instructed and naturalistic learners (e.g. Pica, 1983), (2) compare the success of instructed and naturalistic learners (Long, 1983a) and (3) examine whether attempts to teach specific grammatical structures resulted in their acquisition (e.g. White *et al.*, 1991). These studies showed that, by and large, the order of acquisition was the same for instructed and naturalistic learners (although there were some interesting differences [1]), that instructed learners generally achieved higher levels of grammatical competence than naturalistic learners and that instruction was no guarantee that learners would acquire what they had been taught. These results were interpreted as showing that the acquisitional processes of instructed and naturalistic learning were the same but that instructed learners progressed more rapidly and achieved higher levels of proficiency. This led to the conclusion that it was beneficial to teach grammar but that in order to be effective it was necessary to ensure that it was taught in a way that was compatible with the natural processes of acquisition (Long, 1988).

Subsequent research has borne out the overall effectiveness of grammar teaching (see Norris and Ortega's (2000) meta-analysis of 49 studies). Further, there is evidence that, contrary to Krashen's (1993) continued claims, instruction contributes to both 'acquired' knowledge (see R. Ellis, 2002b) as well as learned knowledge. There is also increasing evidence that naturalistic learning in the classroom (as, for example, in immersion programmes) does not typically result in high levels of grammatical competence (Genesee, 1987). In short, there is now convincing indirect and direct evidence to support the teaching of grammar. Nevertheless, doubts remain about the nature of the research evidence. Many studies (including most of those reviewed by Norris and Ortega) measure learning in terms of 'constrained constructed responses' (e.g. fill-in-the-blanks, sentence joining or sentence transformation), which can be expected to favour grammar teaching. There is only mixed evidence that instruction results in learning when this is measured by means of 'free constructed responses' (e.g. communicative tasks). Also, it remains the case that learners do not always acquire what they have been taught and that for grammar instruction to be effective it needs to take account of how learners develop their interlanguages. As we will see, there is controversy regarding both how interlanguage development occurs and how instruction can facilitate this.

WHAT GRAMMAR SHOULD WE TEACH?

Assuming, then, that grammar teaching can contribute to interlanguage development, the next logical question concerns what grammar we should teach. This question can be broken down into two separate questions:

> What kind of reference grammar should we base teaching on?
> Which grammatical features should we teach?

Linguistics affords a broad selection of grammatical models to choose from, including structural grammars, generative grammars (based on a theory of Universal Grammar) and functional grammars. Traditionally syllabuses have been based on structural or descriptive grammars. Structural syllabuses traditionally have emphasised the teaching of form over meaning (e.g. Lado, 1970). While the influence of structural grammars is still apparent today, modern syllabuses rightly give more attention to the functions performed by grammatical forms. Thus, for example, less emphasis is placed on such aspects of grammar as sentence patterns or tense paradigms and more on the meanings conveyed by different grammatical forms in communication. Some attempt was once made to exploit the insights to be gleaned from generative theories of grammar (see for example Bright's *Patterns and Skills in English*, 1965), but in general syllabus designers and teachers have not found such models useful and have preferred to rely on modern descriptive grammars, such as Celce-Murcia and Larsen-Freeman's (1999)

Grammar Book. This is an especially valuable resource because it not only provides a comprehensive, clear and pedagogically exploitable description of the grammar of English but also identifies the kinds of errors that L2 learners are known to make with different grammatical structures. Such information is important because it helps to identify which structures and which aspects of a structure require special attention. The *Grammar Book* is also ideal in that it presents information not only about linguistic form but also about the semantic and discoursal meanings realised by particular forms. As VanPatten, Williams and Rott (2004) emphasized, the establishment of form-meaning connections is a 'fundamental aspect' of language acquisition. Thus, any reference grammar that fails to describe the form-meaning connections of the target language must necessarily be inadequate. In general, then, the choice of which type of grammar to use as a basis for teaching is not a major source of controversy; descriptive grammars that detail the form-meaning relationships of the language are ascendant.

In contrast, the choice of which grammatical structures to teach is controversial. Two polar positions can be identified and various positions in between. At one end of this continuum is Krashen's minimalist position. Krashen (1982) argued that grammar teaching should be limited to a few simple and portable rules such as 3rd person -*s* and past tense -*ed* that can be used to monitor output from the 'acquired' system. He based his argument on the claim that most learners are only capable of learning such simple rules — that more complex rules are generally not 'learnable' or, if they are learnable, are beyond their ability to apply through monitoring. Krashen's claim, however, is not warranted. There is now ample evidence that many learners are capable of mastering a wide range of explicit grammar rules. Green and Hecht (1992), for example, found that university-level students of English in Germany were able to produce clear explanations for 85% of the grammatical errors they were asked to explain while overall the learners in their study (who included secondary school students) managed satisfactory explanations for 46% of the errors. Macrory and Stone (2000) reported that British comprehensive school students had a fairly good explicit understanding of the perfect tense in French (e.g. they understood its function, they knew that some verbs used *avoir* and some *etre*, they were familiar with the forms required by different pronouns and they were aware of the need for a final accent on the past participle). Hu (2002) found that adult Chinese learners of English demonstrated correct metalinguistic knowledge of prototypical rules of six English structures (e.g. for articles 'specific reference' constituted the prototypical rule) but were less clear about the peripheral rules for these structures (e.g. 'generic reference').

At the other pole is the comprehensive position — teach the whole of the grammar of the target language [2]. This is the position adopted by many course book writers (see for example Walter and Swan's (1990)*The New Cambridge English Course*) or authors of grammar practice materials (see, for example, Murphy's (1994) *English in Use*) . Such a position would also seem unwarranted in that learners are clearly capable of learning a substantial amount of the grammar of an L2 without instruction and also because, in most teaching contexts, there is only limited time available for teaching grammar so some selection is needed.

What then should selection be based on? The answer would seem obvious — the inherent learning difficulty of different grammatical structures. The problem arises in how to determine this. To begin with, it is necessary to distinguish two different senses of 'learning difficulty'. This can refer to the difficulty learners have in understanding a grammatical feature and the difficulty they have in internalizing a grammatical feature so that they are able to use it accurately in communication. These two senses relate to the distinction between learning grammar as explicit knowledge and as implicit knowledge, which is discussed later. Clearly, what is difficult to learn as explicit knowledge and as implicit knowledge is not the same. For example, most learners have no difficulty in grasping the rule for English 3rd person -s but they have enormous difficulty in internalising this structure so they can use it accurately. These two senses of learning difficulty have not always been clearly distinguished in language pedagogy, with the result that even when the stated goal is the development of implicit knowledge, it is the anticipated difficulty students will have in understanding a feature that guides the selection and grading of grammatical structures. For example, 3rd person -*s* is an easy feature to understand and is typically taught very early but it is a late-acquired feature.

How then has learning difficulty been established? Traditionally, factors such as the frequency of specific structures in the input and their utility to learners have been invoked (Mackey, 1965) but these would seem to have more to do with use [3] rather than inherent cognitive difficulty. Here we will consider two approaches that have figured in attempts to delineate the latter.

1. Teach those forms that differ from the learners' first language (L1).

2. Teach marked rather than unmarked forms.

The first approach was, of course, the one adopted in many early structural courses based on a contrastive analysis of the learner's L1 and the target language. While the contrastive analysis hypothesis as initially formulated is clearly not tenable (see Ellis, 1985, Chapter 2), there is still general agreement in SLA that learners transfer at least some of the features of their L1 into the L2. For example, there is ample evidence (Trahey & White, 1993) to show that French learners of English produce errors of the kind:

 * Mary kissed passionately John.

because French permits an adverb to be positioned between the verb and the direct object. Nevertheless, contrastive analysis does not constitute a sound basis for selecting grammatical structures. In many teaching contexts, the learners come from mixed language backgrounds where it would not be possible to provide tailor-made grammar teaching for groups of learners with different L1s. Also, we simply do not yet know enough about when difference does and does not translate into learning difficulty and there are cases where learning difficulty arises even where there is no difference.

The second approach, however, is also problematic. Markedness has been defined in terms of whether a grammatical structure is in some sense frequent, natural and basic or infrequent, unnatural and deviant from a regular pattern (Richards, Platt & Weber, 1985). For example, the use of an infinitive without *to* following *make*, as in:

He made me follow him.

can be considered marked because *make* is one of the few verbs in English that takes this kind of complement and because this pattern occurs only infrequently. The general idea here is that we should teach the marked features and leave the learners to learn the unmarked forms naturally by themselves. The problem here is that, as the above definition suggests, markedness remains a somewhat opaque concept, so that it is often difficult to apply with the precision needed to determine which structures to teach.

The selection of grammatical content, then, remains very problematic. One solution to the kinds of problems referred to above is to base selection on the known errors produced by learners. In this respect, lists of common learner errors such as those available in Turton and Heaton's (1996) *Longman Dictionary of Common Errors* and Swan and Smith's (2001) *Learner English: A Teacher's Guide to Interference and Other Problems* are helpful.

The problems of selection are probably the main reason why grammatical syllabuses are so alike and have changed so little over the years; it is safer to follow what has been done before. Of course the selection of what to teach will also depend on the learner's stage of development. The problems that this involves are discussed in subsequent sections.

WHEN SHOULD WE TEACH GRAMMAR?

There are two competing positions here. According to the first, it is best to give emphasis to the teaching of grammar in the early stages of L2 acquisition. According to the second, it is best to emphasize meaning-focused instruction to begin with and introduce grammar teaching later when learners have already begun to build their interlanguages. I will briefly consider the arguments for both positions.

A key premise of behaviourist theories of language learning is that 'error like sin needs to be avoided at all costs' (Brooks, 1960). The idea here is that once learners have formed incorrect 'habits' they will have difficulty in eradicating them and replacing them with correct 'habits'. Thus, it is necessary to ensure that they develop correct habits in the first place. This was one of the key premises of the audiolingual method (Lado, 1964). Other arguments can be advanced in favour of starting grammar teaching early. The alternative to a form-focused approach is one that emphasises meaning and message creation, as in task-based language teaching (Skehan, 1998) but in the opinion of many teachers it is not possible for beginner learners to engage in meaning-centred activities as they lack the necessary knowledge of the L2 to perform tasks. Thus, they argue that a form-focused approach is needed initially in order to construct a basis of knowledge that learners can then use and extend in a meaning-focused approach. Finally, current connectionist theories of L2 learning, which give primacy to implicit learning processes based on massive exposure to the target language, also provide a basis for teaching grammar to beginners. N. Ellis (2005) has suggested that learning necessarily commences with an explicit representation of linguistic forms, which are then developed through implicit learning. He suggests that there is merit in teaching learners grammar because it provides a basis for the 'real' learning that follows. This seems to echo Lightbown's (1991) metaphor, according to which grammar instruction facilitates learning by providing learners with 'hooks' which they can 'grab' onto. The idea behind this metaphor is that a conscious understanding of how grammatical features work facilitates the kind of processing (for example, attention to linguistic form) required for developing true competence.

The argument against teaching grammar early on derives from research on immersion programmes (e.g.Genesee, 1987), which shows that learners in such programmes are able to develop the proficiency needed for fluent communication without any formal instruction in the L2. For example, learners of L2 Spanish do not need to be taught that adjectives follow nouns in this language; they seem to be able to learn this 'naturally' from exposure to communicative input (Hughes, 1979). Similarly, learners of L2 English can master simple relative clauses (e.g. clauses where the relative pronoun functions as subject and the clause is attached to a noun phrase following the verb). There is ample evidence to show that learners can and do learn a lot of grammar without being taught it. This being so, why bother to teach what can be learned naturally? A second reason for delaying grammar teaching to later stages of development is that early interlanguage is typically agrammatical (Ellis, 1984b; Perdue & Klein, 1993). That is, learners rely on a memory-based system of lexical sequences, constructing utterances either by accessing ready-made chunks or by simply concatenating lexical items into simple strings. Ellis (1984b) gives examples of such utterances in the early speech of three classroom learners:

> Me no (= I don't have any crayons)
> Me milkman (= I want to be the milkman)
> Dinner time you out (= It is dinner time so you have to go out)

Such pidginized utterances rely heavily on context and the use of communication strategies. They are very effective in simple, context-embedded communication. Arguably, it is this lexicalised knowledge that provides the basis for the subsequent development of the grammatical competence needed for context-free communication. This, then, is a strong argument for delaying the teaching of grammar until learners have developed a basic communicative ability.

In general, I have favoured the second of these positions (see R. Ellis, 2002b). Given that many classroom learners will not progress beyond the initial stages of language learning, it seems to me that a task-based approach that caters to the development of a proceduralized lexical system and simple, naturally acquired grammatical structures will ensure a threshold communicative ability and, therefore, is to be preferred to an approach that insists on grammatical accuracy from the start and that, as a consequence, may impede the development of this communicative ability. Task-based language teaching is possible with complete beginners if the first tasks emphasise listening (and perhaps reading), ensure the input is context supported, and allow for non-verbal responses. However, it is possible that such an approach can be usefully complemented with one that draws beginners' attention to some useful grammatical features (e.g. past tense -*ed* in English) that otherwise they might miss. This is the aim of input-processing instruction (VanPatten, 1996, 2003), which is discussed later.

SHOULD GRAMMAR TEACHING BE MASSED OR DISTRIBUTED?

This question is logically independent of the preceding question. That is, irrespective of when grammar teaching commences, we need to consider whether it should be concentrated into a short period of time or spread over a longer period. There is remarkably little research that has addressed this question.

The research that has been undertaken reports on the relative effects of massed and distributed language instruction on general language proficiency rather than the effects on grammar learning. Collins *et al.* (1999) summarise the available research as follows:

> ... none of the language program evaluation research has found an advantage for distributed language instruction. Although the findings thus far lead to the hypothesis that more concentrated exposure to English may lead to better student outcomes, the evidence is not conclusive. (p. 659).

Collins *et al.* then report their own study of three intensive ESL programmes in Canada, one (the distributed programme) taught over the full 10 months of one school year, one (the massed programme) concentrated into 5 months but taught only to above average students and the third (the massed plus programme) concentrated into 5 months, supplemented with out-of-class opportunities to use English and taught to students of mixed ability levels. The main finding was that the massed and especially the massed plus students outperformed the distributed programme students on most of the measures of learning, including some measures of grammatical ability, although this finding might in part have been explained by the fact that the massed programmes provided more overall instructional time.

Collins *et al.*'s study points to the need for further research, especially through studies that compare massed and distributed instruction directed at specific grammatical structures. Ideally what is needed is a study that compares short periods of instruction directed at a particular structure spread over several days with the same amount of instruction compressed into one or two lessons [4]. Received wisdom is that a cyclical approach to grammar teaching (Howatt, 1974) is to be preferred as it allows for the kind of gradual acquisition of grammar that is compatible with what is known about interlanguage development. However, the results of Collins *et al.*'s study suggest, at the very least, that such a position needs to be investigated empirically. Here, then is an issue, about which nothing definitive can be said at the present moment.

SHOULD GRAMMAR TEACHING BE INTENSIVE OR EXTENSIVE?

Intensive grammar teaching refers to instruction that is directed for a sustained period of time (which could be a lesson or a series of lessons covering days or weeks) at a single grammatical structure or, perhaps, a pair of contrasted structures (e.g. English past continuous vs.

past simple). Extensive grammar teaching refers to instruction that is directed at a whole range of structures within a short period of time (e.g. a lesson) so that each structure receives only minimal attention in any one lesson. It is the difference between shooting a pistol repeatedly at the same target and firing a shot-gun in order to spray pellets at a variety of targets. Instruction can be intensive or extensive irrespective of whether it is massed or distributed. This latter distinction refers to how a whole grammar course is staged while the intensive/extensive distinction refers to whether a single or multiple grammatical features is/are addressed within each single lesson.

Grammar teaching is typically viewed as entailing intensive instruction. The present-practice-produce (PPP) model of grammar teaching, which underlies most discussions of grammar teaching in teacher handbooks (see, for example, Hedge (2000) and Ur (1996)), assumes an intensive focus on specific grammatical structures. Although it is acknowledged that learners' 'readiness' to acquire a specific structure limits the effectiveness of teaching (no matter how intensive it is), there is also an underlying assumption that, with sufficient opportunities for practice, learners will eventually succeed in automatizing the structures they are taught. As Ur says:

> The aim of grammar practice is to get students to learn the structures so thoroughly that they will be able to produce them correctly on their own. (p.83).

Thus, the idea that 'practice makes perfect' is the primary justification for the intensive approach. 'Practice', however, must involve both drills and tasks (i.e. opportunities to practice the target structure in a communicative context).

It is perhaps less easy to see how grammar teaching can comprise extensive instruction. It is not likely that a teacher would elect to present and practice a whole range of grammatical structures within a single lesson. Extensive grammar instruction of a kind, however, has always had a place in grammar teaching. Some thirty years ago, while teaching in a secondary school in Zambia, I regularly gave lessons where I illustrated and explained some of the common errors that I had observed my students making in their written compositions. Similarly, in the context of task-based teaching, some teachers have been observed to make a note of the errors learners make and then to address them when the task is over (Basturkmen, Loewen & Ellis, 2004).

Also, extensive grammar teaching can occur within a learning activity, not just as some kind of postscript. Teachers provide corrective feedback in the context of both form-focused and meaning-focused lessons and while feedback in the former may be directed primarily at the structure targeted by the lesson in the latter it is likely to be directed at whatever errors learners happen to make. Studies of corrective feedback (e.g. Lyster & Ranta, 1997; Ellis, Batsurkmen & Loewen, 2001) demonstrate that in communicative lessons a wide variety of grammatical forms are addressed incidentally through corrective feedback.

There is little doubt now that intensive grammar lessons can be effective. While earlier research showed that learners do not always learn what they are taught, especially when learning is measured in terms of spontaneous production (e.g. Kadia, 1987), more recent research (e.g. Spada & Lightbown, 1999) indicates that even if learners are not ready to learn the targeted structure, intensive grammar teaching can help them progress through the sequence of stages involved in the acquisition of that structure. Teaching a marked structure intensively can help learners learn associated less marked structures even if it does not result in acquisition of the marked structure. Intensive instruction also helps learners to use structures they have already partially acquired more accurately (e.g. White *et al.*, 1991).

There are also theoretical arguments and some empirical evidence in favour of an extensive approach. Cook (1989) argued from the perspective of Universal Grammar that learners require minimal evidence in order to set a particular parameter for the grammar they are learning. Other researchers have emphasised the importance of negative evidence through corrective feedback for grammar learning by adults. Loewen (2002) showed that even very brief episodes of corrective feedback are related to correctness on subsequent tests. In this study, Loewen identified the errors that teachers addressed incidentally in the context of communicative language teaching and then developed tailor-made tests, which he administered to the learners who made the specific errors either one day or two weeks later. These tests showed that the learners were subsequently often able to identify and correct their own errors.

Clearly, there are pros and cons for both intensive and extensive grammar instruction. Some structures may not be mastered without the opportunity for repeated practice. Harley (1989), for example, found that anglophone learners of L2 French failed to acquire the distinction between the preterit and imparfait past tenses after hours of exposure (and presumably some corrective feedback) in an immersion programme but were able to improve their accuracy in the use of these two tenses after intensive instruction. However, intensive instruction is time-consuming (in Harley's study the targeted structures were taught over an 8 week period!) and thus there will be constraints on how many structures can be addressed. Extensive grammar instruction, on the other hand, affords the opportunity for large numbers of grammatical structures to be attended to. Also, more likely than not, many of the structures will be addressed repeatedly over a period of time. Further, because this kind of instruction involves a response to the errors each learner makes it is individualized and affords the skilled teacher on-line opportunities for the kind of contextual analysis that Celce-Murcia (2002) recommends as basis for grammar teaching. However, it is not possible to attend to those structures that learners do not attempt to use (i.e. extensive instruction cannot deal effectively with avoidance). Also, of course, it does not provide the in-depth practice that some structures may require before they can be fully acquired.

Arguably, grammar teaching should be conceived of in terms of both approaches. This suggests a need to revise how grammar teaching is conceptualised in teacher handbooks to include the kind of extensive treatment of grammar that arises naturally through corrective feedback.

IS THERE ANY VALUE IN TEACHING EXPLICIT GRAMMATICAL KNOWLEDGE?

The distinction between explicit and implicit knowledge was mentioned briefly earlier. Explicit knowledge consists of the facts that speakers of a language have learned. These facts are often not clearly understood and may be in conflict with each other. They concern different aspects of language including grammar. Explicit knowledge is held consciously, is learnable and verbalizable and is typically accessed through controlled processing when learners experience some kind of linguistic difficulty in the use of the L2. A distinction needs to be drawn between explicit knowledge as analysed knowledge and as metalinguistic explanation. The former entails a conscious awareness of how a structural feature works while the latter consists of knowledge of grammatical metalanguage and the ability to understand explanations of rules. In contrast, implicit knowledge is procedural, is held unconsciously and can only be verbalized if it is made explicit. It is accessed rapidly and easily and thus is available for use in rapid, fluent communication. In the view of most SLA researchers, competence in an L2 is primarily a matter of implicit knowledge.

Whether there is any value in teaching explicit knowledge of grammar has been and remains today one of the most controversial issues in teaching grammar. In order to make sense of the different positions relating to the teaching of explicit knowledge it is necessary to consider three separate questions:

1. Is explicit knowledge of any value in and of itself?
2. Is explicit knowledge of value in facilitating the development of

implicit knowledge?

3. Is explicit knowledge best taught deductively or inductively?

The first question has already been partly addressed when we considered what grammar to teach. We noted that researchers disagree over learners' ability to learn explicit knowledge, with some (e.g. Krashen, 1982) seeing this as very limited and others (e.g. Green & Hecht, 1992) producing evidence to suggest that it is considerable. There is, however, a separate issue related to the first question. This concerns the extent to which learners are able to utilize their explicit knowledge (whatever that consists of) in actual performance. Again, one position is that this is limited. Krashen argues that learners can only use explicit knowledge when they 'monitor' and that this requires that they are focused on form (as opposed to meaning) and have sufficient time to access the knowledge. There is also some evidence that teaching explicit knowledge by itself (i.e. without any opportunities for practising the target feature) is not effective. Studies by VanPatten and Oikennon (1996) and Wong (2004) both indicate that experimental groups that received explicit information alone performed no differently on interpretation and production tests than a control group.

But other positions are also possible. I have argued that explicit knowledge is used in both the process of formulating messages as well as in monitoring and that many learners are adroit in accessing their explicit memories for these purposes, especially if the rules are, to a degree, automatized. However, this does require time. Yuan and Ellis (2003) showed that learners' grammatical accuracy improved significantly if they had time for 'on-line planning' while performing a narrative task, a result most readily explained in terms of their accessing explicit knowledge.

Irrespective of whether explicit knowledge has any value in and of itself, it may assist language development by facilitating the development of implicit knowledge. This is the issue addressed by the second of the two questions above. It concerns what has become known as the interface hypothesis. This addresses whether explicit knowledge plays a role in L2 acquisition. Three positions can be identified. According to the non-interface position (Krashen, 1981a), explicit and implicit knowledge are entirely distinct with the result that explicit knowledge cannot be converted into implicit knowledge. This position is supported by research that suggests that explicit and implicit memories are neurologically separate (Paradis, 1994). The interface position argues the exact opposite. Drawing on skill-learning theory, DeKeyser (1998) argues that explicit knowledge becomes implicit knowledge if learners have the opportunity for plentiful communicative practice. The weak interface position (R. Ellis, 1993a) claims that explicit knowledge can convert into implicit knowledge if the learner is ready to acquire the targeted feature and that this occurs by priming a number of key acquisitional processes, in particular 'noticing' and 'noticing the gap' (Schmidt, 1990). That is, explicit knowledge of a grammatical structure makes it more likely learners will attend to the structure in the input and carry out the cognitive comparison between what they observe in the input and their own output. These positions continue to be argued at a theoretical level. Although there is plentiful evidence that explicit instruction is effective in promoting L2 learning (e.g. Norris & Ortega, 2000) there has been no published study that has directly tested whether this is because explicit knowledge converts directly into implicit knowledge or simply facilitates its development. One reason for this is the problem of measurement, i.e., the difficulty of ascertaining which type of knowledge learners employ when they perform a language task or test.

The three positions support very different approaches to language teaching. The non-interface position leads to a 'zero grammar' approach, i.e. one that prioritizes meaning-centred approaches such as immersion and task-based teaching. The interface position supports PPP — the idea that a grammatical structure should be first presented explicitly and then practiced until it is fully proceduralized. The weak interface position also lends support to techniques that induce learners to attend to grammatical features. It has been used to provide a basis for consciousness-raising tasks that require learners to derive their own explicit grammar rules from data they are provided with (R. Ellis, 1993a; Fotos, 1994). It is likely that all three approaches will continue to attract supporters, drawing on different theories of L2 acquisition and citing research that lends indirect support to the preferred approach. It is unlikely that this controversy will be resolved through research in the near future.

The third question assumes there is value in explicit knowledge and addresses how best to teach it. In deductive teaching a grammatical structure is presented initially and then practiced in one way or another; this is the first P in the present-practice-produce (PPP) sequence. In inductive teaching, learners are first exposed to exemplars of the grammatical structure and are asked to arrive at a metalinguistic generalisation on their own; there may or may not be a final explicit statement of the rule. A number of studies (see Erlam, 2003b for a review) have examined the relative effectiveness of these two approaches to teaching explicit knowledge. The results have been mixed. For example, Herron and Tomosello (1992) found a clear advantage for inductive instruction, Robinson (1996) found that a deductive approach was more effective, while Rosa and O'Neill (1999) found no significant difference. Erlam's own study revealed a significant advantage for the group receiving deductive instruction. Perhaps the main lesson to be learned from the research to date is the need for a differentiated approach to both researching and teaching explicit knowledge. It is likely that many variables impact on which approach learners benefit most from, including the specific structure that is the target of the instruction and the learners' aptitude for grammatical analysis. Simple rules may best be taught deductively while more complex rules may lend themselves to an inductive approach. Learners skilled in grammatical analysis are likely to fare better with an inductive approach than those less skilled.

IS THERE A BEST WAY TO TEACH GRAMMAR FOR IMPLICIT KNOWLEDGE?

To answer this question it is necessary to consider the various instructional options for teaching grammar. I have attempted this in a number of publications (e.g. R. Ellis, 1997, 1998, 2002b; Chapter 13) [5]. I will consider just two here — the difference between input-based and production-based instruction and between different types of corrective feedback.

The case for the input-based option is based on a computational model of L2 acquisition, according to which acquisition takes place as a product of learners comprehending and processing input. Such approaches, when directed at grammar, seek to draw learners' attention to the targeted structure(s) in one or more ways — simply by contriving for numerous exemplars of the structure(s) to be present in the input materials, by highlighting the target structure(s) in some way (e.g. by using bold or italics in written texts), or by means of interpretation tasks (Ellis, 1995b) directed at drawing learners attention to form-meaning mappings. VanPatten (1996, 2003) has developed a version of the input-based option that he calls 'processing instruction'. This is directed at helping learners to overcome the 'default processing strategies' that are a feature of interlanguages (e.g. assuming that the first noun in a sentence is always the agent). A case for the output-based option can be found in both skill-building theory (see previous discussion) or in a sociocultural theory of L2 learning, according to which learning arises out of social interaction which scaffolds learners' attempts to produce new grammatical structures (Ohta, 2001). A number of studies have compared the relative effectiveness of input-based and production-based instruction, with mixed results, resulting in on-going debate about the relative merits of these two options (VanPatten, 2002; DeKeyser *et al.*, 2002). It may be that, in classrooms, this comparison is ultimately meaningless because, in practice, both options are likely to involve input-processing and production. For example, it is quite conceivable that in an input-based approach individual students silently 'produce' the target structure, while in a production-based instruction an utterance produced by one student serves as input for another. It is, therefore, not surprising that both options have been shown to result in acquisition [6].

There a rich descriptive literature on corrective feedback (i.e. teacher responses to learner errors) and an increasing number of studies have investigated the relative effects of different types of feedback on acquisition. Key options are (1) whether the feedback is implicit or explicit and (2) whether the feedback is input- or output-based. Implicit feedback is feedback where the corrective force of the response to learner error is masked, for example, a recast, which reformulates a deviant utterance correcting it while keeping the same meaning:

> NNS: Why he is very unhappy?
> NS: Why is he very unhappy?
> NNS: Yeah why is very unhappy?
> (Philp, 2003).

or, as in this contrived example, a request for clarification

> NNS: Why he is very unhappy?
> NS: Sorry?
> NNS: Why is he very unhappy?

Explicit feedback takes a number of forms, such as direct correction or metalinguistic explanation. There is some evidence that explicit feedback is more effective in both eliciting immediate correct use of the structure by the learner and in subsequent use, e.g. in a post-test (Carroll & Swain, 1993; Lyster, 2004). But there is also some evidence and some strong theoretical reasons in support of implicit feedback (see Long, 1996). Indeed, this type of feedback is more compatible with a focus-on-form approach discussed above as it ensures that learners are more likely to maintain the primary focus on meaning. However, as Muranoi (2000) notes, implicit feedback is probably more effective when it is targeted intensively at a pre-selected form than when it occurs extensively in incidental focus-on-form. In the latter, explicit attention to form may be more effective.

Input-based feedback is feedback that models the correct form for the learner (e.g. by means of a recast). Output-based feedback is feedback that seeks to elicit production of the correct form from the learner (e.g. by means of a request for clarification). Again, there is disagreement about the relative effectiveness of these two feedback options and no clear evidence to choose between them. Some descriptive studies have shown that output-based feedback is more likely to lead to learners correcting their own initial erroneous utterances in what is referred to as 'uptake'. However, uptake is not the same as acquisition.

In short, while considerable progress has been made in identifying those instructional options that are likely to be of psycholinguistic significance, there are, as yet, few conclusions that can be drawn as to which ones are the most effective for acquisition. It is possible to point to studies and theoretical arguments that suggest that each of the major options discussed above can contribute to acquisition.

SHOULD GRAMMAR BE TAUGHT IN SEPARATE LESSONS OR INTEGRATED INTO COMMUNICATIVE ACTIVITIES?

In Ellis (2001) I considered three broad types of form-focused instruction, as shown in Table 1. 'Focus-on-forms' refers to instruction involving a 'structure-of-the-day' approach, where the students' primary focus is on 'form' (i.e. accuracy) and where the activities are directed intensively at a single grammatical structure. This, then, involves teaching grammar in a series of separate lessons. 'Focus-on-form' entails a primary focus on meaning with attention to form arising out of the communicative activity. This can be 'planned', where a focused task is required to elicit occasions for using a pre-determined grammatical structure, as, for example, in Samuda (2001). In this approach, attention to the pre-determined grammatical structures will also be intensive. Alternatively, focus-on-form can be 'incidental', where attention to form in the context of a communicative activity is not pre-determined but rather occurs 'on-line' in accordance with the participants' linguistic needs as the activity proceeds. In this approach, it is likely that attention will be given to a wide variety of grammatical structures during any one task and thus will be extensive. Focus-on-form implies no separate grammar lessons but rather grammar-teaching integrated into a curriculum consisting of communicative tasks.

Table 1: Types of form-focused instruction (Ellis, 2001, p. 17)

Type of FFI	Primary Focus	Distribution
1. Focus-on-forms	Form	Intensive
2. Planned focus-on-form	Meaning	Intensive
3. Incidental focus-on-form	Meaning	Extensive

There is considerable theoretical disagreement regarding which of these types of instruction is most effective in developing implicit knowledge. Long (1988, 1991) and Doughty (2001) have argued strongly that 'focus-on-form' is best equipped to promote interlanguage development because the acquisition of implicit knowledge occurs as a result of learners attending to linguistic form while they are engaged with understanding and producing meaningful messages. Other researchers, however, have argued that a focus-on-forms approach is effective. DeKeyser (1998), for example, has argued that grammatical structures are learned gradually through the automatization of explicit knowledge and that this can be achieved by means of a focus-on-forms approach. This approach acknowledges the value of teaching explicit knowledge and subsequently proceduralizing it by means of activities (drills and tasks) that practice 'behaviors' (i.e. involve meaning) rather than 'structures'. It is worth noting here, however, one point of agreement in these different positions — instruction needs to ensure that learners are able to connect grammatical forms to the meanings they realise in communication. So far, the debate has addressed the difference between focus-on-form and focus-on-forms. There has been little discussion of the relative merits of planned and incidental focus-on-form. In effect, this involves a consideration of whether instruction should be intensive or extensive, a question we have already considered.

CONCLUSION

Grammar has held and continues to hold a central place in language teaching. The 'zero grammar approach' was flirted with but never really took hold as is evident in both the current textbook materials emanating from publishing houses (e.g. Whitney & White, 2001) and in current theories of L2 acquisition. There is ample evidence to demonstrate that teaching grammar works.

While there is now a clear conviction that a traditional approach to teaching grammar based on explicit explanations and drill-like practice is unlikely to result in the acquisition of the implicit knowledge needed for fluent and accurate communication, there continues to be disagreement regarding what should replace this. It seems appropriate, then, to finish with a statement of my own beliefs about grammar teaching, acknowledging that many of them remain controversial:

1. The grammar taught should be one that emphasizes not just form but also the meanings and uses of different grammatical structures.

2. Teachers should endeavour to focus on those grammatical structures that are known to be problematic to learners rather than try to teach the whole of grammar.

3. Grammar is best taught to learners who have already acquired some ability to use the language (i.e. intermediate level) rather than to complete beginners. However, grammar can be dealt with as soon

as learners begin to use the language productively through corrective feedback.

4. A focus-on-forms approach is valid as long as it includes an opportunity for learners to practice 'behaviour' in communicative tasks.

5. Consideration should be given to experimenting with a massed rather than distributed approach to teaching grammar.

6. Use should be made of both input-based and output-based instructional options.

7. A case exists for teaching explicit grammatical knowledge as a means of assisting subsequent acquisition of implicit knowledge. Teaching explicit knowledge can be incorporated into both a focus-on-forms and a focus-on-form approach. In the case of a focus-on-forms approach, a differentiated approach involving sometimes deductive and sometimes inductive instruction may work best.

8. An incidental focus-on-form approach is of special value because it affords an opportunity for extensive treatment of grammatical problems (in contrast to the intensive treatment afforded by a focus-on-forms approach).

9. Corrective feedback is important for learning grammar. It is best conducted using a mixture of implicit and explicit feedback types that are both input-based and output-based.

10. In accordance with the above beliefs, grammar instruction should take the form of separate grammar lessons (a focus-on-forms approach) and also be integrated into communicative activities (a focus-on-form approach).

Many (if not all) of these statements are open to challenge. They constitute a personal interpretation of what the research to date has shown. It may also seem that I am hedging my bets by encompassing a wide number of options and that I am suggesting that 'anything goes'. It is certainly true that I do not believe (and do not think the research demonstrates) that there is just one preferred approach to teaching grammar. The acquisition of the grammatical system of an L2 is a complex process and almost certainly can be assisted best by a variety of approaches. But what is important is to recognize what options are available, what the theoretical rationales for these options are and what the problems are with these rationales. This is the starting point for developing a personal theory of grammar teaching.

The fact that so much controversy exists points to the need for more research. One of the greatest needs is for research that addresses to what extent and in what ways grammar instruction results in implicit knowledge. Ideally, this requires methods of measuring acquisition that tap into learners' ability to use the grammatical structures they have been taught in communication (especially oral communication). Studies that employ such methods are still few and far between. Another need is for longitudinal studies that investigate the effects of instruction over time. While most recently published studies include delayed post-tests they typically incorporate instructional treatments of a relatively short duration. Longitudinal studies that employ qualitative as well as quantitative methods will help to show not just if there is a delayed effect for instruction but also its accumulative effect. The effects of corrective feedback, for example, are most likely to become evident gradually when learners are repeatedly exposed to feedback on the same grammatical structures. Further research, even if it does not succeed in providing clear-cut answers to the questions raised in this article, will deepen our understanding of the issues involved and afford better defined 'provisional specifications' (Stenhouse, 1975), which teachers can experiment with in their own classrooms.

Notes

[1] For example, Pica (1983) notes that some structures (e.g. plural -*s*) were used more accurately by instructed learners and some (e.g. Verb -*ing*) by naturalistic learners. In other structures (e.g. articles) there was no difference.

[2] Of course, it is not possible to specify the 'whole' grammar of a language. While the grammar of a language may be determinate, descriptions

of it are certainly not. The *Longman Grammar of Contemporary English* ran to 1,081 pages (excluding index and bibliography) but doubtlessly does not account for all the known facts of English grammar. Nevertheless, there is a recognized 'canon' of English structures that, in the eyes of syllabus designers and text-book writers, constitutes the grammar of English.

[3] Structures like English articles that are very frequent in the input can impose considerable learning difficulty. Structures such as English conditionals may be very useful to learners but are also difficult to learn.

[4] It might prove much easier to conduct rigorous studies of massed and distributed learning when these are focused on specific grammatical structures, given the problems that arise in controlling extraneous variables in evaluations of entire programmes.

[5] I distinguish between psycholinguistic and methodological options (cf. R. Ellis, 1998). The former consist of options that are related to some model of L2 acquisition. The latter are options evident in instructional materials for teaching grammar. Here I consider only psycholinguistic options.

[6] There is also controversy regarding how to measure the effectiveness of these two (and other) instructional options. Norris and Ortega (2000) have shown that the effectiveness of instruction varies depending on whether it is measured by means of metalinguistic judgements, selected response, constrained constructed response or free constructed response. Most SLA researchers (and teachers too perhaps) would consider the last of these the most valid measure. Chapter 5 reviewed a number of studies that examined the effects of different kinds of instruction on learners' free constructed responses, reporting that instruction can have an effect on this type of language use.

Section D

CONCLUSION

Chapter 18

Teaching Grammar for Learning

INTRODUCTION

My overriding concern in this book has been to examine the relationship between teaching and learning grammar. My research and my pedagogical proposals have been based on the assumption that for grammar teaching to 'work' it has to take account of how learners learn grammar. For this reason my approach has been to draw on what is currently known about how second language (L2) learners develop their interlanguages. Thus all the chapters have been informed by my knowledge of Second Language Acquisition (SLA), a field of study that has shown exponential development from the time of the study reported in Chapter 2 to now. In this final chapter I will try to summarize my own ideas about how grammar teaching can be conducted in a way that promotes learning.

I want to begin by revisiting the 'interface issue'. This is really the central issue and how one thinks grammar should be taught will rest on the position one adopts. Second, I will bring together a number of concrete suggestions from previous chapters about how grammar learning can be facilitated through instruction. Finally, I will provide an example of a lesson that encapsulates the kind of approach to teaching grammar that I think is likely to be effective.

THE INTERFACE ISSUE

The inter-face issue assumes that a clear distinction can be drawn between explicit and implicit knowledge and that the processes involved in learning each of these are also different. The knowledge distinction is now well-established. There is plenty of evidence to suggest that implicit and explicit knowledge are quite distinct. The distinction is not only cognitive (i.e. clearly acknowledged in the field of psychology) but also neurological (i.e. evident in the way the brain organizes and stores information). In Ellis (2008: 755) I drew the following conclusion from my survey of the neuroscientific research:

> The neuroscientific research that has investigated procedural/
> implicit memory and declarative/explicit memory indicates a substantial
> degree of anatomical localization within the brain. It has demonstrated
> that procedural memory is responsible for grammar (both morphology
> and syntax) and that declarative memory is responsible for lexis
> (including those aspects of grammar that are lexical).

If it is accepted that implicit and explicit knowledge are housed in different neurological structures within the brain, the interface issue is a very real issue for teachers.

The key question is whether explicit knowledge 'converts' into implicit knowledge. There are different answers to this question, Krashen (1981) advanced the non-interface hypothesis, which claims that the acquisition of the two types of knowledge draw on different cognitive processes and so are developed separately. According to this view explicit knowledge neither converts nor facilitates the acquisition of implicit knowledge although, to a limited extent, it may assist L2 use when learners employ their explicit knowledge to monitor. DeKeyser (1998) drew on skill-learning theory to argue in favour of the strong interface hypothesis. This claims that explicit knowledge can be 'proceduralized' through practice, especially when this requires learners to engage in meaningful communication. This view of the relationship between the two types of knowledge underlies mainstream approaches to grammar teaching today (e.g. the present-practice-produce sequence). I have argued in favour of the weak interface hypothesis (see Chapter 11). This makes two separate claims. The first is that explicit knowledge converts into implicit knowledge providing the learner is developmentally ready to acquire the target feature. The second claim is that explicit knowledge functions as a 'facilitator' of implicit knowledge by assisting the processes responsible for its acquisition (i.e. noticing, noticing-the-gap, and auto-input). The problem with the first of these claims from a practical standpoint is that learner 'readiness' is very difficult to establish and will also vary from learner to learner. It is not practical to expect teachers to know whether each student is ready to acquire a specific target feature. It is for this reason that I have increasingly emphasized the facilitating role of explicit knowledge.

The interface issue continues to be debated — largely at a theoretical level. There is empirical evidence to support each of the three hypotheses. No single study has conclusively demonstrated which of the three hypotheses can explain the relationship between explicit and implicit knowledge. Indeed, it is very difficult to design such a study as it requires investigating the effects of instruction on a grammatical feature that is entirely 'new' (i.e. the learners have not yet begun to acquire it). In any single group of learners there will be those who have already partially acquired the grammatical feature that is the target of a study.

That said, there is ample evidence to show that teaching a specific grammatical structure is no guarantee it will be acquired (i.e. that learners will incorporate the feature into their implicit knowledge). Chapters 2, 3 and 5 report research that demonstrates this. It is for this reason that my own position has been to emphasize the teacher's role in 'facilitating' the acquisition of grammar rather than 'teaching' it.

FACILITATING L2 ACQUISITION

When grammar teaching is directed at 'facilitating' acquisition the aim becomes not that of trying to implant the target feature into the learner's mental grammar of the L2 so that they can use it correctly but rather that of creating the conditions that will assist the processes involved in its acquisition. There is a fundamental difference in these two views of what grammar teaching should try to achieve. In the case of the former, the aim is to achieve immediate learning (i.e. the expectancy is that, as a result of the instruction, the learner will have learned the target feature). In the case of the latter, however, there is no such expectancy. It is possible that the facilitation will achieve immediate success if the learner is developmentally ready to acquire the feature targeted by the instruction but from what we know of the gradual, incremental nature of grammar learning it is much more likely to lead to only partial restructuring of the learner's mental grammar and its effect may only become apparent later. That is, the effect of the instruction is more likely to be delayed than immediate. Much of this book has focused on how teachers can 'facilitate' acquisition through grammar teaching. I have suggested a number of ways and will review three of these now.

Interpretation Tasks

Interpretation tasks (see Chapter 12) are input-based tasks that aim to draw learners' attention to the target feature. Thus, they seek to teach grammar through input-processing rather than output-processing. They assist learners to notice and comprehend the target structure, not to produce it. Such tasks expose learners to input that has been enriched with the target structure and require them to demonstrate their understanding by means of a non-verbal response (e.g. choosing the correct picture or performing an action). The input is designed in such a way that it can only be understood if the learner processes the grammatical structure. That is, it requires bottom-up processing of the input, not just top-down processing. For example, in a sentence like 'The dog was bitten by Mary' it requires learners to attend to the grammatical features that mark this sentence as passive in order to understand it.

The theoretical rationale for such tasks is that acquisition begins with noticing and creating a form-function mapping (i.e. identifying the semantic or functional meaning of the target structure). Learners cannot produce the target structure until (1) they have created this form-function mapping and (2) integrated the feature into the mental grammar (their interlanguage). Interpretation tasks aim at (1) but not (2) as integration lies under the control of the learner, not the teacher. Thus, the aim is to create the conditions for acquisition to take place, not to guarantee that it will. Such tasks have another advantage. Learners often feel anxious when struggling to produce a grammatical feature that they have not yet acquired. Production is inherently more anxiety-creating than comprehension. Anxiety inhibits learners' ability to hold and rehearse grammatical details in their working memory.

There is now a plethora of studies that show that interpretation tasks assist acquisition. Most of these have been conducted within VanPatten's theoretical framework (e.g. VanPatten, 1996). This proposes that the way in which learners process input is constrained by a number of general principles that inhibit their ability to attend to key grammatical features. For example, the First Noun Principle states that learners will assume that the first noun in a sentence is the agent of the action. This works for many sentences but not for sentences like 'The dog was bitten by Mary'. Processing Instruction involves the use of interpretation tasks, which assist learners to attend to grammatical features that might otherwise be overlooked as learners operate in accordance with the general principles. VanPatten and his co-researchers have conducted a number of studies that show that Processing Instruction can facilitate acquisition and is more effective than traditional production-based instruction (see Chapters 12 and 13).

Consciousness-Raising Tasks

'Consciousness-raising' is a widely used term in SLA-based discussions of grammar teaching. In its broadest sense it refers to attempts to make learners conscious of a grammatical feature. Thus in this sense it would include interpretation tasks and Processing Instruction.However, I have used this term with a narrower definition — to refer to activities directed at helping learners to form an understanding of a grammatical feature — in other words to assist them in developing explicit knowledge.

In this narrower sense, consciousness-raising can involve direct explicit instruction, where the learner is provided with a metalinguistic description of the target feature either by the teacher or via a grammar reference book, or indirect explicit instruction where the learner is assisted to construct a metalinguistic rule for the target structure him- or herself. The means for achieving indirect explicit instruction are consciousness-raising tasks (see Chapters 11, 13 and 14). These provide the learner with data, which when analysed lead to the construction of a metalinguistic rule. They aim to place the burden of formulating explicit rules on the learner and in so doing to encourage the learner to become autonomous. Consciousness-raising tasks cater to a discovery-based approach to teaching grammar.

The rationale for both direct and indirect consciousness-raising is that explicit knowledge of grammatical features is both useful in itself and can assist the process of acquiring implicit knowledge. Explicit knowledge of grammar plays a role in L2 production (but perhaps a lesser role in comprehension). First, learners can draw on their explicit knowledge to help them in the formulation stage (Levelt, 1989). This stage involves the selection of the lexical-grammatical means for expressing the meanings the learner wishes to communicate, which have been decided on in the conceptualisation stage. Effective communication requires that learners have access to implicit knowledge in the formulation stage but if this is lacking it can be compensated for by drawing on explicit knowledge. L2 learners do this all the time. Second, explicit knowledge is available for monitoring the output of the formulation stage either before it is articulated or by self-correcting after articulation. A simplified version of Levelt's model is shown in Figure 1 below, indicating where explicit knowledge has a role to play in production.

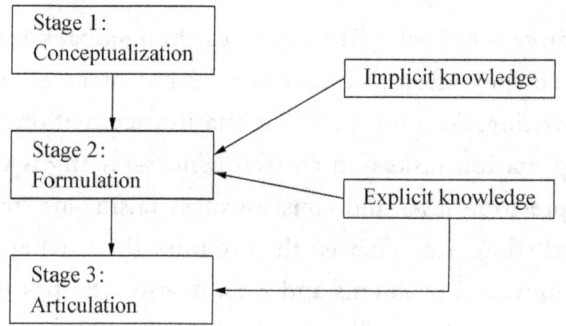

Figure 1: The contribution of explicit knowledge to L2 production

I have also argued that explicit knowledge has a role to play in L2 acquisition. It assists learners to notice grammatical features in the input and also to notice the gap between their own interlanguage production and target language usage. Both noticing and noticing-the-gap are essential acquisitional processes. Thus while explicit knowledge in itself can never compensate for implicit knowledge it can facilitate its development.

Explicit knowledge is declarative — it consists of 'facts' about the target language.It is always easier to teach facts than to teach 'skills'. Facts can be taught incrementally, one at a time. They can be memorized. For this reason a traditional structural syllabus provides a basis for teaching learners explicit knowledge. In contrast, implicit knowledge is procedural and skill-like. It is acquired gradually and involves the slow restructuring of mental procedures over a lengthy period of time. For this reason, I have argued that a structural syllabus cannot serve as a basis for developing implicit knowledge.

Consciousness-raising — direct or indirect — is not a substitute for the kind of instruction needed to develop implicit knowledge. But it can serve the valuable purpose of providing learners with the explicit knowledge that will assist them in the slow and painstaking process of acquiring implicit knowledge.

Corrective Feedback

Corrective feedback (CF) refers to the feedback that learners receive when they attempt to use the L2 but make errors in their speech or writing. As a means of facilitating acquisition, CF differs from interpretation tasks and consciousness-raising is two crucial ways. Interpretation tasks and consciousness-raising are 'pre-emptive' instructional strategies. That is, they require the teacher to identify specific grammatical problems and then devise activities to assist the learner to overcome them. They are also intensive in the sense that they focus on a single target feature at a time, providing the learner with input that is rich in that feature. In contrast, CF is a 'reactive' instructional strategy. Teachers respond to learner errors when they occur. Also, CF is often extensive in the sense that teachers may not focus on correcting a single error type but instead address a variety of different errors within a single lesson. CF, then, complements pre-emptive strategies.

Both oral and written CF can occur in response to errors that learners make in a practice exercises or in communicative tasks. There is particular merit in the latter as this ensures that the CF relates to meanings that the learners themselves are trying to express. A good example of how oral CF can be embedded in a communicative task can be found in Chapter 4, where the teacher responded to past tense errors in a story-telling task with requests for clarification to prod the learners to self-correct. A further example can be found in the lesson described in the next section of this chapter. The theoretical case for incorporating CF into a communicative task is transfer-appropriate-processing:

...according to the principle of transfer appropriate processing, the learning environment that best promotes rapid, accurate retrieval of what has been learned is that in which the psychological demands placed on the learner resemble those that will be encountered later in natural settings. (Segalowitz & Lightbown, 1999, p.51)

CF, then, can be hypothesized to be more effective if is provided in the context of a communicative task as the 'psychological demands placed on the learner' in such a task resemble those found in natural communication much more closely than those arising in practice exercises.

The extent to which CF assists acquisition is, however, a matter of debate. Some theories claim that only positive evidence in the form of 'comprehensible input' (or 'comprehensible output') promotes acquisition and that negative evidence in the form of CF only leads to explicit knowledge. Other theories, however, maintain that learners' make use of the negative evidence that CF provides to restructure their implicit knowledge. Ultimately this debate can only be resolved empirically through studies that investigate whether CF does lead to acquisition. There is, in fact, ample evidence now available to show that both oral and written CF does assist acquisition (see Sheen and Ellis, 2011). CF can help learners acquire new grammatical forms and, perhaps more significantly, lead to greater control over those forms that they have already partially acquired (i.e. to improve the accuracy with which they use these forms).

There are a variety of different types of CF. In Chapter 15 I outlined a typology of written CF types. For example, teachers call elect to provide direct correction (i.e. provide the learner with the correct form), indirect correction (i.e. simply indicate that an error has occurred without correcting it), or metalinguistic correction (i.e. provide learners with information about the target language rule that has been contravened). Written CF can also be unfocused (when it is 'extensive') or focused on a specific error type (when it is 'intensive'). A somewhat similar range of types are evident in oral CF (see Table 1). These differ in two major ways. They can be 'implicit' (i.e. the corrective force of the CF is hidden) or 'explicit' (i.e. the corrective force is clearly evident). They can also be input-providing (i.e. provide the learner with the correct form) or output-prompting (i.e. prompt the learner to self-correct). Permuting these two dimensions of oral CF allows for four basic types: (1) implicit and input-providing, (2) explicit and input-providing, (3) implicit and input-providing and (4) explicit and output-prompting. Table 1 shows the specific CF strategies that belong to each of the four types.

Table 1: A taxonomy of oral CF strategies

	Implicit	Explicit

Input-providing	• Conversational recasts
	e.g. L: I go cinema.
	    T: *You are going to the cinema?*
		• Didactic recasts
		e.g. L: I go cinema tomorrow.
		    T: *Yes, you are going to the cinema tomorrow?*
		• Explicit correction only
		e.g. L: I go cinema yesterday.
		    T: *No. You need 'went'.*
		• Explicit correction with metalinguistic explanation
		e.g. L: I go cinema yesterday.
		    T: *Went. You need past tense.*

Output-prompting	• Repetition
	e.g. L: I go cinema.
	    T: *I go cinema?*
	• Clarification requests
	e.g. L: I go cinema.
	    T: *Sorry?*
		• Metalinguistic clue
		e.g. L: I go cinema yesterday.
		T: *Past tense.*
		• Elicitation
		e.g. L: I go cinema yesterday.
		    T: *You _____?*
		• Paralinguistic signal
		e.g. L: I go cinema yesterday.
		    (T gestures with thumb over right shoulder to indicate past time reference.)

A key issue for language pedagogy is what types of CF strategy are more likely to facilitate acquisition. There is, however, no consensus on this issue among either SLA or L2 writing researchers. Indeed, according to one theory — sociocultural theory — it will not prove possible to identify which type is most effective. This theory argues that CF needs to be tailored to the individual learner so as to enable the learner to achieve self-regulation (i.e. the ability to use the target language form correctly without assistance) and that this is best achieved by searching for the least explicit CF type that will enable the learner to self-correct. Sociocultural theory argues that learning is not just evident in whether the learner can use the target form correctly but also in a reduction of the corrective assistance that is needed for the learner to self-correct. In contrast, cognitive-interactionist theories provide arguments in favour of implicit input-providing CF (i.e. conversational or didactic recasts) while skill-learning theories prioritize output-prompting CF. There are research studies that demonstrate the efficacy of all these different types.

What then can I say to teachers about CF? First, I would suggest that teachers should not be afraid to correct their students' errors both in their writing and their communicative speech. Correction helps but only if students attend to it. For this reason, it seems to me that the students need to know they are being corrected. Thus, second, on balance, explicit forms of correction are likely to be more effective than implicit. Third, many students benefit not just from being given the correct grammatical form but also by developing an understanding of the nature of their error and of the target language rule. Thus, third, providing the students with metalinguistic clues is likely to help. Fourth, on balance (and not surprisingly) CF works better when it is focused (i.e. addresses a single error type). This means that teachers should consider selecting a specific error type for correction in each lesson rather than spraying correction at whatever errors occur. Fifth, teachers should provide time for students to 'uptake' the correction (i.e. to repair their error). This means pausing after correcting a student. Sixth, teachers should recognize that CF can facilitate acquisition when it occurs 'on-line' (i.e. the teacher corrects the student immediately after the error has occurred) and when it is 'delayed' [1], as when the teacher makes a note of the errors that occurred in a communicative activity and goes over them after the activity is completed. These six suggestions constitute guidelines, not prescriptions; above all teachers need to be sensitive to the needs of individual students and to experiment with different ways of conducting CF in their classrooms.

AN EXAMPLE OF A GRAMMAR LESSON

The example I have chosen is Samuda's (2001) account of a task-based lesson designed to teach students epistemic modality (i.e. the use of modal verbs such as 'might' and 'must' to express degrees of possibility and certainty). Samuda distinguishes 'knowledge constructing' activities designed to assist learners to construct new form-meaning mappings and 'fluency stretching activities' designed to refine and stretch learners' existing interlanguage. Pre-testing of the students established that they had very little prior knowledge of this form-meaning mapping. Thus, the lesson she describes constitutes an example of grammar teaching aimed at 'knowledge constructing'. The lesson was based on a communicative task — the Things-in-Pocket Task. I will begin by describing the lesson and the task she used and then discuss what transpired in terms of how it illustrates the facilitative role that grammar teaching can play.

The Lesson

The lesson began with an activity in which learners were told the contents of a mystery person's pocket and were asked to work together in groups, speculating about the person's possible identity. As they did so, each group was asked to complete a chart by suggesting possible identities (e.g. the person could be a smoker because there are matches in his pocket) and by noting how certain they were about these speculations in a table. The first column of this table had the heading 'less than 50 % certain (it's possible)', the second column is headed '90% certain (it's probable)', whilst the third had the heading '100% certain (it's certain'). An analysis of the students' production in the group work stage showed that they mined the input of the task for useful lexis (e.g. 'possible', 'probable' and 'certain') and also mobilized their own somewhat limited interlanguage resources (e.g. used expressions such as 'maybe' and 'I'm not sure') but that they failed to use the target epistemic modal forms.

Once the group work was over, the teacher chaired a class discussion in which she adopted the role of communicator but at the same time attempted to shift the students' focus from meaning to form by interweaving the target forms into the interaction, as in this exchange:

> S: Look (opens matchbox). Many matches so maybe he just keep for friend, not for him.
>
> T: Mmmm I — I guess it's possible he might smoke. It's hard to tell just from this.

Samuda describes the teacher's approach as an implicit one, involving 'precasting' (i.e. the 'systematic mining of pre-established meaning') followed by 'conversational interweaves' (where the target forms are introduced through feedback) to create an interface between meaning and form, as in the example above. However, the students did not uptake the interweaves, a failure that Samuda explains in terms of the intense focus on meaning during this stage of the lesson.

In the next stage, the teacher initiated a more explicit focus on the target forms. In the first place, the teacher tried to focus the students' attention narrowly on the connection between meaning and form, often resorting to metalinguistic comments to do so, as in this example:

> T: 100% 100%? Then you can say he IS a business man (writes on board). When you when you're NOT 100% certain, you can use 'must'. OK? Not he is a business man but he must be a businessman.

It is during this stage that the students began to use the target forms in their speech when prompted. The teacher also now employed corrective feedback when students failed to use the target forms or used them erroneously. Samuda noted that all but one of the teacher's corrective moves were taken up by the students. In the post-task phase of the lesson (where the students collaborated in preparing a poster presentation), the students begin to incorporate the new forms into their production on their own initiative, as in the following example, where a number of learners contribute to the discussion:

> L1: He likes
> L2: Golf
> L3: Tennis
> L4: Art
> L2: Mmm (looking at chart) art just probable and chess
> L4: So probable?
> L5: Probable
> L2: (writing) He *must* like chess?
> L3: and art
> (p. 135).

A post-test administered after the lesson yielded a mean score of 19.01 (out of 26), an increase of 15.28 points from the pre-test suggesting that the learners had successfully acquired the target structure although Samuda was cautious in the claims she made as there was no control group in her study.

Discussion

The title of Smnuda's article is 'Guiding relationships between form and meaning during task performance'. In other words she viewed her approach as that of facilitating the process by which learners acquire new forms (the epistemic medals) and map these on to the meanings they wished to communicate.

Samuda's lesson provides a clear example of how grammar teaching can facilitate learning. It differs markedly from traditional grammar teaching where the teacher first presents the grammatical structure to the students (typically by means of direct explicit instruction) and then practices it, first by means of controlled exercises and then in a communicative activity. It illustrates two of the ways in which I have suggested grammar learning can be facilitated through instruction — consciousness-raising and corrective feedback. I will begin by considering these. I will then suggest how the other way — interpretation tasks — might have been incorporated into the lesson.

In the first stage of the lesson, when the students worked in groups to complete the chart, they were not made aware of the target structure. Instead, a context was created that would make the use of this structure 'natural'. However, given that the students initially had only very limited knowledge of the target structure (as shown by the pre-test) it is not surprising that during this stage they failed to use any modal verbs, relying instead on the input provided by the task (i.e. words like 'possible' and 'probable' contained in the initial chart they completed) and their prior knowledge of formulaic expressions. In the second, teacher-led stage of the lesson, the students were now made aware of the target structure. What Samuda's lesson seems to show is the importance of developing students' metalinguistic understanding of the target structure (i.e. 'understanding'). The teacher in this lesson adopted a number of consciousness-raising strategies to help the students develop a clear understanding of the meaning of the epistemic modals. She explicitly pointed out the meanings of the modals *might* and *must* by showing how they expressed the same meanings as the lexical items 'possible' and 'probable'. She also drew their attention to the form of the modal verbs (e.g. 'You use the simple verb here because *must* is a modal verb — it doesn't change'). These metacomments were inserted into the flow of the class discussion. However, they were not completely effective in enabling the students to use the modal verbs. To address this, the teacher also used the blackboard to underscore the key points. Importantly, it is only when the teacher adopted these explicit strategies for making the students conscious of the target forms that they began to notice the forms in her input and, a little later, to begin using them themselves. Also, interestingly, with the teacher's prompting, they were ultimately able to monitor their errors (e.g. one student self-corrected 'must has' to 'must have').

This lesson, then, demonstrates how developing students' explicit knowledge through consciousness-raising helped to trigger the kinds of processes ('noticing', 'noticing-the-gap' and 'monitoring') that I have hypothesized to play a central role in L2 acquisition. The lesson also suggests that focus-on-form of the more explicit kind, supported by adroit use of metalanguage, is highly effective and, indeed, with some students may be necessary to motivate interlanguage development in task-based interactions.

In my own discussion of consciousness-raising earlier in this chapter I saw it a basis for developing a lesson that was exclusively concerned with developing learners' explicit knowledge (i.e. it was 'pre-emptive'). The lesson Samuda describes shows how consciousness-raising techniques call be incorporated into a task-based lesson, where the main focus is on communicating meaningfully (i.e. the consciousness- raising was 'reactive'). Samuda and Bygate (2008), in their commentary on this lesson, noted the following:

> Whereas teachers have generally focused on form before students need to use it (as in PPP approaches) or after the need has passed (in post-task feedback and practice materials), this approach specifically times the teacher's input so that it occurs at a mid-point during the task, before the task has been completed' (p.144-145)

I see merit in utilizing consciousness-raising in both ways. There are times that learners can benefit from simply developing a metalinguistic understanding of a grammatical feature as a means to using the explicit knowledge to notice and notice-the-gap in subsequent communication. But, as this lesson illustrates, there is also merit in integrating consciousness-raising into a communicative grammar lesson.

The lesson also illustrates how corrective feedback can be used to help learners learn a new grammatical feature. Interestingly, most of the corrections the teacher provided arose not because the teacher failed to understand the students (there were no or very few breakdowns in actual communication) but because the teacher wished to draw their attention to the target forms. Samuda reports that 73% of the teacher's corrective forms addressed problems of form and only 27% problems of meaning. In other words, attention to form arose not because of some communication problem but, didactically, because the teacher wished to ensure that the students focus on some specific linguistic feature. Interestingly, the teacher's recasts of learner utterances, where she attempted to introduce the modal verbs, were not uptaken by the students and did not lead to the use of the target forms in their own utterances. This bears out my earlier comments that corrective feedback of the more explicit kind may be more noticeable and thus more likely to facilitate acquisition.

The lesson did not include an interpretation task. Given that the students obviously had little prior knowledge of epistemic modals (as shown by the results of the pre-test), it was perhaps optimistic to expect them to use these in the initial stage of the lesson when they were working in groups to complete the chart [2]. An alternative might have been to have begun the lesson with an interpretation task that would force them to process the meaning of the modals in input. One way this could have been achieved was by asking the students to listen to sentences such as 'Mary might be married', 'Tom must be a bachelor' and 'Helen is a widow' and ticking boxes in a table for each sentence according to whether the sentences refer to possibility, near certainty or complete certainty.

There is of course no need to incorporate all three of the instructional strategies in a single lesson. This lesson clearly 'worked' as the students were eventually successful in using the modal verbs in their own utterances and demonstrated learning in the post-test. However, while corrective feedback obviously requires some kind of production task, both interpretation tasks and consciousness-raising tasks can be used by themselves. That is, they can serve as the basis for complete lessons. I see interpretation tasks, consciousness-raising, and corrective feedback as instructional options that can be utilized in a variety of different ways.

CONCLUSION

In my introduction to this book (Chapter 1) I recalled a grammar lesson that I had taught many years ago in a secondary school in Zambia, which demonstrated the failure of my attempt to eliminate a common error in my students' production (the overuse of the present progressive). I do not believe this is an unusual occurrence. Many (probably most) teachers have experienced something similar. They teach a grammatical structure in one way or another but the students do not learn it.

Thus, the axiom that informs this whole book is for grammar teaching to work it must accord with how learners learn. However, learning an L2 is an enormously complex task and there are many different theories to explain how it occurs — as apparent in the different positions regarding the interface issue. Thus, there is no consensus on the 'best' way to teach grammar for learning. In this book, I have advanced my own views about how to achieve this, drawing on my own understanding of the research in SLA. Other views are possible and indeed have been strongly advocated. Perhaps what is most important in the long run is that teachers engage actively and consciously in this search. I hope the contents of this book will assist teachers to search for ways in which they can teach grammar for learning.

Notes

[1] Oral CF can occur either online or be delayed. Written CF is almost always delayed (i.e. teachers collect in a piece of writing, correct it, and then hand it back to the students). Thus in the case of writing students see the corrections some time after they made their errors. The fact that written CF has been shown to be effective in helping learners to achieve greater accuracy in subsequent pieces of writing is evidence that delayed CF is effective.

[2] The need for initial input relating to the target features is, however,

disputable. Samuda might well argue that her primary purpose in the chart-filling activity was not to elicit use of the modal verbs but to 'prime' them for the subsequent activities by establishing the meanings that the modal verbs convey. The activity led to the students using lexical markers of certainty (e.g. 'possible' and 'probable') which set the scene for the later introduction of the modal forms. See Batstone and Ellis (2009) for a somewhat different interpretation of Samuda's lesson.

Bibliography

Alanen, R. (1995). Input enhancement and rule presentation in second language acquisition. In R. Schmidt (Ed.), *Attention and awareness in foreign language learning* . Honolulu: University of Hawaii Press.

Allen, P., Swain, M., Harley, B., & Cummins, J. (1990).Aspects of classroom treatment: Toward a more comprehensive view of second language education. In B. Harley, P. Allen, J. Cummins & M. Swain (Eds.).

Allwright, R. (1975). Problems in the study of the language teacher's treatment of learner error. In M. Burt and H. Dulay (Eds.), *ON TESOL'75: New directions in second language learning* . Washington, DC: TESOL.

Allwright, R. (1980). Turns, topics, and tasks: patterns of participation in language learning and teaching. In D. Larsen-Freeman (Ed.), *Discourse analysis in second language research.* Rowley, MA: Newbury House.

Allwright, R. (1988). *Observation in the language classroom.* London: Longman.

Anderson, J. (1983). *The architecture of cognition.* Cambridge, MA: Harvard University Press.

Asher, J. (1977). *Learning another language through actions: The complete teachers' guidebook* . Los Gatos, CA: Sky Oaks.

Asher, J., Kusudo, J., & de la Torre, R. (1974).Learning a second language through commands: The second field test. *The Modern Language Journal, 58,* 24–32.

Ashwell, T. (2000). Patterns of teacher response to student writing in a multiple-draft composition classroom: Is content feedback followed by form feedback the best method? *Journal of Second Language Writing 9*, 227–58.

Aufderstrasse, H., Bock, H., Gerdes, M., & Muller, H. (1983). *Themen*. Munchen: Max Hueber Verlag.

Ausubel, D. (1971). Some psychological aspects of the structure of knowledge. In P. Johnson (Ed.), *Learning: Theory and practice*. New York: Thomas Y. Crowell.

Ayoun, D. (2001). The role of negative and positive feedback in the second language acquisition of Passe Compose and Imparfait. *The Modern Language Journal 85*, 226–243.

Badalamenti, V. and Henner-Stanchina, C. (1993). *Grammar dimensions: Form, meaning and use one*. Boston: Heinle and Heinle.

Bailey, N., Madden, C, & Krashen, S. (1974). Is there a 'natural sequence' in adult second language learning? *Language Learning, 24*, 235–244.

Bardovi-Hardlig, K., & Bofman, T. (1989). Attainment of syntactic and morphological accuracy by advanced language learners. *Studies in Second Language Acquisition, 11*, 17–34.

Basturkmen, H., Loewen, S. & Ellis, R. (2004).Teachers' stated beliefs about incidental focus on form and their classroom practices. *Applied Linguistics 25*, 243– 272.

Batstone, R. (2002). Contexts of engagement: A discourse perspective on 'intake' and 'pushed output. *System 30*, 1–14.

Batstone, R. and Ellis, R. (2009). Principled grammar teaching. *System 37*: 194–204.

Beebe, L. (1980). Measuring the use of communication strategies. In R. Scarcella & S. Krashen (Eds.), *Research in second language acquisition*. Rowley, MA: Newbury House.

Bialystok, E. (1982). On the relationship between knowing and using linguistic forms. *Applied Linguistics*, 3, 181–206.

Bialystok, E. (1991). Achieving proficiency in a second language: a processing description. In R. Phillipson, E. Kellerman, L. Selinker, M. Sharwood-Smith, & M. Swain (Eds.), *Foreign/second language pedagogy research*. Clevedon: Multilingual Matters.

Bialystok, E. & Frohlich, M. (1977). Aspects of second language learning in classroom settings. *Working Papers on Bilingualism, 13*, 2–26.

Bialystok, E. & Sharwood Smith, M. (1985). Interlanguage is not a state of mind: An evaluation of the construct for second language acquisition. *Applied Linguistics 6*, 101–117.

Bley-Vroman, R. (1983). The comparative fallacy in interlanguage studies: The case of systematicity. *Language Learning, 33*, 1–17.

Block, D. (2003). *The social turn in second language acquisition*. Edinburgh: Edinburgh University Press.

Bloomfield, L. (1933). *Language*. New York: Holt, Rinehart and Winston.

Bolitho, R. and Tomlinson, B. (1980). *Discover English*. London: George Allen and Unwin.

Breen, M. (1984). Process in syllabus design and classroom language learning. In C. M. Brumfit (Ed.), *General English syllabus design (ELT Documents No. 118)*. Oxford: Pergamon Press.

Breen, M. (1985). Authenticity in the language classroom. *Applied Linguistics, 6*, 60–70.

Bright, J. (1965). *Patterns and skills in English, book 1* . Arusha: Longman.

Brooks, N. (1960). *Language and language learning*. New York: Harcourt Brace and World.

Brumfit, C. (1979). Communicative language teaching: An educational perspective. In C. Brumfit & K. Johnson (Eds.), *The Communicative approach to language teaching*. Oxford: Oxford University Press.

Brumfit, C. (1984). *Communicative methodology in language teaching*. Cambridge: Cambridge University Press.

Burt, H. (1975). Error analysis in the adult EFL classroom. *TESOL Quarterly, 9*, 53–63.

Byrne, D. (1986). *Teaching oral English. 2nd edition*. London: Longman.

Cadierno, T. (1995). Formal instruction from a processing perspective: An investigation into the Spanish past tense. *The Modern Language Journal, 79*, 179–193.

Calderhead, J. (Ed.). (1988). *Teachers' professional learning*. London: Falmer Press. Cambridge University Press.

Canale, M. (1983). From communicative competence to language pedagogy. In J. Richards and R. Schmidt (eds.). *Language and communication*. London: Longman.

Carr, W., & Kemmis, S. (1986). *Becoming critical: Education, knowledge and action research*. London: Falmer Press.

Carroll, S. (2001). *Input and evidence: The raw material of second language acquisition*. Amsterdam, John Benjamins.

Carroll, S., & Swain, M. (1993). Explicit and implicit negative feedback: An empirical study of the learning of linguistic generalizations. *Studies in Second Language Acquisition 15*, 357–386.

Carroll, S., Swain, M. & Roberge, Y. (1992). The role of feedback in adult second language acquisition: Error correction and morphological generalizations. *Applied Pyscholinguistics 13*, 173–198.

Castagnaro, P. (1991). An experimental study of two interventional packages to improve student production for the notion of relative position. Unpublished manuscript, Temple University Japan, Tokyo.

Celce-Murcia, M. & Larsen-Freeman, D. (1999). *The grammar book 2nd edition*. Boston: Heinle and Heinle.

Celce-Murcia, M. (2002). Why it makes sense to teach grammar through context and through discourse. In E. Hinkel & S. Fotos (Eds.), *New perspectives on grammar teaching in second language classrooms*. Mahwah, N.J.: Lawrence Erlbaum.

Chandler, J. (2003). The efficacy of various kinds of error feedback for improvement in the accuracy and fluency of L2 student writing. *Journal of Second Language Writing, 12*, 267–296.

Chaudron, C. (1985). Intake: On models and methods for discovering learners' processing of input. *Studies in Second Language Acquisition, 7*, 1–14.

Chaudron, C. (1987). *Second language classrooms*. Cambridge: Cambridge University Press.

Chaudron, C. (2003). Data collection in SLA research. In C. Doughty & M. Long (Eds.), *Handbook of second language acquisition*. Oxford: Blackwell.

Clahsen, H. (1980). Psycholinguistic aspects of second language acquisition. In S. Felix (Ed.), *Second language development: Trends and issues*. Tubingen: Gunter Narr.

Clahsen, H. (1984). The acquisition of German word order: A test case for cognitive approaches to L2 development. In R. Andersen (Ed.), *Second languages: A cross-linguistic perspective*. Rowley, MA: Newbury House.

Clahsen, H. (1985). Profiling second language development: A procedure for assessing L2 proficiency. In K.Hyltenstam & M. Pienemann (Eds.), *Modelling and assessing second language acquisition* (pp. 283–332). Clevedon: Multilingual Matters.

Clahsen, H., & Muysken, P. (1986). The availability of universal grammar to adult and child language learners — a study of the acquisition of German. *Second Language Research, 2*, 93–119.

Clarke, M. (1994). The dysfunctions of theory/practice discourse. *TESOL Quarterly, 28*, 9–26.

Clyne, M. (1985). Medium or object — different contexts of (school-based) second language acquisition. In K. Hyltenstam and M. Pienemann (Eds.), *Modelling and assessing second language acquisition*. Clevedon: Multilingual Matters.

Coenen, J., & Van Hout, R. (1987). Word order phenomena in second language acquisition of Dutch. *Linguistics in the Netherlands* (pp. 83–92). Dordrecht: Foris.

Cohen, A. (1989). Reformulation: A technique for providing advanced feedback in writing. *Guidelines, 11* (2), 1–9.

Collins, L., Halter, R., Lightbown, P & Spada, N. (1999). Time and distribution of time in L2 instruction. *TESOL Quarterly 33*, 655–680.

Cook, V. (1989). Universal grammar theory and the classroom. *System 17*, 169–182.

Corder, S. P. (1974). Error analysis. In J. Allen & S. Corder (Eds.), *The

Edinburgh course in applied linguistics, Vol. 3 (pp. 122–154). London: Oxford University Press.

Corder, S. P. (1967). The significance of learners' errors. *International Review of Applied Linguistics 5*, 161–169.

Corder, S. P. (1981). Error analysis and remedial teaching. In S. P. Corder (Ed.), *Error analysis and interlanguage* (pp. 45–55). Oxford: Oxford University Press.

Cronbach, L. (1980). *Toward reform of program evaluation.* San Francisco: Jossey-Bass.

Crookes, G. (1993). Action research and second language teachers: Going beyond teacher research. *Applied Linguistics, 14,* 130–144.

Crookes, G. (1997).SLA and language pedagogy: A socio-educational perspective. *Studies in Second Language Acquisition, 19,* 93–116.

Daniel,I. (1983). On first-year German foreign language learning: A comparison of behavior in response to two instructional methods. Unpublished doctoral dissertation, University of Southern California.

Day, E. and Shapson, S. (1991). Integrating formal and functional approaches to language teaching in French immersion: An experimental study. *Language Learning, 41,* 25–58.

Day, R. R. (1984). Student participation in the ESL classroom. *Language Learning, 34,* 69–89.

De Graaf, R. (1997). *Differential effects of explicit instruction on second language acquisition.* Netherlands: Holland Institute of Generative Linguistics.

DeKeyser, R. (1994). Implicit and explicit learning of L2 grammar: A pilot study. *TESOL Quarterly, 28,* 188–194.

DeKeyser, R. (1995). Learning second language grammar rules: An experiment with a miniature linguistic system. *Studies in Second Language Acquisition, 17,* 379–410.

DeKeyser, R. (1997). Beyond explicit rule learning: Automatizing second language morphosyntax. *Studies in Second Language Acquisition, 19,* 1–39.

DeKeyser, R. (1998). Beyond focus on form: Cognitive perspectives on learning and practicing second language grammar. In C. Doughty & J.

Williams (Eds.), *Focus on form in classroom second language acquisition* (pp. 42–63). Cambridge: Cambridge University Press.

DeKeyser, R., & Sokalski, K. (1996). The differential role of comprehension and production practice. *Language Learning, 46,* 613–642.

DeKeyser, R., Salaberry, R.,Robinson, P. & Harrington, M. (2002). What gets processed in processing instruction? A commentary on Bill VanPatten's "Processing instruction: an update". *Language Learning, 52,* 805–824.

Dickerson, L. (1975). The learner's interlanguage as a system of variable rules'. *TESOL Quarterly, 9,* 401–407.

Diller, K. (1978). *The language teaching controversy.* Rowley, Mass.: Newbury House.

Dornyei, Z. (2001). *Motivational strategies in the language classroom.* Cambridge: Cambridge University Press.

Doughty, C. (1991). Second language instruction does make a difference: Evidence from an empirical study on SL relativization.*Studies in Second Language Acquisition, 13,* 431–469.

Doughty, C. (2001). Cognitive underpinnings of focus on form. In P. Robinson (Ed.). *Cognition and second language instruction.* Cambridge: Cambridge University Press.

Doughty, C. (2003a). Effects of instruction on learning a second language: A critique of instructed SLA research. In B. VanPatten, J. Williams & S. Rott (Eds), *Form-meaning connections in second language acquisition.* Mahwah, New Jersey: Lawrence Erlbaum.

Doughty, C. (2003b). Instructed SLA: Constraints, compensation and enhancement. In C. Doughty & M. Long (Eds.), *The handbook of second language acquisition* (pp. 256–310). Malden, MA: Blackwell.

Doughty, C. & Varela, E. (1998). Communicative focus on form. In C. Doughty & J. Williams (Eds.), *Focus on Form in Classroom Second Language Acquisition* (pp. 114–138). Cambridge: Cambridge University Press.

Doughty, C. & Williams, J. (1998). Issues and terminology. In C. Doughty and J. Williams(Eds.), *Focus on Form in Classroom Second Language Acquisition* (pp. 1–11). Cambridge: Cambridge University Press.

Doughty, C., & Varela, E. (1995, March). Communicative fonF. Paper presented at the annual conference of the American Association of Applied Linguistics,Long Beach, CA.

Douglas, D. (2001). Performance consistency in second language acquisition and language testing: a conceptual gap. *Second Language Research, 17*, 442–456.

Dulay, H., & Burt, M. (1973). Should we teach children syntax? *Language Learning, 23*, 245–258.

Dulay, H., Burt, M. & Krashen, S. (1982). *Language two*. New York: Oxford University Press.

DuPlessis, J., Solin, D., Travis, L, & White, L. (1987). UG or not UG, that is the question: A reply to Clahsen and Muysken. *Second Language Research, 3*, 56–67.

Eastwood, J. (1992). *Oxford Practice Grammar*. Oxford: Oxford University Press.

Eckman, F,Bell, L, & Nelson, D. (1988). On the generalization of relative clause instruction in the acquisition of English as a second language. *Applied Linguistics, 9*, 1–20.

Eckman, F. (1985). Some theoretical and pedagogical implications of the markedness differential hypothesis. *Studies in Second Language Acquisition, 7*, 289–308.

Edmundson, W. (1985). Discourse worlds in the classroom and in foreign language learning. *Studies in Second Language Acquisition, 7*, 159–168.

Elbaum, S. (1996). *Grammar in context book 1. 2nd edition* . Boston: Heinle and Heinle.

Elley, W. (1991). Acquiring literacy in a second language: The effect of book-based programs. *Language Learning, 41*, 375–411.

Ellis, G., & Sinclair, B. (1989). *Learning to learn English*. Cambridge: Cambridge University Press.

Ellis, N. (1993). Rules and instances in foreign language learning:

Interactions of explicit and implicit knowledge. *European Journal of Cognitive Psychology, 5,* 289–318.

Ellis, N. (1996). Sequencing in SLA: Phonological memory, chunking, and points of order. *Studies in Second Language Acquisition, 18,* 91–126.

Ellis, N. (1998). Emergentism, connectionism and language learning. *Language Learning, 48,* 631–664.

Ellis, N. (2002). Frequency effects in language processing: A review with implications for theories of implicit and explicit language acquisition. *Studies in Second Language, Acquisition 24*(2), 143–188.

Ellis, N. (2005). At the interface: How explicit knowledge affects implicit language learning. *Studies in Second Language Acquisition, 27*(2), 303–352.

Ellis, R. (1982). Informal and formal approaches to communicative language teaching. *ELT Journal, 361,* 73–81.

Ellis,R. (1983). Formulaic Speech and Language Teaching. Talk given at 1983 TESOL Convention, Toronto.

Ellis, R. (1984a). Can syntax be taught? A study of the effects of formal instruction on the acquisition of WH questions by children. *Applied Linguistics, 5,* 138–155.

Ellis, R. (1984b). *Classroom second language development.* Oxford: Pergamon.

Ellis, R. (1984c). The role of instruction in second language acquisition. In D.Singleton & D. Little (Eds.), *Language learning in formal and informal contexts.* IRAAL.

Ellis, R. (1985). *Understanding second language acquisition.* Oxford: Oxford University Press.

Ellis, R. (1988a), Investigating language teaching: The case for an educational approach. *System, 16,* 1–11.

Ellis, R. (1988b). The role of practice in second language learning. *Teanga, 8,* 1–28.

Ellis, R. (1989). Are classroom and naturalistic acquisition the same? A study of the classroom acquisition of German word order rules. *Studies in Second Language Acquisition, 11,* 305–328.

Ellis, R. (1990). *Instructed second language acquisition*. Oxford: Basil Blackwell.

Ellis, R. (1991). *Second language acquisition and language pedagogy*. Clevedon: Multilingual Matters.

Ellis, R. (1993a). The structural syllabus and second language acquisition. *TESOL Quarterly, 27,* 91–113.

Ellis, R. (1993b). Interpretation-based grammar teaching. *System, 21,* 69–78.

Ellis, R. (1994a). *The study of second language acquisition*. Oxford: Oxford University Press.

Ellis, R. (1994b). An instructed theory of second language acquisition. In N. Ellis (Ed.), *Implicit and explicit learning of languages*. London: Academic Press.

Ellis, R. (1994c, March). Metalinguistic knowledge and second language pedagogy. Paper presented at the Annual Conference of the American Association of Applied Linguistics, Baltimore.

Ellis, R. (1995a). Modified oral input and the acquisition of word meanings. *Applied Linguistics, 16,* 409–441.

Ellis, R. (1995b). Interpretation tasks for grammar teaching. *TESOL Quarterly, 29,* 87–105.

Ellis, R. (1997). *SLA research and language teaching*. Oxford: Oxford University Press.

Ellis, R. (1998). Teaching and research: Options in grammar teaching, *TESOL Quarterly, 32,* 39–60.

Ellis, R. (1999a). Input-based approaches to teaching grammar: A review of classroom-oriented research. *Annual Review of Applied Linguistics, 19,* 64–80.

Ellis, R. (1999b). Making the classroom acquisition-rich. In R. Ellis (Ed.), *Learning a second language through interaction* (pp. 211–229). Amsterdam: John Benjamins.

Ellis, R. (2001). Introduction: Investigating Form-Focused Instruction. *Language Learning, 51* (s1), 1–46.

Ellis, R. (2002a). Does form-focused instruction affect the acquisition of implicit knowledge? A review of the research. *Studies in Second Language Acquisition, 24*, 223–236.

Ellis, R. (Ed.). (2002b). *Form-focused instruction and second language learning.* Malden, MA: Blackwell.

Ellis, R. (2002c). The place of grammar instruction in the second/foreign language curriuculum. In E. Hinkel & S. Fotos (Eds.), *New perspectives on grammar teaching in second language classrooms* (pp. 17–34). Mahwah, N.J.: Lawrence Erlbaum.

Ellis, R. (2003). *Task-based language learning and teaching.* Oxford: Oxford University Press.

Ellis, R. (2004). The definition and measurement of explicit knowledge. *Language Learning, 54*, 227–275.

Ellis, R. (2005). Measuring implicit and explicit knowledge of a second language: A pyschometric study. *Studies in Second Language Acquisition 27*, 141–172.

Ellis, R. (2006). Researching the effects of form-focused instruction on L2 acquisition. *AILA Review, 19*(1), 18–41.

Ellis, R & Barkhuizen, G. (2005). *Analyzing learner language.* Oxford: Oxford University Press.

Ellis, R., Basturkmen, H. & Loewen, H. (2001).Learner uptake in communicative ESL lessons. *Language Learning, 51*, 281–318.

Ellis, R. and Gaies, S. (1998). *Impact grammar.* Hong Kong: Longman Addison Wesley.

Ellis, R., Loewen, S. and Erlam, R. (2006).Implicit and explicit corrective feedback and the acquisition of L2 Grammar. *Studies in Second Language Acquisition,28*, 339–368.

Ellis, R. & Rathbone, M. (1987). The acquisition of German in a classroom context. Mimeograph report.Ealing College of Higher Education.

Ellis, R. & Sheen, Y. (2006). Re-examining the role of recasts in SLA. *Studies in Second Language Acquisition, 28*, 575–600.

Ellis, R., & Wells, G. (1980). Enabling factors in adult-child discourse. *First Language, 1,* 46–82.

Ely, C. (1986). An analysis of discomfort, risktaking, sociability and motivation in the L2 classroom. *Language Learning, 36,* 1–25.

Eraut, M. (1994). *Developing professional knowledge and competence.* London: Falmer Press.

Erlam, R. (2003a). Evaluating the relative effectiveness of structured input and output-based instruction in foreign language learning. *Studies in Second Language Acquisition, 25,* 559–582.

Erlam, R. (2003b). The effects of deductive and inductive instruction on the acquisition of direct object pronouns in French as a second language. *The Modern Language Journal 87,* 242–260.

Erlam, R. (2006). Elicited imitation as a measure of implicit knowledge: An empirical validation study. *Applied Linguistics, 27,* 464–491.

Eubank, L. (1987). The acquisition of German negation by formal language learners. In B. VanPatten, T. Dvorak, & J. Lee (Eds.), *Foreign language learning: A research perspective* (pp. 33–51). Rowley, MA: Newbury House.

Faerch, C. (1980). Describing interlanguage through interaction: problems of systematicity and permeability. *Working Papers on Bilingualism, 19,* 59–78.

Faerch, C. (1985).Meta talk in FL classroom discourse. *Studies in Second Language Acquisition, 7,* 184–199.

Faerch, C., & Kasper, G. (1986).The role of comprehension in second language acquisition. *Applied Linguistics, 7,* 257–274.

Fathman, A. (1975). The relationship between age and second language productive ability. *Language Learning, 25,* 245–266.

Fathman, A. (1978). ESL and EFL learning: Similar or dissimilar? In C. Blatchford & J. Schacter (Eds.), *On TESOL 78: Policies, programs and practices* (pp. 213–223). Washington DC: TESOL.

Fazio, L. (2001). The effect of corrections and commentaries on the journal writing accuracy of minority- and majority-language students.

Journal of Second Language Writing, 10, 235–249.

Felix, S. (1977). Kreative und reproduktive Kompetenz im Zweitsprachenwerb. In H. Huntfeld (Ed.), *Neue perspektiven der fremdsprachendidaktik.* Kronberg.

Felix, S. (1981).The effect of formal instruction on second language acquisition. *Language Learning, 31,* 87–112.

Ferris, D. (2006). Does error feedback help student writers?New evidence on short- and long-term effects of written error correction. In K. Hyland & F. Hyland (Eds.), *Feedback in Second Language Writing: Contexts and Issues* (pp. 81–104). Cambridge: Cambridge University Press.

Ferris, D. & Roberts, B. (2001). Error feedback in L2 writing classes: How explicit does it need to be? *Journal of Second Language Writing, 10,* 161–184.

Firth, J. (1957). *Papers in Linguistics 1934–1951.* London: Oxford University Press.

Fortune, A. (1998). Survey Review: Grammar practice books. *ELT Journal* 52, 67–79.

Foster, P. (1998). A classroom perspective on the negotiation of meaning. *Applied Linguistics, 19,* 1–23.

Foster, P. (2001). Rules and routines: A consideration of their role in task-based language production of native and non-native speakers. In M. Bygate, P. Skehan & M. Swain (Eds.), *Task-Based Learning: Language Teaching, Learning and Assessment* (pp. 75–97). Harlow: Pearson.

Foster P. & Skehan, S. (1996). The influence of planning on performance in task-based learning. *Studies in Second Language Acquisition, 18,* 299–324.

Fotos, S. (1992). Grammar consciousness-raising tasks: Negotiating meaning while focusing on form. Unpublished doctoral dissertation,Temple University Japan.

Fotos, S. (1993). Consciousness and noticing through focus on form: Grammar tasks performance versus formal instruction. *Applied*

Linguistics, 14, 385–407.

Fotos, S. (1994). Integrating grammar instruction and communicative language use through grammar consciousness-raising tasks. *TESOL Quarterl, 28,* 323–351.

Fotos, S. and Ellis, R. (1991). Communicating about grammar: A task-based approach. *TESOL Quarterly, 25,* 605–628.

Freidson, E. (1977). The futures of professionalization. In M. Stacey, MReid, C. Heath, and R. Dingwall (Eds.), *Health and the division of labor* (pp.14–38). London: Croon Helm.

Gary, J. (1978). Why speak if you don't need to? The case for a listening approach to beginning foreign language learning. In W. Ritchie (Ed.), *Second language acquisition research* (pp. 185–199). New York: Academic.

Gass, S. (1982). From theory to practice. In W. Rutherford & M. Hines (Eds.), *On TESOL '81* (pp. 129–139). Washington, DC: TESOL.

Gattegno, C. (1972). *Teaching foreign languages in schools: The silent way.* New York: Educational Solutions.

Genesee, F. (1987). *Learning through two Languages: Studies of immersion and bilingual education.* Cambridge, MA: Newbury House.

Gower, R. and Walters, S. (1983). *Teaching Practice Handbook.* London: Heinemann Educational.

Green, P and K. Hecht. (1992). Implicit and explicit grammar: An empirical study. *Applied Linguistic, 13,* 168–184.

Gregg, K. (1984). Krashen's monitor and Occam's razor. *Applied Linguistics, 5,* 79–100.

Guenette, D. (2007). Is feedback pedagogically correct? Research design issues in studies of feedback on writing. *Journal of Second Language Writing, 16,* 40–53.

Halliday, M.,McIntosh, A., & Strevens, P. (1964). *The linguistic sciences and language teaching.* London: Longman.

Hammerley, H. (1975). The deduction induction controversy. *The Modern Language Journal, 59,* 15–18.

Han, Z. 2002. A study of the impact of recasts on tense consistency in L2 output. *TESOL Quarterly, 36,* 543–572.

Harley, B. (1989). Funtional grammar in French immersion: A classroom experiment. *Applied Linguistics, 10,* 331–359.

Harley, B. (1998). The role of focus-on-form tasks in promoting child L2 acquisition. In C. Doughty and J. Williams (Eds.), *Focus on Form in Classroom Second Language Acquisition* (pp. 156–174). Cambridge: Cambridge University Press.

Harmer, J. (1983). *The practice of English language teaching.* London: Longman.

Hatch, E. (1978a). Acquisition of syntax in a second language. In J. Richards (Ed.), *Understanding second and foreign language learning* (pp. 34–70). Rowley, MA: Newbury House.

Hatch, E. (1978b). Apply with caution. *Studies in Second Language Acquisition, 2,* 123–143.

Hatch, E. (1978c). Discourse analysis and second language acquisition. In E. Hatch (Ed.), *Second language acquisition.* Rowley, Mass.: Newbury House.

Hatch, E. (1978d). *Second language acquisition.* Rowley, MA: Newbury House.

Hatch, E., & Farhady, H. (1982). *Research design and statistics.* Rowley, MA: Newbury House.

Hawkins, E. (1984). *Awareness of Language: An Introduction.* Cambridge: Cambridge University Press.

Haycraft, J. (1978). *An introduction to English language teaching.* London: Longman.

Hedgcock, J. (1993). Well-formed vs. ill-formed strings in L2 metalingual tasks: Specifying features of grammaticality judgements. *Second Language Research, 9,* 1–21.

Hedge, T. (2000). *Teaching and learning in the language classroom.* Oxford: Oxford University Press.

Herron, C. & Tomosello, M. (1992). Acquiring grammatical structures by guided induction. *French Review, 65,* 708–718.

Higgs, T., and Clifford, R. (1982). The push toward communication. In T. Higgs (Ed.), *Curriculum, competence and the foreign language teacher.* Skikie, IL: National Textbook Company.

Hosenfeld, C. (1976). Learning about language: discovering our students' strategies. *Foreign Language Annals, 9,* 117–129.

Howatt, T. (1974). The background to course design.In J. Allen & S. P. Corder (Eds.), *Techniques in applied linguistics: The Edinburgh course in applied linguistics. Volume 3* (pp. 1–23). Oxford: Oxford University Press.

Hu, G. (2002). Psychological constraints on the utility of metalinguistic knowledge in second language production. *Studies in Second Language Acquisition, 24,* 347–386.

Hubbard, P., Jones, H., Thornton, B. and Wheeler, R. (1983). *A training course for TEFL.* Oxford: Oxford University Press.

Huebner, T. (1979). Order-of-acquisition vs. dynamic paradigm: a comparison of method in interlanguage research. *TESOL Quarterly, 13,* 21–28.

Huebner, T. (1983). *A longitudinal analysis of the acquisition of English.* Ann Arbor, MI: Karoma.

Hughes, A. (1979). Aspects of a Spanish adult's acquisition of English. *Interlanguage Studies Bulletin, 4,* 49–65.

Hulstijn, J. & De Graaf, R. (1994). Under what conditions does explicit knowledge of a second language facilitate the acquisition of implicit knowledge? A research proposal. In J. Hulstijn & R. Schmidt (Eds.), *Consciousness in second language learning.* AILA Review 11.

Hulstijn, J. & DeKeyser, R. (1997). Testing SLA theory in the research laboratory. *Studies in Second Language Acquisition, 19,* 131–143.

Hyland, K. & Hyland, F. (2006). Feedback on second language students' writing. *Language Teaching, 39,* 83–101.

Ingram, F., Nord, J., & Dragt, D. (1975).A program for listening comprehension. *Slavic and East European Journal, 19,* 1–10.

Jespersen, J. (1904). *How to Teach a Foreign Language*. London: George Allen and Unwin.

Johnson, Karen. (1995). *Understanding communication in second language classrooms*. Cambridge: Cambridge University Press.

Johnson, Keith. (1988). Mistake correction. *English Language Teaching Journal, 42*, 89–101.

Johnson, Keith. (1996). *Language teaching and skill learning*. Oxford: Blackwell.

Johnson, K., & Swain, M. (1998). *Immersion education: International perspectives*. Cambridge: Cambridge University Press.

Johnston, M. (1987). Understanding learner language. In D. Nunan (Ed.). *Applying second language acquisition research*. National Curriculum Research Centre (Adelaide, Australia): Adult Migrant Education Program.

Johnston, M. (undated). Second language acquisition research: a classroom perspective. Adult Migrant Eduaction Service, New South Wales, Australia.

Jones, L. (1992). *Communicative grammar practice*. Cambridge: Cambridge University Press.

Jordens, P. (1988).The acquisition of word order in 12 Dutch and German. Unpublished manuscript, Vrije Universiteit, Amsterdam.

Jourdenais, R., Ota, M., Stauffer, S., Boyson, B. & Doughty, C. (1995). Does textual enhancement promote noticing? A think-aloud protocol analysis. In R. Schmidt (Ed.), *Attention and awareness in foreign language learning* (pp. 183–216). Honolulu: University of Hawaii Press.

Kadia, K. (1987). The effect of formal instruction on monitored and spontaneous naturalistic interlanguage performance. *TESOL Quarterly, 22*, 509–515.

Kasper, G, & Rose, K. R. (2002). *Pragmatic development in a second language*. Oxford: Blackwell.

Kim, H., & Mathes, G. (2001). Explicit vs. implicit corrective feedback. *The Korea TESOL Journal, 1,* 1–15.

Kim, S. & Elder, C. (2005). The relationship between teachers' language choice and pedagogic functions in foreign language classrooms. *Language Teaching Research, 9, 355–380.*

Klein, W. & Perdue, C. (1992). *Utterance structure: Developing grammars again.* Amsterdam: John Benjamins.

Krahnke, K. (1987). *Approaches to syllabus design for foreign language teaching.* Englewood Cliffs, NJ: Prentice Hall.

Krashen, S. (1977). Some issues relating to the monitor model. In H. Brown, C. Yorio, & R. Crymes. (Eds.), *On TESOL'77: Teaching and learning English as a second language: Trends in research and practice* (pp. 144–158). Washington DC: TESOL.

Krashen, S. (1981a). *Second language acquisition and second language learning.* Oxford: Pergamon.

Krashen, S. (1981b).Consciousness-Raising and the Second Language Acquirer. A Response to Sharwood-Smith'. Mimeo. University of Southern California.

Krashen, S. (1982). *Principles and practice in second language acquisition.* Oxford: Pergamon.

Krashen, S. (1983). Second language acquisition theory and the preparation of teachers. In J. Alatis, H. Stern, & P. Strevens (Eds.), *Applied linguistics and the preparation of teachers: Toward a rationale* (pp. 255–263). Washington, DC: Georgetown University Press.

Krashen, S. (1985). *The input hypothesis.* London: Longman.

Krashen, S. (1989). We acquire vocabulary and spelling by reading: Additional evidence for the Input Hypothesis. *Modern Language Journal, 73, 440–464.*

Krashen, S. (1993). The effect of grammar teaching: Still peripheral. *TESOL Quarterly, 27, 717–725.*

Krashen, S. (1994). The input hypothesis and its rivals. In N. Ellis (Ed.), *Implicit and explicit learning of languages.* London: Academic Press.

Krashen, S., Jones, C., Zelinski, S. & Usprich, C. (1978). How important is instruction? *ELT Journa, 32, 257–261.*

Krashen, S., Sferlazza, V., Feldman, L, & Fathman, A. (1976). Adult performance on the SLOPE test: More evidence for a natural sequence in adult second language acquisition. *Language Learning, 26,* 145–151.

Kumaravadivelu, B. (1994). The postmethod condition: (E)merging strategies for second/ foreign language teaching. *TESOL Quarterly, 28,* 27–48.

Lado, R. (1964). *Language teaching: A scientific approach.* New York: McGraw Hill.

Lado, R. (1970). *Lado English series. Book 1.* Montreal: Centre Educatif et Culturel.

Lalande, J. F. (1982).Reducing composition errors: An experiment. *The Modern Language Journal, 66,* 140–149.

Lantolf, J. (1996). Second language theory building: Letting all the flowers bloom! *Language Learning, 46,* 713–749.

Lantolf, J. (2000). Second language learning as a mediated process. *Language Teaching, 33,* 79–96.

Larsen-Freeman, D. (1975). The acquisition of grammatical morphemes by adult ESL students. *TESOL Quarterly, 9,* 409–420.

Larsen-Freeman, D. (1991). Teaching grammar. In M. Celce-Murcia (Ed.), *Teaching English as a second or foreign language* (pp. 279–295). Rowley, MA: Newbury House.

Larsen-Freeman, D., & Long, M. H. (1991). *An introduction to second language acquisition research.* London: Longman.

Lee,I. (1997). ESL learners' performance in error correction in writing. *System, 25,* 465–477.

Leeman, J. (2003). Recasts and second language development: Beyond negative evidence.*Studies in Second Language Acquisition, 25*(1), 37–63.

Leeman, J., Arteagoitia,I., Fridman, D & Doughty, C. (1995). Integrating attention to form in content-based Spanish instruction. In R. Schmidt (Ed.), *Attention and awareness in foreign language learning* (pp. 183–216). Honolulu: University of Hawaii Press.

Levelt, W. (1989). *Speaking: From intention to articulation*. Cambridge: Cambridge University Press.

Lightbown, P. (1983). Exploring relationships between developmental and instructional sequences in L2 acquisition. In H. Seliger & M. Long (Eds.), *Classroom oriented research in second language acquisition* (pp. 217–245). Rowley, MA: Newbury House.

Lightbown, P. (1985a). Can acquisition be altered by instruction? In K. Hyltenstam & M. Pienemann (Eds.), *Modelling and assessing second language acquisition* (pp. 101–112). Clevedon: Multilingual Matters.

Lightbown, P. (1985b). Great expectations in second language acquisition research and classroom teaching. *Applied Linguistics, 6*, 263–273.

Lightbown, P. (1991). What have we here? Some observations on the effect of instruction on L2 learning. In R. Phillipson,E. Kellerman, L. Selinker, M. Sharwood Smith, & M. Swain (Eds.). *Foreign/second language pedagogy research* (pp. 197–212) Clevedon, Avon: Multilingual Matters.

Lightbown, P. (1992). Can they do it themselves? A comprehension-based ESL course for young children. In Courchene, R., J. Glidden, J. St. John, & C. Therien (Eds.), *Comprehension-based second language teaching*. Ottawa: University of Ottawa Press.

Lightbown, P. (2000). Anniversary article: Classroom SLA research and second language teaching. *Applied Linguistics, 21*, 431–462.

Lightbown, P. & Spada, N. (1990). Focus-on-form and corrective feedback in communicative language teaching: Effects on second language learning. *Studies in Second Language Acquisition, 12*, 429–448.

Lightbown, P., Spada, N. & Wallace, R. (1980). Some effects of instruction on child and adolescent ESL learners, In R. Scarcella and S. Krashen (Eds.), *Research in second language acquisition*. Rowley, MA: Newbury House.

Littlewood, W. (1981). *Communicative language teaching*. Cambridge: Cambridge University Press.

Loewen, S. (2002). The occurrence and effectiveness of incidental focus on form in meaning-focused ESL lessons. Unpublished PhD Thesis, University of Auckland, New Zealand.

Loewen, S. (2005). Incidental focus on form and second language learning. *Studies in Second Language Acquisition, 27*, 361–386.

Long, M. (1977). Teacher feedback on learner error: Mapping cognitions. In H. Brown, C. Yorio & R. Crymes (Eds.). *On TESOL 77.* Washington D.C., TESOL.

Long, M. (1983a). Does second language instruction make a difference? A review of the research. *TESOL Quarterly, 17*, 359–382.

Long, M. (1983b). Native speaker/non-native speaker conversation and the negotiation of comprehensible input. *Applied Linguistics, 4*, 126–141.

Long, M. (1983c). Native speaker/non-native speaker conversation in the second language classroom. In M.Clarke & J. Handscombe (Eds.). *On TESOL '82: Pacific perspectives on language learning and teaching* (pp. 207–225). Washington, DC: TESOL.

Long, M. (1984). Process and product in ESL program evaluation. *TESOL Quarterly, 18*, 409–425.

Long, M. (1985). A role for instruction in second language acquisition: Task-based language training. In K.Hyltenstam & M. Pienemann (Eds.), *Modelling and assessing second language acquisition* (pp. 77–100). Clevedon: Multilingual Matters.

Long, M. (1988). Instructed interlanguage development. In L. Beebe (Ed.). *Issues in second language acquisition: Multiple perspectives* (pp. 115–141). New York: Newbury House.

Long, M. (1991). Focus on form: A design feature in language teaching methodology. In K. de Bot, R. Ginsberg & C. Kramsch (Eds.), *Foreign language research in cross-cultural perspective* (pp. 39–52). Amsterdam: John Benjamin.

Long, M. (1996). The role of the linguistic environment in second language acquisition. In W. Ritchie & T. Bhatia (Eds.), *Handbook of second language acquisition* (pp. 413–468). San Diego: Academic Press.

Long, M. (2007). Chapter 5: Recasts in SLA: The story so far. In M. Long. *Problems in SLA*. Mahwah, NJ: Lawrence Erlbaum.

Long, M. H., & Crookes, G. (1991). Three approaches to task-based syllabus design. *TESOL Quarterly, 26* (1), 27–56.

Long, M. and Robinson, P. (1998). Focus on form: Theory, research and practice. In C. Doughty & J. Williams (Eds). *Focus on form in classroom second language acquisition* (pp. 15–41). Cambridge: Cambridge University Press.

Long, M., Inagaki, S. & Ortega, L. (1997). The role of implicit negative feedback in SLA: Models and recasts in Japanese and Spanish. *The Modern Language Journal, 82,* 357–371.

Loschky, L.and R. Bley-Vroman. (1990). Creating structure-based communication tasks for second language development. University of Hawaii Working Papers in ESL 9, 161–209.

Loschky, L. and Bley-Vroman, R. (1993). Grammar and task-based methodology. In G. Crookes and S. Gass (Eds.), *Tasks and Language Learning: Integrating Theory and Practice* (pp. 123–167). Clevedon, Avon: Multilingual Matters.

Louden, W. (1992). Understanding reflection through collaborative research. In A. Hargreaves & M. Fullan (Eds.), *Understanding teacher development*. New York: Teachers College Press.

Lyster, R. (1994). The role of functional-analytic language teaching on aspects of French immersion students' sociolinguistic competence. *Applied Linguistics, 15,* 263–287.

Lyster, R. (1998). Negotiation of form, recasts, and explicit correction in relation to error types and learner repair in immersion classrooms. *Language Learning, 48,* 183–218.

Lyster, R. (2004) . Differential effects of prompts and recasts in form-focused instruction. *Studies in Second Language Acquisition, 26,* 399–432.

Lyster, R. & L. Ranta. (1997). Corrective feedback and learner uptake: Negotiation of form in communicative classrooms. *Studies in Second Language Acquisition, 19,* 37–66.

Mackey, A. (1999). Input, interaction and second language development: An empirical study of question formation in ESL. *Studies in Second Language Acquisition, 21,* 557–587.

Mackey, A. & Philp, J. (1997). Conversational interaction and second language development: Recasts, responses and red herrings? *The Modern Language Journal, 82,* 338–356.

Mackey, W. (1965). *Language teaching analysis.* London: Longman.

Mackey, W. (1976). *Language teaching analysis.* London: Longman.

Macrory, G. & Stone, V. (2000). Pupil progress in the acquisition of the perfect tense in French: The relationship between knowledge and use. *Language Teaching Research, 4,* 55–82.

Makino, T. (1980). Acquisition order of English morphemes by Japanese secondary school students. *Journal of Hokkaido University of Education, 30,* 101–148.

McLaughlin, B. (1978). The monitor model: Some methodological considerations. *Language Learning, 23,* 309–332.

McLaughlin, B. (1990). Restructuring. *Applied Linguistics, 11,* 113–128.

McTear, M. (1975). Structures and categories of foreign language teaching sequences. In R. Allwright (Ed.), Working papers: Language teaching classroom research. University of Essex, Department of Language and Linguistics.

Meisel, J. (1983). Strategies of second language acquisition: More than one kind of simplification. In R. Andersen (Ed.), *Pidginization and creolization as language acquisition* (pp. 120–157). Rowley, MA: Newbury House.

Meisel, J., Clahsen, H., & Pienemann, M. (1981). On determining developmental stages in natural second language acquisition. *Studies in Second Language Acquisition, 3,* 109–135.

Milton, J. (2006). Resource-rich Web-based feedback: Helping learners become independent writers. In K. Hyland & F. Hyland (Eds.), *Feedback in second language writing: Contexts and issues.* (pp. 123–139). Cambridge: Cambridge University Press

Monfries, H. (1969). *Oral drill in sentence patterns*. London: Macmillan.

Moore, A. (1989). Review of Second language grammar: Learning and teaching. *English Language Teaching Journal, 43,* 155–157.

Moulton, W. (1961). Linguistics and language teaching in the United States, 1940–1960. In C. Mohrman, A. Sommerfelt, & J. Whatmough (Eds.), *Trends in European and American linguistics, 1930–1960* (pp. 82–109). Utrecht, Netherlands: Spectrum.

Munby, J. (1968). *Read and think: Training in intensive reading skills*. London: Longman.

Muranoi, H. (2000). *Focus on form through interaction enhancement: Integrating formal instruction into a communicative task in EFL classrooms. Language Learning, 50,* 617–673.

Murphy, R. (1994). *English in use: A self-study reference and practice book for intermediate students. 2nd edition*. Cambridge: Cambridge University Press.

Myles, F. (2004). From data to theory: The over-representation of linguistic knowledge in SLA. *Transactions of the Philological Society, 102,* 139–168.

Myles, F., Mitchell, R., & Hooper, J. (1998). Rote or rule? Exploring the role of formulaic language in classroom foreign language learning. *Language Learning, 48,* 323–363.

Myles, F., Mitchell, R., & Hooper, J. (1999). Interrogative chunks in French L2: A basis for creative construction? *Studies in Second Language Acquisition, 21,* 49–80.

Nagata, N. (1993). Intelligent computer feedback for second language instruction. *The Modern Language Journal* 77, 330–339.

Nagata, N. (1997). An experimental comparison of deductive and inductive feedback generated by a simple parser. *System ,* 25, 515–534.

Naiman, N., Fröhlich, M., Stern, H., & Todesco, A. (1978).The good language learner. *Research in education Series No 7.* Toronto: The Ontario Institute for Studies in Education.

Newmark, L. (1966). How not to interfere in language learning.

International Journal of American Linguistics, 32, 77–87.

Nicholas, H., Lightbown, P., & Spada, N. (2001). Recasts as feedback to language learners. *Language Learning, 51,* 719–758.

Nobuyoshi, J., & Ellis, R. (1993). Focused communication tasks. *English Language Teaching Journal,* 47, 203–210.

Norris, J. & Ortega, L. (2000).Effectiveness of L2 Instruction: A Research Synthesis and Quantitative Meta-analysis. *Language Learning, 50,* 417–528.

Norris, J. & Ortega, L. (2003). Defining and measuring SLA. In C. Doughty & M. Long (Eds.), *Handbook of Second Language Acquisition* (pp. 717–760). Oxford: Blackwell.

Nunan, D. (1990). The teacher as researcher. In C. Brumfit & R. Mitchell (Eds.), *Research in the language classroom, ELT documents, 133* (pp. 16–32). London: Modern English Publications.

Nunan, D. (1989). *Designing tasks for the communicative classroom.* Cambridge: Cambridge University Press.

Nystrom, N. (1983). Teacher-student interaction in bilingual classrooms: Four approaches to error feedback. In H. Seliger & M. Long (Eds.), *Classroom-oriented research in second language acquisition* . Rowley, Mass.: Newbury House.

Ohta, A.S. (2001). *Second language acquisition processes in the classroom: Learning Japanese.* Mahwah, NJ: Lawrence Erlbaum.

Palmer, H. (1917). *The scientific study and teaching of languages.* London: Harrap.

Paradis, M. (1994). Neurolinguistic aspects of implicit and explicit memory: Implications for bilingualism and SLA. In N. Ellis (Ed.), *Implicit and explicit learning of languages* (pp. 393–419). San Diego: Academic Press.

Parker, K. & Chaudron, C. (1987). The effects of linguistic simplifications and elaborative modifications on L2 comprehension.*University of Hawaii' Working Papers in ESL, 6,* 106–133.

Pavesi, M. (1986). Markedness, discoursal modes and relative clause formation in a formal and informal context. *Studies in Second Language Acquisition, 8*, 38–55.

Pawley, A., & Syder, F. (1983). Two puzzles for linguistic theory: Nativelike selection and nativelike fluency. In J. Richards & R. Schmidt (Eds.), *Language and communication* (pp. 191–225). London: Longman.

Pennington, M., & Richards, J. (1997). Reorienting the teaching universe: The experience of five first-year teachers of English in Hong Kong. *Language Teaching Research, 1*, 149–178.

Perdue, C. & Klein, W. (1993). Concluding remarks. In C. Perdue (Ed.), *Adult second language acquisition: cross-linguistic perspectives. Volume 2. The Results* (pp. 253–272) Cambridge: Cambridge University Press.

Philp, J. (2003). Constraints on "noticing the gap": Non-native speakers' noticing of recasts in NS-NNS interaction. *Studies in Second Language Acquisition, 25*, 99–126.

Pica, R. (1987), Second-language acquisition, social interaction and the classroom. *Applied Linguistics, 8*, 3–21.

Pica, T. (1983). Adult acquisition of English as a second language under different conditions of exposure. *Language Learning, 33*, 465–497.

Pica, T. (1992). The textual outcomes of native speaker-nonnative speaker negotiation: What do they reveal about second language learning. In C. Kramsch & S. McConnell-Ginet (Eds.), *Text and context: Cross-disciplinary perspectives on language study* (pp. 198–237). Lexington, MA: D. C. Heath.

Pienemann, M. (1980). The second language acquisition of immigrant children. In S. Felix (Ed.), *Second language development: Trends and issues* (pp. 41–56). Tubingen: Gunter Narr.

Pienemann, M. (1984). Psychological constraints on the teachability of languages. *Studies in Second Language Acquisition, 6*, 186–214.

Pienemann, M. (1985). Learnability and syllabus construction. In K. Hylstenstam & M. Pienemann (Eds.), *Modelling and assessing second language acquisition* (pp. 23–76). Clevedon: Multilingual Matters.

Pienemann, M. (1986). Is language teachable? Psycholinguistic experiments and hypotheses. *Australian Working Papers in Language Development, 1,* 1–41.

Pienemann, M. (1989). Is language teachable? Psycholinguistic experiments and hypotheses. *Applied Linguistics, 10,* 52–79.

Pienemann, M. (1999). *Language Processing and Second Language Development: Processability Theory.* Amsterdam: John Benjamins.

Pienemann, M., &Johnston, M. (1987). Factors influencing the development of language proficiency. In D. Nunan (Ed.), *Applying second language acquisition research* (pp. 45–141). Adelaide, Australia: Adult Migrant Education Program.

Pienemann, M., Johnston, M. and Brindley, G. (1988). An acquisition-based procedure for second language assessment. *Studies in Second Language Acquisition, 10,* 217–243.

Pinker, S. (1989). Rresolving a learnerability paradox in the acquisition of the verb lexicon. In M. Rice & R. Schiefelbusch (Eds.), *The teachability of language.* Baltimore: Paul H. Brookes.

Prabhu, N. (1987). *Second language pedagogy: A perspective.* Oxford: Oxford University Press.

Reber, A. (1976). Implicit learning of synthetic learners: the role of instructional set. *Journal of Experimental Psychology, Human Learning and Memory, 2,* 88–94.

Reber, A. (1989). Implicit learning and tacit knowledge. *Journal of Experimental Psychology: General, 118,* 219–235.

Richards, J. (Ed.). (1974). *Error analysis.* London: Longman.

Richards, J., Platt, J., & Weber, H. (1985). *Longman dictionary of applied linguistics.* London: Longman.

Rivers, W. & Temperley, M. (1978). *A practical guide to the teaching of English.* New York: Oxford University Press.

Robb, T., Ross, S., & Shortreed,I. (1986). Salience of feedback on error and its effect on EFL writing quality. *TESOL Quarterly, 20,* 83–93.

Robinson, P. (1996). Learning simple and complex rules under implicit, incidental rule-search conditions, and instructed conditions. *Studies in Second Language Acquisition, 18,* 27–67.

Robson, C. (1973). *Experiment, design and statistics in psychology.* London: Penguin.

Rosa, E. & Leow, R. P. (2004).Awareness, different learning conditions, and second language development. *Applied Psycholinguistics 25,* 269–292.

Rosa, E. & O'Neill, D. (1999). Explicitness, intake, and the issue of awareness: Another piece to the puzzle. *Studies in Second Language Acquisition, 21,* 511–553.

Rose, K. & Kasper, G. (Eds). (2002). *Pragmatics in language teaching.* Cambridge: Cambridge University Press.

Rutherford, W. (1987). *Second language grammar: Learning and teaching.* London: Longman.

Rutherford, W., & Sharwood-Smith, M. (1985). Consciousness-raising and universal grammar. *Applied Linguistics, 6,* 274–281.

Ryle, G. (1949). *The concept of mind.* London: Hutchinson.

Sachs, R. & Polio, C. (2007). Learners' use of two types of written feedback on an L2 writing task. *Studies in Second Language Acquisition, 29,* 67–100.

Sajavaara, K. (1981).The nature of first language transfer: English as 12 in a foreign language setting. Paper presented at the first European-North American Workshop in Second Language Acquisition Research, Lake Arrowhead, California.

Salaberry, M. (1997). The role of input and output practice in second language acquisition. *Canadian Modern Language Review, 53,* 422–451.

Samuda, V. (2001). Getting relationship between form and meaning during task performance: The role of the teacher. In M. Bygate, P. Skehan, & M. Swain (Eds.), *Task-based learning: Language teaching, learning and assessment* (pp. 119–140). Harlow: Pearson.

Samuda, V. and M. Bygate. (2008). *Tasks in second language learning.* Basingstoke: Palgrave McMillan.

Sanz, C. (2003). Computer delivered implicit vs. explicit feedback in processing instruction. In VanPatten, B. (Ed.), *Processing instruction: Theory, research, and commentary (Second language acquisition research)*. Mahwah, NJ: Lawrence Erlbaum.

Schapers, R., Luscher, R., & Gluck, M. (1980). *Grundkurs Deutsch*. Munchen: Verlag fur Deutsch.

Scherer, A., & Wertheimer, M. (1964). *A psycholinguistic experiment in foreign language teaching*. New York: McGraw-Hill.

Schmidt, R. (1990). The role of consciousness in second language learning. *Applied Linguistics, 11*, 129–158.

Schmidt, R. (1992). Awareness and second language acquisition. *Annual Review of Applied Linguistics, 13,* 206–226.

Schmidt, R. (1993). Consciousness, learning and interlanguage pragmatics.In G. Kasper & S. Blum-Kulka (Eds.), *Interlanguage pragmatics* (pp. 21–42). Oxford University Press.

Schmidt, R. (1994). Deconstructing consciousness in search of useful definitions for applied linguistics. In J. Hulstijn & R. Schmidt (Eds.). *Consciousness in second language learning. AILA Review 11.*

Schmidt, R. (2001). Attention. In P. Robinson (Ed.), *Cognition and second language instruction*. Cambridge: Cambridge University Press.

Schmidt, E., & Frota, S. (1986). Developing basic conversational ability in a second language: A case-study of an adult learner. In R. Day (Ed.), *Talking to learn: Conversation in second language research* (pp. 237–326). Rowley, MA: Newbury House.

Schoenberg,I. (1994). *Focus on grammar*. Reading, MA.: Longman Addison Wesley.

Schumann, J. (1978a). Second language acquisition: The pidginization hypothesis. In E. Hatch (Ed.), *Second language acquisition* (pp. 256 – 271). Rowley, MA: Newbury House.

Schumann, J. (1978b). *The pidginization process: A model for second language acquisition*. Rowley, MA: Newbury House.

Schwartz, B. 1993. On explicit and negative data effecting and affecting competence and linguistic behavior. *Studies in Second Language*

Acquisition 15, 147–163.

Schwartz, J. (1980). The negotiation of meaning: repair in conversations between second language learners of English. In D. Larsen-Freeman (Ed.), *Discourse analysis in second language research.* Rowley, MA: Newbury House.

Scott, V. (1989). An empirical study of explicit and implicit teaching strategies in French. *The Modern language Journal, 73,* 14–22.

Segalowitz, N., & Lightbown, P. (1999). Psycholinguistic approaches to SLA . *Annual Review of Applied Linguistics, 19,* 43–63.

Seliger, H. (1975). Inductive method and deductive method in language teaching: A re-examination. *International Review of Applied Linguistics, 13,* 1–18.

Seliger, H. (1977), Does practice make perfect? A study of interaction patterns and L2 competence. *Language Learning, 27,* 263–275.

Seliger, H. (1979). On the nature and function of language rules in language teaching. *TESOL Quarterly, 13,* 359–369.

Selinker, L. (1972). Interlanguage. *International Review of Applied Linguistics, 10,* 209–331.

Sharwood Smith, M. (1981). Consciousness-raising and the second-language learner. *Applied Linguistics, 2,* 159–169.

Sharwood Smith, M. (1993). Input enhancement in instructed SLA: Theoretical bases. *Studies in Second Language Acquisition, 15,* 165–179.

Sheen, Y. (2004). Corrective feedback and learner uptake in communicative classrooms across instructional settings. *Language Teaching Research, 8,* 263–300.

Sheen, Y. (2006). Exploring the relationship between characteristics of recasts and learner uptake. *Language Teaching Research, 10,* 361–392.

Sheen, Y. (2007). The effect of focused written corrective feedback and language aptitude on ESL learners' acquisition of articles. *TESOL Quarterly, 41,* 255–283.

Sheen, Y. and Ellis, R. 2011. Corrective feedback in language teaching. InE. Hinkel (Ed.), *Handbook on research in second language teaching and learning (Second edition)*. Mahwah: NJ: Lawrence Erlbaum.

Siegel, S. (1956). *Nonparametric statistics for the behavioral sciences*. New York: McGraw-Hill.

Sinclair, J. & Coulthard, M. (1975). *Towards an analysis of discourse*. Oxford: Oxford University Press.

Skehan, P. (1998). *A cognitive approach to language learning*. Oxford: Oxford University Press.

Slimani, A. (1989). The role of topicalization in classroom language learning. *System, 17*, 223–234.

Slimani, A. (1992). Evaluation of classroom interaction. In J. Alderson & A. Beretta (Eds.), *Evaluating second language education*. Cambridge: Cambridge University Press.

Smith, P. (1970). *A comparison of the audiolingual and cognitive approaches to foreign language instruction: The Pennsylvania Foreign Language Project*. Philadelphia: Center for Curriculum Development.

Sorace, A. (1996). The use of acceptability judgements in second language acquisition research. In W. Ritchie & T. Bhatia (Eds.), *Handbook of second language acquisition*. San Diego: Academic Press.

Spada, N. & Lightbown, P. (1993). Instruction and the development of questions in classrooms. *Studies in Second Language Acquisition, 15*, 205–224.

Spada, N. and Lightbown, P. (1999). First language influence and developmental readiness in second language acquisition. *The Modern Language Journal, 83*, 1–21.

Stenhouse, L. (1975). *An introduction to curriculum research and development*. London: Heinemann.

Stern, H. (1983). *Fundamental concepts of language teaching*. Oxford: Oxford University Press.

Stern, H. (1992). *Issues and options in language teaching*. In P. Allen & B. Harley, (Eds.). Oxford: Oxford University Press.

Sternberg, R. (2002). The theory of successful intelligence and its implications for language aptitude testing. In P. Robinson (Ed.).

Individual differences and instructed language learning (pp. 13–43). Amsterdam: John Benjamins.

Stevick, E. W. (1980). *A way and ways.* Rowley, MA: Newbury House.

Swain, M. (1985). Communicative competence: Some roles of comprehensible input and comprehensible output in its development. In S. Gass & C. Madden (Eds.), *Input in second language acquisition* (pp. 235–252). Rowley, MA: Newbury House.

Swain, M. (1995). Three functions of output in second language learning. In G. Cook & B. Seidhofer (Eds.), *For H. G. Widdowson: Principles and practice in the study of language.* Oxford: Oxford University Press.

Swain, M. (2000). The output hypothesis and beyond: Mediating acquisition through collaborative dialogue. In J. Lantolf (Ed.), *Sociolcultural and second language learning.* Oxford: Oxford University Press.

Swan, M. & Smith, B. (2001). *Learner English: A teacher's guide to interference and other problems 2nd Ed.* Cambridge: Cambridge University Press.

Tanaka, K. (2004). Language learning beliefs and language proficiency of Japanese learners of English in New Zealand. Doctoral thesis, University of Auckland.

Tanaka, Y. (1996). The comprehension and acquisition of relative clauses by Japanese high school students through formal instruction. Unpublished doctoral dissertation, Temple University Japan, Tokyo.

Terrell, T. D. (1991). The role of grammar instruction in a communicative approach.*Modern Language Journal, 75, 52–63.*

Tickoo, M. (Ed.). (1993). *Simplification: Theory and application.* Singapore: SEAMEO Regional Language Centre.

Tomasello, M & Herron, C. (1988). Down the garden path: Inducing and correcting overgeneralization errors in the foreign language classroom. *Applied Psycholinguistics, 9, 237–246.*

Trahey, M. (1996). Positive evidence in second language acquisition: Some long term effects. *Second Language Research. 12,* 111–139.

Trahey, M. & White, L. (1993). Positive evidence and preemption in the second language classroom. *Studies in Second Language Acquisition 15,* 181–204.

Truscott, J. (1996). Review article: The case against grammar correction in L2 writing classes. *Language Learning, 46,* 327–369.

Turner, D. (1979). The effect of instruction on second language learning and second language acquisition. In R. Andersen (Ed.), *The acquisition and use of Spanish as first and second language* (pp. 78–91). Washington, DC: TESOL.

Turton, J. & Heaton, N. (Eds.). (1996). *Longman dictionary of common errors.* London: Longman.

Tuz, L. (1992). Comparison of two grammar teaching options: Comprehension-based instruction vs. production-based instruction. Unpublished manuscript, Temple University Japan.

Ur, P. (1988). *Grammar practice activities: A practical guide for teachers.* Cambridge: Cambridge University Press.

Ur, P. (1996). *A course in language teaching.* Cambridge: Cambridge University Press.

van Lier, L. (1991). Inside the classroom: Learning processes and teaching procedures. *Applied Language Learning, 2,* 29–69.

VanPatten, B. (1990). Attending to content and form in the input: an experiment in consciousness. *Studies in Second Language Acquisition, 12,* 287–301.

VanPatten, B. (1993). Grammar teaching for the acquisition-rich classroom. *Foreign Language Annals, 26,* 435–450.

VanPatten, B. (1996). *Input processing and grammar instruction in second language acquisition.* Norwood, NJ: Ablex.

VanPatten, B. (2002). Processing instruction: An update. *Language Learning, 52,* 755–804.

VanPatten, B. (2003). *From input to output: A teacher's guide to second language acquisition.* New York: McGraw-Hill.

VanPatten, B. (2004). Input-processing in second language acquisition. In

B. VanPatten (Ed.), *Processing instruction: Theory, research, and commentary* (pp. 5–31). Mahwah, NJ.: Erlbaum.

Van Patten, B., & Cadierno, T. (1993).SLA as input processing: A role for instruction. Unpublished manuscript.

VanPatten, B. & Oikennon, S. (1996) Explanation vs. structured input in processing instruction. *Studies in Second Language Acquisition, 18,* 495–510.

VanPatten, B. & Sanz, C. (1995). From input to output: Processing instruction and communicative tasks. In F. Eckman, D. Highland, P. Lee, J. Mileham, & R. Weber (Eds.), *Second language acquisition theory and pedagogy.* Mahwah, N. J.: Lawrence Erlbaum.

VanPatten, B., Williams, J., & Rott, S. (2004). *Form-meaning connections in second language acquisition.* Mahwah, NJ.: Lawrence Erlbaum.

Vygotsky, L. (1962). *Thought and language.* Cambridge, MA: MIT Press.

Walter, C. & Swan, M. (1990). *The new English Cambridge course.* Cambridge: Cambridge University Press.

Weinert, R. (1987). Processes in classroom second language development: The acquisition of negation in German. In R. Ellis (Ed.), *Second language acquisition in context* (pp. 83–99). London: Prentice-Hall.

Weiss, C. (Ed.). (1977). *Using social research in public policy making.* Lexington: DC Heath.

Wells, G. (1980). Apprenticeship in meaning. In K. Nelson (Ed). *Children's language,* Vol. 2. New York: Gardner Press.

Wells, G. (1985). *Language development in the pre-school years* . Cambridge: Cambridge University Press.

Wesche, M. (1981). Language aptitude measures in streaming, matching students with methods, and diagnosis of learning problems. In K. Diller (Ed.), *Individual differences and universals in language learning aptitude.* Rowley, Mass.: Newbury House.

Westmoreland, R. (1983). *L2 German acquisition by instructed adults.* Unpublished manuscript, University of Hawaii at Manoa.

White, L. (1987). Against comprehensible input: The input hypothesis and the development of second-language competence. *Applied Linguistics, 8,* 95–110.

White, L. (1995). Input, triggers, and second language acquisition. Can binding be taught? In R. Eckman, D.Highland, P. Lee, & R. Weber (Eds.), *Second language acquisition theory and pedagogy.* Mahwah, N.J.: Lawrence Erlbaum.

White, L., Spada, N, Lightbown, P. & Ranta, L. (1991). Input enhancement and question formation. *Applied Linguistics, 12,* 416–432.

Whitney, N & White, L. (2001). *Team up: Students Book 1.* Oxford: Oxford University Press.

Widdowson, H. (1968). The teaching of English through science. In J. Dakin, B. Tiffen, & H. Widdowson (Eds.), *Language in education* (pp. 115–175). London: Oxford University Press.

Widdowson, H. (1990). *Aspects of language teaching.* Oxford: Oxford University Press.

Wilkins, D. (1976). *Notional syllabuses.* Oxford: Oxford University Press.

Williams, J. (1995). Focus on form in communicative language teaching: Research findings and the classroom teacher. *TESOL Journal, 4*(3), 12–16.

Williams, J. (2005). Learning without awareness. *Studies in Second Language Acquisition, 27,* 2.

Williams, J. & Evans, J. (1998). What kind of focus and on which forms? In C. Doughty & J. Williams (Eds.). *Focus on form in classroom second language acquisition* (pp. 139–155). Cambridge: Cambridge University Press.

Winitz, H. (Ed.). (1981). *The comprehension approach to foreign language instruction.* Rowley, MA: Newbury House.

Wlodkowski, R. (1986). *Enhancing adult motivation to learn .* San Francisco, CA.: Jossey-Bass.

Wode, H. (1980). *Learning a second language: An integrated view of language acquisition.* Tübingen, Germany: Gunter Narr.

Wong, W. (2004). Processing instruction in French: The roles of explicit information and structured input. In B. VanPatten (2003) (Ed.), *From input to output: A teacher's guide to second language acquisition* (pp. 187–205). New York: McGraw-Hill.

Yalden, J. (1983). *The communicative syllabus: Evolution, design and implementation*. Oxford: Pergamon Press.

Young, R. & Doughty, C. (1987). Negotiation in Context: a review of research. In J. Lantolf & A. Labarca (Ed.), *Research in second language learning: Focus on the classroom*. Norwood, N.J: Ablex.

Yuan, F. & Ellis, R. (2003). The effects of pre-task planning and on-line planning on fluency, complexity and accuracy in L2 oral production. *Applied Linguistics, 24,* 1–27.

Zobl, H. (1983). Markedness and the projection problem. *Language Learning, 33,* 293–313.

Zobl, H. (1985). Grammars in search of input and intake. In S. Gass & C. Madden (Eds.), *Input in second language acquisition* (pp. 329–344). Rowley, MA: Newbury House.

Index